CALL in a climate of change: adapting to turbulent global conditions

Short papers from EUROCALL 2017

Edited by Kate Borthwick,
Linda Bradley & Sylvie Thouësny

Published by Research-publishing.net, not-for-profit association
Contact: info@research-publishing.net

© 2017 by Editors (collective work)
© 2017 by Authors (individual work)

CALL in a climate of change: adapting to turbulent global conditions – short papers from EUROCALL 2017
Edited by Kate Borthwick, Linda Bradley, and Sylvie Thouësny

Rights: This volume is published under the Attribution-NonCommercial-NoDerivatives International (CC BY-NC-ND) licence; individual articles may have a different licence. Under the CC BY-NC-ND licence, the volume is freely available online (https://doi.org/10.14705/rpnet.2017.eurocall2017.9782490057047) for anybody to read, download, copy, and redistribute provided that the author(s), editorial team, and publisher are properly cited. Commercial use and derivative works are, however, not permitted.

Disclaimer: Research-publishing.net does not take any responsibility for the content of the pages written by the authors of this book. The authors have recognised that the work described was not published before, or that it was not under consideration for publication elsewhere. While the information in this book are believed to be true and accurate on the date of its going to press, neither the editorial team, nor the publisher can accept any legal responsibility for any errors or omissions that may be made. The publisher makes no warranty, expressed or implied, with respect to the material contained herein. While Research-publishing.net is committed to publishing works of integrity, the words are the authors' alone.

Trademark notice: product or corporate names may be trademarks or registered trademarks, and are used only for identification and explanation without intent to infringe.

Copyrighted material: every effort has been made by the editorial team to trace copyright holders and to obtain their permission for the use of copyrighted material in this book. In the event of errors or omissions, please notify the publisher of any corrections that will need to be incorporated in future editions of this book.

Typeset by Research-publishing.net

Cover design based on © Josef Brett's, Multimedia Developer, Digital Learning, http://www.eurocall2017.uk/, reproduced with kind permissions from the copyright holder.

Cover layout by © Raphaël Savina (raphael@savina.net)
Photo "frog" on cover by © Raphaël Savina (raphael@savina.net)

Fonts used are licensed under a SIL Open Font License

ISBN13: 978-2-490057-04-7 (Ebook, PDF, colour)
ISBN13: 978-2-490057-05-4 (Ebook, EPUB, colour)
ISBN13: 978-2-490057-03-0 (Paperback - Print on demand, black and white)
Print on demand technology is a high-quality, innovative and ecological printing method; with which the book is never 'out of stock' or 'out of print'.

British Library Cataloguing-in-Publication Data.
A cataloguing record for this book is available from the British Library.

Legal deposit: Bibliothèque Nationale de France - Dépôt légal: décembre 2017.

University of Southampton

Table of contents

ix   Programme committee

xii   Preface
       Kate Borthwick

1   Developing a vocabulary size test measuring two aspects of receptive vocabulary knowledge: visual versus aural
     Kazumi Aizawa, Tatsuo Iso, and Paul Nadasdy

7   Learning by design: bringing poster carousels to life through augmented reality in a blended English course
     Mehrasa Alizadeh, Parisa Mehran, Ichiro Koguchi, and Haruo Takemura

13   Empowering language learners through the use of a curriculum-integrated information literacy programme: an action research project
     Sahar Alzahrani

19   Transforming learning, conceptualisation and practices through a MOOC on English as a Medium of Instruction for Academics
     Robert Baird, Kate Borthwick, and Mary Page

24   Foreign language anxiety on a massive open online language course
     Zsuzsanna Bárkányi and Sabela Melchor-Couto

30   LMOOCs, classifying design: survey findings from LMOOC providers
     Elaine Beirne, Mairéad Nic Giolla Mhichíl, and Gearóid Ó Cleircín

35   Learners' perceptions of a reading section without instruction
     Alessandra Belletti Figueira Mulling

40   Mobile resources for integration: how availability meets the needs of newly arrived Arabic-speaking migrants in Sweden
     Nataliya Berbyuk Lindström, Sylvana Sofkova Hashemi, Lorna Bartram, and Linda Bradley

Table of contents

46   The assessment of digital project work in the EFL classroom
Jan Berggren and Christopher Allen

51   Normalisation in flux: teachers' and learners' digital literacy in the Japanese university context
Thomas E. Bieri and Darren Elliott

56   An evaluation of TTS as a pedagogical tool for pronunciation instruction: the 'foreign' language context
Tiago Bione, Jennica Grimshaw, and Walcir Cardoso

62   An exploratory study of feedback practices for written and oral tasks in an online English course
Laia Canals and Jackie Robbins

67   Can an interactive digital game help French learners improve their pronunciation?
Walcir Cardoso, Avery Rueb, and Jennica Grimshaw

73   Automatically generating questions to support the acquisition of particle verbs: evaluating via crowdsourcing
Maria Chinkina, Simón Ruiz, and Detmar Meurers

79   Computer-assisted English learning system based on free conversation by topic
Sung-Kwon Choi, Oh-Woog Kwon, and Young-Kil Kim

86   The potential of elicited imitation for oral output practice in German L2
Frederik Cornillie, Kristof Baten, and Dirk De Hertog

92   Emerging affordances in videoconferencing for language learning and teaching
Aparajita Dey-Plissonneau

99   Developing a cross-platform web application for online EFL vocabulary learning courses
Kazumichi Enokida, Tatsuya Sakaue, Mitsuhiro Morita, Shusaku Kida, and Akio Ohnishi

105	Goofy Guide Game: affordances and constraints for engagement and oral communication in English *Kaisa Enticknap-Seppänen*
110	Data-driven learning and the acquisition of Italian collocations: from design to student evaluation *Luciana Forti*
116	Determining factors in student retention in online courses *Kolbrún Friðriksdóttir and Birna Arnbjörnsdóttir*
122	Designing a MOOC for learners of Spanish: exploring learner usage and satisfaction *Ana Gimeno-Sanz*
128	OER use in intermediate language instruction: a case study *Robert Godwin-Jones*
135	Teacher perspectives on the integration of mobile-assisted language learning *Jennica Grimshaw, Walcir Cardoso, and Laura Collins*
140	Online study: postgraduate student perceptions of core skills development *Patricia E. Grounds and Caroline Moore*
146	Evaluating lexical coverage in Simple English Wikipedia articles: a corpus-driven study *Clinton Hendry and Emily Sheepy*
151	A chatbot for a dialogue-based second language learning system *Jin-Xia Huang, Kyung-Soon Lee, Oh-Woog Kwon, and Young-Kil Kim*
157	Motivational factors in telecollaborative exchanges among teenagers *Kristi Jauregi and Sabela Melchor-Couto*
163	The TeCoLa project: pedagogical differentiation through telecollaboration and gaming for intercultural and content integrated language teaching *Kristi Jauregi and Sabela Melchor-Couto*

170 Students' views on the helpfulness of multimedia components of digital flashcards in mobile-assisted vocabulary learning
Regina Kaplan-Rakowski and Barbara Loranc-Paszylk

177 The comparison of the impact of storytelling and digital storytelling assignments on students' motivations for learning
Naoko Kasami

184 A Facebook project for pre-service language teachers
Liliia Khalitova, Gulnara Gimaletdinova, Gulnara Sadykova, and Albina Kayumova

189 Using a learning management system to enhance an extensive reading program
Cory J. Koby

194 Exploring meaning negotiation patterns in synchronous audio and video conferencing English classes in China
Chenxi (Cecilia) Li, Ligao Wu, Chen Li, and Jinlan Tang

200 Re-mediating postmillennial posters
Paul A. Lyddon and Jaime Selwood

205 Designing and developing a blended course: toward best practices for Japanese learners
Parisa Mehran, Mehrasa Alizadeh, Ichiro Koguchi, and Haruo Takemura

211 Listening difficulty detection to foster second language listening with a partial and synchronized caption system
Maryam Sadat Mirzaei, Kourosh Meshgi, and Tatsuya Kawahara

217 Can you understand me? Speaking robots and accented speech
Souheila Moussalli and Walcir Cardoso

222 Improving expressive writing in EFL through blogging
Rana Namouz, Hagit Misher-Tal, and Orly Sela

229 Criteria for evaluating a game-based CALL platform
Neasa Ní Chiaráin and Ailbhe Ní Chasaide

Table of contents

235 Designing for ab initio blended learning environments: identifying systemic contradictions
Oisín Ó Doinn

242 How "blended" should "blended learning" be?
Boguslaw Ostrowski, Scott Windeatt, and Jill Clark

248 'L2 assessment and testing' teacher education: an exploration of alternative assessment approaches using new technologies
Salomi Papadima-Sophocleous

254 MALL with WordBricks – building correct sentences brick by brick
Marina Purgina, Maxim Mozgovoy, and Monica Ward

260 Collective designing and sharing of open educational resources: a study of the French CARTOUN platform
Nolwenn Quere

265 Harnessing the power of informal learning: using WeChat, the semi-synchronous group chat, to enhance spoken fluency in Chinese learners
Marion Sadoux

271 ESL learners' online research and comprehension strategies
Noridah Sain, Andy Bown, Andrew Fluck, and Paul Kebble

277 Combining formal and informal learning: the use of an application to enhance information gathering and sharing competence in a foreign language
Yukiko Sato, Irene Erlyn Wina Rachmawan, Stefan Brückner, Ikumi Waragai, and Yasushi Kiyoki

283 An open-sourced and interactive ebook development program for minority languages
Emily Sheepy, Ross Sundberg, and Anne Laurie

289 Reception of Japanese captions: a comparative study of visual attention between native speakers and language learners of Japanese
Eline C. Sikkema

Table of contents

294   The potential of automated corrective feedback to remediate cohesion problems in advanced students' writing
Carola Strobl

300   A dynamic online system for translation learning and testing
Yan Tian

306   The use of MOOC as a means of creating a collaborative learning environment in a blended CLIL course
Svetlana Titova

312   Language students learning to manage complex pedagogic situations in a technology-rich environment
Riikka Tumelius and Leena Kuure

317   Exploring AI language assistants with primary EFL students
Joshua Underwood

322   Construction and evaluation of an integrated formal/informal learning environment for foreign language learning across real and virtual spaces
Ikumi Waragai, Tatsuya Ohta, Shuichi Kurabayashi, Yasushi Kiyoki, Yukiko Sato, and Stefan Brückner

328   ICALL's relevance to CALL
Monica Ward

333   Developing multimedia supplementary materials to support learning beginning level Chinese characters
Lisha Xu

339   Roles of mobile devices supporting international students to overcome intercultural difficulties
Xiaoyin Yang and Xiuyan Li

345   Enhancing grammatical structures in web-based texts
Leonardo Zilio, Rodrigo Wilkens, and Cédrick Fairon

351   Author index

Programme committee

Programme chairs

- Peppi Taalas (chair), *University of Jyvaskylä, Finland*
- John Gillespie (co-chair), *University of Ulster, United Kingdom*

Committee members

- Christine Appel, *Universitat Oberta de Catalunya, Spain*
- David Barr, *Ulster University, United Kingdom*
- Becky Bergman, *Chalmers University of Technology, Sweden*
- Claire Bradin Siskin, *Consultant, United States*
- Angela Chambers, *University of Limerick, Ireland*
- Suzanne Cloke, *University of Padova, Italy*
- Jozef Colpaert, *Universiteit Antwerpen, Belgium*
- Vera Menezes, *Universidade Federal de Minas Gerais, Brazil*
- Charlotte Everitt, *University of Southampton, United Kingdom*
- Ana Gimeno, *Universidad Politecnica de Valencia, Spain*
- Muriel Grosbois, *Université Paris Sorbonne – ESPE, France*
- Nicolas Guichon, *Lyon 2, Laboratoire ICAR, France*
- Sarah Guth, *University of Padova, Italy*
- Marie-Josee Hamel, *University of Ottawa, Canada*
- Mirjam Hauck, *The Open University, United Kingdom*
- Francesca Helm, *University of Padova, Italy*
- Phil Hubbard, *Stanford University, United States*
- Sake Jager, *University of Groningen, Netherlands*
- Leena Kuure, *University of Oulu, Finland*
- Dominique Macaire, *Université de Lorraine, France*
- Liam Murray, *University of Limerick, Ireland*
- Susanna Nocchi, *Dublin Institute of Technology, Ireland*
- Robert O'Dowd, *University of León, Spain*
- Sue Otto, *University of Iowa, United States*
- Luisa Panichi, *University of Pisa, Italy*
- Salomi Papadima-Sophocleous, *Cyprus University of Technology, Cyprus*
- Hans Paulussen, *KU Leuven KULAK, Belgium*
- Pascual Pérez-Paredes, *University of Cambridge, United Kingdom*

Programme committee

- Alessia Plutino, *University of Southampton, United Kingdom*
- Mathias Schulze, *San Diego State University, United States*
- Oranna Speicher, *University of Nottingham, United Kingdom*
- Glenn Stockwell, *Waseda University, Japan*
- Sylvie Thouësny, *Research-publishing.net, Ireland*
- Cornelia Tschichold, *Swansea University, United Kingdom*
- Steven White, *University of Southampton, United Kingdom*
- Shona Whyte, *Université Côte d'Azur, France*

Peer-reviewing committee (full articles)

- Christopher Allen, *Linnaeus University, Sweden*
- Birna Arnbjörnsdóttir, *University of Iceland, Iceland*
- Elena Bárcena, *UNED, Spain*
- Zsuzsanna Barkanyi, *The Open University, United Kingdom*
- David Barr, *Ulster University, United Kingdom*
- Elaine Beirne, *Dublin City University, Ireland*
- Nataliya Berbyuk Lindström, *University of Gothenburg, Sweden*
- Jan Berggren, *Linnaeus University, Sweden*
- Alex Boulton, *University of Lorraine, France*
- Laia Canals, *Universitat Oberta de Catalunya, Spain*
- Frederik Cornillie, *KU Leuven & imec, Belgium*
- Aparajita Dey-Plissonneau, *Dublin City University, Ireland*
- Martina Emke, *The Open University, United Kingdom*
- Charlotte Everitt, *University of Southampton, United Kingdom*
- Marta Fondo Garcia, *Universitat Oberta de Catalunya, Spain*
- Luciana Forti, *University for Foreigners of Perugia, Italy*
- Jonás Fouz González, *Universidad Católica San Antonio, Spain*
- Kolbrún Friðriksdóttir, *University of Iceland, Iceland*
- Christina Nicole Giannikas, *Cyprus University of Technology, Cyprus*
- John Gillespie, *University of Ulster, Northern Ireland*
- Ana Gimeno-Sanz, *Universidad Politécnica de Valencia, Spain*
- Luis Gonzalez, *Université de Lausanne, Switzerland*
- Nasser Jabbary, *Texas A&M University, United States of America*
- Kristi Jauregi, *Utrecht University, Netherlands*
- Elis Kakoulli Constantinou, *Cyprus University of Technology, Cyprus*
- Regina Kaplan-Rakowski, *Independent researcher, United States of America*
- Leena Kuure, *University of Oulu, Finland*
- Bruce Lander, *Matsuyama University, Japan*
- Paul Lyddon, *Osaka Jogakuin College, Japan*

Programme committee

- Chris McGuirk, *University of Central Lancashire, United Kingdom*
- Parisa Mehran, *Osaka University, Japan*
- Antje Neuhoff, *TU Dresden, Germany*
- Neasa Ní Chiaráin, *Trinity College, Ireland*
- Mairéad Nic Giolla Mhichí, *Dublin City University, Ireland*
- Susanna Nocchi, *Dublin Institute of Technology, Ireland*
- Breffni O'Rourke, *Trinity College, Ireland*
- Marina Orsini-Jones, *Coventry University, United Kingdom*
- Nolwenn Quere, *Université de Bretagne Occidentale, France*
- Timothy Read, *UNED, Spain*
- Marion Sadoux, *University of Nottingham Ningbo China, China*
- Cédric Sarré, *Université Paris-Sorbonne, France*
- Müge Satar, *Bogazici University, Turkey*
- Shannon Sauro, *Malmö University, Sweden*
- Jaime Selwood, *Hiroshima University, Japan*
- Eline Sikkema, *Dublin City University, Ireland*
- Adam Smith, *Future University Hakodate, Japan*
- Oranna Speicher, *University of Nottingham, United Kingdom*
- Elena Volodina, *University of Gothenburg, Sweden*
- Monica Ward, *Dublin City University, Ireland*
- Ciara Wigham, *Clermont Université – LRL, France*

Preface

Kate Borthwick[1]

Welcome to the EUROCALL short papers 2017!

2017 saw the 25th conference for the European Association of Computer-Assisted Language Learning (EUROCALL). Every year, EUROCALL serves as a rich venue to share research, practice, new ideas, and to make new international friends – and this year was no different. It is an innovative and inspiring conference in which researchers and practitioners share their novel and insightful work on the use of technology in language learning and teaching. This volume of short papers captures the pioneering spirit of the conference and you will find here both inspiration and ideas for theory and practice.

EUROCALL 2017 was hosted by Modern Languages and Linguistics, at the University of Southampton, in the UK. Between the 23-26 August, we welcomed over 280 delegates from 32 countries. This year's theme was 'CALL in a climate of change', a topic which seemed to become more eerily appropriate by the day, as 2017 passed by. The theme encompassed the notion of how practice and research in CALL is responding to shifting global circumstances which impact on education, including developments arising from economic, political, or environmental change. It cut across areas including considerations for teacher training, competitive educational models, open education, new models for blended learning, collaboration, mobile learning, creative and innovative pedagogy, data analytics, students' needs and sustainability – and crucially, it looked to the future with optimism.

The programme was packed with over 200 sessions related to this topic and it included a large number of workshops, pecha kucha, posters, and symposia. This

---

1. University of Southampton, Southampton, United Kingdom; k.borthwick@soton.ac.uk

How to cite: Borthwick, K. (2017). Preface. In K. Borthwick, L. Bradley & S. Thouësny (Eds), *CALL in a climate of change: adapting to turbulent global conditions – short papers from EUROCALL 2017* (pp. xii-xiv). Research-publishing.net. https://doi.org/10.14705/rpnet.2017.eurocall2017.678

volume offers a snapshot of this dynamic landscape and 60 of the papers appear here.

Our keynote speakers, who came from CALL and non-CALL disciplines, helped us to explore the current and changing climate that CALL research and practice finds itself in. They offered us expert and illuminating perspectives on the digital environment of the 21st century, and how this environment impacts on practitioners in education. They suggested ways in which it may influence our approaches in the future.

Steven Thorne was our Graham Davies keynote speaker and he opened the conference with characteristic energy and enthusiasm, offering us a dazzling array of ideas to ponder. He discussed cultural-historical approaches to language learning and existing notions of how we learn language 're-wilding' and gave examples of using technology-enhanced approaches, such as mobile augmented reality games, to contextualise language use in ways highly relevant to learners. He presented a vision of language education which encompasses social justice, uses methods of linguistic and data analysis, and uses approaches designed to accommodate a range of language learners, including indigenous peoples and foreign and second language learners.

David Millard joined us from the discipline of web and computer science and posed the provocative title 'People Like You Like Presentations Like This'. The discipline of web science aims to understand the dynamics of human interaction online and this title reflects what we learn and what we *think* we learn when studying the web. He explored how we have moved from the utopian ideals behind the web's creation to today's concerns over fake news, mass surveillance, and anti-social behaviour. He emphasised the need for knowledge and understanding about how the web works, in order to use technology to shape the world in positive and beneficial ways.

Our final keynote speaker was Shannon Sauro, who presented her work on the practices and interactions in fan-networks (fandoms). She outlined how networks of fans have used technology and the web to collaborate in creative and varied ways, often moving beyond the source material (of which they are fans) and generating novel and sophisticated responses. Online networks of fans have also come together to respond to global socio-political challenges. Shannon suggested that we should look to fandoms for inspiration and motivation in understanding the effective use of social aspects of the web and particularly in responding to socio-political challenges. During her presentation, it also became clear that most of the delegates were Harry Potter fans!

More information about these keynote addresses, as well as the full programme and session abstracts, may be found at the conference website (http://www.eurocall2017.uk/).

We offer an enormous thank you to all of the presenters and participants at the EUROCALL 2017 conference. Every participant made an essential contribution to an event that was thought-provoking, inspiring, and very enjoyable.

The production of this volume has been a collaborative effort by the EUROCALL community and we would like to thank all of our authors and reviewers. All submissions for this volume have been rigorously reviewed: submissions received an average of two external reviews and were then subjected to further meta-reviewing.

This volume reflects the wide variety of topics featured at the conference and the high quality of contributions. We hope you will enjoy reading it as much as we – the editors – have during its preparation; it contains the essence of EUROCALL 2017.

We look forward to seeing you at future EUROCALL conferences!

Developing a vocabulary size test measuring two aspects of receptive vocabulary knowledge: visual versus aural

Kazumi Aizawa[1], Tatsuo Iso[2], and Paul Nadasdy[3]

Abstract. Testing learners' English proficiency is central to university English classes in Japan. This study developed and implemented a set of parallel online receptive aural and visual vocabulary tests that would predict learners' English proficiency. The tests shared the same target words and choices – the main difference was the presentation of the target words. Test results showed that for both the Aural Test (AT) and the Visual Test (VT), average scores from 1,000 to 4,000 of the JACET8000 word list's frequency bands decreased in proportion to word frequency. More detailed analyses highlighted gaps between visual and aural aspects of receptive vocabulary knowledge of frequency of 4,000 and beyond. It further indicated that the aural version of the test was a better predictor of English proficiency. For future directions, we need to develop other sets of the VT and the AT to improve the reliability of the tests, and this is especially important in order to satisfy the needs of educational institutes that demand high accuracy in vocabulary testing.

Keywords: vocabulary knowledge, computerized tests, test format, English proficiency.

1. Introduction

The popularity of English as a broad, global subject has been growing in recent times. University students rely on clear measuring of their English ability through systematic testing, and this is a factor that contributes to their final grade upon

---

1. Tokyo Denki University, Tokyo, Japan; aizawa@cck.dendai.ac.jp
2. Tokyo Denki University, Tokyo, Japan; tiso@mail.dendai.ac.jp
3. Tokyo Denki University, Tokyo, Japan; nadasdy@cck.dendai.ac.jp

How to cite this article: Aizawa, K., Iso, T., & Nadasdy, P. (2017). Developing a vocabulary size test measuring two aspects of receptive vocabulary knowledge: visual versus aural. In K. Borthwick, L. Bradley & S. Thouësny (Eds), *CALL in a climate of change: adapting to turbulent global conditions – short papers from EUROCALL 2017* (pp. 1-6). Research-publishing.net. https://doi.org/10.14705/rpnet.2017.eurocall2017.679

graduation. As this is the case, it is fundamental that Japanese students' English ability is tested as accurately as possible. Therefore, universities usually give placement tests to freshmen. According to the questionnaire survey on university placement tests (Aizawa, Iso, & Sasao, 2015), 72% of universities give placement tests to new students upon entering university. Among them, about 80% of those universities purchase placement tests provided by reliable outside sources – *Test of English for International Communication* (TOEIC) 40%, *TOEIC Bridge* 20%, *Test of English as a Foreign Language* 10%, *Assessment of Communicative English* 10%. Moreover, 48% out of the 80% responded that they would be interested in quick and easy-to-use placement tests if they are available.

In the area of vocabulary testing, it has been traditionally the case that only the visual aspects of vocabulary have been measured. A test like TOEIC, for example, is 50% listening questions and therefore relies on students recognizing words within multiple-choice questions. As the demands increase for more accurate measurement of student vocabularies, new innovations in testing need to be developed and considered. Current research suggests that the ways to evaluate the level of an individual's vocabulary is still relatively limited (Pignot-Shahov, 2012). Various tests, however, have been popular for some time, and several vocabulary tests have been developed for research and educational purposes. Among them the *English as a Foreign Language Vocabulary Test* (Meara, 1992) and the *Vocabulary Levels Test* (Nation, 1990) have been widely used. As for these tests, Milton (2009) outlines the positive aspects of the former: speed and ease of use, a large number of items, reliability, multiple versions, less boredom, and better student concentration; and the negative aspects: increased guessing, faced with complex decisions, and overestimation. However, regarding aural vocabulary tests, there is only a limited amount available: the dictation form of Nation's (1990) *Vocabulary Levels Test* (Fountain & Nation, 2000) and *AuralLex* (Milton & Hopkins, 2005). As tests like these are limited in number, the current study aims to provide an alternative option for those wishing to concurrently test vocabulary both aurally and visually.

2. Methods

2.1. Test development

In the development of vocabulary tests, it is important to first decide what the exact definition of knowing a word is. There have been several attempts at this, most notably by Richards (1976), Palmberg (1987), and Nation (1990). However, there is yet to be a conclusive answer to what clearly constitutes vocabulary knowledge. In this paper, we broadly define knowing a word as having an ability to choose, among the list, the corresponding word with the meaning assigned.

The 15 target words and 45 distractor words were randomly chosen from each frequency band of JACET8000 words to construct four multiple-choice questions. Each set of questions consisted of one key and three distractors (the same parts of speech) from eight different frequency bands of 1,000 words each. In total, there were 15 questions of four multiple choices for each eight bands, totaling 120 questions. The AT and the VT are parallel in terms of test format, target words, and choices: the only difference is the mode of target word presentation. In both tests, the target words are presented prior to the four choices (Figure 1). In the AT, each target word was presented aurally, while in the VT, the common target words are shown in a written form. The time length of presenting words (five seconds) and choices (ten seconds) were almost identical. If test takers did not choose an answer for each question, the answer became invalid and the test proceeded to the next question.

Figure 1. Sample screens of AT and VT

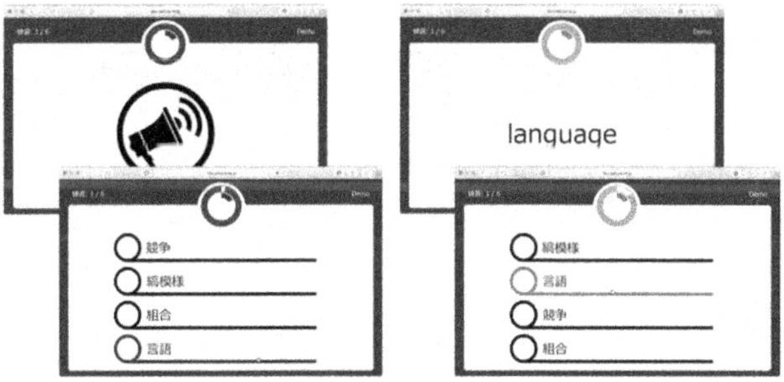

Left: The target word 'language' is being presented aurally followed by four multiple choices.

Right: The same target word is presented visually followed by the same multiple choices.

2.2.   Purpose and procedure

The purpose of this study is to identify the gaps in average scores between aural and visual tests of receptive vocabulary knowledge. It is also designed to find out whether the test can be used to predict students' TOEIC score. The participants were 140 lower-intermediate engineering students who were taking English as part of their course study. The participants voluntarily took the tests: the AT in the first week, followed by the VT in the third week to avoid the priming effect, since both tests share the same target words as described above. It took about 15 minutes to complete each test.

3. Results and discussion

The descriptive statistics are shown in Table 1. The mean score of the VT was slightly higher than that of the AT (88.56 and 78.16, respectively). Figure 2 shows that the frequency band scores of the AT and the VT declined until frequency level 5,000, but from level six and upward the gaps did not follow this pattern. On every frequency band, the scores of the VT were statistically significantly higher than those of the AT. The gaps in scores between the VT and the AT became larger up until level six, but the differences were not straightforward on levels seven and eight. A further analysis of scores suggested that the AT better predicted TOEIC scores as seen in Figure 3 with a correlation coefficient of $r=.57$ as opposed to .44 of the VT. Furthermore, the multiple regression analysis revealed that the AT score of level three most reliably accounted for the TOEIC score, followed by level five of the AT. The VT scores were not deemed as estimating factors.

Table 1. Descriptive statistics of the tests

		Mean	SD	MAX	MIN
Vocabulary Test	VT	88.58	10.75	104	44
	AT	78.16	12.24	115	59
TOEIC	Listening	225.30	55.84	375	100
	Reading	165.73	52.53	295	45
	Total	**391.03**	**98.83**	**610**	**180**

Figure 2. Means of scores by JACET8000 levels

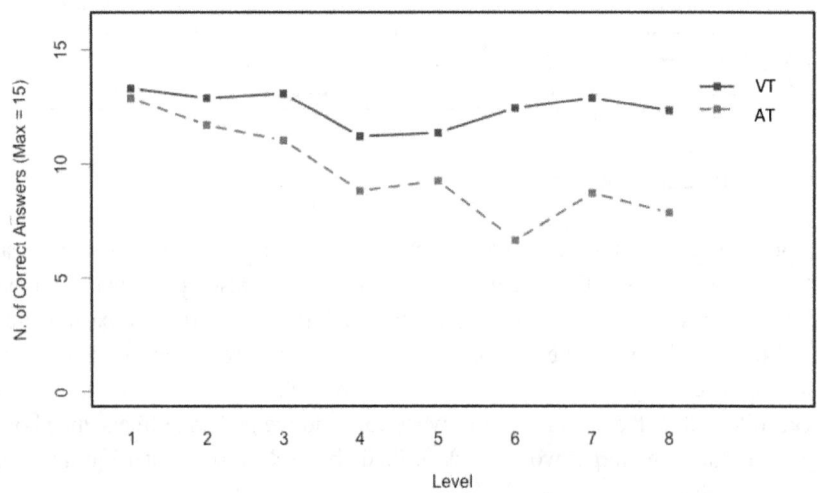

Figure 3. Correlations of TOEIC, AT, and VT

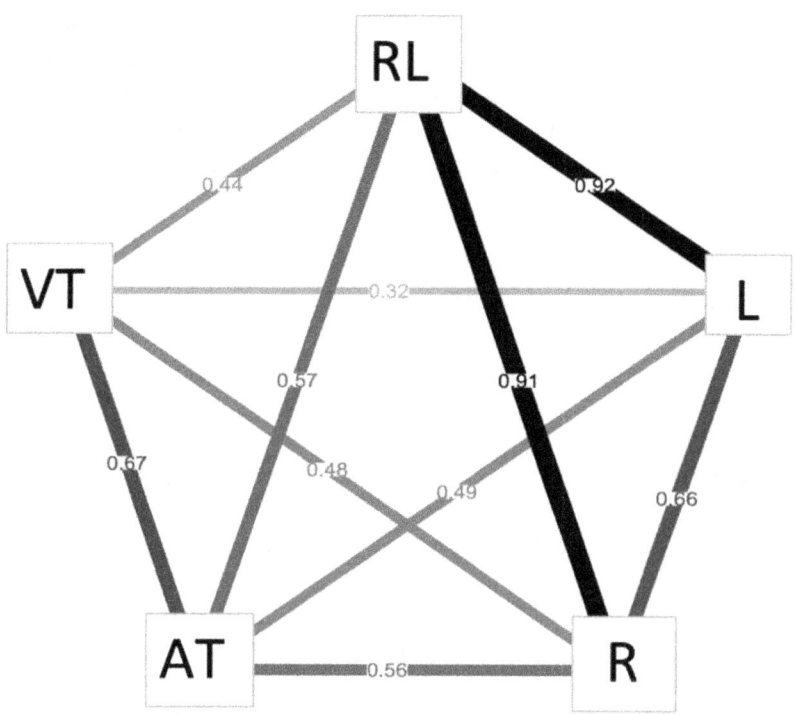

The declining pattern in the AT scores is not observed in the VT scores, which seem to plateau at level five. A possible explanation is the overall ceiling effect in the VT. Another is the inherent problem found in the word list itself – it has been reported elsewhere that levels five and after of the JACET8000 words contain a certain number of loan words and derivational forms of higher frequency words. Some of those could be inadvertently used as target words.

The current study showed that the AT was a better predictor of the TOEIC score. This is an important finding as no previous studies directly compared the results of visually and aurally tested vocabulary sizes.

4. Conclusion

Testing in Japanese educational institutions is fundamental for placing students in suitable levels and for evaluating ability and progress. We have strived to create testing instruments that will predict most accurately the vocabulary sizes of a small group of Japanese students, and though there was a considerable amount of success in the data returned, more research is needed and more refinement of the instruments is necessary if we are to provide high levels of reliability in vocabulary testing. Further experimentation using refined versions of the same tools will be carried out in subsequent research projects, and we would invite others that are interested in measuring the accuracy of their students' vocabulary levels to do the same.

5. Acknowledgements

This work was supported by JSPS Research Grant (No. 26580114).

References

Aizawa, K., Iso, T., & Sasao, Y. (2015). *Developing an online placement test (interim report)*. Foreign Language Teaching Expo 2015, Tokyo.

Fountain, R., & Nation, I. S. P. (2000). A vocabulary-based graded dictation test. *RELC Journal 31*, 29-44. https://doi.org/10.1177/003368820003100202

Meara, P. (1992). *EFL vocabulary tests*. University College Swansea.

Milton, J. (2009). *Measuring second language vocabulary acquisition*. Multilingual Matters.

Milton, J., & Hopkins, N. (2005). *AuralLex*. Swansea University.

Nation, I. S. P. (1990). *Teaching and learning vocabulary*. Heinle and Heinle.

Palmberg, R. (1987). Patterns of vocabulary development in foreign language learners. *Studies in Second Language Acquisition, 9*, 201-220. https://doi.org/10.1017/S0272263100000474

Pignot-Shahov, V. (2012). Measuring L2 receptive and productive vocabulary knowledge. *Language Studies Working Papers, 4*, 37-45.

Richards, J. C. (1976). The role of vocabulary teaching. *TESOL Quarterly, 10*, 77-89. https://doi.org/10.2307/3585941

Learning by design: bringing poster carousels to life through augmented reality in a blended English course

Mehrasa Alizadeh[1], Parisa Mehran[2],
Ichiro Koguchi[3], and Haruo Takemura[4]

> **Abstract.** In recent years, there has been a burgeoning interest in Augmented Reality (AR) technologies, especially in educational settings to edutain (i.e. educate and entertain) students and engage them in their learning. This study reports the results of the use of an AR application called BlippAR to augment poster carousel tasks in a blended English course offered at Osaka University. Both quantitative and qualitative data were collected through a usage experience questionnaire, an open-ended feedback form, and observations. The implemented AR application is described, and the overall positive user experience is reported, along with displaying a sample of collaborative student-generated AR posters. The rewards and challenges of having students design AR content are also discussed.
>
> **Keywords**: augmented reality, AR, BlippAR, situated learning, learning by design, learner-generated AR content.

1. Introduction

AR, a technology that allows virtual objects to be superimposed onto the actual world in real time, has emerged as one of the most promising technologies for education, which can edutain students and engage them in their learning. AR apps, such as Aurasma, Wikitude, Layar, and Augment, are a type of mobile application that allow users to overlay digital information onto the physical world by attaching photos, texts, audio, and/or videos. These applications are gaining popularity among English language teaching practitioners and researchers (e.g. Reinders &

---

1. Osaka University, Osaka, Japan; alizadeh.mehrasa@lab.ime.cmc.osaka-u.ac.jp
2. Osaka University, Osaka, Japan; mehran.parisa@lab.ime.cmc.osaka-u.ac.jp
3. Osaka University, Osaka, Japan; ikoguchi@lang.osaka-u.ac.jp
4. Osaka University, Osaka, Japan; takemura@cmc.osaka-u.ac.jp

How to cite this article: Alizadeh, M., Mehran, P., Koguchi, I., & Takemura, H. (2017). Learning by design: bringing poster carousels to life through augmented reality in a blended English course. In K. Borthwick, L. Bradley & S. Thouësny (Eds), *CALL in a climate of change: adapting to turbulent global conditions – short papers from EUROCALL 2017* (pp. 7-12). Research-publishing.net. https://doi.org/10.14705/rpnet.2017.eurocall2017.680

Lakarnchua, 2014), as AR use is aligned with recent learning theories: for example, constructivist learning, situated learning, game-based learning, and inquiry-based learning.

2. Project description: an AR-based exploratory case study at Osaka University

A fifteen-week blended course of English for General Academic Purposes (EGAP), titled Osaka University Global English Online (OUGEO), was designed, developed, and implemented at Osaka University for second-year undergraduate students. Out of the 15 weeks, ten weeks were purely online, and five were face-to-face. Poster presentation carousel was selected as the term project, which allowed the students to go around, visit posters, listen to their peers' presentations, ask/answer questions, and develop their oral fluency. An AR app, called BlippAR, was also chosen to be introduced to the learners to create learner-generated (aka learnAR-generated) AR posters.

Initially, through a technology survey, it was found that all of the students owned a smartphone. A face-to-face training session both on poster presentations and on using BlippAR to create Blipps was then held (the slides are available at https://www.slideshare.net/parisamehran/blippar-tutorial), and the students formed 14 groups of five to six members each to present at two poster sessions. For the purpose of this paper, we focused on data collected during the first poster session where seven groups presented their posters in three rounds to three different listener groups (see Figure 1).

Figure 1. Class arrangement for the first poster session

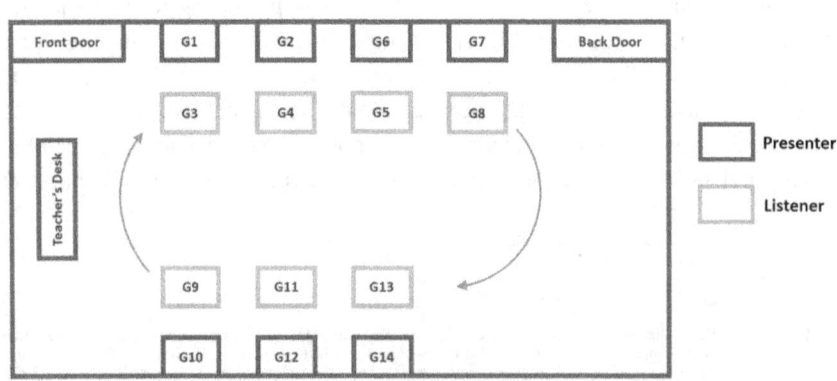

Each presenting group was asked to select a global theme, create a poster based on the topic, and find or make a video related to the content to overlay on the poster using BlippAR. This paper reports on the past AR experiences of the learners, their views on the use of AR, specifically BlippAR, and their estimate of AR use for their future projects. Some samples of learner-generated AR content are also provided.

3. Method

3.1. Participants

The total number of the students participating in the current study was 71, of which 35 (49.3%) were males and 36 (50.7%) were females, with a mean age of 19 (ranging from 18 to 22). The participants were all undergraduate students majoring in humanities, mainly from the Faculties of Letters, Law, and Economics. Fifty-six of them (78.9%) reported that they had never experienced using AR, and 67 of them (94.4%) said that they had not known about BlippAR.

3.2. Instrumentation

A usage experience questionnaire (adapted from Chow, Thadani, Wong, & Pegrum, 2015; Davis, 1989; Venkatesh, Morris, Davis, & Davis, 2003), an open-ended feedback form, and observations were utilized to collect data on respondents' attitude toward the use and experience of AR.

4. Findings

After being trained on Blipp creation, the students designed and generated their interactive AR-based posters. Figure 2 illustrates a sample of student-generated AR content.

Despite the fact that about half of the students found BlippAR difficult to use, the majority of them believed that working with BlippAR was fun and that it made learning English more interesting, which led to their overall positive usage experience with BlippAR. However, a majority of the students felt that using BlippAR would not directly contribute to the improvement of their English. Table 1 shows the responses to the usage experience questionnaire.

Figure 2. Sample student-generated AR-based poster[5]

Mother's Day
Group 14

Introduction
Today, we would like to introduce Mother's Day of the world. In Japan, we have the Mother's Day on second Sunday of May. We give carnation or some gifts for mother and say mother "Thank you." because mothers work and do housework for their family. By the way, in other countries, are their mother's days? When? How? We searched Mother's Day of the world.

https://goo.gl/ayzwxR

America
During the Civil War, a woman called Ann Jarvis worked to help the soldiers regardless of enemies or allies. On 12th May,1907,her daughter Anna held a party in memory of her mother and gave the participant white carnations. This is the origin of Mother's Day. In 1914,it is enacted as a national holiday to honor mothers held on the second Sunday in May. These days, people give their mothers various presents including carnations.

https://goo.gl/JdF9Gw

France
The last Sunday in May or the first Sunday in July. In 1806, Napoleon I (1769-1821) created a national holiday for mothers. However, he created this holiday to praise the role of giving birth rather than to thank mothers because the population had been decreasing through many wars. In 1950, Mother's Day is established officially affected by American mother's day.
French send flowers as same as Japan, but they never send carnations because carnations are regarded as flowers to offer on a grave. There aren't particular flowers, but people often give roses, Chinese peonies(芍薬 in Japanese) and chrysanthemums(菊 in Japanese) to their mothers.

https://goo.gl/pmCrXh

China
Background:
Mother's day is generally celebrated on the second Sunday in May in China. It is a holiday that was first celebrated regionally in Hong Kong and Macau. After the Chinese economic reform in 1979, the Chinese mainland began to embrace this holiday. As the imported holiday of Mother's Day aligned with traditions of filial piety in China, it became popular soon during people who are born after 1980s.

Activities:
- Schools and colleges arrange campaigns to raise funds to meet the needs of their mother.
- Project Happiness, one aimed at helping poor mothers, was launched in 1995 by the China Population Welfare Foundation, Family Planning Association of China and China Population News.
- The Meng Mu Culture Festival in Taigu, Shangxi Province, was held on May 12, 2013 to celebrate and promote Mother's Day in China.

https://goo.gl/xHMym1

Egypt
Mother's day in Egypt is on 21st March. It begins in 1956. Mustafa Amin ;she is Egyptian journalist , wrote American Mother's Day in her books. It is origin. On Mother's day, children gives present for mother. In Egypt, children is often dancing for mother on this day.

https://goo.gl/y9SJkz

Summary
In Japan, the origin of Mother's Day is "Mother's Day" of America. And there are various Mother's Days in the world. The date of Mother's Day and customs are different.
However, many countries have Mother's Day. Although there are some differences, we respect our mother and appreciate mother's hard work.

---

5. To watch the poster come to life, download and install the mobile application BlippAR, then go to settings and enter the following code: 238935. Finally scan the image shown by a red arrow in Figure 2 to watch the video overlayed on it.

Table 1. Usage experience questionnaire results

Items	Strongly Disagree	Disagree	Agree	Strongly Agree
I find BlippAR easy to use.	7.0%	43.7%	43.7%	5.6%
BlippAR makes learning English more interesting.	4.2%	26.8%	57.7%	11.3%
Working with BlippAR is fun.	2.9%	22.5%	57.7%	16.9%
I do not like working with BlippAR.	11.3%	57.7%	26.8%	4.2%
My overall usage experience with BlippAR is good.	2.8%	38.0%	56.3%	2.9%
Using BlippAR would improve my English.	8.4%	62.0%	26.8%	2.8%

Regarding the subsequent use of BlippAR, about half of the students (52.1%) were not sure whether they would use BlippAR again outside the class, and 28.2% of them said they were not intending to.

The qualitative data (i.e. open-ended feedback and observations), also revealed that, to a large number of students, AR could make the process of English learning interesting and fun, but it could not directly improve their English. A few students believed that AR could improve their English skills as it provided more opportunities for getting exposed to English and it engaged all their auditory and visual senses.

5. Discussion

Overall, considering both quantitative and qualitative findings, a fairly positive AR user experience was reported by the participants of this study. This result is roughly in line with those of previous studies (e.g. Chow et al., 2015; Küçük, Yılmaz, & Göktaş, 2014) which investigated the attitude of students toward the use of AR and showed a more positive attitude compared to the findings of this study. The participants of the current study found their AR experience as interesting and pleasant, however about half of them also found it difficult to use due to technical glitches (e.g. the long loading time for some overlayed videos). Li, Chen, Whittinghill, and Vorvoreanu's (2014) study also revealed that technical issues decreased users' satisfaction and diverted their attention from the learning task. Despite having technical challenges, this study suggests that AR could to some extent engage students and motivate them to learn (items 2 and 3). As pointed out by Chow et al. (2015), AR can improve the level of students' engagement in learning, and as mentioned by Reinders and Lakarnchua (2014), AR has the potential to increase students' motivation, and boosting engagement and motivation can eventually facilitate the improvement of English language skills.

6. Concluding remarks and future vision

In this study, AR was used to augment poster carousel tasks in a blended English course. Notwithstanding the technical difficulties, by and large, the quantitative findings and the qualitative feedback and observations indicated that a majority of the participants engaged in AR and found the activity a rather enjoyable experience. Further research will determine how using AR and getting students involved with generating their own AR-based content may improve the effectiveness of language learning, as well as learners' motivation. With advances in new technologies, it will be increasingly easier to bring more of AR to the classroom in the near future, and interactive, engaging learning environments can be created to enhance learning and meet the needs of students in the 21st century.

References

Chow, E. H. C., Thadani, D. R., Wong, E. Y. W., & Pegrum, M. (2015). Mobile technologies and augmented reality: early experiences in helping students learn about academic integrity and ethics. *International Journal of Humanities, Social Sciences and Education, 2*(7), 112-120.

Davis, F. D. (1989). Perceived usefulness, perceived ease of use, and user acceptance of information technology. *MIS Quarterly, 13*(3), 319-340. https://doi.org/10.2307/249008

Küçük, S., Yılmaz, R. M., & Göktaş, Y. (2014). Augmented reality for learning English: achievement, attitude and cognitive load levels of students. *Education and Science, 39*(176), 393-404. https://doi.org/10.15390/EB.2014.3595

Li, S., Chen, Y., Whittinghill, D. M., & Vorvoreanu, M. (2014). A pilot study exploring augmented reality to increase motivation of Chinese college students learning English. Paper presented at the 2014 ASEE Annual Conference, Indianapolis, IN. https://goo.gl/LLm3GX

Reinders, H., & Lakarnchua, O. (2014). Implementing mobile language learning with an augmented reality activity. *Modern English Teacher, 23*(2), 42-50. http://innovationinteaching.org/wp-content/themes/default/images/met2014.pdf

Venkatesh, V., Morris, M. G., Davis, G. B., & Davis, F. D. (2003). User acceptance of information technology: toward a unified view. *MIS Quarterly, 27*(3), 425-478.

Empowering language learners through the use of a curriculum-integrated information literacy programme: an action research project

Sahar Alzahrani[1]

Abstract. This paper implements and evaluates a curriculum-integrated information literacy programme in an Arabic primary school in the United Kingdom to empower learners and develop life-long learning skills. It reports on an action research project with a reflective practice approach used at the beginning of the semester to identify potential problems before planning the action. A focus group interview and learners' written output were used to answer three research questions about learners' awareness, attitudes, and confidence about information literacy skills. Enhancement was found in these three aspects.

Keywords: information literacy skills, learner empowerment, technology enhanced language learning, language learner autonomy.

1. Introduction

In the last few decades, a large number of sources of information have appeared, and thus learning information search skills is important (Sasikala & Dhanraju, 2011). To help learners cope with this change, we need to enhance their autonomy by equipping them with the needed skills (Schwienhorst, 2008). Learners' use of information literacy skills effectively helps to improve their performance in schools (Ilogho & Nkiko, 2014). Information literacy skills are essential for the development of life-long learning (Wallace, Shorten, & Crookes, 2000). As such, helping learners to become life-long learners and more autonomous entails empowering them with opportunities for experimentation with authentic language learning material through the use of search tools (Schwienhorst, 2008).

---

1. University of Southampton, Southampton, United Kingdom; saharmatar2@gmail.com

How to cite this article: Alzahrani, S. (2017). Empowering language learners through the use of a curriculum-integrated information literacy programme: an action research project. In K. Borthwick, L. Bradley & S. Thouësny (Eds), *CALL in a climate of change: adapting to turbulent global conditions – short papers from EUROCALL 2017* (pp. 13-18). Research-publishing.net. https://doi.org/10.14705/rpnet.2017.eurocall2017.681

The context of this study is an Arabic primary school run by volunteering individuals in the United Kingdom. In this school, soft copies of the textbooks are used via technology. Learners in this school are proficient at their L2 (English) and they are learning writing and reading in their L1 (Arabic). Because information search skills are believed to be important for the enhancement of learners' awareness of, attitude towards, and confidence in information exploration (Dunn, 2002), this study presents the results for their empowerment in language learning and for the development of their life-long learning skills. It also seeks to answer three research questions:

- To what extent are learners aware of search skills on the internet after the training?

- What are learners' attitudes towards search skills after the training?

- To what extent are learners confident with looking for and using information after the training?

2. Method

2.1. Study design

"Reflective practice can be a useful precursor to action research. It is not identical to it" (McMahon, 1999, p. 163). In reflective practice, teachers do not learn how to perform actions, but they learn from their experience and they should be sensitive to the needs of their own and of their context as well as the educational philosophies adopted by their institutions (McMahon, 1999). In this study, I have adopted a reflective practice approach (a thinking approach to practice) which led to a strategic action characterising the undertaken action research. Reflective practice was used during the first two weeks of the study to identify potential problems that might suppress learners' life-long learning skills. I looked at learners' needs and the existing resources and found that printed textbooks are not available for those learners. They have limited competence at information search and are used to receiving information from teachers and textbooks. After the reflective practice, the strategic action was planned to solve this problem.

This paper reports on an action research that implements and evaluates a curriculum-integrated information literacy programme in a primary school. The planned action was to provide eight-week training on the information literacy skills to develop learners' search skills on the internet to enhance their awareness and performance and to provide a non-graded task at the end of each class to search for a given topic (e.g. food etiquette). These eight tasks provide opportunities to explore information outside the classroom. Five search skills – appropriate for the young age of those learners – were used as the focus of the training: defining the topic; choosing a search tool; defining keywords; using search building techniques (e.g. synonyms, limiters, and refining); and knowing how to read the search results.

2.2. Data collection

An interpretive approach is exploited in this study in which qualitative data is used to explore the potential change in aspects of learning after being exposed to the training and after being given the tasks. Learners' feedback on the tasks and on the skills practiced during the course were collected at the beginning of the training and after the last task in the training.

To answer the research questions, a Focus Group (FG) interview was used at two different times (FG1 after the first task and FG2 after the last task) to collect learners' feedback on the course tasks and skills which were practiced during the course. Moreover, learners' written output was collected every week to evaluate the impact of the training and the tasks.

3. Results and discussion

The instructional methodology contributed to the development of a set of lifelong learning skills. The activity theory – in which a unity between consciousness and activity is achieved – is used to explain the findings.

3.1. Awareness

- To what extent are learners aware of search skills on the internet after the training?

This section presents evidence found in learners' data in the FG regarding learners' enhanced awareness of search skills. In FG2, steps can be identified in the explanation of the search process they used. Additionally, longer and richer description of the process was provided in FG2 and there was less mention of parents' support in FG2.

3.2. Attitude

- What are learners' attitudes towards search skills after the training?

This question was answered using the FG. The first two learners in Table 1 started and ended with a positive attitude (easy to look for information on the internet) perhaps because they knew beforehand how to use the computer and to code. It was difficult for Learner 3 in Task 1 – though he was excited to learn it – but this has become easier after the course. Five other learners started with a negative attitude. Three of them (4, 5, and 6) have enhanced their attitude as they have benefited from the training, but two others (7 and 8) were the least contributing learners and maintained their negative attitude.

Table 1. Learners' attitudes towards information search

St.	Before the training	Reasons	After the training	Reasons
1	Easy	Coding experience	Easy	Coding experience
2	Easy	Coding experience	Easy	Coding experience
3	Difficult, but excited	Likes to explore	Easy	Practice (he is a good student)
4	Difficult, sought parents' help	Result selection, reading, and writing	Easier, with difficulties	Reading and rewriting information
5	Difficult, sought parents' help	New kind of jobs	Easier, with difficulties	Reading and rewriting information
6	Difficult, sought parents' help	Hard job	Easier, with difficulties	Using English Keyboard to type Arabic
7	Difficult, sought parents' help	Don't know how to write	Difficult	The least contributing
8	Difficult, sought parents' help	Need to write a lot	Difficult	The least contributing

3.3. Confidence

- To what extent are learners confident with looking for and using information after the training?

This question was answered using the FG and learners' written output. The first two learners started and ended the course with great confidence which was attributed to their experience in coding. The rest of the learners lacked confidence before the training. Four of them (3, 4, 5, and 6) reported greater confidence after it due to the practice they had. Nonetheless, two learners were the least contributing learners and they still lacked confidence after the course (Table 2).

Table 2. Learners' confidence about the use of information search

St.	Before the training	Reasons	After the training	Reasons
1	Great	Coding experience	Great	Coding experience
2	Great	Coding experience	Great	Coding experience
3	No	Lots of information	Better	Practice
4	No	Lack of skills and awareness of steps	Better	Practice
5	No	Don't know how to do it	Better	Learned
6	No	Hard job	Better	Used it
7	No	Need mum's help	Lack	Don't know how to do it
8	No	Lots of details	Lack	Scared

To ensure validity of confidence findings, FG was triangulated with learners' written output in the tasks performed at the beginning and at the end to identify evidence for the potential improvement in learners' confidence. In the last task, learners were found using longer sentences and their writing length in the tasks increased. In addition, the bullet points used in writing the first task were changed into full paragraphs in the last task.

4. Conclusions

In short, the implemented curriculum-integrated information literacy programme, designed for an Arabic primary school in the United Kingdom, seems to show effectiveness in developing learners' awareness of information literacy skills, enhancing their attitudes, and promoting their confidence about their information literacy competence, as was argued by Dunn (2002). Future research can implement a similar programme with learners in higher education.

5. Acknowledgements

I would like to thank the principal of the Arabic School in Southampton, UK and the students for helping with this study.

References

Dunn, K. (2002). Assessing information literacy skills in the California State University: a progress report. *Journal of Academic Librarianship, 28*(1-2), 26-35. https://doi.org/10.1016/S0099-1333(01)00281-6

Ilogho, J., & Nkiko, C. (2014). Information literacy search skills of students in five selected private universities in Ogun State, Nigeria: a survey. *Library Philosophy and Practice (e-journal)*. Paper 1040.

McMahon, T. (1999). Is reflective practice synonymous with action research? *Educational Action Research, 7*(1), 163-169. https://doi.org/10.1080/09650799900200080

Sasikala, C., & Dhanraju, V. (2011). Assessment of information literacy skills among science students of Andhra University. *Library Philosophy and Practice (e-journal)*. Paper 626.

Schwienhorst, K. (2008). *Learner Autonomy and CALL Environments*. Routledge.

Wallace, M. C., Shorten, A., & Crookes, P. A. (2000). Teaching information literacy skills: an evaluation. *Nurse Educ Today, 20*(6), 485-9. https://doi.org/10.1054/nedt.1999.0439

Transforming learning, conceptualisation and practices through a MOOC on English as a Medium of Instruction for Academics

Robert Baird[1], Kate Borthwick[2], and Mary Page[3]

Abstract. One of the oft-cited advantages of Massive Open Online Courses (MOOCs) is that they provide access opportunities for learners that they might not otherwise have, for example, offering continuing professional development, complementing traditional courses of study, or opening up new areas of knowledge (Ferguson & Sharples, 2014; Hollands & Tirthali, 2014; Zheng, Rosson, Shih, & Carroll, 2015). We report on our experiences designing the FutureLearn MOOC *English as a Medium of Instruction for Academics*, and reflect upon how a free, online platform, operating across a global network, has the potential to enhance learning and practice in English Medium Instruction (EMI) domains. We consider how EMI, a topic with transient, contextual, and emergent themes, can profit from contextualisation through global online dialogues in ways that benefit wider understanding of EMI while simultaneously informing educators about the field.

Keywords: MOOC, EMI, English language, open education.

1. Introduction

MOOCs have been a growing phenomenon in UK higher education for some years now and researchers are still developing an understanding of their value, purpose, and impact as an educational experience. Practitioners have identified potential benefits to this kind of free, open, large-scale course, including continuing professional development, complementing traditional courses of study with additional educational material, or accessing new areas of knowledge (Ferguson &

---

1. University of Southampton, Southampton, United Kingdom; r.d.baird@soton.ac.uk
2. University of Southampton, Southampton, United Kingdom; k.borthwick@soton.ac.uk
3. University of Southampton, Southampton, United Kingdom; m.w.page@soton.ac.uk

How to cite this article: Baird, R., Borthwick, K., & Page, M. (2017). Transforming learning, conceptualisation and practices through a MOOC on English as a Medium of Instruction for Academics. In K. Borthwick, L. Bradley & S. Thouësny (Eds), *CALL in a climate of change: adapting to turbulent global conditions – short papers from EUROCALL 2017* (pp. 19-23). Research-publishing.net. https://doi.org/10.14705/rpnet.2017.eurocall2017.682

Sharples, 2014; Hollands & Tirthali, 2014; Zheng et al., 2015). This paper focusses on the potential of the Futurelearn MOOC platform in the area of EMI from the perspectives of the designers. The next phase of our MOOC will see further empirical research carried out around the MOOC's users' experiences.

2. Method

2.1. The approach

The MOOC 'English as a Medium of Instruction for Academics' was made in collaboration with FutureLearn, a UK-based MOOC platform provider (www.futurelearn.com). The FutureLearn course model is designed "according to principles of effective learning, through storytelling, discussion, visible learning, and using community support to celebrate progress" (https://www.futurelearn.com/using-futurelearn/why-it-works). It is informed by a particular learning design based on a conversational model of learning which promotes social activity as an integral part of learning. A core intention is to create a learning community and involve learners as participants in sharing their own experiences and knowledge.

We considered conversational activity as more important than any pre-made course content, and so courses were designed to foster discussion of ideas and encourage online social interaction. This was stimulated through a range of functions and activities designed to elicit such insights and interaction, with each step of the course inviting comments and some prioritising such input as the step's content. Participants were invited to engage with polls and quizzes; share resources, examples and experiences with others; evaluate and reflect on informative content (e.g. articles or videos) from their own contextual and professional experiences; and to engage with debates ranging from contextual best practice to the status of English and other languages. Together, we tried to design each step to position the voices, experiences, and participation of the 'learners' as the course content, with provided resources seeking to stimulate dissemination of ideas rather than guide thought.

2.2. The focus

EMI refers to courses that are taught through English in 'international' contexts (Dearden, 2014). In the pursuit of perceived benefits associated with internationalisation, some universities are pushing to implement EMI despite challenges they face in doing so effectively (Kirkpatrick, 2017). Such challenges can relate to developing infrastructure and support across populations with diverse roles and needs, and various communicative issues facing students and staff when using English in their contexts.

Jenkins (2014) observes that English is prevalent in higher education discourses around the world and Baird (2013) highlighted that 'EMI' can refer to a vast range of educational scenarios, with materials, assessments, goals, contextual communication, and student/staff populations all providing points of potential variation in how EMI is realised. This creates a need for the development of networks that can establish an enduring channel of communication between academics working in these areas. An open online course was perceived as an ideal place for such dialogues to be initiated and developed.

2.3. The 'E' of EMI

Language changes with users and uses, and English as a Lingua Franca (ELF) researchers have highlighted the complex, pragmatic, and dynamic ways in which communication can take place between speakers who do not share a first language (Baird, Baker, & Kitazawa, 2014; Jenkins, 2015; Mauranen, 2012). We see accessing experiences of actual EMI language practices as essential to understanding what the 'E' in EMI can refer to and in developing educators' abilities to engage with 'it' in their settings.

The recent work of Jenkins (2017) has gone beyond 'which kind of English?' to consider the role of multilingualism in ELF and EMI contexts. Different approaches to English and multilingualism in EMI settings are directly accessible through the abovementioned conversational approaches of this MOOC, which allows content to be grounded in diverse experiences, identities, and practices rather than presented by experts who have never worked in or been to many settings in which these educators operate.

3. Discussion

There are clear challenges presented by EMI to individuals and institutions, but not everybody has equal opportunities to engage in professional development, networking or critical reflection. In order to bring people together who are involved with EMI in its various realisations, we needed a platform that was accessible, free, inclusive, and which did not have constraints on participation times (with participants in different time zones). This inclusivity was not only convenient for reaching people, but was a key design principle for collaborative learning within a complex field of practice. With EMI involving such diversity, networked knowledge-sharing is an essential part of understanding, contextualising, and processing ideas and practices.

One concern was how to allow for the development of an individual's self-belief and simultaneously allow space for shifts in perception within the structure of the MOOC. In our experience, confidence and self-efficacy can be the most obvious barriers that many EMI educators face, and this can be inhibited by pacifying EMI educators through instructing them or setting objective targets. Our 'bottom-up' approach was also a way of addressing this. Reflective practice was core to the design of learners' online experience, and rather than prescribing an EMI template ("this is what you have to say and do in your classroom"), we encouraged participants to contribute to discussions of their own and others' practice. By doing this, we attempted to embrace the diversity of the EMI environment and assign shared responsibility for determining what might be appropriate practice in each setting.

4.   Conclusions

The Futurelearn MOOC design enabled us to encourage participants to reflect on their environments, explore alternatives, and justify their rationales for approaching EMI in their chosen ways. Initial participant data shows that interaction on the course was good: it attracted nearly 4000 learners, of whom 55% posted at least one comment. We sought to create a transformative learning community in which all participants provide, negotiate, and co-construct knowledge across the various EMI contexts and practices. Participants were seen as experts within their own localities and specialities, equipped with relevant knowledge and skills to share and discuss strategies and approaches that could benefit their learners. An open, dialogic learning model uniting globally-located learners suited this purpose. This allowed us to embrace learning as co-constructed rather than transmitted, and allowed us to identify, define, and negotiate contextually relevant practices and constructs through dialogue, which is fitting for an emergent field such as EMI and for communication in ELF settings, as both have various realisations and contextual influences on their use. Through the course's discussion areas, insights were sustained by the community in a way that we hope enhanced educators' awareness, autonomy, and confidence within their roles. Further in-depth analysis of participant data and responses is underway.

References

Baird, R. (2013). *Investigating perceptions of Master's students on English-as-a-medium-of-instruction programmes in East Asia*. PhD thesis. University of Southampton. https://www.researchgate.net/publication/299657278_Investigating_Perceptions_of_Master%27s_Students_on_English-as-a-medium-of-instruction_Programmes_in_East_Asia

Baird, R., Baker, W., & Kitazawa, M. (2014). The complexity of ELF. *The Journal of English as a Lingua Franca, 3*(1), 171-196. https://doi.org/10.1515/jelf-2014-0007

Dearden, J. (2014). *English as a medium of instruction–a growing global phenomenon*. British Council. https://www.britishcouncil.org/sites/default/files/e484_emi_-_cover_option_3_final_web.pdf

Ferguson, R., & Sharples, M. (2014). Innovative pedagogy at massive scale: teaching and learning in MOOCs. In *Open Learning and Teaching in Educational Communities: 9th European Conference on Technology Enhanced Learning, EC-TEL 2014, Graz, Austria, September 16-19, 2014, Proceedings, Lecture Notes in Computer Science. Springer International Publishing* (pp. 98–111). https://doi.org/10.1007/978-3-319-11200-8_8

Hollands, F.M., & Tirthali, D. (2014). *MOOCs: expectations and reality, Report for the Center for Benefit-cost Studies of Education*. Columbia University.

Jenkins, J. (2014). *English as a Lingua Franca in the International University. The politics of academic English language policy*. Routledge.

Jenkins, J. (2015). Repositioning English and multilingualism in English as a Lingua Franca. *Englishes in Practice, 2*(3), 49-85. https://doi.org/10.1515/eip-2015-0003

Jenkins, J. (2017). *Mobility and English language policies and practices in higher education*. In S. Canagarajah (Ed.), *The Routledge handbook of migration and language* (pp. 502-518). Routledge.

Kirkpatrick, A. (2017). 談亞洲地區大學專業領域以英語授課: 議題與政策 (Asian Universities and English as a Medium of instruction: Topics and policies). *The Way of Language: Learning, Assessment and Culture, 8*, 5-11. https://www.lttc.ntu.edu.tw/Journal.htm

Mauranen, A. (2012). *Exploring ELF: academic English shaped by non-native speakers*. Cambridge University Press.

Zheng, S., Rosson, M. B., Shih, P. C., & Carroll, J. M. (2015). Understanding student motivation, behaviors and perceptions in MOOCs. In *Proceedings of the 18th ACM Conference on Computer Supported Cooperative Work & Social Computing* (pp. 1882-1895). ACM. https://doi.org/10.1145/2675133.2675217

Foreign language anxiety on a massive open online language course

Zsuzsanna Bárkányi[1] and Sabela Melchor-Couto[2]

Abstract. This paper examines learner attitudes, self-efficacy beliefs, and anxiety in a beginners' Spanish Language Massive Open Online Course (LMOOC) by answering three research questions: (1) how do learners feel about acquiring speaking skills on an LMOOC?; (2) do they experience anxiety with regards to speaking?; and (3) do their self-efficacy beliefs remain unchanged during the LMOOC? Data was collected from over 900 participants registered on two Spanish for Beginners programmes offered by The Open University (UK). Quantitative data was collected through reflective questionnaires (11 items) and participants' comments were obtained on two discussion forums. Results indicate that learners have positive attitudes towards LMOOCs and present higher speaking self-efficacy beliefs by the end of the course. Although spoken interactions in this environment are not synchronous, most participants report feeling intimidated by the idea of posting their recordings on the course forum.

Keywords: LMOOC, self-efficacy beliefs, foreign language anxiety.

1. Introduction

LMOOCs are massive open online courses for teaching and learning second and foreign language with unrestricted access and unlimited participation. LMOOCs are unique in that language learning is skill-based rather than knowledge-based and acquiring these skills involves interaction with other speakers, which might not be easy to achieve on a Massive Open Online Course (MOOC). The Spanish for Beginners programme offered by The Open University comprises six four-week courses covering level A1 – Common European Framework of Reference for languages (CEFR). Interaction is possible in the discussion areas, where dialogue

1. The Open University, Milton Keynes, United Kingdom; zsuzsanna.barkanyi@open.ac.uk
2. University of Roehampton, London, United Kingdom; s.melchor-couto@roehampton.ac.uk

How to cite this article: Bárkányi, Z., & Melchor-Couto, S. (2017). Foreign language anxiety on a massive open online language course. In K. Borthwick, L. Bradley & S. Thouësny (Eds), *CALL in a climate of change: adapting to turbulent global conditions – short papers from EUROCALL 2017* (pp. 24-29). Research-publishing.net. https://doi.org/10.14705/rpnet.2017.eurocall2017.683

and peer feedback is shared. The only way of 'speaking' to peers and instructors is by recording one's own voice and uploading the file to the forum.

LMOOCs present an interesting and unexplored context to observe affective variables such as Foreign Language Anxiety (FLA) or self-efficacy beliefs, which is the aim of this study. FLA is a specific type of anxiety that can be experienced by learners across all language activities and most scholars concur that it is mainly negative for learners (MacIntyre, 2017). The most widely used instrument to measure FLA is Horwitz, Horwitz, and Cope's (1986) Foreign Language Classroom Anxiety Scale (FLCAS); other questionnaires measure the anxiety experienced in specific language activities, such as writing or reading.

Self-efficacy beliefs refer to people's perceived ability to perform in specific contexts (Bandura & Schunk, 1981). Research indicates that users feel they perform better when interactions are via Computer-Mediated Communication (CMC) environments instead of face-to-face (F2F) (Tanis & Postmes, 2007). Similar conclusions have been found in CALL research (Henderson, Huang, Grant, & Henderson, 2009). Most of the instruments available for measuring self-efficacy in language learning consist of items that ask students overtly to rate their competence on specific skills.

2. Method

The first course of the Spanish for Beginners programme had 4,903 fully participating learners, completing at least 50% of the activities, out of the total 49,120 registered students; the last course had 301 participants.

Quantitative data was collected through reflective pre- and post-course questionnaires (11 questions). Post-course surveys have 10% of responses as compared to pre-course surveys, and respondents often skip questions, resulting in uneven data. Responses from various courses were merged into two pre-course and post-course sets. Comparing learners' answers at the beginning and at the end of a course would require a repeated measures analysis like ANOVA or a paired t-test. However, due to the nature of our courses and ethical reasons (anonymity of answers), it is not possible to match the pre- and post-course data. Therefore, both sets have been treated as two groups, and, following Boone and Boone's (2012) recommendation to analyse Likert-type data, a Pearson's chi-square test was applied. Qualitative data was obtained from comments on the questionnaires and discourse in the discussion forum. A total of 207 responses to open-ended questions were provided, mostly on attitudes and habits regarding the speaking activities proposed in the LMOOC.

All responses were analysed and coded according to topic, which resulted in four broad categories referring to technical issues, motivational factors for completing the activities, lack of motivation, and anxiety experienced.

3. Results and discussion

3.1. Learner beliefs and behaviours

Most participants have a positive view of LMOOCs. When it comes to speaking specifically, pronunciation and understanding were seen by the majority as very easy or fairly easy to learn online (44.7% and 60.1%), whereas fluency was described as fairly or very difficult to learn online (49.3%). Accuracy presents responses spread evenly amongst the three options.

3.2. Self-efficacy beliefs

When asked at the start of the course, most participants rated their speaking ability, grammatical accuracy in spoken Spanish, fluency, and vocabulary as very or fairly poor. However, when compared with the results collected at the end of the course, a shift towards the positive end of the spectrum is observed across all parameters, particularly in pronunciation and vocabulary (Figure 1).

Figure 1. Speaking self-efficacy beliefs: start (n=907) and end (n=270)

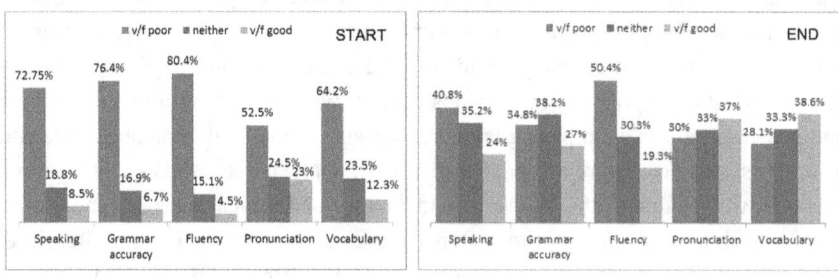

The Pearson's chi-square test administered indicates that the differences between the data recorded at the start and end of the course are significant in all cases

(p<.001). This suggests an improvement in participants' self-efficacy beliefs after completing the LMOOC (see Table 1).

Table 1. Self-efficacy beliefs Pearson's chi square test

Overall speaking	$X2 = 110.51, df = 4, p<0.001$
Grammatical accuracy	$X2 = 196.36, df = 4, p<0.001$
Fluency	$X2 = 132,73, df = 4, p<0.001$
Pronunciation	$X2 = 83.91, df = 4, p<0.001$
Vocabulary	$X2 = 150.99, df = 4, p<0.001$

3.3. Foreign language anxiety

The data available in this category is more limited than in previous sections, yet it presents interesting findings. Participants report feeling insecure when recording themselves but are not particularly anxious when faced with audio materials that they do not understand and feel more comfortable when shielded by their computer in speaking activities. In fact, most learners prefer CMC interactions. Unlike their perceived self-efficacy beliefs, learners' fear of synchronous speaking situations shows a similar level at the beginning and at the end of the course. It is interesting to note that, at the beginning of the course, learners do not show so much appreciation for the advantages of CMC interactions as compared to the end of the course. A Pearson's chi-square test was applied to identify statistically significant data. These have been signalled with an asterisk in the Table 2 below. Students' comments also reflect this anxiety, as they report not being confident enough to record themselves or they feel intimidated and embarrassed.

Table 2. Pre- and post-course answers to anxiety-related questions (n=182 and n=26, respectively)

	Strongly agree / agree		Neither		Strongly disagree / disagree	
	START	END	START	END	START	END
I never feel quite sure of myself when I have to record my voice.	57.14%	44.00%	21.98%	28.00%	20.88%	28.00%
I don't worry about making mistakes in Spanish.	45.36%	46.15%	21.86%	7.69%	32.79%	46.15%
It frightens me when I don't understand the audios and the videos in the course material.	24.16%	7.69%	38.76%	38.46%	37.08%	53.85%

I get nervous when I don't understand every word in the audios and videos of the course material.	26.97%	11.54%	31.46%	19.23%	41.57%	69.23%
I would not be nervous speaking Spanish to native speakers.	31.84%	34.62%	24.58%	26.92%	43.58%	38.46%
I would probably feel comfortable around native speakers of Spanish.	34.64%	42.31%	36.31%	23.08%	29.05%	34.62%
It's easier to speak into a computer than face-to-face* (X-squared = 9.658, df = 2, p-value = 0.008)	40.98%*	73.08%*	35.52%*	19.23%*	23.05%*	7.69%*
The lack of physical presence makes me feel more comfortable.	35.52%	53.85%	44.81%	38.46%	19.67%	7.69%
The lack of physical presence makes me feel more nervous* (X-squared = 7.5394, df = 2, p-value = 0.019)	10.44%*	0.00%*	43.41%*	26.92%*	46.15%*	73.08%*

Over half of the participants (54.1%; n=133) recorded the speaking activities, although the majority chose not to post them (62.35%; n=85) because they felt intimidated by it (46.6%) despite the fact that it is an asynchronous activity. This indicates that FLA is present in online courses and it can have inhibitory effects.

4. Conclusion

In line with Rubio (2014), the data analysed indicates that LMOOC learners have positive attitudes towards this type of (spoken) language learning environment. By the end of the course, participants present higher self-efficacy beliefs in terms of speaking competence. A majority of learners feel more comfortable interacting in the foreign language via a CMC environment than F2F (in accordance with earlier literature, e.g. Wehner, Gump, & Downey, 2011) and, although spoken activities are not synchronous, most learners report to be intimidated, not confident enough, and even embarrassed by the option of posting their recordings. This shows that FLA is not only present in F2F classrooms but also in online courses. A novel finding of the present research is that due to FLA, learners on LMOOCs can also experience an inhibitory effect.

References

Bandura, A., & Schunk, D. H. (1981). Cultivating competence, self-efficacy, and intrinsic interest through proximal self-motivation. *Journal of Personality and Social Psychology, 41*(3), 586-598.

Boone, H. N. & D. A. Boone (2012). Analyzing likert data. *Journal of Extension, 49*(2). http://www.joe.org/joe/2011april/a6.php

Henderson, M., Huang, H., Grant, S., & Henderson, L. (2009). Language acquisition in Second Life: improving self-efficacy beliefs. In R. J. Atkinson & C. McBeath (Eds), *Same places, different spaces. Proceedings Ascilite Auckland 2009*. University of Auckland.

Horwitz, E. K., Horwitz, M. B., & Cope, J. (1986). Foreign language classroom anxiety. *The Modern Language Journal, 70*, 125-132. https://doi.org/10.1111/j.1540-4781.1986.tb05256.x

MacIntyre, P. D. (2017). *New insights into language anxiety: theory, research and educational implications (second language acquisition)*. Multilingual Matters.

Rubio, F. (2014). Teaching pronunciation and comprehensibility in a Language MOOC. In E. Bárcena & E. Marín-Monje (Eds), *Language MOOCs: providing learning, transcending boundaries* (pp. 143-160). De Gruyter. https://doi.org/10.2478/9783110420067.9

Tanis, M., & Postmes, T. (2007). Two faces of anonymity: paradoxical effects of cues to identity in CMC. *Computers in Human Behavior, 23*, 955-970. https://doi.org/10.1016/j.chb.2005.08.004

Wehner, A., Gump, A. W., & Downey, S. (2011). The effects of second Life on the Motivation of undergraduate students learning a foreign language. *Computer-Assisted Language Learning, 24*(3), 277-289. https://doi.org/10.1080/09588221.2010.551757

LMOOCs, classifying design: survey findings from LMOOC providers

Elaine Beirne[1], Mairéad Nic Giolla Mhichíl[2], and Gearóid Ó Cleircín[3]

Abstract. Many of the major Massive Open Online Course (MOOC) platforms support learning approaches which can be roughly categorised as transmission-based and asynchronous (Morris & Lambe, 2014), with limited forms of interactive elements. Language learning is viewed within this study as an active process which includes knowledge, skills, and cultural competencies. Designing a Language-learning MOOC (or LMOOC) that facilitates this view of the language learning process is challenging, however, particularly considering the predominance of learning templates within the MOOC platforms that are designed from a mainly knowledge-transmission perspective. Using Conole's (2014) classification of MOOCs, a sample of LMOOC providers self-report in a survey on the pedagogical approach implemented within their LMOOC's learning design. These findings are reported in this paper. This study is timely as the number of LMOOCs being offered is increasing, although the proportion of LMOOCs is still low in terms of the wider MOOC landscape. The paper concludes by considering whether LMOOCs can be aligned with this classification tool or whether an extension to this classification is required to cater for the nuances of MOOC-based language learning.

Keywords: language learning MOOCs, classification of MOOCs, language learning design, LMOOCs.

---

1. Dublin City University, Dublin, Ireland; elaine.beirne4@mail.dcu.ie
2. Dublin City University, Dublin, Ireland; mairead.nicgiollamhichil@dcu.ie
3. Dublin City University, Dublin, Ireland; gearoid.ocleircin@dcu.ie

How to cite this article: Beirne, E., Nic Giolla Mhichíl, M., & Ó Cleircín, G. (2017). LMOOCs, classifying design: survey findings from LMOOC providers. In K. Borthwick, L. Bradley & S. Thouësny (Eds), *CALL in a climate of change: adapting to turbulent global conditions – short papers from EUROCALL 2017* (pp. 30-34). Research-publishing.net. https://doi.org/10.14705/rpnet.2017.eurocall2017.684

1. Introduction

There has been significant growth of MOOCs over the past decade. LMOOCs, however, have been slower than other disciplinary areas to engage with the potential of this new learning model. In 2014, Bárcena and Martín-Monje (2014) conducted an analysis of the availability of LMOOCs on the major MOOC platforms, revealing 26 LMOOCs. A review of the current offering of LMOOCs, conducted by this research team in June 2017, based on the methodology of Bárcena and Martín-Monje (2014), noted an increase of LMOOCs to 143. Chinese joined English and Spanish as the most popular languages in LMOOCs. The provision of other languages is also increasing, with courses for languages such as Norwegian, Malay, Frisian, and Sanskrit now available. The majority of courses are aimed at the beginner level. However, an increasing number of courses are aimed at more advanced learners who want to improve their language skills, particularly in specific domains such as language for business or academic purposes. This emerging language learning model raises important issues for course designers and developers concerning the rationale for adopting a particular pedagogical approach that caters for the specificities of foreign language learning. MOOCs are typically categorised as either xMOOC or cMOOC based on the pedagogical design of the course. xMOOCs tend to adopt a behaviourist learning approach and reflect more of a transmission approach to learning, while cMOOCs support connectivist pedagogy and are focused around learner generated content and interactive media (Morris & Lambe, 2014). The majority of the major MOOC platforms have xMOOC templates and are predominantly focussed on knowledge acquisition. Language learning, however, is an active process that requires both skill development and knowledge acquisition (Bárcena & Martín-Monje, 2014; Sokolik, 2014) situated within cultural contexts. Learning a language requires the use of higher order thinking skills as well as high levels of engagement and interaction. In addition, after infancy there is a need for a more rule-based cognitive approach (Meltzoff & Prinz, 2002). This paper examines how the current supply of LMOOCs are addressing learning within MOOC environments. Using Conole's (2014) classification of MOOCs, the paper explores the approach to (1) learning, (2) technology, and (3) learner support as reported by a sample of LMOOC providers from a variety of the major MOOC platforms.

2. Method

Data for this study was collected by means of a structured, online questionnaire containing 24 items, divided into three sections using both closed and open questions.

The questions were constructed to correspond to Conole's (2014) classification criteria. The questionnaire was piloted with two LMOOC providers prior to the main study. Participants self-reported (1) contextual information, (2) information relating to the participants, and finally (3) the pedagogical approach adopted in the LMOOC. The questionnaire was distributed to a sample of 40 LMOOC providers identified by the research based on a sampling methodology adopted from Bárcena and Martín-Monje (2014). Twenty-one completed questionnaires were classified. To aid with the analysis, three dimensions were developed by the researchers to group responses as low, medium, and high with respect to each criterion (Conole, 2014), an example of this criterion is outlined in Table 1.

Table 1. Example of criterion parameters

Dimension	Low	Medium	High
Massive	0 – 1,000	1,000 – 5,000	More than 5,000
Multimedia	Course is limited to the use of one media type e.g. video	Course utilises a limited number of multimedia types	Course uses a wide range of multimedia and interactive media

3. Findings from the classification of LMOOCs

Table 2 illustrates the finding of the classification of each LMOOC's responses to the questionnaire, where each response represents one LMOOC in the table. In terms of context, the LMOOCs demonstrate examples of low, medium, and high degrees of size and openness, with openness being viewed as a continuous construct rather than a binary state (Wiley, 2009). With regard to pedagogy, the majority of courses demonstrated high degrees of reflection, multimedia usage, learner autonomy, and communication. The type of communication is predominantly learner to learner interaction whilst learner to instructor communication is not facilitated to the same extent. The LMOOCs demonstrated a lower degree of collaboration. The courses that encourage collaboration facilitate it through platform tools but tend not to link it to the learning content. Interestingly, while most MOOCs are not formally credentialed, many LMOOCs self-reported medium to high degrees of course formality. Certification is provided on completion of most of the LMOOCs in the sample, often for an additional fee. While reflection is encouraged in many courses, further investigation is required to reveal its nature and extent. With many courses promoting an asynchronous approach to learning, learner autonomy was reported as high. The LMOOCs in the sample self-reported high quality with quality assurance mechanisms being implemented by the major MOOC platforms. The categorisation of the diversity of the participants or the nature of the learning pathways within each LMOOC is not reported as it did not align with the scale used by the researchers in their analysis.

Table 2. Classification of LMOOCs

Dimension	Low	Medium	High
Open	2	10	8
Massive	5	5	10
Multimedia	1	7	13
Collaboration	10	9	2
Communication	1	9	11
Quality	1	2	18
Reflection	3	-	18
Formal Learning	5	8	6
Certification	2	16	3
Autonomy	2	10	9

4. Discussion and conclusion

The classification schema is used to describe MOOCs, but it is also in use as a checklist to guide the design process and as a means of evaluating a MOOC's learning design (Conole, 2014). With regard to LMOOCs, however, in order to fully investigate the way in which language acquisition is supported within the course, further dimensions are required. Based on the literature pertaining to the key characteristics of effective LMOOCs (Bárcena & Martín-Monje, 2014), the researchers recommend at least the addition of two further dimensions to Conole's (2014) categorisation: language skills and instructor presence. Facilitating and assessing the development of all four language skills (reading, writing, speaking, and listening) is fundamental to the effective design of online second language courses (Don, 2005). The existing classification does not address any specific aspects of course content. As a result, the extent to which language skills and cultural competencies are dealt with by the course was not examined. In addition, the literature acknowledges the importance of instructor presence and support in developing language learner confidence and participation (Don, 2005; Kop, 2011; Moreira-Teixeira & Mota, 2014). While instructor presence is alluded to by the existing dimensions of autonomy and communication, it is not an exclusive component of these categories. The classification, therefore, does not specifically address the extent of instructor presence in the course. Designing an LMOOC that addresses the specificities of foreign language learning is challenging. The adaptations to Conole's (2014) classification recommended by this paper could make a useful tool in assisting LMOOC course designers.

5. Acknowledgements

This study was supported by the Department of Arts, Heritage and the Gaeltacht, Republic of Ireland under the Twenty-year Strategy for the Irish Language.

References

Bárcena, E., & Martín-Monje, E. (2014). Language MOOCs: an emerging field. In E. Bárcena & E. Martín-Monje (Eds), *Language MOOCs: providing learning, transcending boundaries*. Degruyter Open.

Conole, G. (2014). A new classification schema for MOOCs. *The international journal for Innovation and Quality in Learning, 2*(3), 65-77.

Don, M. R. (2005). An investigation of the fundamental characteristics in quality online Spanish instruction. *CALICO Journal 22*(2), 285-306.

Kop, R. (2011). The challenges to connectivist learning on open online networks: learning experiences during a massive open online course. *The International Review of Research in Open and Distributed Learning, 12*(3), 19-38. https://doi.org/10.19173/irrodl.v12i3.882

Meltzoff, A. N., & Prinz, W. (Eds). (2002). *The imitative mind: development, evolution and brain bases (Vol. 6)*. Cambridge University Press. https://doi.org/10.1017/CBO9780511489969

Moreira-Teixeira, A. M., & Mota, J. (2014). A proposal for the methodological design of collaborative language MOOCs. In E. Bárcena & E. Martín-Monje (Eds), *Language MOOCs: providing learning, transcending boundaries*. Degruyter Open. https://doi.org/10.2478/9783110420067.3

Morris, N., & Lambe, J. (2014). *Studying a MOOC: a guide*. Palgrave Macmillan.

Sokolik, M. (2014). What Constitutes an Effective Language MOOC? In E. Bárcena & E. Martín-Monje (Eds), *Language MOOCs: providing learning, transcending boundaries*. Degruyter Open. https://doi.org/10.2478/9783110420067.2

Wiley, D. (2009, November 16). *Defining open*. https://opencontent.org/blog/archives/1123

Learners' perceptions of a reading section without instruction

Alessandra Belletti Figueira Mulling[1]

Abstract. This study highlights learners' perceptions about their experience with self-access materials with a qualitative orientation as the best way to understand nuances of how students learn and what they need from learning materials. This paper presents English as a foreign language learners' attitudes when interacting with the computer-reading section *Catching a Glimpse* (CaG) – which consists of texts written for pedagogic purposes accompanied by a bilingual glossary, an audio version of the text, and a text illustration. Learners' perceived experience with CaG was addressed through stimulated recall in semi-structured interviews with 24 participants who commented on and explained how and why they interacted with CaG. Furthermore, respondents shared their impressions of the fact that there was no initial or follow-up question instructing learners on what to do. The findings suggest the absence of instruction or set goals fostered an authentic interaction with the texts, however, CaG's instructional design does not properly benefit from computer-assisted language learning technology.

Keywords: self-access, learners' impressions, reading without instruction, qualitative data.

1. Introduction

This paper is a fraction of the on-going evaluation of the digitally delivered and self-access English learning material English M1, developed by the Brazilian Ministry to students and members of staff at beginner level of English in vocational schools. The material comprises 18 lessons, each ending with the reading section CaG.

---

1. University of Portsmouth, Portsmouth, United Kingdom; alessandra.mulling@port.ac.uk

How to cite this article: Belletti Figueira Mulling, A. (2017). Learners' perceptions of a reading section without instruction. In K. Borthwick, L. Bradley & S. Thouësny (Eds), *CALL in a climate of change: adapting to turbulent global conditions – short papers from EUROCALL 2017* (pp. 35-39). Research-publishing.net. https://doi.org/10.14705/rpnet.2017.eurocall2017.685

CaG has no instruction or follow-up activity and learners are given no specific goal to guide them on how to interact with it. All texts were written for pedagogic purposes and contain a maximum of 600 words. Texts are accompanied by (1) a bilingual (English-Portuguese) glossary; (2) a user-activated audio version of the text, and (3) a text illustration.

By giving voice to learners' often-overlooked opinions (Conole, 2008; Levy, 2016), this paper focusses on their perceived experience and their own approach to engage with CaG.

2. Method

2.1. Participants

Twenty-four users of the material participated in face-to-face interviews. They were 14 school staff-members (adult learners) and ten secondary-level students. All participants but one expressed they had previously studied English.

2.2. Data collection and instrument

Participants were prompted to interact with two previously selected CaG sections on a computer screen as a way of recalling their original experiences and impressions about the reading section. This was also an opportunity to build a rapport so learners would feel at ease to share their opinion.

Stimulated recall was combined with recorded semi-structured interviews in learners' L1 (Portuguese) in order to investigate detailed information about learner's perceived benefits in reading the texts and how they interacted with CaG as a whole. For instance, with the intent of capturing learners' chosen approach, participants were asked to describe their steps for interaction with CaG (e.g. whether they started reading straight away, or first observed the illustration, the glossary, or played the audio) and share their opinion on the reasons why they approached CaG the way they did.

For a more efficient coding management system during the analytical process of the qualitative data, the software Nvivo was employed. Nvivo allows the researcher to trace codes in a transparent way, increasing integrity and coherence when interpreting data across participants and within an individual. After looking for patterns, categories emerged based on frequencies, such as learners' positive claims about the absence of an instruction and a follow-up activity related to the text.

3. Results and discussion

Despite being digitally delivered, an analysis (see McGrath, 2002 for a difference between analysis and evaluation) of CaG suggests it makes little use of the interactivity, the usability, and the functionality supported by digital tools and usually regarded as one of the advantages in using computer technologies for language learning (Chapelle, 2003; Dziemianko, 2012).

Participants' reports regarding their experience with the glossary confirmed such suggestions. Even though learners said they used the glossary when reading the texts, critical comments revealed its benefits were limited, as it did not contain all the words needed. Learners mentioned using Google or electronic dictionaries owing to a more comprehensive number of word entries. For instance, Participant 16 kept an electronic dictionary open on his computer screen and Participant 2 preferred accessing the vocabulary lists previously presented in the material because they contained word visuals and examples of the word in use. Also, three participants described the glossaries as a threshold level type of words-list they were allowed to not know the meaning, implying they should know the others not in the list. This reveals the potentially negative impact of glossaries, as learners might feel frustrated if led into believing their lexical knowledge is below expected.

The audio tool is the one feature in CaG that capitalizes on computer technology to support a multi-media experience for learners. However, only four respondents used the tool, all for the same reason: checking words pronunciation. Learners made no reference to using the audio for listening comprehension purposes. Participant 6 said it disrupted her trying to make sense of the text because "the audio came before my line of thought and interrupted it […] it mixed my understanding of the text with my understanding of pronunciation".

Despite respondents' perceptions of the glossary and the audio tool as not especially useful in supporting reading and comprehension, data suggested they were interested in the texts. Learners reported that the absence of instruction or follow-up activity generated a relaxed attitude towards the texts and freedom to act independently under relaxed conditions. For instance, Participant 2 compared CaG readings to when she reads in the L1. Nine respondents described CaG as an "entertainment" (Participant 2), because the section did not present new linguistic content.

In this sense, data analysis revealed learners focused on text meaning. Participants (e.g. 7) shared how after an extensive lesson with rules and learning activities, reading about culture-related content felt good. Participant 10 explained how he felt about CaG:

> "I finished everything about this lesson, now I will relax a little bit reading this text [...] I had already done the activities, everything was ready, before moving on I read the text".

Another indication of focus on meaning is learners' examples of how some of the information read in the texts is useful for their lives. For instance, Participant 26, a Spanish teacher, was pleased to read about Thanksgiving as she found it interesting to compare with her knowledge about celebrations in Spanish speaking countries.

The illustration also encouraged focus on meaning. Four respondents said they used the visual input to confirm whether their comprehension of the text was plausible. They did not observe the illustration before, but during and after reading. They also explained that observing the image before reading could lead them into plausible interpretation of the image but incoherent with the text.

4. Conclusions

When it comes to self-access materials, giving voice to learners through qualitative analysis of data can reveal impressions that are very particular to learners' experience (Bahumaid, 2008; Ellis, 1997; McGrath, 2002). This study presented learners' opinion about a reading section that had no instruction or demanded outcome and their approach to interacting with it.

Learners' positive impressions support Masuhara's (2013) claims that follow-up comprehension questions or keeping linguistic outcomes in mind might lead students to feel apprehensive about reading. This study extends Masuhara's (2013) assertion proposing learners have also enjoyed not being given a reason to read the texts, which allowed them to be creative in their approach.

Undeterred by the few advantages taken from its digital delivery, which could have provided better learning experience through, e.g. a multimedia glossary, participants reported experience with CaG was positive. This study concludes that not having an instruction conferred a sense of authenticity to reading, as learners were the ones who ultimately decided whether to read or not, the extent to which they committed to comprehending, and most importantly, how they approached the texts (like whether they used online support, or listened to the audio before, during, or after reading). Furthermore, the absence of a demanded linguistic outcome led learners' attention to the meaning of the language in the texts, one of Chapelle's (2001) criteria for CALL task appropriateness.

Further research in the field should address the extent to which focus on meaning is a corollary effect of reading without instruction or a demanded linguistic outcome in self-access materials for beginners and how these conditions affect learners' efforts to comprehend.

References

Bahumaid, S. (2008). TEFL materials evaluation: a teacher's perspective. *Poznan Studies in Contemporary Linguistics, 44*(4), 423-32. https://doi.org/10.2478/v10010-008-0021-z

Chapelle, C. A. (2001). *Computer applications in second language acquisition.* Cambridge University Press. https://doi.org/10.1017/CBO9781139524681

Chapelle, C. A. (2003). *English language learning & technology: lectures on applied linguistics in the age of information and communication technology.* John Benjamins. https://doi.org/10.1075/lllt.7

Conole, G. (2008). Listening to the learner voice: the ever changing landscape of technology use for language students. *ReCALL, 20*(2), 124-140. https://doi.org/10.1017/S0958344008000220

Dziemianko, A. (2012). On the use(fullness) of paper and electronic dictionaries. In S. Granger & M. Paquot (Eds), *Electronic Lexicography* (pp. 319-342). Oxford Scholarship Online. https://doi.org/10.1093/acprof:oso/9780199654864.003.0015

Ellis, R. (1997). The empirical evaluation of language teaching materials. *ELT Journal, 51*(1), 36-42. https://doi.org/10.1093/elt/51.1.36

Levy, M. (2016). The role of qualitative approaches to research in CALL contexts: closing in on the learner's experience. *Calico Journal 32*(3), 554-568. https://doi.org/10.1558/cj.v32i3.26620

Masuhara, H. (2013). Materials for developing reading skills. In B. Tomlinson (Ed.), *Developing materials for language teaching* (pp. 365-390). Bloomsbury.

McGrath, I. (2002). *Materials evaluation and design for language teaching.* Edinburgh University Press.

Mobile resources for integration: how availability meets the needs of newly arrived Arabic-speaking migrants in Sweden

Nataliya Berbyuk Lindström[1], Sylvana Sofkova Hashemi[2], Lorna Bartram[3], and Linda Bradley[4]

Abstract. The paper reports on the availability and use of mobile resources by newly arrived Arabic migrants in Sweden, and how the resources meet migrants' integration needs. Analysis of websites and applications (hereafter apps) in combination with focus group interviews is used. Results show that though a variety of resources are available, translation and vocabulary apps are primarily used. Possible reasons are lack of connection in language training resources to migrants' immediate needs such as employment and education, accommodation, contact with locals and societal information (Ager & Strang, 2008). Cultural differences might be influential for Arabic-speakers' low use of chat apps for communication with locals.

Keywords: integration, Arabic, migrants, mobile learning, Sweden.

1. Introduction

During the past two years, about 200 000 people have sought asylum in Sweden, many coming from Arabic-speaking countries (Swedish Migration Agency, 2017). Host societies face challenges in supporting the migrants' integration (Sunderland, 2016). Many newly arrived migrants have smartphones (Bradley, Berbyuk Lindström, & Sofkova Hashemi, 2017), which are potential bridging tools to the host society (Collin & Karsenti, 2012). Though mobile learning "can

---

1. University of Gothenburg, Gothenburg, Sweden; nataliya.berbyuk.lindstrom@gu.se
2. University of Gothenburg, Gothenburg, Sweden; sylvana.sofkova.hashemi@gu.se
3. Chalmers University of Technology, Gothenburg, Sweden; bartram@chalmers.se
4. Chalmers University of Technology, Gothenburg, Sweden; linda.bradley@chalmers.se

How to cite this article: Berbyuk Lindström, N., Sofkova Hashemi, S., Bartram, L., & Bradley, L. (2017). Mobile resources for integration: how availability meets the needs of newly arrived Arabic-speaking migrants in Sweden. In K. Borthwick, L. Bradley & S. Thouësny (Eds), *CALL in a climate of change: adapting to turbulent global conditions – short papers from EUROCALL 2017* (pp. 40-45). Research-publishing.net. https://doi.org/10.14705/rpnet.2017.eurocall2017.686

enhance, extend and enrich the concept and activity of learning itself" (Traxler, Barcena, & Laborda, 2015, p. 1236), existing resources are not always adapted to the needs of the users (Epp, 2017). Further, an overview of mobile resources, hereafter resources, consisting of mobile apps and mobile websites for integration is lacking.

The study investigates the availability of resources for integration purposes and how they are used in relation to the needs expressed by newly arrived Arabic-speaking migrants in Sweden. Research questions concern:

- What resources are available?
- How are they used?
- What integration needs do the migrants have?
- How are the available resources meeting these needs?

2. Method

The study is based on a combination of focus group interviews and analysis of available resources for integration. Six semi-structured interviews with 27 literate Arabic-speaking migrants (14 male and 13 female) enrolled in 'Swedish for immigrants' courses were conducted. The majority (23) were from Syria, three from Iraq, and one from Algeria.

Respondents were asked about their experiences and perceptions of necessary information to be integrated in Sweden and the use of resources. The focus group interviews were conducted in groups of four to six people. They were carried out in Arabic (four groups) and Swedish and English (two groups), and audio-recorded. Thematic content analysis (Braun & Clarke, 2006) was used for analysis.

The analysis of available resources comprised a search for websites and apps on the Swedish market through several media channels (newspapers, TV, the Internet) and via the App Store and Google Play Store (November 2016-April 2017). Both Swedish and Arabic search words were used, e.g. 'nyanländ' (newly arrived), 'al-suwīd' (Sweden). Criteria for inclusion were resources supporting Arabic-Swedish or only Swedish, analysed in terms of:

- primary function;
- accessibility (pricing, platform, user interface language);
- reliability (technical problems).

3. Results and discussion

We found 48 resources: 39 apps and nine websites adapted to mobile use. Table 1 presents examples of the resources[5].

Table 1. Primary function and accessibility (platform)

Primary function	Accessibility (Platform/examples)						Total
	Android	iOS	Android/ iOS	Web	Android/ iOS/Web	iOS/Web	
Language training	11 Rādiyū taʿallam al-luġa l-suwīdiyya (Radio Learn Swedish 100)	3 Marhaba (Hello)	7 Språkkraft Läscoach (Language power Reading coach)	2 Akelius svenska (Akelius Swedish)	3 Hejsvenska (Hello Swedish)	1 Speakify	27
Translation & vocabulary	3 Qāmūs ʿarabī suwīdī bidūn intarnit (Arabic-Swedish dictionary without Internet)	1 SayHi Translate	3 Språk i vården (Language in health care)		2 Lexin		9
Societal information	2 Sweden Arabs			3 Mobilearn	1 Information om Sverige (Information about Sweden)		6
Contact with locals			2 Welcome App	4 Kompis Sverige (Friend Sweden)			6
Total	16	4	12	9	6	1	48

---

5. A complete annotated list can be found at https://research-publishing.box.com/s/ryr3andyr9ks1u6vgehrtf58v4y0ov70

As to primary function, 'language training' represents the majority of the resources (56%), followed by 'translation & vocabulary' (19%), 'societal information' (12.5%), and 'contact with locals' (12.5%). Concerning accessibility, Android apps dominate (33%), followed by apps developed for both Android and iOS (25%) and Web (19%). Moreover, a high degree (92%), were available either as a whole or in part in Arabic. Only three websites and one of the cross-platform resources were entirely in Swedish. Regarding pricing, the vast majority (83%) of all apps were free of charge (including those free to download and use and those which were free but contained advertisements). Seven apps (15%) were paid services (paid to download and free apps with in-app purchases). At the time of the review, the majority of the resources indicated good *reliability*. Six resources (13%) exhibited reliability issues, such as incorrect representation of the Arabic orthography, freezing problems, and lengthy loading times. Four (8%) apps were considered inaccessible due to password requirements or partially missing content.

Concerning mobile usage in the focus group interviews, 'translation & vocabulary' resources *Google Translate* and *Lexin* were used on a daily basis, while only a few respondents mentioned using 'language training' resources, e.g. *Duolingo* and *Lingio*. Lack of time and motivation for using 'language training' apps as well as a wish for adding societal information to their content were expressed. None acknowledged using 'societal information' and 'contacts with locals'.

In regard to integration needs and how the available resources meet these needs, the migrants mentioned learning Swedish as the key factor for integration together with employment, education, and getting accommodation. Validating one's education and finding employment "to become financially secure" in order to "give back" to the Swedish society was prioritised. However, many participants experienced lack of knowledge about the job application process. Further, unconfirmed working experience from home countries and limited experience in Sweden were considered as having a detrimental effect on their job prospects. Contact with Swedes and learning about Sweden, its laws, culture, and health care were also emphasised. Many were concerned about little contact with Swedes, some experienced rejection, while others had positive experiences. The respondents described Syrians as "very social", while Swedes were regarded as more reserved, which complicated initial contacts.

4. Conclusion

Successful integration is essential for both host societies and migrants, and mobile technologies have potential to support this process (Bobeth et al., 2013; Borkert,

Cingolani, & Premazzi, 2009). Designing resources for migrants, understanding of target group characteristics and its immediate needs are essential to ensure usability. Our study shows that there are distinct discrepancies in relation to the available resources on the market, the use of resources by the newly arrived migrant's and their needs. Though most of the available resources are represented by reliable 'language training' apps and thus could meet the expressed linguistic needs (i.e. learning Swedish), primarily 'translation & vocabulary' resources for solving immediate communication needs rather than for systematic language training are used. A probable reason for low use of 'language training' apps could be their weak relation to the migrants' social and economic integration needs, i.e. managing employment, education, and accommodation (Ager & Strang, 2008), resulting in a lack of motivation for learners. Future studies should explore reasons for the low use of 'social information' and 'contact with locals' apps – possible explanations could be lack of knowledge about them as well as cultural factors, e.g. preferences of oral face-to-face communication (Zaharna, 1995) over written distance communication.

5. Acknowledgements

The authors wish to acknowledge the support of the Asylum, Migration and Integration Fund (AMIF) and to particularly thank all the respondents for their participation.

References

Ager, A., & Strang, A. (2008). Understanding integration: a conceptual framework. *Journal of refugee studies, 21*(2), 166-191. https://doi.org/10.1093/jrs/fen016

Bobeth, J., Schreitter, S., Schmehl, S., Deutsch, S., & Tscheligi, M. (2013). User-centered design between cultures: designing for and with immigrants. In P. Kotzé, G. Marsden, G. Lindgaard, J. Wesson, & M. Winckler (Eds), *Human-computer interaction – INTERACT 2013*. Lecture Notes in Computer Science, vol 8120. Springer. https://doi.org/10.1007/978-3-642-40498-6_65

Borkert, M., Cingolani, P., & Premazzi, V. (2009). *The state of the art of research in the EU on the uptake and use of ICT by immigrants and ethnic minorities*. European commission, Joint Research Centre, Institute for Prospective Technological Studies, Seville.

Bradley, L., Berbyuk Lindström, N., & Sofkova Hashemi, S. (2017). Integration and language learning of newly arrived migrants using mobile technology. *Journal of Interactive Media in Education,2017*(1): 1-9. https://doi.org/10.5334/jime.434

Braun, V., & Clarke, V. (2006). *Using thematic analysis in psychology. Qualitative Research in Psychology, 3*(2), 77-101. https://doi.org/10.1191/1478088706qp063oa

Collin, S., & Karsenti, T. (2012). Facilitating linguistic integration of immigrants: an overview of ICT tools. *Issues in Informing Science and Information Technology, 9*, 243-251. http://iisit.org/Vol9/IISITv9p243-251Collin086.pdf

Epp, C. D. (2017). Migrants and mobile technology use: gaps in the support provided by current tools. *Journal of Interactive Media in Education, 2017*(1), 1-13. http://doi.org/10.5334/jime.432

Sunderland, J. (2016). For Europe, integrating refugees is the next big challenge. *World Politics Review*. https://www.hrw.org/news/2016/01/13/europe-integrating-refugees-next-big-challenge

Swedish Migration Agency. (2017). http://www.migrationsverket.se

Traxler, J., Barcena, E., Laborda, J. G. (2015). Mobile technology for foreign language teaching: building bridges between non-formal and formal scenarios. *Journal of Universal Computer Science, 21*(10), 1234-1247.

Zaharna, R. (1995). Understanding cultural preferences of Arab communication patterns. *Public Relations Review, 21*(3), 241-255. https://doi.org/10.1016/0363-8111(95)90024-1

The assessment of digital project work in the EFL classroom

Jan Berggren[1] and Christopher Allen[2]

Abstract. This paper reports on a project aiming at describing professional practice in the assessment of collaborative digital projects among a group of in-service English as a Foreign Language (EFL) teachers within the context of a single workplace, a technologically well-resourced upper secondary school in Sweden. In a previous project (Allen & Berggren, 2016), teachers were provided with an overview of the digital literacy concept as described by Dudeney, Hockly, and Pegrum (2013) as part of an initiative to better integrate information communication technology into their classroom practice. The current study addresses the need expressed in previous projects for developing assessment practices among the teachers working with digital projects, making use of a practical overview of the assessment of digital projects (Dudeney et al., 2013) trying out an assignment. Afterwards, a focus group interview was conducted focusing on teachers' experiences of digital project assessment. The results indicate that while the teaching and assessment of collaborative digital projects are not aligned, the teaching of digital literacy making use of digital resource may augment 'traditional' assessment. Following this conclusion, a necessity of further collaboration among EFL teachers appears, aiming at developing the assessment of the collaborative aspect of digital projects.

Keywords: digital literacy, assessment, exploratory practice, in-service training.

---

1. Linnaeus University, Kalmar, Sweden; jan.berggren@ksgyf.se
2. Linnaeus University, Kalmar, Sweden; christopher.allen@lnu.se

How to cite this article: Berggren, J., & Allen, C. (2017). The assessment of digital project work in the EFL classroom. In K. Borthwick, L. Bradley & S. Thouësny (Eds), *CALL in a climate of change: adapting to turbulent global conditions – short papers from EUROCALL 2017* (pp. 46-50). Research-publishing.net. https://doi.org/10.14705/rpnet.2017.eurocall2017.687

1. Introduction

1.1. Background

Individually targeted testing and assessment have been at the cornerstone of language teaching performance measurement since the introduction of the *Cambridge First Certificate* course in English over one hundred years ago. As contemporary workplaces increasingly adopt team- and project-based practices in the digital era, the question is how language teachers can begin assessing collaborative digital project work as a departure from more traditional individualised proficiency testing.

This paper describes and discusses an initiative to assess collaborative digital project work in advanced EFL teaching at a technologically well-resourced school within the context of the *digital literacy* framework as set out by Dudeney et al. (2013).

1.2. Digital literacy practices and collaborative assessment

In a series of publications (Dudeney et al., 2013; Hockly, 2012), the notion of digital literacy applied to language teaching has been advanced as a means of combining the promotion of foreign language proficiency and skills in the use of digital tools and resources. The wholesale adoption of digital practices in EFL teaching necessitates the alignment of teaching with assessment involving not only the final digital artefact, but also the entire collaborative working process with groups of learners leading up to the product (Palloff & Pratt, 2009).

Moreover, combining EFL teaching with the preparation of learners for real-world application of their language proficiency and making use of digital tools is to be considered as involving Task-Based Language Assessment (TBLA), interpreted as "the elicitation and evaluation of language use (across all modalities) for expressing and interpreting meaning, within a well-defined communicative context (and audience), for a clear purpose, toward a valued goal or outcome" (Norris, 2016, p. 232). This is especially so in the case of the *History Hunt* project, which focusses on the evaluation of communicative proficiency within a well-defined context with a clear purpose. In all, the procedure of the *History Hunt* project is essentially one of TBLA at the intersection of purely performance-based assessment and collaborative process-and-product assessment.

2. Method

2.1. The teaching activity

A pilot group of five EFL teachers at an upper secondary school in southern Sweden were tasked with teaching and assessing a mobile-assisted language learning project in English based loosely on the *History Hunt* lesson activity as described in Dudeney et al. (2013). This activity involved 140 learners tasked with the creation of digital map 'trails' based on *Google Maps* highlighting urban locations with historical or cultural significance. Learners augmented maps with textual, video and audio material recorded on hand-held devices[3].

2.2. The assessment matrix

Teachers were initially provided with a digital assessment grading matrix as described by Dudeney et al. (2013). Based on this input, teachers adopted the principle that the project assessment should cover both process and product aspects of the learning activity. It was also decided that teachers would use the assessment matrix in the digital literacies resource book (Dudeney et al., 2013, p. 344) in conjunction with the syllabus and the grading system for English adopted by the *Swedish National Agency for Education* (LGY 2011), thus establishing an assessment matrix for the project.

In another step, teachers created together a task description for the project and defined their own set of grading criteria for the assessment of this specific project[4]. The teachers also decided on which aspects of process and product were to be assessed by the teacher and/or peer groups. This step involved deciding on the balance between teacher and peer assessment.

3. Results

3.1. Assessment of the collaborative process

Pupils' self-assessment turned out to be the most common way of assessing the collaborative process, even though teachers initially had an ambition to include

---
3. https://larskaggskolan.wordpress.com/2017/01/16/te16bjan/
4. https://larskaggskolan.wordpress.com/category/english-6/

peer assessment, that is pupils assessing the work of other pupils, as well. The reason given for the lack of peer assessments was a practical problem of groups not working at the same pace. Some teachers then replaced peer assessments with meetings between the teacher and pupils.

Thus, based on pupils' self-assessments, three teachers arranged for seminars in which pupils presented to their teacher and another group of pupils how far they had reached and what problems they were working with in their group. Two teachers did not set up formal meetings, but communicated in the classroom continuously with pupils about their plans, problems, and progress. These meetings, however, were not used in the process of grading pupils. Instead, teachers said their main aim in their meetings with pupils was to promote pupils' communication, making them organise themselves more effectively.

3.2. Assessment of the collaborative product

Assessing the product, all teachers made use of the matrix they had created collectively. However, reflecting on important aspects to focus on in a digital project, they considered it hard for a language teacher to assess technical skills as such. Their professional role is instead to assess to what extent digital resources are made good use of in communicating a reliable content fulfilling the demands of the assignment.

At the same time, the matrix, as well as teacher focus group comments, make clear that in assessing the vodcasts, more traditional components were primarily focussed on by the teachers, such as structure, lexis, grammar, pronunciation, and intonation. To a lesser degree, there was an assessment of the use of digital resources, that is the assignment demanded pupils to exhibit their vodcasts on a digital map, presenting relevant information from different sources, mainly the internet.

4. Discussion and conclusion

Promoting the development of assessment practices working with collaborative digital projects (c.f. Dudeney et al., 2013, p. 342) is a process in several steps, as indicated by the *History Hunt* project. The results suggest that there is a lack of alignment in Palloff and Pratt's (2009) terms between teaching, demanding collaboration on process and product, and assessment in the project. Peer assessment did not occur as planned and teachers did not grade the collaborative process. In the future, a solution might be to make members of groups interact in the classroom on the topic of process and be graded on this by the teacher. Meanwhile, teachers could at regular intervals offer formative feedback on process.

There is to some extent also a lack of alignment of assessment and teaching, since teachers focussed mostly on individual skills of foreign language proficiency and only to some degree on pupils' collaborative skills in making use of a vodcast to communicate. Teachers tend to fall back on traditional assessment of the language product, saying assessing pupils' individual language proficiency is their field of expertise.

A conclusion may be that to perfectly align assessment with teaching activities in digital projects is not possible, or even necessary in EFL teaching. The *History Hunt* project indicates that teaching digital literacy making use of digital resources augments traditional assessment, helping to ensure authenticity, preparing pupils for a future making good use of digital resources communicating a reliable content, and, according to the teachers, heightening motivation among pupils. Finally, through working together with colleagues, inspired by Dudeney et al. (2013), results obtained from the interview suggest the necessity among EFL teachers of incorporating development of assessment practices working with digital projects alongside busy teaching schedules and administrative demands. Teachers have collectively begun to develop an awareness of what is relevant when assessing a digital project.

References

Allen, C., & Berggren, J. (2016). Digital literacy and sustainability – a field study in EFL teacher development. In S. Papadima-Sophocleous, L. Bradley & S. Thouësny (Eds), *CALL communities and culture – short papers from EUROCALL 2016* (pp. 14-19). Research-publishing.net. https://doi.org/10.14705/rpnet.2016.eurocall2016.531

Dudeney, G., Hockly, N., & Pegrum, M. (2013). *Digital literacies*. Pearson Education.

Hockly, N. (2012). Digital literacies. *ELT Journal, 66*(1), 108-112. https://doi.org/10.1093/elt/ccr077

Norris, J. (2016). Current uses for task-based language assessment. *Annual Review of Applied Linguistics, 36,* 230-244. https://doi.org/10.1017/S0267190516000027

Palloff, R., & Pratt, K. (2009). *Assessing the online learner: resources and strategies for faculty.* Jossey-Bass.

Normalisation in flux: teachers' and learners' digital literacy in the Japanese university context

Thomas E. Bieri[1] and Darren Elliott[2]

Abstract. Although subsequent research suggests a more nuanced reality, Prensky's (2001) concept of the digital native remains a compelling and influential metaphor, continuing to shape thinking in education and beyond. This paper addresses self-reported digital literacy of 54 teachers and 477 learners in Japanese tertiary education. An online survey was administered to measure how often both groups use particular types of tools and perform certain tasks, and how comfortable they feel using technology. For initial analysis, some items were grouped into constructs labeled work, creative, and social. The researchers found that teachers appear to be both more comfortable and more frequent users of technology. This is particularly apparent with 'work' applications. According to the data, students report lower levels of comfort even for those tools which they use as frequently as teachers. In this paper, the authors speculate on why this might be and discuss implications for classroom practice.

Keywords: digital native, normalisation, Japan, digital literacy.

1. Introduction

Innovations in technology have created incredible opportunities for language teachers and learners, and yet there are often many obstacles to overcome. Amongst these obstacles, fear, resistance, and misunderstanding from teachers, learners, and institutions can have a negative impact on the successful implementation of pedagogically sound uses of technology in language classes (Selwyn, 2013). In this research, the authors investigate the relationships between teacher, learner, and technology in the Japanese university context.

---

1. Nanzan University, Nagoya, Japan; bieritho@ic.nanzan-u.ac.jp
2. Nanzan University, Nagoya, Japan; delliott@ic.nanzan-u.ac.jp

How to cite this article: Bieri, T. E., & Elliott, D. (2017). Normalisation in flux: teachers' and learners' digital literacy in the Japanese university context. In K. Borthwick, L. Bradley & S. Thouësny (Eds), *CALL in a climate of change: adapting to turbulent global conditions – short papers from EUROCALL 2017* (pp. 51-55). Research-publishing.net. https://doi.org/10.14705/rpnet.2017.eurocall2017.688

The authors take as their starting point two widely cited concepts in the field: Prensky (2001) and Bax (2003, 2011). While Prensky's (2001) theory of the 'digital native' has been thoroughly examined and found wanting since its initial publication (e.g. Thomas, 2011, for an excellent deconstruction of Prensky's work), the idea of the digital native has taken hold in the mainstream. Bax posited and further developed a theory of 'normalisation' which he defined as the point at which technology is no longer seen as novel and is incorporated into language learning processes without comment (Bax, 2003, 2011). Both theories have an important place in seeking to understand the success or failure of technologies used for language education. The authors pursued two lines of inquiry suggested by these concepts. The first was to ascertain if and how teachers and learners differ and converge in their uses and perceptions of technology, and the second was to investigate if and how teachers and learners differ in their understanding of what is 'normalised'.

2. Method

Participants from universities across Japan were invited to complete an online survey[3]. Basic demographic data was collected, followed by items to ascertain ease of access to a number of mainstream technological tools, frequency of use of said tools, and the self-reported comfort levels of respondents in using those tools and performing common tasks using technology. Other than a few demographic items, teachers and students encountered the same questions, all of which were presented in both Japanese and English. Thirteen multi-item, Likert scale questions, totalling 154 discrete items, were presented, as well as three open-ended questions.

A link to the survey was distributed by the researchers in their own classes and in the classes of colleagues at other Japanese universities, as well as via social networks (Facebook and Twitter) and email. Though 714 respondents began the questionnaire, due to disqualifications and abandonment of the survey, the number completed was 477 by students and 54 by instructors, all at universities in Japan.

For initial analysis, we grouped some items into constructs labeled 'work', 'creative', and 'social'. Although not exclusively work-related, items associated with word processing, spreadsheet, presentation and email applications formed the 'work' construct. Software used to capture and edit audio, video, and photo files were gathered together as the 'creative' construct, and microblogging, social networking, chat, and messaging application items were considered as the 'social' construct.

---

3. See supplementary material: https://research-publishing.box.com/s/1nj5bf658r8xea5mb213829rftocn0kv

For data analysis, numerical values were assigned to the Likert item responses. Items related to usage ranged from 0 ('Never') to 4 ('Every Day'), and items related to comfort ranged from 0 ('I Never Use') to 4 ('Very Comfortable').

3. Results and discussion

Teachers appear to be both more comfortable and more frequent users of technology than students (Table 1), particularly 'work' tools (Table 2), which matches reports that students in Japan are not often expected to use these tools in their studies. Kubota (2014) noted that Japanese students often arrive at university with having only recently acquired a computer and with less experience using ICT for study than other countries. Murray and Blyth (2011) found that 55.1% of university students in Japan reported never or almost never using word processing software, rising to 78.5% for presentation software and 85.7% for spreadsheets. Therefore, it is not surprising that respondents who are not working (i.e. students) would be less likely to use, and therefore less comfortable with, technology designed to perform office tasks. Meanwhile, students do express interest in using these tools in language learning, and it seems likely that students recognise the need to master the technology they will need in the workplace and want to overcome the lack of comfort they feel.

Table 1. General use and comfort levels

	Students	Teachers
Use	1.774	2.329
Comfort	2.001	3.009

Table 2. Work construct use and comfort levels

	Students	Teachers
Use	1.465	2.826
Comfort	1.924	3.492

Even when students report higher average rates of usage relative to teachers (when teacher-reported rates are considered equal to one) they do not report higher levels of comfort on any item (Table 3). The highest comfort level reported by students, touchscreen text input, is only .97 times the reported comfort level of instructors. Students report writing text with pen and paper at a rate 1.17 times that of teacher responses, yet their comfort level is reported at only .84 times that which teachers report. Students are also more likely to write on paper than teachers, while teachers are more likely to use a keyboard or speech-to-text software than students. One explanation would be that students, in Japanese tertiary education, are often asked to use pen and paper in class and teachers are more likely to own (or have exclusive use of) desktop and laptop computers. There are suggestions that contemporary students are less adept at touch-typing than their predecessors due to their increased use of touchscreen devices, but whether this can be ascribed to preference or necessity we cannot be certain. It may be that today's students 'grow into' keyboards as they join the workforce.

Table 3. Student levels of usage and comfort compared to teachers', where teacher levels equal one

	Use	Comfort
Overall	.76	.65
Application installer	1.01	.64
Video streaming	1.01	.85
Taking photographs	1.01	.86
Photo editing	1.03	.86
Text-based chat	1.03	.86
Inputting text with a touchscreen	1.06	.97
Writing text with pen and paper	1.12	.84
Video recording	1.14	.84
Blogging/Microblogging/Sharing	1.17	.84

Teachers need to be aware that what is 'normalised' for them (e.g. word processing and email software) may not be for students. Whether teachers provide specific training, or allow students time to figure things out for themselves, a lack of student comfort with commonly used software needs to be considered when designing tasks, lessons, and curricula. However, that does not mean that teachers should switch to using tools which students report being more experienced or comfortable with. For example, students report using some creative and social tools at higher or identical levels to teachers, such as microblogging sites Twitter and Instagram. Although students use tools in the social construct frequently, they report less interest in using them for language learning than 'work' tools or 'creative' tools. It is possible that they would like to keep social tools for themselves, and may resent an encroachment upon technology they see as personal.

4. Conclusions

Although the survey had a fairly high attrition rate, length and online delivery may possibly have resulted in a pool of participants skewed towards those more comfortable with technology. The data suggests that university students in Japan are less frequent and less comfortable users of technology than their teachers. Increasing self-confidence and changing ways of working may be more important than date of birth – the younger teachers in our sample are, by Prensky's (2001) definition, digital natives themselves.

The next step in our research will be to conduct interviews with many of the teacher participants, and richer description is expected to emerge at that stage. We also believe that replicating the study with a paper based survey may yield different data and that investigating in other contexts would prove enlightening.

5. Acknowledgements

We would like to thank Nanzan University, Nagoya, Japan. This research has been supported by the Nanzan University Pache Research Subsidy I-A-2 for the 2017 academic year.

References

Bax, S. (2003). CALL – past, present and future. *System, 31*(1), 13-28. https://doi.org/10.1016/S0346-251X(02)00071-4
Bax, S. (2011). Normalisation revisited: the effectiveness of technology in language education. *International Journal of Computer-Assisted Language Learning and Teaching, 1*(2), 1-15. https://doi.org/10.4018/ijcallt.2011040101
Kubota, M. (2014). The passive usage of ict by Japanese undergraduate students. *International Journal for Educational Media and Technology, 8*(1), 41-55.
Murray, A., & Blyth, A. (2011). A survey of Japanese university students' computer literacy levels. *The JALT CALL Journal, 7*(3), 307-318.
Prensky, M. (2001). Digital natives, digital immigrants part 1. *On the horizon, 9*(5), 1-6. https://doi.org/10.1108/10748120110424816
Selwyn, N. (2013). *Distrusting educational technology: critical questions for changing times.* Routledge.
Thomas, M. (Ed.) (2011). *Deconstructing digital natives: young people, technology, and the new literacies.* Routledge.

An evaluation of TTS as a pedagogical tool for pronunciation instruction: the 'foreign' language context

Tiago Bione[1], Jennica Grimshaw[2], and Walcir Cardoso[3]

Abstract. Despite positive evidence demonstrating the pedagogical benefits of Text-To-Speech (TTS) synthesisers for second/foreign language learning (Liakin, Cardoso, & Liakina, 2017), there is a need for up-to-date formal evaluations, specifically regarding its potential to promote learning. This study evaluates the voice quality of a TTS system in comparison with a human voice, and examines its pedagogical potential for use in an English as a Foreign Language (EFL) setting in terms of speech quality, ability to be understood by L2 users, and potential to focus on a specific language form. EFL learners in Brazil completed four tasks to evaluate the quality of TTS-generated texts. Results suggest that the TTS voice performed equally as well as the human voice in almost every assessment measure, demonstrating a high level of intelligibility and the ability to provide learners with opportunities to notice linguistic forms.

Keywords: text-to-speech synthesis, TTS, pronunciation, English as a foreign language.

1. Introduction

Second language (L2) researchers and practitioners have explored the pedagogical capabilities of TTS synthesisers – a type of speech technology that creates a spoken version of any written text – for their potential to enhance the acquisition of writing (Kirstein, 2006), vocabulary, reading (Proctor, Dalton, & Grisham, 2007), and pronunciation (Liakin et al., 2017). Despite positive evidence demonstrating the

---

1. Concordia University, Montréal, Canada; tiagobione@gmail.com
2. Concordia University, Montréal, Canada; jennica.grimshaw@gmail.com
3. Concordia University, Montréal, Canada; walcir.cardoso@concordia.ca

How to cite this article: Bione, T., Grimshaw, J., & Cardoso, W. (2017). An evaluation of TTS as a pedagogical tool for pronunciation instruction: the 'foreign' language context. In K. Borthwick, L. Bradley & S. Thouësny (Eds), *CALL in a climate of change: adapting to turbulent global conditions – short papers from EUROCALL 2017* (pp. 56-61). Research-publishing.net. https://doi.org/10.14705/rpnet.2017.eurocall2017.689

pedagogical benefits of TTS, there is a need for up-to-date formal evaluations, specifically regarding the potential for TTS to promote the conditions under which languages are acquired, particularly in an EFL environment, as recommended by Cardoso, Smith, and Garcia Fuentes (2015).

The objective of this study is to evaluate the voice quality of a standard TTS system in comparison with that of a human. It also examines the pedagogical potential of using TTS-based input in an EFL setting in terms of its speech quality, ability to be understood by L2 users, and potential to focus on specific language features according to the following criteria:

- text comprehension (an intelligibility test to assess users' ability to understand a text and answer comprehension questions);

- intelligibility (the extent to which a message is actually understood, measured by a dictation activity; Derwing & Munro, 2005);

- users' ratings of holistic pronunciation features (comprehensibility, naturalness and accuracy; Derwing & Munro, 2005); and

- users' ability to identify a linguistic feature (i.e. the aural identification of English regular past tense endings).

This study is guided by the following research question: how does the quality of speech produced by a TTS system compare to a human voice?

2. Method

Twenty-nine adult Brazilian EFL learners (native speakers of Brazilian Portuguese) were recruited in Recife, Brazil (age range: 18-33; M=23.6, SD=4.9). Their proficiency in English was intermediate, determined by a triangulation of methods (placement at their language school, self-ratings, and the researcher's assessment during the experiment).

Data were collected in one-shot individual sessions in which each participant completed a set of tasks designed to assess each criterion pertinent to evaluating the quality of TTS and human speech. For intelligibility, participants completed a 'dictation task' in which they were asked to transcribe sentences. In addition, they listened to two short stories and answered six multiple-choice questions covering each story's main points. To evaluate pronunciation holistically, participants rated the quality of speech based on comprehensibility, naturalness, and pronunciation accuracy using a six point Likert scale. Participants rated not only the two short stories, but also 12 decontextualised short sentences (e.g. 'The boy watched the clock ticking on the wall'). The rationale for the inclusion of these decontextualised sentences was that they could yield different results due to the low cognitive load required for their processing, as the participants need to concentrate solely on speech quality, not understanding. Finally, for the ability to focus on grammatical forms, participants performed an aural identification task for 16 sentences, in which they judged whether the target feature (past tense marker -ed) appeared in the input or not. Participants had to determine whether the action took place in the past (e.g. 'I called my mother') or not (e.g. 'I visit my cousin Sam') and check their response on the answer sheet.

For all tasks, participants listened to speech samples alternately produced by TTS and a human. The TTS voice, by NeoSpeech, was based on a female North American speaker, and the human was a North American female native-speaker with similar speech patterns. The material presented to participants was organised in two randomised sequences (A, B) in a way that both sequences contained the same target sentences or texts, but were produced by different voice sources. Participants who received Sequence A heard the same sentences as participants in Sequence B; however, all the sentences produced by the TTS in Sequence A were recorded by human voice in Sequence B, and vice-versa. At the end of the session, participants were interviewed about their insights on the quality of the TTS-generated voices. This paper reports the findings from the analysis of the quantitative data gathered from the four tasks.

3. Results

Participants' ratings of speech quality (comprehensibility, naturalness and accuracy) in short stories and sentences, story comprehension results, percentage of correct words transcribed in the dictation task (intelligibility), and participants' accuracy in identifying present/regular past verbs (to measure TTS's ability to provide noticeable input) were tallied and the means of matched voice pairings from both randomised sequences (A, B) were compared. Parametric statistics were used for data sets that met normality assumptions (namely data from the short story comprehension tasks and ratings). For every other set, non-parametric tests were conducted. Paired sample t-tests and Wilcoxon Signed-Rank tests were used, respectively, with an alpha level of .05 to determine statistical significance. An adjusted alpha of .004 was calculated using a false detection rate post-hoc method. Table 1, Table 2, and Table 3 below show the descriptive statistics and results according to each task.

Table 1. Descriptive statistics and parametric results: story rating, story comprehension (intelligibility)

	TTS		Human		t	p
Story ratings	Mean	SD	Mean	SD		
Comprehensibility	4.42	.02	4.92	.30	-2.59	.235
Naturalness	3.12	.74	4.58	.41	-6.35	.099
Accuracy	5.04	.15	5.31	.13	-27.00	.024
Comprehension test (intelligibility)	4.57	.81	4.74	.75	-4.25	.147

Table 2. Descriptive statistics and nonparametric results: sentence rating, dictation (intelligibility)

	TTS	Human	Z	p
Sentence ratings	Median	Median		
Comprehensibility	5.06	5.10	-.628	.530
Naturalness	3.45	5.13	-3.06	.002*
Accuracy	4.93	5.10	-2.85	.004*
Dictation task (Intelligibility)	59.65	55.05	-.153	.878

*$p < .004$

Table 3. Descriptive statistics and nonparametric test results for feature identification test

	Median	Z	p
TTS	.67	-1.67	.094
Human	.83		

The statistical analyses showed that foreign language learners rated or performed similarly regardless of the voice (TTS or human), except for naturalness and accuracy at sentential levels. The findings correspond to previous studies (e.g. Cardoso et al., 2015) and to those obtained in Kang, Kashiwagi, Treviranus, and Kaburagi (2008), who found that non-native English learners do not recognise a significant difference between synthetic and human voices. Contrary to previous studies, such as Bailly (2003), this study found that artificial and human speech were equally intelligible and comprehensible. Finally, echoing the results of Cardoso et al. (2015), both TTS and human samples helped participants notice past tense forms, confirming our hypothesis that TTS can provide learners with alternative ways to access or identify target linguistic forms.

4. Conclusions

As recommended by Cardoso et al. (2015), evaluations of TTS systems should be conducted in EFL environments where language exposure is limited to determine their effectiveness as pedagogical tools in providing students with additional opportunities for practice. The speech synthesis evaluated in this study has generally performed equally to a human voice, demonstrating a high level of intelligibility and the ability to provide learners with opportunities to notice aural linguistic forms such as the regular past -ed. This finding indicates that a change in learning environment (from second to foreign) can positively affect learners' perceptions and attitudes towards TTS-produced input, and suggests that EFL learners may be less sensitive to distinctions between natural and artificial voices than ESL students. Future research should reinforce these results by evaluating TTS in other EFL settings to verify if students in these contexts could also benefit from its adoption.

Our findings suggest that TTS systems are ready for L2 pedagogy, as they can enhance learners' access to the target language anytime and anywhere, promote autonomous learning (e.g. where students select their own materials), and facilitate teacher-supervised instruction (e.g. where teachers develop personalised materials for their students, based on their needs).

References

Bailly, G. (2003). Close shadowing natural versus synthetic speech. *International Journal of Speech Technology, 6*(1), 11-19. https://doi.org/10.1023/A:1021091720511

Cardoso, W., Smith, G., & Garcia Fuentes, C. (2015). Evaluating text-to-speech synthesizers. In F. Helm, L. Bradley, M. Guarda, & S. Thouësny (Eds), *Critical CALL – Proceedings of the 2015 EUROCALL Conference, Padova, Italy* (pp. 108-113). Research-publishing.net. https://doi.org/10.14705/rpnet.2015.000318

Derwing, T. M., & Munro, M. J. (2005). Second language accent and pronunciation teaching: a research-based approach. *TESOL Quarterly, 39*(3), 379-397. https://doi.org/10.2307/3588486

Kang, M., Kashiwagi, H., Treviranus, J., & Kaburagi, M. (2008). Synthetic speech in foreign language learning: an evaluation by learners. *International Journal of Speech Technology, 11*(2), 97-106. https://doi.org/10.1007/s10772-009-9039-3

Kirstein, M. (2006). *Universalizing universal design: applying text-to-speech technology to English language learners' process writing.* Doctoral dissertation. University of Massachusetts, Boston, USA.

Liakin, D., Cardoso, W., & Liakina, N. (2017). The pedagogical use of mobile speech synthesis (TTS): focus on French liaison. *Computer Assisted Language Learning, 30*(3-4), 348-365. https://doi.org/10.1080/09588221.2017.1312463

Proctor, C. P., Dalton, B., & Grisham, D. (2007). Scaffolding English language learners and struggling readers in a universal literacy environment with embedded strategy instruction and vocabulary support. *Journal of Literacy Research, 39*(1), 71-93.

An exploratory study of feedback practices for written and oral tasks in an online English course

Laia Canals[1] and Jackie Robbins[2]

Abstract. This paper explores teachers' feedback practices in an online language teaching course. We examine several variables that could have an impact on providing effective and meaningful feedback essential to account for students' rate of completion of a one-semester course. Classroom size, amount of teacher-student and student-student interactions, and teachers' experience levels are considered when examining 43 upper-intermediate online English classrooms. These practices were checked against students' completion rates over the semester to identify the variables that may account for student progress. The data analysis helped assess the effect of a small teacher professional development intervention and indicates that student engagement is crucial in online language learning.

Keywords: online language learning, whole-class feedback, teacher and student engagement, teacher professional development.

1. Introduction

Technology enhanced language teaching in fully-online settings offers challenges and opportunities, including regarding teachers' feedback practices in asynchronous oral and written tasks (Dysthe, Lillejord, Wasson, & Vines, 2010). Teachers must provide feedback in the manner and amount that students can learn most effectively from whilst following up on its effects on their progress and engagement with the subject. Equally important in online settings where several instructors teach the same course is providing teachers with continuous professional development activities which foster standardised marking and feedback practices. This is particularly important for guiding novice teachers in effective feedback practices (Samburskiy & Quah, 2014) and when engaging more seasoned teachers in

---

1. Universitat Oberta de Catalunya, Barcelona, Spain; ecanalsf@uoc.edu
2. Universitat Oberta de Catalunya, Barcelona, Spain; jrobbins@uoc.edu

How to cite this article: Canals, L., & Robbins, J. (2017). An exploratory study of feedback practices for written and oral tasks in an online English course. In K. Borthwick, L. Bradley & S. Thouësny (Eds), *CALL in a climate of change: adapting to turbulent global conditions – short papers from EUROCALL 2017* (pp. 62-66). Research-publishing.net. https://doi.org/10.14705/rpnet.2017.eurocall2017.690

reflecting on their experiences. The aim of this research is to unveil the factors that determine successful teaching practices which have an impact on students' progress in computer-assisted language learning settings. Our hypothesis is that successful feedback practices contribute to a higher number of learners completing the course and have a positive impact on learners' proficiency development in the target language.

2. Methodology

We examine feedback and classroom interaction practices taking place in two asynchronous communication spaces in the Virtual Learning Environment (VLE) which facilitate written and oral communication interactions between teachers and learners, and amongst peers themselves: written discussion forums and oral discussion spaces. Additionally, we identify which other variables can account for successful classroom feedback practices by combining quantitative and qualitative data analysis methods.

The participants in this study are 42 teachers (27 females, 15 males) teaching upper-intermediate (B2 level) English university courses online. Twenty-six (62%) are experienced online teachers who have been teaching the course for over three semesters, ten (23%) have been teaching for one or two terms, and six (14%) are teaching in this mode for the first time. All teachers are experienced English as a foreign language teachers who have completed basic intensive online language training in methodologies and pedagogies employed in the 43 classrooms of this course (task-based language teaching).

The data was collected by an online questionnaire to gather information on teachers' beliefs and behaviours regarding feedback practices adopted in the previous term and about the effectiveness of those practices (i.e. the teachers' accounts about their actual behaviour and the number of feedback posts and the spaces used). The two communicative spaces are the discussion forums and oral discussion spaces that host students' communicative practices based on task prompts provided by the teacher.

Data collection was conducted as part of a teacher professional development activity engaging the teachers in reflecting on their group-feedback practices using the different asynchronous communication spaces in the classroom with the aim of giving specific guidance to novice teachers and standardising group feedback practices. The questionnaire sent after the professional development activity was initiated with a forum discussion amongst all teachers and an explanation of its purpose. Since the point was to collect responses about specific classroom practices, the questionnaire was not anonymous although the data was subsequently anonymised. The researchers double-checked some of the information gathered against the data obtained from the VLE.

Descriptive and inferential statistics were run after the dependent and independent variables were identified (see http://bit.ly/CanalsRobbinsAnnex). The dependent variable, classroom type, is a construct that helped determine what a successful classroom looked like defined both in terms of previous studies on teacher and student engagement (Samburskiy & Quah, 2014; Sockalingam, 2016) and according to the availability of the VLE data. This variable was informed by another independent variable: a higher than average completion rate, as in the proportion of students who completed the course, that is who submitted all the assignments regardless of whether they failed or passed the course. Finally, we established which classrooms showed higher than average percentages of completion rates. Of the 43 classrooms, 18 (42%) were deemed successful according to the previous calculations and 25 (58%) were considered average classrooms.

3. Findings and discussion

3.1. Successful versus average classrooms

The two classroom types showed similar classroom sizes and similar experience levels on the part of the teachers. The successful classroom group had a higher number of students on average (46.89 versus 45.52). Overall, the successful classroom group had slightly more experienced teachers than the average classroom group (1.72 versus 1.32 experience level on a scale of 0-3, where 0 is one semester, 1 is two semesters and 2 is over three semesters). There were no novice teachers in successful classrooms: all six were in average classrooms. However, there was a case which disturbed our data: one teacher teaching two classrooms turned out to have a successful classroom and an average one.

Successful classrooms showed a higher number of both students' and teachers' posts in the written communication space (953 and 73.5) than average classrooms (777 and 71.2) and a higher number of overall posts to the oral communication space (448) compared with the average classroom (352). The average classroom, however, showed a higher number of teachers' posts to the oral communication space (http://bit.ly/CanalsRobbinsAnnex, part 1).

Out of the differences reported above and after running a one-way ANOVA, only two of the variables showed significant differences between the two types of classrooms. The overall number of messages in the written communication space and the overall number of comments in the oral communication space showed a main effect $F(1,41)=7,664$, $p=.008$ and $F(1,41)=18,075$, $p=.001$ on classroom success (http://bit.ly/CanalsRobbinsAnnex, part 2). Although failing to reach a significance level, teachers' experience levels seem to play a role not as determinant as the other two factors: number of messages in the written communication space and overall number of comments in the oral communication space. The number of teachers' comments on the oral and written spaces and classroom size do not indicate a significant effect on classroom success.

3.2. Teachers' feedback practices

Besides self-reporting the number of messages in each space, the questionnaire also asked about teachers' beliefs regarding whole-class feedback and revealed how these beliefs changed during and after the teacher development activity. Teachers appreciated these reflective activities and indicated that they helped them engage learners more effectively and led to improving the learning process, also observed by Sockalingam (2016).

Teachers in successful classrooms indicated that they changed the way they gave feedback to provide more meaningful group feedback for learners by creating specific folders in the forum, using consistently the same space to give feedback, or providing shorter and more focused feedback messages.

On the other hand, teachers in average classrooms recognised they should have given more feedback and adjusted the tone of messages to foster learners' engagement with the learning process, although some indicated that time constraints limit this.

4. Conclusions

The study allows us to draw tentative conclusions regarding the main findings, the validity of our instruments and the effect of a teacher development intervention which will serve as the basis of a wider study. We will specifically look into whole-class feedback practices to determine which prove most successful in fostering student engagement with the learning process and teacher engagement in their professional development, which are key determiners of group cohesion and online course success (Garrison & Cleveland-Innes, 2005).

First, student participation in both communication spaces tends to confirm that successful teachers foster learners' engagement in group interaction and communicative activities which results in higher numbers of students completing the course and fewer students dropping out, consistent with previous findings (Robbins, Malicka, Canals, & Appel, 2015).

Teachers can learn to be more successful; experience partly accounts for determining successful learning experiences. The findings confirm the need for continuous teacher development activities which contribute to raising teachers' awareness of the effects of their teaching practices and improving their online teaching skills.

Regarding the limitations of the study, the questionnaire proved to be suitable for tapping into teachers' beliefs and behaviours regarding group feedback practices only to a certain extent, therefore we will need to refine the questions asked in future investigations. An additional finding whereby the same teacher had both an average and a successful classroom indicates that there are other variables (group dynamics, students' major and English proficiency) that were left out given the limited scope of this study which could play a role in determining success in online language courses.

References

Dysthe, O., Lillejord, S., Wasson, B., & Vines, A. (2010). Productive e-feedback in higher education. Two models and some critical issues. In S. Ludvigsen, A. Lund, I. Rasmussen, & R. Säljö (Eds), *Learning across sites: new tools, infrastructures and practices* (pp. 243-258). Routledge.

Garrison, R., & Cleveland-Innes, M. (2005). Facilitating cognitive presence in online learning: interaction is not enough. *The American Journal of Distance Education, 19*(3), 133-148. https://doi.org/10.1207/s15389286ajde1903_2

Robbins, J., Malicka, A., Canals, L., & Appel, C. (2015). Online communication in a higher education EFL course: the role of student and teacher activity in student retention. In E. K. Sorensen, A. Szucs, & M. S. Khalid (Eds), *Proceedings of the 1st International Conference: Innovations in Digital Learning for Inclusion* (pp. 152-158). Aalborg Universitetsforlag.

Samburskiy, D., & Quah, J. (2014). Corrective feedback in asynchronous online interaction. *CALICO Journal, 31*(2), 158-178. https://doi.org/10.11139/cj.31.2.158-178

Sockalingam, N. (2016). Engaged teaching to enhance teaching and learning. *Asian Journal of the Scholarship of Teaching and Learning, 6*(2), 122-128.

Can an interactive digital game help French learners improve their pronunciation?

Walcir Cardoso[1], Avery Rueb[2], and Jennica Grimshaw[3]

Abstract. This study examines the effects of the pedagogical use of an interactive mobile digital game, *Prêt à Négocier* (PàN), on improving learners' pronunciation of French as a Second Language (FSL), using three holistic measures: comprehensibility, fluency, and overall pronunciation. Two groups of FSL learners engaged in different types of game-playing over one month: while the experimental group played PàN, the control group engaged in paper-based gamified information gap activities. Following a pre-test/post-test research design, our findings revealed no statistically significant differences between the two groups.

Keywords: digital gaming, L2 pronunciation, French.

1. Introduction

Second/foreign language (L2) pronunciation is often evaluated based on at least three criteria (e.g. Derwing, Rossiter, Munro, & Thomson, 2004): users' intelligibility (the extent to which non-native speech can be understood by others), comprehensibility (the listener's perceptions of how difficult to understand the speech is), and fluency (one's ability to speak in an efficient, effortless manner). In L2 pedagogy, one of the key recommendations for developing pronunciation is practice, preferably involving repetition and the recycling of already-acquired features (Nation & Newton, 2009), in an interactive environment (Zielinski, 2012). However, because of time constraints, these goals are not easily achievable. One way to fulfill these recommendations and circumvent time constraints is via the use of tools that promotes interaction among interlocutors, motivates learners to reuse their linguistic skills, and allows them to practice on their own in a meaningful, fun

---

1. Concordia University, Montreal, Canada; walcir.cardoso@concordia.ca
2. Vanier College, Montreal, Canada; rueba@vaniercollege.qc.ca
3. Concordia University, Montreal, Canada; jennica.grimshaw@gmail.com

How to cite this article: Cardoso, W., Rueb, A., & Grimshaw, J. (2017). Can an interactive digital game help French learners improve their pronunciation? In K. Borthwick, L. Bradley & S. Thouësny (Eds), *CALL in a climate of change: adapting to turbulent global conditions – short papers from EUROCALL 2017* (pp. 67-72). Research-publishing.net. https://doi.org/10.14705/rpnet.2017.eurocall2017.691

environment. We believe that PàN (developed by Avery Rueb, Walcir Cardoso, and Affordance Studio – http://app.readytonegotiate.com) fulfills these criteria.

PàN is a digital information gap activity designed to help French students develop their oral interaction skills. It can be played on mobile and static devices, both in face-to-face interactions in the classroom or at home via chat. To succeed in game-playing, students are required to exchange information about a product to buy/sell (e.g. a cell phone), and negotiate with a partner to arrive at a final price within a three minute time frame. Figure 1 illustrates the seller's version of the game's interface in English.

Figure 1. PàN interface

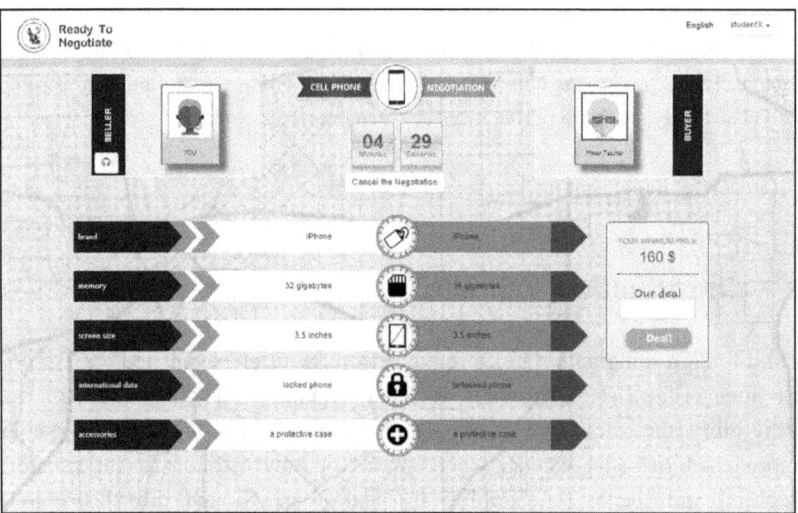

Our goal was to examine the effects of the pedagogical use of PàN on improving French learners' pronunciation, which we hypothesised to positively impact its development (see Hwang et al., 2016 for the rationale, in the context of L2 speaking). Accordingly, the study was guided by the following question: Can PàN help French learners improve their pronunciation on three measures of oral ability – comprehensibility, fluency, and overall pronunciation?

2. Method

The participants were 40 students (average age: 20) enrolled in an intermediate-level FSL class in a pre-university institution (cégep) in Québec, Canada. The goal of the course was to develop French language skills to prepare beginner students for more advanced courses.

The participants were stratified into two groups: while the experimental group (n=22) played PàN, the control group (n=12) engaged in paper-based gamified information gap activities (e.g. Perfect Partner, where students moved around the classroom asking questions to find students with similar information on their card, under time constraints to emulate most features of PàN). These game-playing sessions lasted approximately 25 minutes each, and were conducted biweekly over a period of four weeks, for a total of approximately 200 minutes of gameplay.

The study followed a pre-/post-/delayed post-test design and measured the participants' improvement in French pronunciation in three dimensions, as assessed by 16 judges: comprehensibility, fluency, and overall pronunciation abilities (an impressionistic evaluation of speech combining segmental and prosodic features such as stress, rhythm, and intonation).

The judges were asked to rate ten second randomised excerpts of speech by participants performing a picture-narrative task based on the "Suitcase Story" (Derwing et al., 2004), over the three testing phases. After listening to each excerpt, the judges were asked to indicate, on a six item Likert scale, how they rated that participant's pronunciation based on the three dimensions adopted.

3. Results

Based on a six point Likert scale, judges' ratings for comprehensibility, fluency, and overall pronunciation abilities were examined at the pre-, post-, and delayed post-tests (see Table 1 for means and standard deviations).

As the data are non-parametric, a Wilcoxon Signed-Rank test was conducted based on a student's mean rater score for each of the three measures between two given tests. A summary of the findings is provided below:

- For comprehensibility, the treatment group showed no significant difference between pre- and post-tests (Z=-1.39, p=0.16), nor between the pre- to delayed post-tests (Z=-0.73, p=0.17). Similarly, the control group showed no improvement between pre- and post-tests (Z=-0.311, p=0.76), nor between the pre- to delayed post-tests (Z=-0.47, p=0.64).

- For fluency, the treatment group showed no significance between pre- and post-tests ($Z=-1.92$, $p=0.055$), nor pre- and delayed post-tests ($Z=-1.48$, $p=0.14$). The control group also showed no improvement between pre- and post-tests ($Z=-0.59$, $p=0.56$), nor between the pre- to delayed post-tests ($Z=-0.24$, $p=0.81$).

- For overall pronunciation abilities, again we see no significance for the treatment group between pre- and post-tests ($Z=-0.98$, $p=0.33$), nor pre- and delayed post-tests ($Z=-1.37$ $p=0.17$). The control group also showed no improvement between pre- and post-tests ($Z=-1.10$, $p=0.27$), nor between the pre- to delayed post-tests ($Z=-1.03$, $p=0.30$).

Table 1. Judges' ratings

		Pre-test		Post-test		Delayed post-test	
Measure	Group	M	SD	M	SD	M	SD
Comprehensibility	Treatment	2.85	0.92	3.25	0.91	3.08	1.00
	Control	2.98	0.83	3.10	1.13	2.82	0.81
Fluency	Treatment	2.18	0.65	2.55	0.88	2.53	0.93
	Control	2.33	0.74	2.45	0.91	2.41	0.61
Pronunciation	Treatment	2.27	0.66	2.50	0.76	2.59	0.80
	Control	2.41	0.60	2.60	0.86	2.29	0.65

Mann-Whitney U tests were also conducted to compare improvement between groups for each measure in each test. Results (displayed in Table 2) indicate no significant difference.

Table 2. Mann-Whitney U between-groups comparison

	Pre-test		Post-test		Delayed post-test	
Measure	U	p-value	U	p-value	U	p-value
Comprehensibility	127.00	0.86	125.50	0.82	111.00	0.45
Fluency	117.00	0.59	131.50	0.99	127.00	0.86
Pronunciation	120.50	0.68	113.00	0.49	108.50	0.40

In summary, despite a trend toward significance found for fluency between pre- and post-tests ($p=.055$), these results show that game-playing had no effect on improving the participants' overall pronunciation, considering the three measures employed in the study: comprehensibility, fluency, and overall pronunciation abilities.

4. Discussion and conclusions

We hypothesised that the motivation and 'forced output' engendered by interactive games such as PàN would encourage learners to practice language and, via systematic repetition (Nation & Newton, 2009) and negotiation with their interlocutors (Swain & Lapkin, 1995), improve their L2 linguistic knowledge, particularly in terms of fluency – the use of language in an efficient, effortless manner. However, the results of the three pronunciation tests adopted to assess L2 pronunciation skills suggested that, based on listeners' perceptions, game-playing had no effect on the improvement of FSL learners' pronunciation, despite a trend towards significance for oral fluency. It is possible that these results are due to the brevity of the one month treatment, which seems insufficient for the development of the three aspects of pronunciation in this study. Focusing on fluency, the non-significance observed might be due to the nature of the impressionistic measures adopted, based merely on judges' ratings.

In future studies, we aim to triangulate the analysis by incorporating other quantitative measures to assess L2 pronunciation development, including temporal measures, such as rate of speech and pause length. It is also possible that the information gap activity model used for both experimental and control groups was equally effective (though not statistically significant), with the digital component having little effect on the outcomes. Indeed, the trend in increased fluency for the experimental group suggests that digital game-playing placed more pressure on students to speak faster than its paper-based counterpart, as having an on-screen countdown may be more effective than watching a wall clock.

Despite the lack of significance for L2 pronunciation, based on a previous study (Rueb, Cardoso, & Grimshaw, 2016), we believe that PàN has the potential of enhancing the learning of FSL, at least in areas such as vocabulary acquisition (forthcoming research), the development of negotiation skills in speaking and listening, and the overall learning experience in a fun, gamified environment that can take place whenever and wherever learners feel *prêt à négocier*.

References

Derwing, T., Rossiter, M., Munro, M., & Thomson, R. (2004). Second language fluency: Judgments on different tasks. *Language Learning, 54*(4), 655-679. https://doi.org/10.1111/j.1467-9922.2004.00282.x

Hwang, W.-Y., Timothy, K., Ma, Z.-H., Shadiev, R., & Chen, S.-Y. (2016). Evaluating listening and speaking skills in a mobile game-based learning environment with situational contexts. *Computer Assisted Language Learning, 29*(4), 639-657. https://doi.org/10.1080/09588221.2015.1016438

Nation, I., & Newton, J. (2009). *Teaching ESL/EFL listening and speaking.* Routledge.

Rueb, A., Cardoso, W., & Grimshaw, J. (2016). Developing oral interaction skills with a digital information gap activity game. In S. Papadima-Sophocleous, L. Bradley & S. Thouësny (Eds), *CALL communities and culture – short papers from EUROCALL 2016* (pp. 397-402). Research-publishing.net. https://doi.org/10.14705/rpnet.2016.eurocall2016.595

Swain, M., & Lapkin, S. (1995). Problems in output and the cognitive processes they generate: a step towards second language learning. *Applied Linguistics, 16,* 371-391.

Zielinski, B. (2012). The social impact of pronunciation difficulties: confidence and willingness to speak. In J. Levis & K. LeVelle (Eds), *Proceedings of the 3rd pronunciation in second language learning and teaching conference* (pp.18-26). Iowa State University.

Automatically generating questions to support the acquisition of particle verbs: evaluating via crowdsourcing

Maria Chinkina[1], Simón Ruiz[2], and Detmar Meurers[3]

> **Abstract.** We integrate insights from research in Second Language Acquisition (SLA) and Computational Linguistics (CL) to generate text-based questions. We discuss the generation of wh- questions as functionally-driven input enhancement facilitating the acquisition of particle verbs and report the results of two crowdsourcing studies. The first study shows that automatically generated questions are comparable to human-written ones. The second study investigates different types of questions, their perceived quality, and the responses they elicit.
>
> **Keywords**: automatic question generation, crowdsourcing, particle verbs.

1. Introduction

Questioning is habitually used by language teachers to test comprehension and check understanding of grammar and vocabulary. As argued in Chinkina and Meurers (2017), questions can facilitate the acquisition of different linguistic forms by providing a kind of functionally-driven input enhancement, i.e. by ensuring that the learner notices and processes the form. The CL task of automatic Question Generation (QG) has explored different types of questions: from factual (Heilman, 2011) to deeper ones (Labutov, Basu, & Vanderwende, 2015). For this study, we generate text-based wh- questions and gap sentences targeting particle verbs as they represent a considerable learning load (Schmitt & Redwood, 2011). For instance, given the source text (1), our system generated the question item (1a).

---

1. University of Tübingen, Tübingen, Germany; maria.chinkina@uni-tuebingen.de
2. University of Tübingen, Tübingen, Germany; simon.ruiz-hernandez@uni-tuebingen.de
3. University of Tübingen, Tübingen, Germany; detmar.meurers@uni-tuebingen.de

How to cite this article: Chinkina, M., Ruiz, S., & Meurers, D. (2017). Automatically generating questions to support the acquisition of particle verbs: evaluating via crowdsourcing. In K. Borthwick, L. Bradley & S. Thouësny (Eds), *CALL in a climate of change: adapting to turbulent global conditions – short papers from EUROCALL 2017* (pp. 73-78). Research-publishing.net. https://doi.org/10.14705/rpnet.2017.eurocall2017.692

(1) Source text[4]: Cancellations "ticked up slightly and unexpectedly" in early April amid press coverage about the coming increases, the Netflix letter said.

(1a) Computer: According to the Netflix letter, what did cancellations do? Cancellations _____ slightly and unexpectedly in early April amid press coverage about the coming increases.

Given a sentence parsed using Stanford CoreNLP (Manning et al., 2014), our algorithm detects particle verbs, identifies syntactic components, and applies transformation rules to generate a question.

The performance of QG systems is commonly assessed by human judges – from university students (Zhang & VanLehn, 2016) to crowd workers (Heilman & Smith, 2010). Using crowdsourcing to compare computer-generated and human-written questions seemed like a logical next step in this line of research. Thus, we conducted two crowdsourcing studies[5] to answer the following research questions:

- Are computer-generated questions perceived as similar to human-written ones in terms of well-formedness and answerability?

- Are wh- questions with a gap sentence perceived better in terms of well-formedness and answerability than open-ended wh- questions?

- Do wh- questions with a gap sentence elicit more particle verbs than open-ended wh- questions?

2. Study 1

2.1. Methodology

The goal of this study was to evaluate our question generation system against the gold standard of human-written questions. Given a corpus of 40 news articles, an English teacher and our system each produced 69 questions targeting particle verbs. Questions (2a) and (2b) below are examples of well-formed human-written and computer-generated questions.

---

4. http://www.reuters.com/article/us-netflix-results/netflix-customer-growth-slows-amid-price-hike-shares-plunge-idUSKCN0ZY2H4
5. http://crowdflower.com

(2) Source text[6]: Beijing's drive to make the nation a leader in robotics through its "Made in China 2025" initiative launched last year has set off a rush as municipalities up and down the country vie to become China's robotics center.

(2a) Human: What has the "Made in China 2025" initiative done since it was launched last year? It has _____ a rush for municipalities to become China's robotics center.

(2b) Computer: According to the article, what has Beijing's drive done? Beijing's drive has _____ a rush as municipalities up and down the country vie to become China's robotics center.

To acquire high-quality judgements from proficient English speakers, we limited the countries participating in our crowdsourcing study to English-speaking and some European ones (e.g., Sweden, the Netherlands). We also included so-called test questions to ensure the contributors understood the task at hand and were able to tell well-formed from ill-formed questions.

In the study, the participants were presented with a source text one to three sentences long and a question about it. They had to rate each question on two separate five-point scales (well-formedness and answerability). Additionally, the participants were required to answer the question and to make a guess as to whether it was produced by an English teacher or a computer. We collected 1380 judgements from 364 contributors.

2.2. Results

We first calculated the IntraClass Correlation (ICC) between the contributors' ratings. As the ICC was smaller than .1 (.08 for well-formedness and .09 for answerability), we could ignore the dependencies among the observations and use a simple t-test.

The results showed that human-written questions were slightly better-formed than computer-generated ones (Cohen's d=0.13, t=2.06, p=.03). On the answerability scale, the results were non-significant (d=0.02, t=-0.42, p=.1). To quantify the similarity of the two types of questions, we conducted equivalence tests (d=0.5, alpha level of .05). All results were statistically significant on both scales (p≤.001),

---

6. http://www.reuters.com/article/us-china-debt-robotics-insight/chinas-robotics-rush-shows-how-its-debt-can-get-out-of-control-idUSKCN10E0EV

which indicates that computer-generated and human-written questions are equivalent given the aforementioned parameters[7]. A mixed-effects model revealed a strong correlation between rating a question high and thinking it was human-written (well-formedness: d=0.8, t=17.12, p<0.001; answerability: d=0.7, t=11.71, p<0.001). This indicates that participants expect automatically generated questions to be more ungrammatical and unnatural.

3. Study 2

3.1. Methodology

In the second crowdsourcing study, we wanted to find out i) whether adding a gap sentence to an otherwise open-ended wh- question improves its rating, and ii) whether wh- questions with a gap sentence elicit more particle verbs than open-ended wh- questions. Given the 40 news articles used in the first study, we generated 60 questions and included two types of each question in the dataset – a wh- question with and without a gap sentence. We did not intend to evaluate our system in this study and excluded all ungrammatical or unanswerable questions. In the end, the data consisted of 96 human-written and 96 computer-generated questions.

To imitate a study with non-proficient English learners, we selected contributors with a high reliability but did not limit the participation based on their level of English. The participants were required to answer the questions and rate them on two separate five-point scales (well-formedness and answerability). We collected 960 responses from 477 contributors.

3.2. Results

The agreement among non-proficient English speakers was moderate. The ICC was 0.34 and 0.37 for well-formedness and answerability, respectively, so we opted for mixed-effect models. The results showed that adding a gap sentence improved both well-formedness (d=0.133, t=2.27, p<.01) and answerability (d=0.14, t=2.33, p<.05). To investigate which types of questions elicited more particle verbs, we randomly selected 20% of the responses, excluded nonsensical and non-English answers, and annotated and analysed the remaining questions. We found that

---

[7]. In equivalence testing, the null and the alternative hypothesis are reversed. Therefore, statistically significant results indicate that the two samples are equivalent.

the questions containing an additional gap sentence elicited more particle verbs ($d=0.16$, $t=2.97$, $p<.01$) and more correct responses ($d=0.12$, $t=2.5$, $p=.01$).

4. Conclusions

The results of two crowdsourcing studies showed that computer-generated questions are comparable to human-written ones. We also found that the addition of a gap sentence to a wh- question significantly improves its perceived well-formedness and answerability. Moreover, the responses elicited by wh- questions with a gap sentence contain significantly more correct answers, particle verbs among them, than those elicited by open-ended wh- questions.

From the CL perspective, these findings imply that QG systems can benefit from leveraging different types of questions. Combining a wh- question with a more specific gap sentence helps avoid the pitfalls of the two question types: it maximises the grammaticality and minimises the ambiguity of a question while keeping the task communicative. Such combined question items also elicit more target linguistic forms, which is crucial for functionally-driven input enhancement, as discussed in Chinkina and Meurers (2017).

Interestingly, the participants associated the well-formedness and answerability of a question with it being human-written. This shows that people, and teachers in particular, are often not aware of the state-of-the-art in CL technology and could benefit more from intelligent computer-assisted language learning tools.

5. Acknowledgements

This research was supported by the LEAD Graduate School & Research Network [GSC1028], a project of the Excellence Initiative of the German federal and state governments. We would like to thank our LEAD colleagues Michael Grosz and Johann Jacoby for sharing their expertise in statistical analysis.

References

Chinkina, M., & Meurers, D. (2017). Question generation for language learning: from ensuring texts are read to supporting learning. In *Proceedings of the 12th Workshop on Innovative Use of NLP for Building Educational Applications*.

Heilman, M. (2011). *Automatic factual question generation from text.* Doctoral dissertation, Carnegie Mellon University.

Heilman, M., & Smith, N. A. (2010). Rating computer-generated questions with Mechanical Turk. In *Proceedings of the NAACL HLT 2010 Workshop on Creating Speech and Language data with Amazon's Mechanical Turk* (pp. 35-40).

Labutov, I., Basu, S., & Vanderwende, L. (2015). Deep questions without deep understanding. In *Proceedings of ACL* (pp. 889-898). https://doi.org/10.3115/v1/P15-1086

Manning, C. D., Surdeanu, M., Bauer, J., Finkel, J. R., Bethard, S., & McClosky, D. (2014). The Stanford CoreNLP natural language processing toolkit. In *Proceedings of ACL* (pp. 55-60). https://doi.org/10.3115/v1/P14-5010

Schmitt, N., & Redwood, S. (2011). Learner knowledge of phrasal verbs: a corpus-informed study. In F. Meunier, S. De Cock, G. Gilquin & M. Paquot (Eds), *A taste for corpora: in honour of Sylviane Granger* (pp. 173-209). John Benjamins Publishing. https://doi.org/10.1075/scl.45.12sch

Zhang, L., & VanLehn, K. (2016). How do machine-generated questions compare to human-generated questions? *Research and Practice in Technology Enhanced Learning, 11*(7), 1-28. https://doi.org/10.1186/s41039-016-0031-7

Computer-assisted English learning system based on free conversation by topic

Sung-Kwon Choi[1], Oh-Woog Kwon[2], and Young-Kil Kim[3]

Abstract. This paper aims to describe a computer-assisted English learning system using chatbots and dialogue systems, which allow free conversation outside the topic without limiting the learner's flow of conversation. The evaluation was conducted by 20 experimenters. The performance of the system based on a free conversation by topic was measured by the success rate of the dialogue turn. The average success rate of the dialogue turn was 80.86% and the success rate of dialogue turns for each topic was as follows: (1) 'purchasing New York city tour tickets': 71.86%; (2) 'ordering food': 71.06%; (3) 'talking about health habits': 85.41%; and (4) 'thinking about future currency': 95.09%. Additionally, the precision and recall of English grammar error correction was 66.7% and 31.9% respectively.

Keywords: dialogue system, computer-assisted language learning, free conversation, topic.

1. Introduction

A dialogue system is a system that allows conversation between a user and a system in a natural voice. The dialogue system, which provides an educational environment similar to that of receiving English conversation education from a native speaker by combining the English education field with the dialogue system, is said to be a computer-assisted English learning system. The Korea Electronics and Telecommunications Research Institute has developed GenieTutor, a computer assisted English learning system from 2010 to 2015 (Choi, Kwon, Kim, & Lee, 2016). While GenieTutor asks questions based on a given topic, talks to the learner according to the scenario of the topic, and provides feedback on grammar errors,

---

1. Electronics and Telecommunications Research Institute, Daejeon, Korea; choisk@etri.re.kr
2. Electronics and Telecommunications Research Institute, Daejeon, Korea; ohwoog@etri.re.kr
3. Electronics and Telecommunications Research Institute, Daejeon, Korea; kimyk@etri.re.kr

How to cite this article: Choi, S.-K., Kwon, O.-W., & Kim, Y.-K. (2017). Computer-assisted English learning system based on free conversation by topic. In K. Borthwick, L. Bradley & S. Thouësny (Eds), *CALL in a climate of change: adapting to turbulent global conditions – short papers from EUROCALL 2017* (pp. 79-85). Research-publishing.net. https://doi.org/10.14705/rpnet.2017.eurocall2017.693

it has the disadvantage of limiting the learner's flow of conversations and does not allow free conversation outside the topic. To overcome these drawbacks, the computer-assisted English learning system described in this paper has been developed: GenieTutorPlus (Kwon et al., 2015). It allows free conversation outside the topic without limiting the learner's flow of dialogue and feedback on grammatical errors.

2. Free talk by topic

GenieTutorPlus, as opposed to GenieTutor, aims to help learners continue their English learning by returning to the topic without interrupting their learning, even if they are talking with the dialogue system outside the topic. Therefore, the newly developed English learning system is a system that allows free conversation by topic. GenieTutor and GenieTutorPlus are summarised in Table 1.

Table 1. Comparison between GenieTutor and GenieTutorPlus

GenieTutor	GenieTutorPlus
• System-initiative	• Mixed-initiative between learner and system
• No free conversation outside the topic	• Free conversation outside the topic
	• Chatbot dialogue

Figure 1, below, is an example of GenieTutorPlus for the topic of 'ordering food'.

Figure 1. Example of GenieTutorPlus for the topic of 'ordering food'

```
1. [System] Hi. What would you like?
2. [Learner] Do you have menu?
3. [System] Here you are. What would you like to have?
4. [Learner] I would like cheese omelette.
5. [Tutor] I would like to have a cheese omelette.
6. [System] Okay, there are side dishes you can order.
          Would you like something with your omelette?
7. [Learner] I want to take the coffee.
8. [System] Is this to go or will you be dining in?
9. [Learner] For here. How much is it?
10. [System] That will be 12 dollars and 55 cents, please.
11. [Learner] I have no money.
12. [System] What a pity! 12 dollars and 55 cents, please.
13. [Learner] Here you are.
14. [System] Thanks. Here's your order. Have a nice day.
15. [Learner] Goodbye
```

For instance, [Tutor] refers to the result of recommending the correct sentence by operating the grammar error correction function of the [System]. The second line of Figure 1 shows a [Learner]'s utterance that is related to the topic but is not in the learning corpus. Line 11 shows a learner's utterance that has nothing to do with the topic. While GenieTutor has an 'awkward' or 'wrong' system answer to the learner utterance in these two situations, GenieTutorPlus responds correctly as shown in Figure 1.

3. Processing of free talk by topic

3.1. How does GenieTutorPlus recognise that user utterance is off the topic?

Whether or not the learner's utterance is out of the topic is determined by the topic recognition. Topic recognition is done by comparing a dialogue intention generated from a morphological analysis and a named entity recognition of user utterance with a dialogue intention learned from dialogue maps of topic (Choi et al., 2016).

If a dialogue intention of the user utterance is not included in dialogue intentions by topic, the user utterance is considered to be outside the topic. A dialogue intention is obtained by machine learning and consists of dialogue act and slot. When the user utterance is out of topic, the chatbot responds to the user utterance.

3.2. What is the overall flow of GenieTutorPlus?

Figure 2 illustrates GenieTutorPlus's flow, which starts from the learner's utterance to determine whether it is topic-oriented or chatbot-oriented, and/or whether it has grammar errors.

When a learner makes an utterance, GenieTutorPlus first confirms whether it is topic-oriented. If the utterance is not a topic conversation, GenieTutorPlus responds with the chatbot and then returns to the topic conversation. Otherwise, if the learner's utterance is topic-oriented, GenieTutorPlus in turn processes suitability of content, grammar error detection, and error severity. If a grammatical error is detected, GenieTutorPlus provides feedback on the grammatical error and responds to the contextual sentence within the topic.

Figure 2. Overall flow of GenieTutorPlus

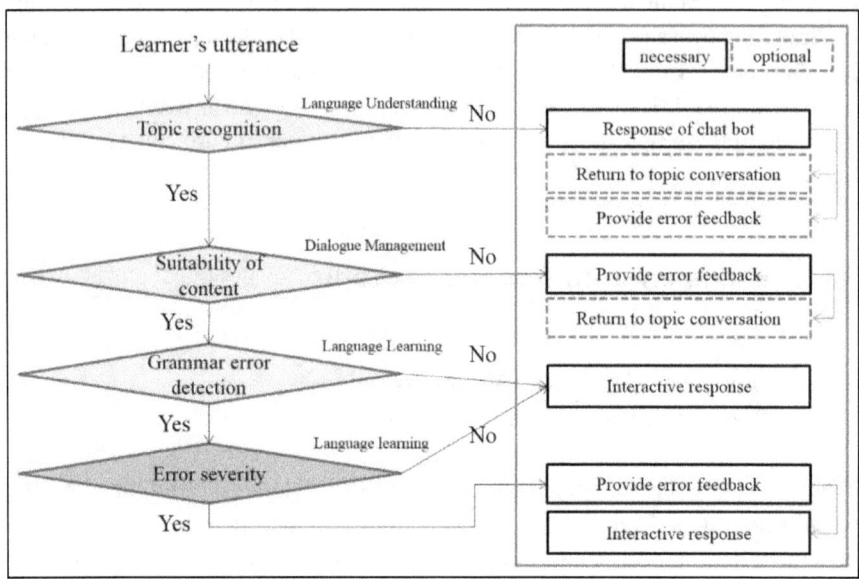

3.3. How does GenieTutorPlus provide feedback on grammar errors?

The language learning module of GenieTutorPlus automatically detects and corrects grammatical errors that may be included in the learner's utterances. Therefore, GenieTutorPlus aims to improve the learner 's ability to speak a foreign language by feeding back the corrected result to the learner.

- Detection of grammar errors: grammatical errors are detected in sentences which are spoken by the learner, and are limited to grammatical errors defined in the system, and multiple grammatical errors can be detected in one sentence.

- Correction of grammar errors: grammar error correction information is generated by using the part of the error vocabulary and surrounding context information.

- Feedback of grammar errors: indicates learner's errors, gives better expression, and uses explicit and implicit feedback effectively in context.

4. Evaluation

The English language education institute is building the free conversation by topic for discussion and learning. Among these topics, we chose four topics to evaluate GenieTutorPlus. The selected topics and evaluation methods were as follows:

- Topics for evaluation: (1) purchasing tickets for New York city tour, (2) ordering food, (3) talking about health habits, and (4) thinking about future currency.

- There were 20 participants. Participants' English level was beginners (ten) and intermediate (ten). Participants were aged in the 10's (one), 20's (15), and 30's (4). There were 11 males and nine females.

- Experimental method: the participants randomly chose a mission by topic. They communicated freely with GenieTutorPlus to accomplish their mission. Participants performed ten missions on four topics, each taking an average of 50 minutes per person.

- Success rate of dialogue turn (%)=(number of correct system's responses to learner's utterance)/(total number of learners' utterances) × 100.

- Success rate of chatbot (%) = (number of correct system's responses to learner's out-of-topic utterance)/(number of learners' out-of-topic utterances) × 100.

- Precision of grammar error correction = (number of words correctly corrected by the system)/(total number of words the system attempted to correct for grammatical errors) × 100.

- Recall of grammar error correction = (number of words that the system corrects correctly)/(actual grammatical error of the evaluation set total words) × 100.

5. Results and discussion

As illustrated in Table 2, the success rate of dialogue turn on the four topics is 80.86%. The chatbot dialogue rate equals to 10.44% and the success rate of chatbot dialogue turn is 31.49%. Even though chatbot dialogue rate is occasional in the free dialogue (10.44%), the success rate of chatbot dialogue turnout is rather low. This is mostly due to the fact that generating chatbot responses which are still suitable for the topic of dialogue is difficult to achieve.

Table 2. Evaluation of GenieTutorPlus

Topic	Experimental group	Success rate of Dialogue turn	Rate of Chatbot dialogues	Success rate of Chatbot
Buying New York City Tour Tickets	beginner	73.75%	7.50%	16.67%
	intermediate class	70.11%	9.20%	75.00%
	Total	71.86%	8.38%	50.00%
Ordering Food	beginner	73.66%	6.99%	15.38%
	intermediate class	68.66%	11.94%	33.33%
	Total	71.06%	9.56%	27.03%
Health Habits Dialogue	beginner	80.53%	12.39%	42.86%
	intermediate class	90.00%	14.17%	23.53%
	Total	85.41%	13.30%	32.26%
Thinking About Future Currency	beginner	96.45%	14.18%	15.00%
	intermediate class	93.75%	6.94%	20.00%
	Total	95.09%	10.53%	16.67%
	Total	80.86%	10.44%	31.49%

Moreover, 500 sentences were extracted from log data from the above experiment. Precision and recall of the English grammar error correction was calculated (see Table 3).

Table 3. English grammar error correction

	Precision	Recall
English grammar error correction	66.7%	31.9%

6. Conclusions

In this paper, we describe an English learning system using chatbots and dialogue systems that help learners continue a dialogue in English even if they are outside of a given topic, and then return to the topic again. The system determines whether the learner's utterance is out of topic by comparing the topic itself with the dialogue intention. The performance of the English learning system using chat bot and dialogue system was measured by the success rate of the dialogue turn and the success rate of the chatbot. The success rate of total dialogue turns reached 80.86% and the success rate of the chatbot was 31.49%. Precision and recall of grammar error correction equaled 66.7% and 31.9% respectively.

In the future, we will investigate how the English learning system handles multiple turns when dialogue goes beyond the predefined discussion topic (Dingli & Scerri, 2013).

7. Acknowledgements

This work was supported by the Institute for Information & communications Technology Promotion (IITP) grant funded by the Korea government (MSIT) (R0126-15-1117, Core technology development of the spontaneous speech dialogue processing for the language learning).

References

Choi, S. K., Kwon, O. W., Kim, Y. K., & Lee, Y. K. (2016). Using a dialogue system based on dialogue maps for computer assisted second language learning. In S. Papadima-Sophocleous, L. Bradley & S. Thouësny (Eds), *CALL communities and culture – short papers from EUROCALL 2016* (pp. 106-112). Research-publishing.net. https://doi.org/10.14705/rpnet.2016.eurocall2016.546

Dingli, A., & Scerri, D. (2013). Building a hybrid: chatterbot-dialog system. *Proceedings of 16th International Conference of Text, Speech, and Dialogue* (pp. 145-152). https://doi.org/10.1007/978-3-642-40585-3_19

Kwon, O. W., Choi, S. K., Roh, Y. H., Kim, Y. K., Park, J. G., & Lee, Y. K. (2015). Trends of spontaneous speech dialogue processing. *Electronics and Telecommunications Trends*, 26-35, in Korean.

The potential of elicited imitation for oral output practice in German L2

Frederik Cornillie[1], Kristof Baten[2], and Dirk De Hertog[3]

Abstract. This paper reports on the potential of Oral Elicited Imitation (OEI) as a format for output practice, building on an analysis of picture-matching and spoken data collected from 36 university-level learners of German as a second language (L2) in a web-based assessment task inspired by Input Processing (VanPatten, 2004). The design and development of OEI for output practice faces two key challenges: learners must be engaged in meaningful language processing rather than in mere repetition of oral stimuli, and the task must eventually provide individualized and qualitative corrective feedback that helps learners to notice gaps between their interlanguage and the target language. Results show that learners attended to meaning and that a commercially available speech recognition tool was able to transcribe learner speech remarkably well.

Keywords: computer-assisted practice, elicited imitation, speaking, morphosyntax, input processing, speech recognition technology.

1. Introduction

In many instructed foreign language learning contexts, opportunities for spoken practice with individualized feedback are scarce. A candidate task for such practice is OEI. In its most basic form, OEI requires learners to repeat oral stimuli (typically sentences) as exactly as possible. It has been mainly used for language assessment, building on the assumption that learners can only accurately repeat sentences they have comprehended and parsed, and will access corresponding mental representations (internalized lexicons and grammars) to reproduce the stimuli. Previous research has shown that OEI can measure implicit knowledge (Erlam,

---

1. KU Leuven & imec, Kortrijk, Belgium; frederik.cornillie@kuleuven.be
2. Ghent University & FWO Vlaanderen, Ghent, Belgium; kristof.baten@ugent.be
3. KU Leuven & imec, Kortrijk, Belgium; dirk.dehertog@kuleuven.be

How to cite this article: Cornillie, F., Baten, K., & De Hertog, D. (2017). The potential of elicited imitation for oral output practice in German L2. In K. Borthwick, L. Bradley & S. Thouësny (Eds), *CALL in a climate of change: adapting to turbulent global conditions – short papers from EUROCALL 2017* (pp. 86-91). Research-publishing.net. https://doi.org/10.14705/rpnet.2017.eurocall2017.694

2009) and oral proficiency (Tracy-Ventura, McManus, Norris, & Ortega, 2014). Additionally, language technology researchers have shown that OEI tests can be automated through Automatic Speech Recognition (ASR) technology (Graham et al., 2008). These findings open opportunities for computer-assisted oral output practice.

However, two preconditions need to be fulfilled for OEI to be a useful task for output practice. First, OEI-based practice must engage learners in meaningful language processing, otherwise the risk is that learners simply parrot what they hear (Erlam, 2009). Therefore, the instructional design of OEI-based practice must rely on sound principles of L2 teaching and learning. Secondly, the task must give automated corrective feedback that can help learners to notice gaps between their speech and the target language. This requires language technology that can accurately recognize learner speech and detect mismatches between learner output and the target language.

The current study investigated the potential of automating OEI for output practice in German L2 while taking these two requirements into account. Research questions include:

- Did the participants attend to meaning?

- How accurately does a state-of-the-art ASR transcribe the participants' production?

2. Method

We designed and developed a web-based and meaning-focused OEI test inspired by Erlam's (2009) implementation of OEI as well as by VanPatten's (2004) theoretical framework of Input Processing. Learners were required to choose between competing visual representations of the oral stimulus before speaking. Immediately after the oral stimulus, two pictures were shown, visualizing alternative interpretations of the stimulus (see Figure 1). This served two purposes: pairing oral stimuli with pictures would stimulate syntactic and semantic processing. Secondly, inserting the picture-matching between the listening and speaking phases results in a time interval, potentially 'flushing' learners' auditory working memory. This is a critical design choice if we do not want learners to draw on their short-term memory when speaking but rather on their internalized lexicon and grammar.

Figure 1. Pictures representing competing interpretations of the ungrammatical stimulus *Der Mann gibt die Frau den Apfel*

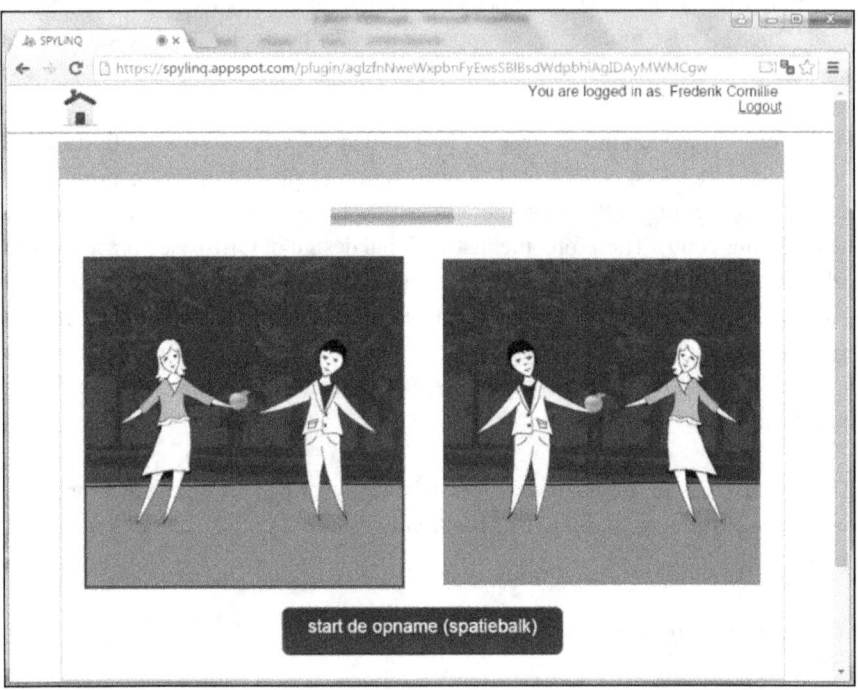

Picture-matching data and spoken data were collected from 36 university-level learners of German L2. Eleven students were in their second year of the academic bachelor program in languages, ten in the third bachelor year, and 15 in the master's program. Their level of proficiency according to the Common European Framework of Reference for languages (CEFR) was estimated between B2 and C1. Eleven students had had an Erasmus stay in a German-speaking country.

Each student was presented with 48 stimuli (comprising grammatical and ungrammatical sentences) that aimed to assess knowledge of case marking and word order; 16 sentences focused on transitives (e.g. *Der Hund verfolgt den Mann*, 'the dog chases the man'), 16 on ditransitives (e.g. *Die Lehrerin schenkt dem Direktor die Blumen*, 'the teacher gives the headmaster flowers'), and another 16 on prepositional phrases (e.g. *Der Mann spaziert durch den Tunnel*, 'the man walks through the tunnel'). Length of the stimuli ranged between five and eight words. The software logged students' interpretations of the sentences; their speech was recorded with Audacity. Students wore headsets throughout the experiment.

After the experiment, the speech data were transcribed manually and through Google's ASR software (Cloud Speech API). This ASR was selected because it is known to work relatively well, can be easily plugged into applications through its API, and recognizes over 80 languages and variants, allowing to scale the solution to other languages.

For the first research question, we analyzed scores on the picture-matching tasks (assessing meaning recognition). If the participants did not attend to meaning during the OEI task, average scores at about the chance level (50%) could be expected. Also, higher-level students were hypothesized to have higher scores. Additionally, we assessed linguistic variation in the learners' responses through manual inspection of the corpus. If semantic variation occurred in addition to (morpho-)syntactic variation, then chances were higher that the learners had also processed the stimuli for meaning.

For the second research question, distance metrics were computed between the manually and automatically transcribed data. We used Levenshtein distance at the word level, which reflects the number of changed, inserted, or deleted words (for each response). As ASR performance may have been affected by the learners' linguistic level, mean Levenshtein distance per student was regressed on the students' year of study and their Erasmus experience.

3. Results

The average percentage of correct responses overall was 78%. Students in the second bachelor year scored 78.1% on average, in the third year 74.4%, and students in the master's program 80.3%. A one-way ANOVA proved the difference between the groups insignificant ($F(2,33)=0.88$, $p=0.42$).

Manual inspection of the corpus revealed instances of semantic variation (e.g. *Der Mann ist gegen den Baum gefahren > Der Mann ist gegen den Baum gefallen*), morphological variation (e.g. *Die Lehrerin schenkt dem Direktor die Blumen > *Die Lehrerin schenkt den Direktor den Blumen*), syntactic variation (e.g. *Dem Direktor schenkt die Lehrerin die Blumen > Die Lehrerin schenkt dem Direktor die Blumen*), and combinations of these (e.g. *Dem Sohn zeigt der Vater die Brille > *Der Vater schenkt der Junge den Junge die Brille*). In addition, there were instances of self-correction (e.g. *Das Mädchen kommt aus der Shop - dem Shop*), disfluencies (e.g. *Der Doktor verklauf verkauft dem Clown das Buch*) and multiple repetitions of the sentence, with or without self-corrections (e.g. *Die Frau gibt den Mann den Apfel. Die Frau gibt dem Mann den Apfel.*)

Levenshtein distance between the manually and automatically transcribed responses ranged between 0 (perfect recognition) and 6 (six words changed, inserted, or deleted). The mean was 0.55 and the median was 0. Out of a total number of 1487 automatically transcribed responses, 979 had zero edit distance. The regression analysis did not reveal any effects of year of study or Erasmus experience ($F(3,27)=0.3917$, $p=.76$, adjusted $R^2=-0.06$).

4. Discussion and conclusions

This study aimed to assess the potential of OEI for output practice in German L2. First, high scores on the picture matching task as well as instances of semantic variation in learner speech suggest that the assessment task stimulated meaningful language processing, even if it was constrained and rather form-focused.

Secondly, Google's ASR service performed remarkably well on the non-native speech. These results bode well for the further development of the task. However, it must be taken into account that the study was limited to higher-level students whose mother tongue is phonetically rather similar to the target language; lower-level students from different mother tongue backgrounds may speak less fluently or in more accented ways, potentially affecting ASR performance.

The next step will be to go beyond simple distance metrics and automatically detect the different types of linguistic variation in order to develop feedback modules for an implementation of this task for L2 practice. This will be done with a view to conducting an experiment that aims to examine the effect of automated feedback on accuracy, fluency, and perhaps complexity (lexical diversity).

5. Acknowledgements

We would like to thank MA student Wouter Vanacker for collecting and preparing the data.

References

Erlam, R. (2009). The elicited oral imitation test as a measure of implicit knowledge. In R. Ellis, S. Loewen, C. Elder, R. Erlam, J. Philp & H. Reinders (Eds), *Implicit and explicit knowledge in second language learning, testing and teaching* (pp. 65-93). Multilingual Matters.

Graham, C. R., Lonsdale, D., Kennington, C., Johnson, A., & McGhee, J. (2008). Elicited imitation as an oral proficiency measure with ASR scoring. *Proceedings of the 6th International Conference on Language Resources and Evaluation* (pp. 1604-1610). http://repository.dlsi.ua.es/242/1/pdf/409_paper.pdf

Tracy-Ventura, N., McManus, K., Norris, J. M., & Ortega, L. (2014). "Repeat as much as you can": elicited imitation as a measure of oral proficiency in L2. In P. Leclercq, A. Edmonds & H. Hilton (Eds), *Measuring L2 proficiency: perspectives from SLA* (pp. 143-166). Multilingual Matters.

VanPatten, B. (Ed.). (2004). *Processing instruction: theory, research, and commentary*. Lawrence Erlbaum Associates.

Emerging affordances in videoconferencing for language learning and teaching

Aparajita Dey-Plissonneau[1]

Abstract. The theory of affordances (Gibson, 1977) came into focus in human-computer interactions and ecological interactive design to explore design strategies to support the actor in direct perception of action possibilities in the operation of things. However, few studies have analysed the basis of affordances in the cultural-historical development of human activity in systems that have substantial socio-cultural, pedagogical, and technological components. This study aims to identify the designed and emerging affordances in an asymmetrical (tutor-learner) videoconferencing environment for language learning. Following Engeström's (2014) Cultural Historical Activity Theory (CHAT) and an ecological Computer Assisted Language Learning (CALL) perspective, I analyse interactions between the design for language learning and technology use at the macro, meso, and micro levels of a videoconferencing project between French tutors and Irish students. I investigate how the designed technological, linguistic, and educational affordances are perceived and acted upon by the tutor-learner activity systems triggering the emergence of new affordances.

Keywords: activity theory, CALL affordances, L2 learning, desktop videoconferencing.

1. Introduction

The term 'affordance' designates an action possibility that is offered by an environment or an object to an actor in the environment either "for good or ill" (Gibson, 1977, p. 68). This relational property depends not just on the 'action possibilities' afforded by the characteristic features of the tool or the environment, but also on the users' perception and action capabilities. CALL affordances are said

---

1. Dublin City University, Dublin, Ireland; aparajita.deyplissonneau2@mail.dcu.ie

How to cite this article: Dey-Plissonneau, A. (2017). Emerging affordances in videoconferencing for language learning and teaching. In K. Borthwick, L. Bradley & S. Thouësny (Eds), *CALL in a climate of change: adapting to turbulent global conditions – short papers from EUROCALL 2017* (pp. 92-98). Research-publishing.net. https://doi.org/10.14705/rpnet.2017.eurocall2017.695

to be a unique combination of social, educational, pedagogical, and technological affordances (Blin, 2016).

An ecological CALL focuses on the interactions between language use, technology use, and language learning by learners, teachers, and other users across multiple timescales and spaces. As mentioned elsewhere (Dey-Plissonneau & Blin, 2016), "educational [and linguistic] affordances are engineered through, for example, the design of lesson plans, learning activities [...], and resources, while others emerge in moment-to-moment interactions between learners or between learners and [tutors]" (p. 298), responding to emerging 'disturbances' during the interaction. These are mediated by the enactment of technological affordances (e.g. text chat, webcam).

So far, mainly micro level studies have analysed tutor/learner interactions using webcam, text chat, synchronous, and asynchronous feedback, etc. and the resulting pedagogical strategies in the language learning via videoconferencing environments (Guichon & Tellier, 2017). Instead of focussing on one particular technological affordance, this study investigates how the designed technological affordances trigger new action possibilities at the micro, meso, and macro level interactions. The following research questions are thus proposed:

- What are the designed technological affordances in the learning environment?

- How do these mediate other CALL affordances for micro, meso, and macro interactions?

- What new affordances emerge in the process?

2. Method

2.1. Context

Masters' students of teaching French as a Foreign Language (FLE) from the University of Lyon 2 (France) tutored online undergraduate Business students from Dublin City University (Ireland) learning French. Six 40-minute weekly interactions were conducted via the videoconferencing platform Visu. These sessions were recorded and incorporated into a rich multimodal corpus: ISMAEL (Guichon, Blin, Wigham, & Thouësny, 2014) (Figure1).

Figure 1. Tutor-tutee dyads and triads (ISMAEL Corpus)

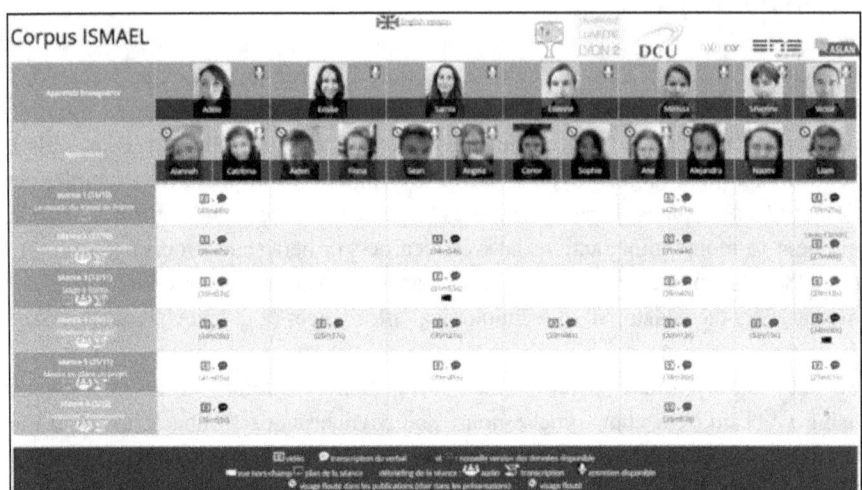

2.2. Data analysis

The designed technological affordances for the videoconferencing platform Visu were identified and categorised. Three consecutive sessions' lesson plans for four tutor-tutee groups (three triads and one dyad) were uploaded to the qualitative analysis software ATLAS.ti and the designed linguistic and educational affordances were coded inductively. The transcripts of the tutors' debriefing sessions were uploaded on ATLAS.ti and coded deductively associating the defined technological, linguistic, and educational affordances to the tutors' perceptions and active interpretations of them. The video recordings of the online instantiations were coded deductively on ELAN to identify the different enactments of these designed affordances. This revealed the emergence of new affordances in the three way interaction between actors, tools, and pedagogical environments.

3. Findings and discussion

3.1. Macro, meso, and micro levels of the interacting activity systems

The macro level is set at the project level where the videoconferencing sessions were integrated on both universities' programme objectives. The meso level is set at the weekly session level where the French tutors' designed lesson plans were implemented. The micro level is set at the moment-to-moment interactions that took place within each session (Figure 2).

Figure 2. Macro, meso, and micro levels of the videoconferencing for language learning and teaching (adapted from Blin, 2016)

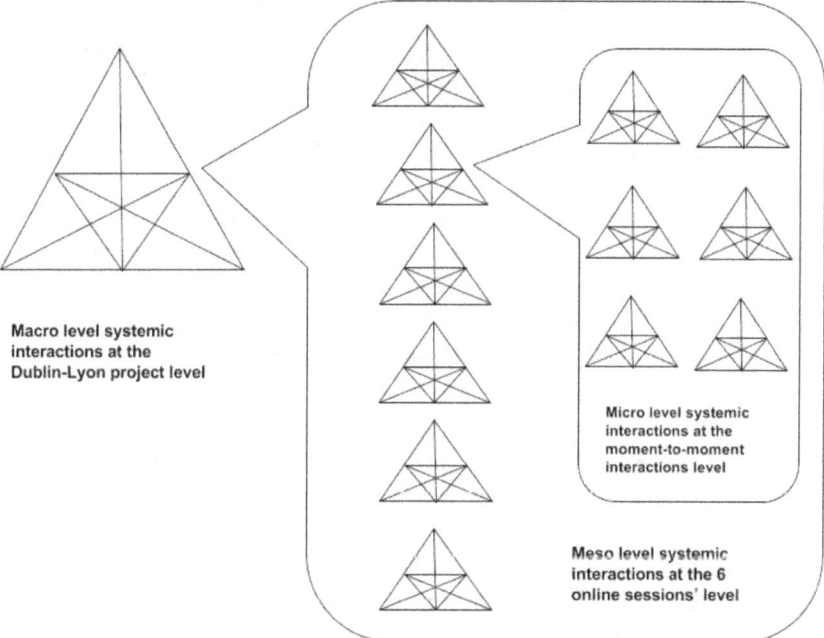

The findings reveal that the tutor-tutee interaction with one another and with the various components within each activity system (technology use, language use, language learning, pedagogical design) deviate from the designed script, as they perceive and enact the affordances differently.

3.2. Technological affordances

Using Cormier, Oleynik, and Lewis's (2014) affordance statement, Visu's designed technological affordances were identified and categorised as follows:

- *Information and Communication affordances* allow for the multimedia management of audio, video, images, online chats, and interactivity content forms allowing learners to process information through auditory and visual channels. Uploading lesson designs was possible, however, sharing and group editing of lesson designs was not afforded.

- *Traceability and Temporal affordances* allow tutor-operated instant or delayed feedback. Visu offers interaction-traces (automatic recording of sessions, chats, shared docs), marker-based traces (tutor ad hoc notes during VC session, markers for localising errors), comment-based traces (post-session multimodal feedback by tutors) allowing the replay of sessions to reflect on teaching practice, viewing session plans, and sending multimodal feedback (Bétrancourt, Guichon, & Prié, 2011).

- *Navigational and Spatial affordances* allow visually guided movement through local online spaces, such as maximising and minimising windows, navigating from one window to another, moving around in on-screen spaces (tabs), such as synchronised, memo, and retrospective spaces.

3.3. Emerging affordances at the interacting micro, meso, and macro levels

Mediated by the aforementioned technological affordances, videoconferencing afforded questioning, explaining, image and video sharing, gesturing, and synchronous and asynchronous corrective feedback, etc. as possibilities for multimodal interactions. Furthermore, tutor and student agencies came into play and enacted the designed affordances differently either to overcome an unexpected 'disturbance' in the activity system or simply to reinterpret the aforementioned technological affordances, thus leading to emerging affordances.

Micro/Meso: disturbances such as tutors' insufficient explaining techniques, students' inarticulate responses, and repetitiveness in lesson plans emerged over the sessions. Role plays, question-answer, and task-based activities were employed through discussions. However, discussion as a pedagogical tool could not afford critical exploratory exchange. This is not easy to implement in synchronous settings, especially in L2 (second language) for B2 (intermediate) level students. The challenge lies in designing questions that can lead to deeper thinking. It was observed that discussions where the students could relate their experiences resulted in greater risk-taking. It is recommended that at the meso level, tutors work on a performative questions framework affording expert questioning rather than teaching-by-telling, reading, or watching videos. However, only training tutors to question may not always induce deep reflective dialogues. Students' feedback expressed that they often lacked vocabulary and content knowledge on the discussed topics. A flipped class approach at the meso level helped counter this problem for one tutor implementing it. However, only the more competent of the two students benefitted from it. From an educational affordance perspective, with access to resources in the pre-session phase, students could familiarise themselves with the vocabulary and ideas, affording deeper reflexive discussions.

Macro: repetitiveness and a lack of coherence between lesson plans were observed. Individual tutor pairs planned a lesson autonomously while integrating feedback from both Lyon and Dublin instructors. The final lesson plan was then shared with the other tutors before the online session. Tutors faced difficulty in appropriating these lesson plans to their respective activity systems. To avoid this, lesson plans could be designed collaboratively on a dedicated discussion forum affording group document sharing and concerted editing. All six lesson plans could have been analysed beforehand to have a sense of inter-session coherence.

4. Conclusion

The desktop videoconferencing environment's affordances are sometimes designed directly, sometimes triggered by the users' agencies, or sometimes occur due to situational deviations, tensions, etc. in the pedagogical interactions. A user may perceive an affordance but may not enact it at all or may not perceive an affordance at all. Despite the inconvenience of being mainly tutor-centred, Visu's technological affordances were inscribed within broader educational affordances which afforded linguistic, socio-cultural, and educational action possibilities. New action possibilities, as demonstrated by some tutors, show the way to a more democratic use of the platform.

A taxonomy of the designed and emerging CALL affordances, along with user perceptions, pedagogical actions, and strategies in desktop videoconferencing for language learning, needs to be further developed in order to inform online language learning, teacher training, and innovation in CALL pedagogy.

5. Acknowledgements

I would like to thank Professors Françoise Blin & Nicolas Guichon for allowing me to use the ISMAEL corpus for this study funded by the Irish Research Council, Ireland.

References

Blin, F. (2016). The theory of affordances. In M.-J. Hamel & C. Caws (Eds), *Language-learner computer interactions: theory, methodology and CALL applications* (pp. 41-64). John Benjamins Publishing. https://doi.org/10.1075/lsse.2.03bli

Bétrancourt, M., Guichon, N., & Prié, Y. (2011). Assessing the use of a trace-based synchronous tool for distant language tutoring. *Computer-Supported Collaborative Learning, 1*, 478-485.

Cormier, P., Oleynik A., & Lewis, K. (2014). Towards a formalisation of affordance modelling for engineering design. *Research in Engineering Design, 25*(3), 259-277. https://doi.org/10.1007/s00163-014-0179-3

Dey-Plissonneau, A., & Blin, F. (2016). Emerging affordances in telecollaborative multimodal interactions. In S. Jager, M. Kurek, & B. O'Rourke (Eds), *New directions in telecollaborative research and practice: selected papers from the second conference on telecollaboration in higher education* (pp. 297-304). Research-publishing.net. https://doi.org/10.14705/rpnet.2016.telecollab2016.521

Engeström, Y. (2014). *Learning by expanding: an activity-theoretical approach to development research* (2nd edition, originally published in 1987). Cambridge University Press. https://doi.org/10.1017/CBO9781139814744

Gibson, J. J. (1977). The theory of affordances. In R. Shaw & J. Bransford (Eds), *Perceiving, acting, and knowing: toward an ecological psychology* (pp. 67-82). Lawrence Erlbaum.

Guichon, N., Blin, F., Wigham, C. R., & Thouësny, S. (2014). *ISMAEL learning and teaching corpus*. Dublin, Ireland: Center for Translation and Textual Studies & Lyon, France: Laboratoire Interactions, Corpus, Apprentissages & Représentations.

Guichon, N., & Tellier, M. (2017). *Enseigner l'oral en ligne. Une approche multimodale.* Editions Didier.

Developing a cross-platform web application for online EFL vocabulary learning courses

Kazumichi Enokida[1], Tatsuya Sakaue[2], Mitsuhiro Morita[3], Shusaku Kida[4], and Akio Ohnishi[5]

Abstract. In this paper, the development of a web application for self-access English vocabulary courses at a national university in Japan will be reported upon. Whilst the basic concepts are inherited from an old Flash-based online vocabulary learning system that had been long used at the university, the new HTML5-based app comes with several new features that are expected to assist students with effective vocabulary learning. Not only is it now made compatible with smartphones, it also enables students to visually check their own progress and their ranking in the class. According to the questionnaire survey conducted among its pilot users, almost 30% of them used the app on their smartphones. Overall, the users found the app beneficial – they especially liked features such as listening to word pronunciation, and checking their own ranking within the class. However, there is room for improvement regarding the usability of the app.

Keywords: mobile learning, CALL, vocabulary learning, software development.

1. Background

Learning a list of word forms and their meanings is still an essential part of English as a Foreign Language (EFL) vocabulary acquisition (c.f. Webb & Nation, 2017). In Japan's tertiary-level EFL education, list learning is a realistic and efficient way of providing learners with a broad range of English words and phrases, considering the extremely limited hours of face-to-face English classes. Utilizing Web-

---

1. Hiroshima University, Higashihiroshima, Japan; kenokida@hiroshima-u.ac.jp
2. Hiroshima University, Higashihiroshima, Japan; tsakaue@hiroshima-u.ac.jp
3. Hiroshima University, Higashihiroshima, Japan; mmorita@hiroshima-u.ac.jp
4. Hiroshima University, Higashihiroshima, Japan; skida@hiroshima-u.ac.jp
5. Version2 Inc., Sapporo, Japan; a-ohnishi@ver2.jp

How to cite this article: Enokida, K., Sakaue, T., Morita, M., Kida, S., & Ohnishi, A. (2017). Developing a cross-platform web application for online EFL vocabulary learning courses. In K. Borthwick, L. Bradley & S. Thouësny (Eds), *CALL in a climate of change: adapting to turbulent global conditions – short papers from EUROCALL 2017* (pp. 99-104). Research-publishing.net. https://doi.org/10.14705/rpnet.2017.eurocall2017.696

Based Training (WBT) for list learning has shown positive effects on vocabulary development (c.f. Burston, 2015) and is expected to avoid the monotony of mechanical self-learning as well as visualize learner progress.

Hiroshima University, a national university in western Japan with 11 faculties and 10,887 undergraduate students (as of May 2017), has implemented large-scale, web-based EFL vocabulary courses since 2011. Each year, approximately 1,000 first-year students of non-English majors take these online courses, such as 'Communication Basic I' and 'Communication Basic II'. In these courses, the students are required to learn 3,000 words per semester (15 weeks) and 6,000 per year on a self-study basis. A vocabulary list of 6,000 essential words with two levels (standard and advanced) was developed for the courses. With this list, learners can build up their vocabulary for daily communication as well as for academic and business situations.

At Hiroshima University, an original WBT system for vocabulary learning called the 'VP System' has been long used for courses involving online self-learning. Developed with Macromedia Flash (currently owned by Adobe) in 2001, it enables the students to learn a large amount of target words in small steps and then review them repeatedly. The system is designed to be easily used by students with different computer-based skills, and to be accessible anytime and anywhere. Detailed records of progress are stored in the server, so that the instructors can use them to assess each student's WBT performance. Whilst these online courses have been found effective in actually expanding students' vocabulary, the old-fashioned VP System running on Flash Player has become increasingly problematic in recent years. The materials are not available on mobile devices, such as smartphones, which enjoy a high penetration rate among university students, and some of the popular PC web browsers are starting to block the Flash plugin by default for security reasons. In order to give these students a wider choice of platforms so that the materials can be accessed from diverse devices, including smartphones and tablets, and to avoid coping with security issues involving Flash Player, a new cross-platform web application had to be developed by exploiting the HTML5 technology. Hence, the purposes of this paper will be to explain the features of this new application, and then to report on which features the users found useful.

2. The HiroTan app: system development

The new application was named HiroTan – a portmanteau of 'Hiroshima' and 'Tango' (a Japanese word meaning 'word'). HiroTan was designed as a web-based app that is optimized for mobile devices as well as PCs. It inherits all the concepts from the old VP System: as is explained in Enokida (2009), a total of 100 words are provided in each chapter, which is broken down into 16 units. Students can learn the form, meaning, and pronunciation of ten words each in the first ten units, and the next five units are devoted to practising them again. The form and translation of each target word are displayed on the screen, where the pronunciation can be heard by clicking/tapping on each word. Then students can check their vocabulary knowledge by matching each word with the correct choice of translation (Figure 1). The final unit is for the review test, where students cannot proceed to the next chapter until they gain a pass level with a minimum of 80%. There are 30 chapters to be learned in one semester, containing 3,000 words in total. Students are given a time limit to finish each unit.

Figure 1. Learning a unit of ten words on HiroTan

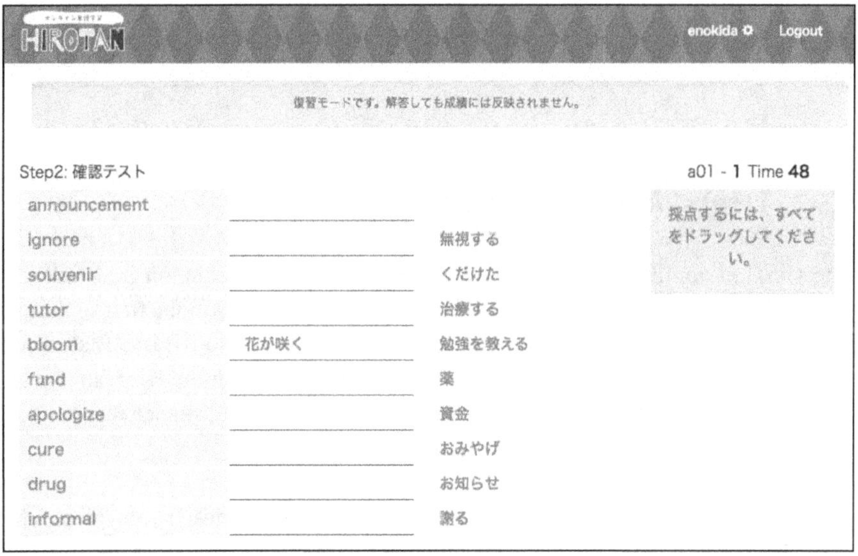

HIROTAN			enokida Logout
	復習モードです。解答しても成績には反映されません。		
Step2: 確認テスト			a01 - 1 Time **48**
announcement			採点するには、すべてをドラッグしてください。
ignore		無視する	
souvenir		くだけた	
tutor		治療する	
bloom	花が咲く	勉強を教える	
fund		薬	
apologize		資金	
cure		おみやげ	
drug		お知らせ	
informal		謝る	

HiroTan also comes with several new features. In the user dashboard, learners can check their own progress, such as the number of words they have learned over the past seven days ('This week'), the number of words they have learned each week ('Weekly'), and their ranking among the whole group of students ('Your position') (Figure 2). These features are intended to encourage learners to set their own pace for successful self-learning, and to improve their learning by comparing their performance with their classmates. The app also supports multiple languages based on Unicode, whilst the VP System only supported Japanese and English.

Figure 2. 'This week', 'Weekly', and 'Your position' in the dashboard

3. Users' feedback and discussion

The HiroTan application was released for pilot use and evaluation in Academic Year 2017. It was used in several vocabulary building courses in the first semester, including part of Communication Basic I. In Communication Basic I, students were required to learn 3,000 words, as mentioned above, with the HiroTan app by the end of the semester. Grades were based on the online performance recorded on the server, and the score of the paper-based final exam.

A questionnaire survey was conducted at the end of the semester to evaluate the app. The question items were: (1) on which platform they mainly used the HiroTan app (PC, smartphone, or both)?; (2) how usable they found the app?; and (3) to what extent they found each of the following functions useful: audio pronunciation, 'This week' (latest learning contents), 'Weekly' (weekly learning contents), and 'Your position' (ranking in your class)? The students were requested to answer Questions 2 and 3 on a six-point Likert scale. There were 151 respondents.

As for Item 1 (the main platform to access HiroTan), 70.2% of the respondents answered "PC", followed by "both PC and smartphone" (17.9%) and "smartphone" (11.9%). Nearly 30% of them incorporated mobile devices into their vocabulary learning. It is not surprising that 70% of them still chose the PC, given the fact that all the first-year students at Hiroshima University are now required to bring their own laptop to campus: they found it easier to do their coursework on devices with a larger screen. The results of Items 2 and 3 (user-friendliness, pronunciation, latest learning contents, weekly learning contents, and ranking in your class) are presented as diverging stacked bar charts in Figure 3.

Figure 3. Survey results: questions 2 and 3 ($N=151$)

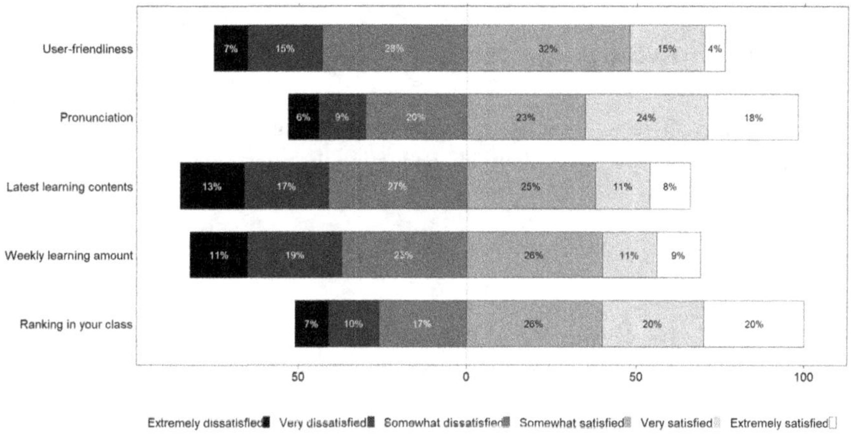

	Extremely dissatisfied	Very dissatisfied	Somewhat dissatisfied	Somewhat satisfied	Very satisfied	Extremely satisfied
User-friendliness	7%	15%	28%	32%	15%	4%
Pronunciation	6%	9%	20%	23%	24%	18%
Latest learning contents	13%	17%	27%	25%	11%	8%
Weekly learning amount	11%	19%	23%	26%	11%	9%
Ranking in your class	7%	10%	17%	26%	20%	20%

Although positive feedback was found on features such as audio playback of word pronunciation and displaying their ranking in class, the popularity of the latest learning contents and weekly learning amount was relatively weak. The students tend to be more interested in comparing their performance with that of their classmates than monitoring their own achievements as an individual learner. Future users of the app could be encouraged to use more the information in 'This week' and 'Weekly' for the latter purpose. Also, there is room for improvement regarding the usability of the app, as is shown in the split opinions on user-friendliness. Further bug fixes and updates will enable them to focus more on learning rather than technology. Overall, however, the pilot version of HiroTan was found beneficial enough to its users.

4. Conclusion and future directions

The HiroTan app was made available to all the 1,000 students taking the Communication Basic I/II courses from the second semester of 2017. Further improvements are to be made on the usability and functionality of the app, based on the feedback from its users. New features planned for future versions of the app include dictation quizzes to check listening and spelling abilities, and cloze tests to practice new vocabulary in context. Questions regarding the effectiveness of WBT-based list learning should also be addressed, such as: (1) what vocabulary knowledge and skills do the learners acquire as a result of list learning?; and (2) to what extent will learning an enormous word list contribute to long-term retention and appropriate use of these words in communicative contexts?

5. Acknowledgements

The authors wish to acknowledge Kunihiro Kusanagi and Lisa Yoshikawa at Hiroshima University for their help in conducting the questionnaire survey.

References

Burston, J. (2015). Twenty years of MALL project implementation: a meta-analysis of learning outcomes. *ReCALL, 27*(1), 4-20. https://doi.org/10.1017/S0958344014000159

Enokida, K. (2009). Classroom practice in English classes based on Hiroshima University's "Campus Ubiquitous Project". *JACET News, 170*, 4-7. http://www.jacet.org/newsletter/jacet170.pdf

Webb, S., & Nation, P. (2017). *How vocabulary is learned*. Oxford University Press.

Goofy Guide Game: affordances and constraints for engagement and oral communication in English

Kaisa Enticknap-Seppänen[1]

Abstract. This study investigates tourism undergraduates' perceptions of learning engagement and oral communication in English through their experiences of testing a pilot purpose-designed educational digital game. Reflecting the implementation of digitalization strategy in universities of applied sciences in Finland, it examines whether single instances of digital gameplay afford oral communication in the L2. Sociocultural and ecological language learning theories were the framework of the study. The data consist of the teacher researcher's observations of gameplay sessions, learning diaries and preliminary and post-gameplay online questionnaires. The learning diaries and open questionnaire responses were analyzed with qualitative content analysis using the preliminary questionnaire responses for comparison. The results showed that once-off gameplay sessions afforded engagement and oral communication in the L2. However, the questionnaire responses and learning diaries implied that the students had high expectations of learning engagement and oral skills development which were not completely fulfilled due to game design constraints. This suggests that although much occurs during single instances of gameplay, a participatory approach involving education professionals and learners in educational game design is warranted to fully optimize L2 appropriation within the game environment.

Keywords: digital educational game, engagement, learning, oral communication.

1. Introduction

In Finland, higher education has embraced digitalization by integrating computer assisted and web based learning into curriculum design. Within this context, Kajaani University of Applied Sciences enabled the '*Simppeli, Simulator and game*

---

1. Kajaani University of Applied Sciences, Kajaani, Finland; kaisa.enticknap-seppanen@kamk.fi

How to cite this article: Enticknap-Seppänen, K. (2017). Goofy Guide Game: affordances and constraints for engagement and oral communication in English. In K. Borthwick, L. Bradley & S. Thouësny (Eds), *CALL in a climate of change: adapting to turbulent global conditions – short papers from EUROCALL 2017* (pp. 105-109). Research-publishing.net. https://doi.org/10.14705/rpnet.2017.eurocall2017.697

expertise application in teaching' project (Rantaharju, 2016). Simppeli allowed one language teacher researcher to design and pilot a digital educational game, with the assistance of game design experts. This interdisciplinary collaboration produced a digital educational game in the L2 (English) specifically for tourism students, which was piloted in an on-campus game laboratory.

The aim of this study was to examine whether a purpose-built educational digital game (Goofy Guide Game) afforded learner engagement and face-to-face oral communication in English among players during single instances of gameplay. The research is situated in a period of rapid change in language learning due to digitalization, which has also broadened the focus of Second Language Acquisition (SLA) research from the formal classroom setting into informal spaces such as online gaming (Cornillie, Thorne, & Desmet, 2012).

2. Method

In autumn 2016, two groups of first year tourism students were split into eight teams of four to six persons and played the game two teams at a time, during four gameplay sessions. The game laboratory, equipped with computers, virtual reality hand and headsets, cameras, audio and lighting equipment, and screens and touch screen devices, offered an exciting non-classroom setting for piloting the game. The two teams were arranged in front of a large screen around two touch-screen devices.

The game consists of a 2D online audio-visual animation made with the widely available online animation software, Go Animate. It presents seven tourist guiding events where the guide behaves inappropriately in customer service situations. These include meeting the tourist group, explaining the itinerary, safety procedures, recommending places to eat, informing, describing monuments, and dealing with an emergency. Of each event, there are four alternative versions (A, B, C, and D) which the players had to slide into the order of best to worst from a customer service perspective, using the touch screen devices.

The players watched and listened to the animation, discussed the different versions in English and then had twenty seconds to agree, slide the answers into position and lock them. They also had to interpret tourism and customer service lexis and differentiate between the levels of politeness communicated by the game's guide character, including deictic cues such as non-verbal expressions. After locking answers, the game displayed the teams' scores on a leaderboard. Each gameplay session took approximately forty minutes to complete. The teacher-researcher organized and observed the gameplay sessions. A video about the game is available at https://youtu.be/idPmuJT2H3Y.

The data were collected with (1) observation, (2) an anonymous pre- and post-game questionnaire created, shared, and gathered via Google forms, and (3) individual learning diaries returned to the Moodle learning management platform after the game sessions. The data were analyzed manually with qualitative content analysis. First the teacher researcher's observations, open responses to the pre- and post-game questionnaires were read, searching for themes, then the learning diaries. The themes that emerged: enjoyment, collaboration, deixis, physical environment, duration of gameplay, soundscape, humor, speaking English, listening comprehension, vocabulary acquisition, professional competence awareness and development, and learning engagement were combined and categorized under the higher order headings of game design, physical environment and interaction. The affordances and constraints for learning and speaking English that arose from the data were then investigated through these headings.

To frame the analysis, this case study employed the sociocultural and ecological approach (Lantolf & Thorne, 2006; van Lier, 2010) to language learning to interpret the social interactions of gameplay. It was a useful theoretical approach for considering English L2 use and appropriation among Finnish higher education students who, as young adults, are encouraged to be active and take responsibility for their own learning within a curriculum involving collaborative work and projects. Sociocultural and ecological learning places students at the center of an environment that provides learning opportunities both inside and outside the formal classroom setting. These affordances can be mediated through physical tools such as digital devices, in this case the game on the screen and the touch screens, and cultural tools such as language, here English L1 spoken by the guide and the tourists (L2) in the game, and the students themselves (L2). The affordances can be appropriated, in other words adopted, by the students through meaningful social activity, such as interaction during face-to-face gameplay.

3. Results and discussion

Within this theoretical framework, the appropriation of learning opportunities can occur through interactions between experts and novices, such as teachers and students, peers with more or less English language competence, and between technology and learners. According to the teacher researcher's observations, the open answers to the post-game questionnaires and the content of the learning diaries; interactions occurred between the team members, and between the game technology, content and players, within the physical environment of the game laboratory.

The outcome of the analysis revealed a contradiction between the teacher researcher's observations and how the players construed learning and speaking English. During the brief once-off gameplay sessions, the students were seen to actively engage with the game content by watching, listening to and discussing issues relevant to deciding how to order their answers on the touch-screens. However, although the players reported that they spoke English, they mentioned a lack of oral utterances and oral communication development. Their explanation for this lack of development lay in the use of deictic communication strategies, such as focusing gaze at other team-mates, nodding and shaking their heads, or pointing, and using short interjections such as 'yes', 'no' or 'over here'. This situation was exacerbated by the limited time the game allowed for discussion, deciding and locking the answers, and by the size of the teams, which prevented some team members from fully participating in the discussions.

On the other hand, the players reported that they had acquired tourism lexis and an awareness of how not to behave in guiding situations. Others mentioned that their L2 listening comprehension improved, although using multiple senses simultaneously distracted from speaking. The players desired more time to discuss the answers, for gaps in the guide-tourist dialogues requiring correct fillers for the game to progress. They also found the gameplay and teamwork enjoyable and appreciated the humour inspired by the unprofessional guide. The learning diaries showed that the game provided a space to reflect on learner and emerging tourism professional identity. For instance, although prior familiarity with subject and linguistic content was mentioned, others felt they could apply it later in working life. Although mainly emphasizing multiplayer online role-playing games, previous research provides somewhat similar outcomes. They indicate that gaming possibly reduces emotional barriers to communication, involves motivating and collaborative features, and rich linguistic environments which benefit L2 learning and promote oral communication and engagement (Cornillie et al., 2012).

4. Conclusions

The players recalled the multiple actions occurring during gameplay and could reflect on its linguistic and professional benefits. However, their experiences of language learning during the game did not match their expectations, which were reported in terms of separate skills, lexis and professional competence development. As above, although the players felt their confidence to speak, pronunciation, listening comprehension, and customer service competence improved, further scaffolding, such as integrated structured speaking tasks employing the lexis in the game, could provide a more positive learning experience. These results are relevant within the discourses of digitalization and game-based learning and can help educators to employ a participatory approach also involving students in game purchase decision-making and design for solutions covering a broad range of learner needs.

5. Acknowledgements

I would like to thank the Simppeli project, KAMK's School of Information Systems, and students of the School of Tourism and Sports for this opportunity to create a digital education game with game design experts and to conduct this research and Ph.D. student Kirsi Korkealehto for her assistance with the research questionnaires and reporting the results.

References

Cornillie, F., Thorne, S. L., Desmet, P. (2012). Digital games for language learning: challenges and opportunities, from hype to insight. *ReCALL, 24*(3), 243-256. https://doi.org/10.1017/S0958344012000134

Lantolf, J. P., & Thorne, S. L. (2006). Sociocultural theory and second language learning. In B. Van Patten & J. Williams (Ed.), *Theories in second language acquisition. An introduction* (2nd edition). Routledge.

Rantaharju, T. (2016). PowerPoint presentation simppeli project (1.1.2015-31.12.2017). https://www.kamk.fi/loader.aspx?id=205115d3-27c2-4aa5-8a48-530c844b5ae5

Van Lier, L. (2010). The ecology of language learning: practice to theory, theory to practice. *Procedia Social and Behavioral Sciences, 3*, 2-6. https://doi.org/10.1016/j.sbspro.2010.07.005

Data-driven learning and the acquisition of Italian collocations: from design to student evaluation

Luciana Forti[1]

Abstract. This paper looks at how corpus data was used to design an Italian as an L2 language learning programme and how it was evaluated by students. The study focuses on the acquisition of Italian verb-noun collocations by Chinese native students attending a ten month long Italian language course before enrolling at an Italian university. It describes how an Italian native corpus, the Perugia Corpus (PEC), and an Italian learner corpus, the Longitudinal Corpus of Chinese Learners of Italian (LoCCLI), were used to build a data-driven learning programme for an eight week long Italian language course. The paper shows how different kinds of data can make a contribution not only to the creation of learning materials, but also to the definition of learning aims and the construction of assessment tools, and it presents the results of an end-of-course student questionnaire.

Keywords: Italian, data-driven learning, collocations.

1. Introduction

The integration of authentic corpus data in second language teaching was first reported by McKay (1980) and further developed by Johns (1991). When Johns (1991) formulated the expression Data-Driven Learning (DDL), the reference was also to a precise teaching methodology based on the guided-discovery of patterns in concordance lines. Since then, DDL has seen a plethora of versions in terms of teaching strategies and tools used (Boulton, 2017).

---

1. University for Foreigners of Perugia, Perugia, Italy; luciana.forti@unistrapg.it

How to cite this article: Forti, L. (2017). Data-driven learning and the acquisition of Italian collocations: from design to student evaluation. In K. Borthwick, L. Bradley & S. Thouësny (Eds), *CALL in a climate of change: adapting to turbulent global conditions – short papers from EUROCALL 2017* (pp. 110-115). Research-publishing.net. https://doi.org/10.14705/rpnet.2017.eurocall2017.698

The view of language as largely formulaic and primed has risen from the increasingly powerful analysis of large corpora containing instances of real language use in a variety of contexts. Knowing a word entails knowing the company it keeps (Firth, 1957), with clear implications for second language pedagogy.

This paper presents a pilot method to design a language learning programme tailored for the acquisition of Italian verb-noun collocations, and the effect it had on students. Two corpora were used: an Italian native reference corpus, the PEC (Spina, 2014), and an Italian non-native corpus, the LoCCLI. The corpus data was used to select learning aims, design learning activities, and build a proficiency test.

2. Method

2.1. Selecting learning aims

The PEC is used through the DICI-A, a PEC-based dictionary of collocations built for learners of Italian L2 (Spina, 2010), in order to identify the list of verb-noun collocations that are mostly used in Italian.

The LoCCLI is used to analyse the errors made in verb-noun collocations, and to serve as a basis for the creation of classroom activities based on error correction, as well as for the selection of distractors in the multiple-choice section of the collocational proficiency test.

Each weekly lesson focused on a set of eight collocations. A list of 32 collocations more frequently used with errors in LoCCLI was made. Errors were tagged according to whether they involved the noun, the determiner, the verb, or the whole combination (Nesselhauf, 2005; Wang, 2016). This initial list was then grouped into eight topics, corresponding to the general weekly topics that each lesson was based on. The missing spots for each weekly set were then filled by selecting collocations from DICI-A and according to the following three main criteria: highest frequency and dispersion values; thematic relevance to the identified topics; and presence of a delexicalised verb.

This two-stage selection process resulted in a list of thematically linked collocations sets. Each set was used to create experimental and traditional activities, as well as devise an appropriate take-home assignment.

2.2. Designing learning activities

Data from LoCCLI was used in error correction activities where learners needed to decide, in their groups, whether the sentences shown contained an error or not. Most activities, however, drew on data extracted from PEC, for designing both traditional as well as concordance-based DDL activities on paper.

Being a sample of multiple instances of a single collocation, the concordance allows the construction of a variety of guided-discovery activities aimed at fostering the interiorisation of a verb-noun collocation, in its specific context of occurrence and in relation to its structural and semantic pattern.

2.3. Building a proficiency test

In order to try to capture both definitional and transferable knowledge of collocations in a balanced manner, the proficiency test was divided into three parts:

- 32 multiple choice items, using the language and the errors found in LoCCLI as distractors;
- 32 gap-fill items, with sentences adapted from PEC, with the omission of the verb collocate;
- a collocational table like the one designed by Gyllstad (2005).

Similarly to Supatranont's (2005) work, the first set of 32 items was aimed at eliciting definitional knowledge, while the second set of 32 items looked at transferable knowledge. The table was aimed at assessing decontextualised transferable knowledge.

3. Results and discussion

An end-of-course questionnaire, composed by closed and open questions, was administered to all eight classes who were exposed to the data-driven experimental lessons. Here we will focus on the 50 questionnaires collected from the experimental classes, and particularly on the closed questions dealing with the specifics of concordance-based materials, all of which were based on a 6-point Likert scale (see Table 1).

An even-numbered scale was chosen in order to avoid a neutral middle option, thus guiding the students to make an accurate choice (Dörnyei & Taguchi, 2010, pp. 28, 114). A balanced mix of both positively and negatively worded items were formulated in order to avoid the tendency of the respondents to select options from only one side of the scale (Dörnyei & Taguchi, 2010, p. 43).

Table 1. Questionnaires collected from the experimental classes; mean based on 6-point scale

Item 1. Reading groups of sentences containing the same combination confused me				
ANSWER		%	MEAN	SD
1	Totally disagree	10%	3.60	1.56
2	Disagree	22%		
3	Partially disagree	10%		
4	Partially agree	26%		
5	Agree	20%		
6	Totally agree	12%		
Item 2. The observation of groups of sentences containing the same combination has helped me to understand how to use that combination in the future				
ANSWER		%	MEAN	SD
1	Totally disagree	2%	5.20	1.14
2	Disagree	4%		
3	Partially disagree	2%		
4	Partially agree	6%		
5	Agree	36%		
6	Totally agree	50%		
Item 3. The groups of sentences will help me make less errors in the future				
ANSWER		%	MEAN	SD
1	Totally disagree	0%	5.08	0.92
2	Disagree	2%		
3	Partially disagree	4%		
4	Partially agree	12%		
5	Agree	42%		
6	Totally agree	40%		
Item 4. A new smartphone application with groups of sentences for word combinations would be useless				
ANSWER		%	MEAN	SD
1	Totally disagree	28%	2.64	1.55
2	Disagree	30%		
3	Partially disagree	14%		
4	Partially agree	14%		
5	Agree	6%		
6	Totally agree	8%		

The proposal of looking at groups of sentences showing how a single combination is used turned out to be, to some extent, challenging, with 60% of respondents stating it was somewhat confusing, although the mean and *SD* values show that answers fall into an evenly distributed in-between area.

On the other hand, responses are more polarised when most students indicate that the groups of sentences they initially found confusing did in fact help them to understand how to use the combination in future, decreasing the perceived likelihood of producing errors. Furthermore, the respondents appear to largely favour the idea of a smartphone app based on concordance lines.

The data from the questionnaire clearly indicates a need to improve the concordance-based activities. One major issue, in fact, is to make concordance lines and pattern hunting tasks more effective for learners. These kinds of improvements would minimise the chances of causing confusion, while strengthening the positive outcomes that have already been observed.

4. Conclusions

Despite the growing body of research in the field of DDL, practicalities related to how corpus data can actually be selected and integrated in second language pedagogy are still often overlooked. This paper attempted to provide a contribution in this direction, by describing a method followed to ease the acquisition of Italian verb-noun collocations, through concordance-based work. The questionnaire results seem to show some promise, especially in relation to possible mobile-assisted language learning applications.

Chinese learners are one of the largest learning populations of Italian as a second/foreign language learning. As a result, the challenges they face have become central in the debate concerning educational effectiveness and innovation in methods and materials design. The position of Italian as an underrepresented language in corpus-based pedagogical research makes it an ideal candidate for future work and development in this sense.

References

Boulton, A. (2017). Research timeline. Corpora in language teaching and learning. *Language Teaching, 50*(4), 483-506. https://doi.org/10.1017/S0261444817000167

Dörnyei, Z., & Taguchi, T. (2010). *Questionnaires in second language research. Construction, administration, and processing* (2nd ed.). Routledge.

Firth, J. R. (1957). *Papers in linguistics 1934-1951*. Oxford University Press.

Gyllstad, H. (2005). Words that go together well: developing test formats for measuring learner knowledge of English collocations. *The Department of English in Lund: Working Papers in Linguistics, 5*, 1-31.

Johns, T. (1991). Should you be persuaded - two examples of data driven learning materials. *Classroom Concordancing, English Language Research Journal 4*, 1-13.

McKay, S. (1980). Teaching the syntactic, semantic and pragmatic dimensions of verbs. *TESOL Quarterly, 14*(1), 17-26. https://doi.org/10.2307/3586805

Nesselhauf, N. (2005). *Collocations in a learner corpus*. John Benjamins Publishing Company. https://doi.org/10.1075/scl.14

Spina, S. (2010). The dictionary of Italian collocations: design and integration in an online learning environment. In *LREC 2010 Proceedings, Malta* (pp. 3202-3208).

Spina, S. (2014). Il Perugia Corpus: una risorsa di riferimento per l'italiano. Composizione, annotazione e valutazione. In *Proceedings of the First Italian Conference on Computational Linguistics CLiC-it 2014 & the Fourth International Workshop EVALITA 2014litica* (Vol. 1, pp. 354-359). Pisa University Press.

Supatranont, K. (2005). *A comparison of the effects of the concordance-based and the conventional teaching methods on engineering students' English vocabulary learning*. Doctoral dissertation. Chulalongkorn University, Thailand.

Wang, Y. (2016). *The idiom principle and L1 influence. A contrastive learner-corpus study of delexical verb+noun collocations*. John Benjamins Publishing Company. https://doi.org/10.1075/scl.77

Determining factors in student retention in online courses

Kolbrún Friðriksdóttir[1] and Birna Arnbjörnsdóttir[2]

Abstract. The rapid growth of online education courses, especially Massive Open Online Courses (MOOCs), has called attention to the issue of student retention and low overall completion rates (Gaebel, 2013). The impact of different modes of delivery on retention has also received attention with a blended learning mode being deemed most effective in retaining students (Harker & Koutsantoni, 2005). Fischer (2007) underscores the need for computer-based tracking data to expose students' progress online. The study presented here is part of a larger study on student retention in online language learning courses and draws on tracking data from over 43,000 learners on 'Icelandic Online' (IOL), an open online course in Icelandic as a second language. Previous findings reveal that completion rates on IOL are low and vary by mode of delivery, revealing regular attrition patterns across all modes of delivery. This paper demonstrates the importance of re-examining parameters for measuring retention and to correlate student retention to views on course content and platform. Further surveys based on the tracking data will elicit more in-depth knowledge about student engagements.

Keywords: student retention, tracking data, self-reports, Icelandic Online.

1. Introduction

IOL offers seven courses in Icelandic as a second language for adults. The courses, developed at the University of Iceland, have been offered since 2004. These self-instructed online courses attract thousands of learners worldwide; providing the opportunity to learn Icelandic, unhindered by limits of geography. Two of the IOL courses (IOL 1 and 2) are offered in three delivery modes; as (1) an open and free, self-directed course, (2) a distance course, and (3) a blended course.

---

1. University of Iceland, Reykjavík, Iceland; kolbrunf@hi.is
2. University of Iceland, Reykjavík, Iceland; birnaarn@hi.is

How to cite this article: Friðriksdóttir, K., & Arnbjörnsdóttir, B. (2017). Determining factors in student retention in online courses. In K. Borthwick, L. Bradley & S. Thouësny (Eds), *CALL in a climate of change: adapting to turbulent global conditions – short papers from EUROCALL 2017* (pp. 116-121). Research-publishing.net. https://doi.org/10.14705/rpnet.2017.eurocall2017.699

The proliferation of MOOCs has called attention to the issue of student retention and concern about low overall completion rates (Gaebel, 2013). It has been pointed out that retention is commonly measured without accounting for student intentions (Koller, Ng, & Chen, 2013) and that no student is obliged to complete or engage in a MOOC (Sokolik, 2014).

Researchers have suggested that traditional approaches to measuring retention may not apply to MOOCs. The field of learning analytics have a significant role to play in providing valuable teaching and learning insights, and researchers (Long & Siemens, 2011) have called for more studies using this methodology on why students decide to leave online courses.

This paper presents an analysis of tracking data on student retention collected over eight years on 43,000 users of IOL. It also introduces a follow-up survey-based study, currently underway, which seeks to provide a more in-depth understanding of why students decide to stay on or leave online courses.

2. Method

This is a three phased, mixed method study. A tracking system is an integral part of IOL and monitors learners' engagement as they move through the course(s). The main objective of the first phase of the study is to analyse the large amount of tracking data by (1) mapping out overall retention rates for all the seven IOL courses, (2) exploring the effect of different modes on student retention, and (3) investigating what the overall engagement patterns on IOL suggest about the nature of retention.

The next two survey-based phases will gather evidence from self-reports from the same students on their use of the IOL programme as measured by the tracking data, with a view to investigate why online learners decide to leave, as well as stay, to the end of the programme. The focus is on learners on IOL 2 who have covered 40-100% of the course in the three different modes of delivery: blended, distance, and open. The survey includes a large number of factors associated with instructional features of the programme and different learning environments. The goal is to investigate (1) whether certain course content factors on IOL serve to encourage or discourage retention, (2) why the blended mode is more effective than other modes in retaining students, and (3) whether learners' intentions and motivations for taking the course are important factors in retention. Regression analysis is used to determine which variables affect retention.

3. Results

3.1. Overall retention on IOL and the effect of different modes of delivery

The data on overall retention on IOL reveal that overall completion rates are low across the seven courses: from 2.4% to 18.2%, depending on courses (Friðriksdóttir, 2017). Furthermore, when studying the effect of different modes of delivery on retention in two of the courses (IOL 1 and 2), the blended learning mode is the most effective in keeping learners in both courses. Table 1 shows the effects of the three modes on retention on IOL 2.

Table 1. Course completion in different modes of delivery in IOL 2

	Open Self-directed Course	Distance Course	Blended Course
N of beginners in a course	3,462	62	281
N of completers in a course	152	3	40
Completion rates	4.4%	4.8%	14.2%

The blended learning mode, with 14.2% completion rates, is more effective in retaining students than both the distance mode (4.8% completion rates), and the open self-directed mode (4.4% completion rates). The completion rates on the three different modes of delivery on IOL 1 revealed similar findings.

3.2. Overall engagement patterns on IOL

The retention data were broken down to reveal when non-completers dropped out. Two of the courses (IOL 1 and 2) were examined specifically for this purpose. Figure 1 shows that the tracking data revealed a regular drop-out pattern across all modes of delivery among the learners who did not remain to the end of IOL 2, showing concentrations of drop-outs at specific junctures in the course and large drop-out rates initially, irrespective of modality. The drop-out pattern in IOL 1 revealed similar findings.

The drop-out patterns exposed in Figure 1 raise further questions on the overall online engagement patterns of non-completers. IOL 1 and 2 were first investigated by using different parameters for coverage of a course. Table 2 reveals quite a different pattern when the parameters for coverage of course content are re-evaluated; completion rates are about (1) two times higher in all the three modes on IOL 2 when the parameters for course completions are modified from 100% coverage of course content to 90%, (2) three to five times higher in all modes when adjusted to 75% coverage, and (3) four to eight times higher in all modes when changed to 50% coverage of course content. The results show similar engagement patterns when data from IOL 1 are examined. The findings presented in Table 2 reveal immense impact on retention when the parameters used to measure retention are adjusted.

Figure 1. Drop-out patterns across the three different modes of delivery in IOL 2

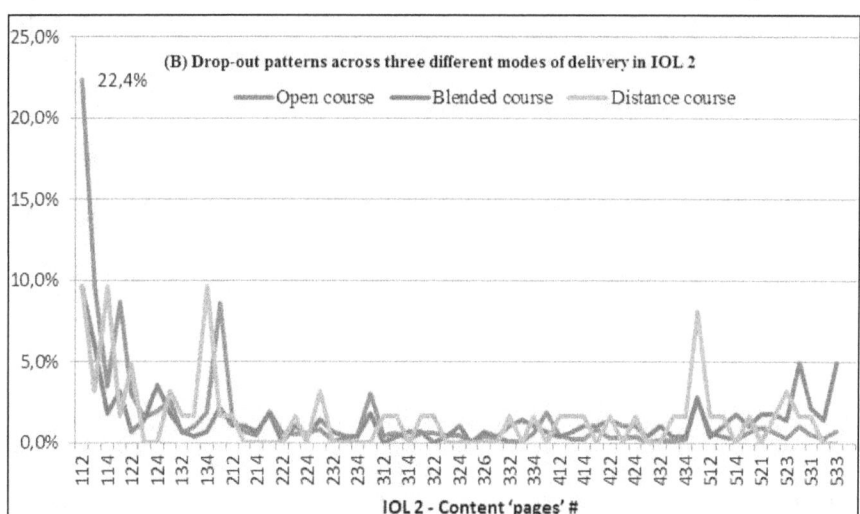

Table 2. Retention in view of different coverage of course content in different modes of delivery in IOL 2

		Content coverage 100%	Content coverage 90%	Content coverage 75%	Content coverage 50%
Blended Course	Completion rates	14.2%	29.2%	40.6%	53.4%
Distance Course	Completion rates	4.8%	6.5%	25.8%	40.3%
Open Course	Completion rates	4.4%	7.3%	14.2%	20.4%

These findings raise further questions on student engagement patterns on all the IOL courses. They were analysed further for a more nuanced picture of the overall engagement patterns. Figure 2 exposes the patterns on all seven IOL courses showing that the majority of learners on IOL complete less than 50% of a course's content.

Figure 2. Overall engagement patterns in all seven courses of IOL in terms of different parameters for coverage of course content

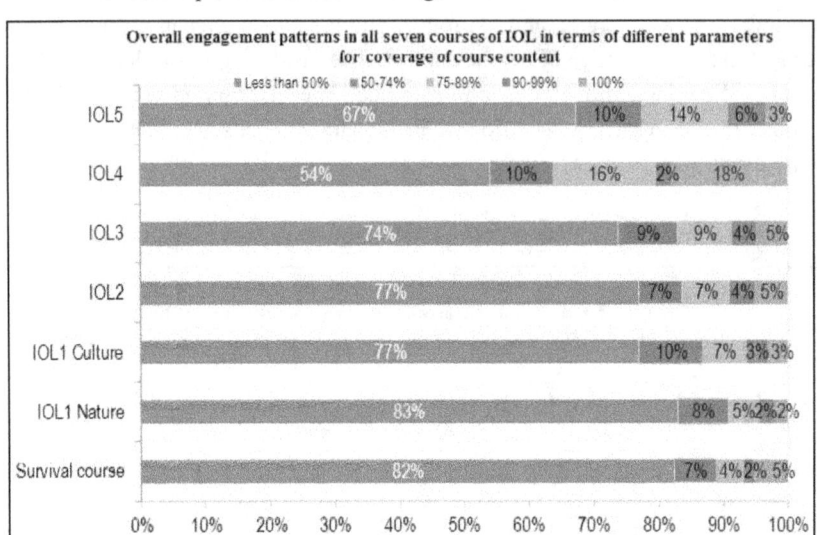

4. Discussion

The results of the tracking data analysis support findings of previous studies on overall low completion rates in online courses (Gaebel, 2013) and that blended learning is most effective in retaining students (Harker & Koutsantoni, 2005). These findings reveal regular attrition patterns across all modes of delivery, with sharp drop-outs initially and concentrations of drop-outs at certain junctures in the courses, and that once parameters for measuring retention are adjusted, a different picture of retention is revealed. The findings give reason to ask what it really means to 'complete a course'.

5. Conclusions

The analysis of IOL's tracking data revealed interesting engagement patterns across courses and calls for a re-evaluation of how retention is measured in MOOCs. The next two phases of this study will gather self-reports from the same tracked students on their use of IOL to gain a deeper understanding of why online learners decide to leave, or complete, a programme.

References

Fischer, R. (2007). How do we know what students are actually doing? Monitoring students' behavior in CALL. *Computer Assisted Language Learning, 20*(5), 409-442. https://doi.org/10.1080/09588220701746013

Friðriksdóttir, K. (2017). The impact of different modalities on student retention and overall engagement patterns in open online courses. *Journal of Assisted Language Learning,* Special issue: analytics in online language learning and teaching, 1-19. http://dx.doi.org/10.1080/09588221.2017.1381129

Gaebel, M. (2013). MOOCs – Massive Open Online Courses. *European University Association* (EUA), Jan. 2013. http://www.eua.be/Libraries/publication/EUA_Occasional_papers_MOOCs

Harker, M., & Koutsantoni, D. (2005). Can it be as effective? Distance versus blended learning in a web-based EAP programme. *ReCALL, 17*(2), 197-216. https://doi.org/10.1017/S095834400500042X

Koller, D., Ng, A., & Chen, Z. (2013). Retention and intention in massive open online courses: in depth. *EDUCAUSE Review.* http://er.educause.edu/articles/2013/6/retention-and-intention-in-massive-open-online-courses-in-depth

Long, P., & Siemens, G. (2011). Penetrating the fog: analytics in learning and education. *EDUCAUSE Review.* http://er.educause.edu/~/media/files/article-downloads/erm1151.pdf

Sokolik, M. (2014). What constitutes an effective language MOOC? In E. Martín-Monje & E. Bárcena (Eds), *Language MOOCs. Providing learning, transcending boundaries* (pp. 16-32). De Gruyter Open. https://doi.org/10.2478/9783110420067.2

Designing a MOOC for learners of Spanish: exploring learner usage and satisfaction

Ana Gimeno-Sanz[1]

Abstract. The authors of the *Learn Spanish: Basic Spanish for English Speakers* Massive Open Online Course (MOOC) explored how registered users interacted amongst themselves, providing peer-support and becoming 'tutors' to their peers. The analysis was based on data collected through two surveys, as well as through comments on a learner-initiated private Facebook group and course-specific forum posts. Instances of learner usage and learner satisfaction are addressed.

Keywords: massive open online courses, Spanish as a foreign language, learner satisfaction, LMOOC design.

1. Introduction

MOOCs specifically designed for language learning – or Language MOOCs (LMOOCs) as they are more commonly termed – are attracting an increasing number of studies. These studies examine them from various points of view: from analysing what constitutes an effective LMOOC (Sokolik, 2014) to ethical and aesthetic considerations (Álvarez, 2014), through aspects such as learner motivation (Beaven, Codreanu, & Creuzé, 2014), the role of the instructor (Castrillo de Larreta-Azelain, 2014), accessibility (Rodrigo, 2014), and design methodology (Moreira Teixeira & Mota, 2014; Gimeno-Sanz, Navarro-Laboulais, & Despujol-Zabala, 2017). This paper focusses on a recently designed 16-week LMOOC, *Learn Spanish: Basic Spanish for English Speakers*, published on the edX[2] platform (Gimeno-Sanz & Navarro-Laboulais, 2015), which attracted over 100,000 learners from 210 different countries from all five continents, within the 25 to 40 age range. This paper briefly addresses: (1) the fact that learners spontaneously had the initiative of interacting amongst themselves beyond the

---

1. Universidad Politécnica de Valencia, Valencia, Spain; agimeno@upvnet.upv.es
2. edX is a non-profit and open source MOOC provider.

How to cite this article: Gimeno-Sanz, A. (2017). Designing a MOOC for learners of Spanish: exploring learner usage and satisfaction. In K. Borthwick, L. Bradley & S. Thouësny (Eds), *CALL in a climate of change: adapting to turbulent global conditions – short papers from EUROCALL 2017* (pp. 122-127). Research-publishing.net. https://doi.org/10.14705/rpnet.2017.eurocall2017.700

scope of the course; (2) how peer support naturally emerged; and (3) the add-ons that were implemented as a result of the comments posted by learners in the forum after the MOOC had been launched.

2. Method

Before taking part in the LMOOC, registered users were asked to complete a questionnaire[3] that sought to gather information on learner profile and expectations. After completion, they were again asked to submit another questionnaire, this time focussing on learner satisfaction. The data[4] reported here is taken from both of these sources (1,313 respondents), as well as from the comments posted on the MOOC forum and the Facebook group that was set up by the students themselves on the very same day the MOOC was launched (15th September 2015).

3. Results and discussion

The questionnaires highlighted a number of issues. First and foremost, that the learners had registered on the course primarily out of pleasure for learning Spanish (35% - 460), followed by the will to improve their job prospects (15% - 197), both reasons adding up to half of the respondents. To a lesser extent, users included reasons such as transversal skills and to boost their CV (11% - 144), to supplement their studies (6% - 79), and lastly, 5% (66) because of the University's prestige. The fact that most of the respondents took the course for pleasure rather than as an obligation correlates with the fact that it was seen as a leisure activity and, as such, a way to facilitate engagement in social interaction. This need for interaction is therefore in line with the will to incorporate social media to promote more personalised interaction among users. It is also a way of creating a sense of belonging to a community with a shared interest, i.e. learning Spanish.

When asked whether they had completed the course, under half of the respondents (536, 41%) agreed to have done so, whilst 59% (777) had not. The reasons given for not completing the course are displayed in Figure 1.

---

3. Powered by LimeSurvey, a free open-source online survey tool (https://www.limesurvey.org). The questionnaires were designed by the UPV MOOC Unit.
4. Data collected between 15 September 2015 and 16 April 2016.

Figure 1. Reasons for not completing the MOOC

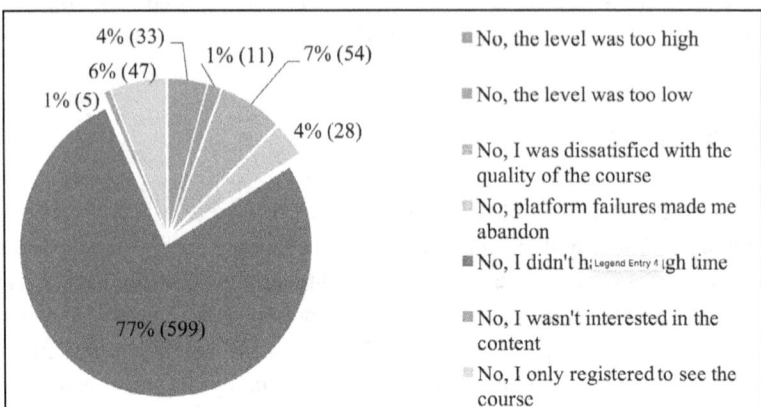

As illustrated in Figure 1, the vast majority of the respondents reported that lack of time was the main reason for not having fulfilled all the course activities nor completed the mid-term and final tests. Despite the MOOC being organised into 16 weeks (estimated at an average of three to four hours of commitment per week), it was available on a self-paced[5] basis during 15 months. This hindered tutor support and feedback but was balanced by having a teaching assistant permanently responding to learner queries and doubts.

Figure 2. Learner perception regarding efficiency and speed in resolving queries

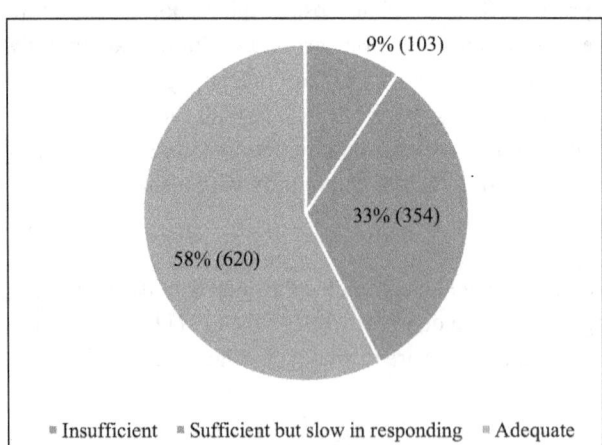

---

5. Self-paced courses do not follow a set schedule. Course materials do not become available according to a schedule, but are completely available as soon as the course begins.

As we can see in Figure 2, despite nearly two-thirds of the respondents being satisfied with the quality of the replies to solve queries and problems encountered during the course of the MOOC, there was still a non-negligible 42% who were somewhat dissatisfied either with the quality or the speed of the response. This factor may also imply that the perception of a certain lack in instructor/teaching assistant involvement was also one of the main reasons for many of the participants deciding to turn to fellow peers for support and, thus, engage in interaction outside the MOOC. This motivated the instructors to become members of and participate in the Facebook group to provide further guidance.

One of the first things that became apparent once the MOOC was launched was that the learners had an urge to interact amongst themselves and provide peer support as a natural reaction, i.e. without being instigated by their instructors. This was conducted by creating the private Facebook group mentioned above, which was promptly joined by (1) the most active and enthusiastic learners, and (2) users with a higher proficiency level who were willing to give fellow learners advice, provide explanations to language queries, and share reinforcement learning resources. The course designers thus realised that it was necessary to supply learners with supplementary materials in order to foster learner engagement and motivation. These supplementary materials had the four following functions.

(1) To decrease learner anxiety and frustration by:

- using the *Translectures*[6] tool to provide videos with automatic transcriptions in Spanish and automatic translations of these into the source language, English;

- allowing learners to reduce playback rate in all of the audio files if they so wished.

(2) To support vocabulary acquisition by:

- adding a link to the Multidict[7] dictionary interface with over 100 languages catered for, interconnected to sundry (monolingual and bilingual) free online dictionaries;

---

6. Translectures is a tool allowing us to generate, edit, and download automatic video captions and translations, developed by the Machine Learning and Language Processing Research Group at the Universidad Politécnica de Valencia. For further information, go to https://www.translectures.eu and http://www.mllp.upv.es
7. Available from http://www.multidict.net

- incorporating automatically generated glossaries for each of the 16 study units inserted into the Multidict dictionary interface, thus allowing learners to quickly seek translations into more than 100 languages – a true asset when considering that participants came from 210 countries around the world.

(3) To provide speaking practice by:

- designing and embedding a voice recording tool (Language Lab) in all of the exercises containing audio, allowing learners to compare their utterances to the models provided by native speakers;

- organising scheduled instructor-led Google Hangouts[8] sessions to support synchronous oral interaction;

- organising learner-driven speaking practice sessions using the Talkabout[9] discussion planner, a tool that serves the purpose of organising speaking practice encounters so that students can interact live among themselves and practise the language together through a Google Hangouts video conference.

(4) To provide additional materials and further practice by:

- curating all the resources recommended by the students themselves through the forum and the Facebook group and providing a list of freely available supplementary materials, organised by language skill;

- integrating a link to Duolingo[10] in order to take advantage of its gamification features.

4. Conclusions

The study yielded interesting data. The lessons learnt are the following:

- It is necessary to enrich an LMOOC with extra resources in order to intensify learner support, which in turn translates into increased motivation.

---

8. For more information, go to https://hangouts.google.com
9. For more information, go to https://talkabout.stanford.edu/welcome
10. For more information, go to https://en.duolingo.com

- Students become more engaged and motivated when they perceive that there are fellow course participants whom they can interact with, either in writing (Facebook) or speaking (one-to-one or group video conferencing).

- The sense of belonging to a community with shared interests can often drive students to turn to their peers rather than to the instructors or teaching assistants for guidance.

- Self-access MOOC participants need to be given incentives in order to become efficient autonomous learners and to keep motivation alive.

References

Álvarez, I. (2014). Ethical and aesthetic considerations in language MOOCs. In E. Martín-Monje & E. Bárcena (Eds), *Language MOOCs: providing learning, transcending boundaries* (pp. 127-142). De Gruyter Open. https://doi.org/10.2478/9783110420067.8

Beaven, T., Codreanu, T., & Creuzé, A. (2014). Motivation in a language MOOC: issues for course designers. In E. Martín-Monje & E. Bárcena (Eds), *Language MOOCs: providing learning, transcending boundaries* (pp. 48-66). De Gruyter Open. https://doi.org/10.2478/9783110420067.4

Castrillo de Larreta-Azelain, M. D. (2014). Language teaching in MOOCs: the integral role of the instructor. In E. Martín-Monje & E. Bárcena (Eds), *Language MOOCs: providing learning, transcending boundaries* (pp. 67-90). De Gruyter Open. https://doi.org/10.2478/9783110420067.5

Gimeno-Sanz, A., & Navarro-Laboulais, C. (2015). *Learn Spanish: Basic Spanish for English Speakers.* MOOC available from https://www.edx.org/course/basic-spanish-1-getting-started-upvalenciax-bsp101x

Gimeno-Sanz, A., Navarro-Laboulais, C., & Despujol-Zabala, I. (2017). In C. Delgado Kloos et al. (Eds), *Digital education: out to the world and back to the campus, EMOOCs 2017 conference proceedings, lecture notes in computer science*, Vol. 10254, pp. 48-57. Springer. https://doi.org/10.1007/978-3-319-59044-8_6

Moreira Teixeira, A., & Mota, J. (2014). In E. Martín-Monje & E. Bárcena (Eds), *Language MOOCs: providing learning, transcending boundaries* (pp. 33-47). De Gruyter Open. https://doi.org/10.2478/9783110420067.3

Rodrigo, C. (2014). Accessibility in language MOOCs. In E. Martín-Monje & E. Bárcena (Eds), *Language MOOCs: providing learning, transcending boundaries* (pp. 106-126). De Gruyter Open.

Sokolik, M. (2014). What constitutes an effective language MOOC? In E. Martín-Monje & E. Bárcena (Eds), *Language MOOCs: providing learning, transcending boundaries* (pp. 16-32). De Gruyter Open. https://doi.org/10.2478/9783110420067.2

OER use in intermediate language instruction: a case study

Robert Godwin-Jones[1]

Abstract. This paper reports on a case study in the experimental use of Open Educational Resources (OERs) in intermediate level language instruction. The resources come from three sources: the instructor, the students, and open content repositories. The objective of this action research project was to provide student-centered learning materials, enhance student motivation, and encourage learner autonomy. The content modules, designed to complement and supplement materials from the commercial textbook used, represent a variety of disciplines and genres. Grammar tutorials cover the structures typically introduced in intermediate language study. Also included are modules on language self-study, which feature annotated guides to online language resources. To accommodate further student personal or professional interest, students were asked to find and curate additional reading or multimedia content.

Keywords: OER, student motivation, learner autonomy.

1. Introduction

At many institutions of higher learning in the United States, there is a language requirement for graduation, often consisting of completion of a four semester sequence of courses in the target language. This is the case currently at my institution, a large public university on the East Coast. After completing the required course sequence, the majority of students do not enroll in further instruction in the target language. This reflects both a practical impediment – the need to complete coursework in their major field of study – and a lack of interest in learning a second language. Because students generally do not continue language study beyond the fourth semester, most do not achieve a functional ability at a level sufficient for interpersonal or professional use. For the most part, they fail to see a connection between proficiency in a second language and their own lives now or in the future.

---

1. Virginia Commonwealth University, Richmond, USA; rgjones@vcu.edu

How to cite this article: Godwin-Jones, R. (2017). OER use in intermediate language instruction: a case study. In K. Borthwick, L. Bradley & S. Thouësny (Eds), *CALL in a climate of change: adapting to turbulent global conditions – short papers from EUROCALL 2017* (pp. 128-134). Research-publishing.net. https://doi.org/10.14705/rpnet.2017.eurocall2017.701

A goal of this project was to motivate students to continue their study of the target language, in this case German, beyond that required by the university curriculum. That further language study could occur through enrollment in subsequent German courses, or more likely, through other avenues such as participation in study abroad or use of online language learning resources. Several approaches were used to motivate students and to equip them with the know-how to use online tools and services. That involved first making available a wider choice of learning materials than is generally the case, particularly if relying exclusively on a print textbook. That variety was designed to offer the possibility for students to connect with content of potential individual interest (see Tomlinson, 2016). Additionally, students created their own learning materials through finding, curating, and describing online resources for learning German, thus engaging in "participatory action research" (Zuber-Skerrit, 2002). Finally, learning modules were developed which targeted the use of online language learning resources and approaches. The goal was to provide students with specific resources for learning German, but also to give them the knowledge and skills to be informed online learners.

2. Method

In recent studies, OERs have been shown to be widely accepted by students, given reduced costs and local adaptability (Hilton, 2016). In this instance, OERs were used to expand areas of content and to engage students with resources useful in online language learning. The modules were developed based on materials taken from open sources and annotated for students at the intermediate level. Materials from OER repositories were integrated into the format used in all modules, based on a basic HTML template. Students had access through the course site in Blackboard and also on the open web. Additionally, students participated in a web site curation blog, designed to encourage students to discover, share, and learn from resources of personal interest (Gilmore, 2007).

3. Discussion

3.1. Grammar tutorials

Grammar tutorials supplemented the as-needed grammar sections of the textbook. As is normally the case today, the textbook did not provide comprehensive presentations of grammar, but rather used a chunked approach, introducing selected aspects of the grammar at a time, with an emphasis on functional use in the context of unit content. This approach works well for the majority of students and integrates grammar functionally into task-based learning. However, for some adult learners, a more comprehensive and systematic grammar presentation aligns better to their analytical learning style. Others may prefer a more inductive approach using discovery learning (Boulton & Cobb, 2017). The online tutorials provide both options. Each starts with corpus-derived examples, inviting students to induce patterns (see Figure 1). Next, explicit rules are discussed, contrasting English and German usage, while walking the learner through multiple, annotated usage examples. At the end of each section, formative assessments provide immediate feedback. The tutorials cover areas typically introduced at the intermediate level and also include review modules.

Figure 1. Grammar tutorial

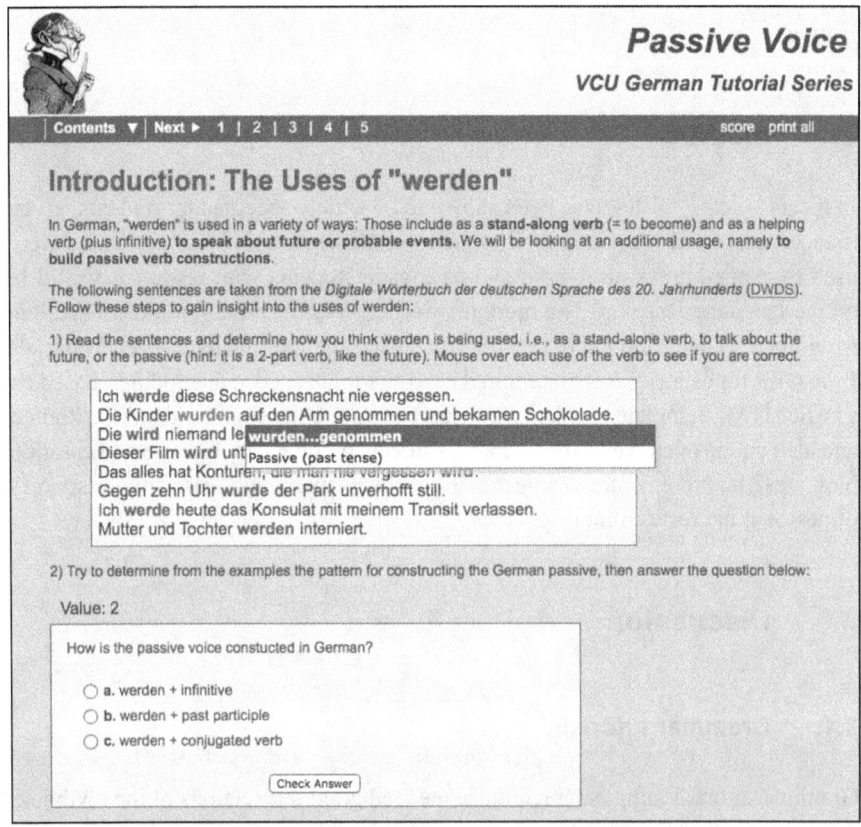

3.2. Content modules

The content modules were designed to extend the range of topics and genres of texts. Students enrolled in this course come from a variety of academic majors. In order to show the relevance of German to different fields, texts and media introduced in the modules come from a variety of areas, such as music history, politics, physics, and engineering. The texts, taken from open content sources, represent a variety of genres, from fairytale to scientific treatise and vary in length and difficulty level. The resources are annotated for language and culture. Each text is accompanied by comprehensive questions and interactive exercises. They also include annotated vocabulary lists, along with flashcards and exercises. Whenever possible, the modules incorporate audio and video; streaming video was used as well.

Figure 2. Content module

Figure 2 shows a module on a Grimm Brothers' fairytale. The story is previewed using a YouTube video presenting a dramatic reading of the story followed by the text itself accompanied by audio recordings of native speakers reading the text. Some of the language used in this case is in Bavarian dialect. Other variations of German are included in the modules, so as to expose students to the reality of dialect forms in German. The option of incorporating this kind of variety of texts, genres, and language variance is one of the advantages online OER has over conventional language textbooks.

3.3. Student-created materials

In addition to the modules created by the instructor or linked from OER sites, students in the course also worked with resources curated by the students themselves. Students were asked to find sites which aligned with course content. A class blog allowed sharing of the resources found (see Figure 3). Once a site was identified, students tagged the resource and provided a description in German. Students were assigned to read each other's posts and rate them; they also wrote comments. The student-curated sites expanded the range of content and genres. Sites curated included personal blogs, YouTube channels, websites for children, news reports, travel logs, food descriptions, and scientific reports.

Figure 3. Curation blog

3.4. Modules on tools and services

Language learners today have a wide range of possible online resources for gaining and maintaining language proficiency. These range from simple flashcard programs or tourist glossaries to full-featured language learning programs such as Duolingo. Social media and online gaming provide opportunities to engage with others in language-mediated activities. However, the very wealth of choices can be a problem. It's been increasingly recognized how important a role language teachers play in guiding students to appropriate resources (Hubbard, 2013). For this project, students had access to an annotated list of tools/services. Additionally, they worked with a series of tutorials focused on online language learning sites/apps. That included vocabulary learning programs, online dictionaries/concordances, machine translation programs, and tandem-learning services. Whenever possible, the modules incorporated materials from open sources. The tutorial on Google Translate, for example, included a walk-through and exercises created by the Open University specifically for learners of German.

4. Conclusion

The modules used in the course provided a wider choice of topics than is generally the case in language instruction at this level in the US. As discussed in Godwin-Jones (2017a), students found the materials to be engaging and motivating; according to student questionnaires, the modules "helped increase interest in German and led them to explore other online language learning resources" (p. 10).

All content was available outside the course-restricted learning management systems/virtual learning environments so as to be available for possible future use after the course was over or even after the students leave the university. The modules on language learning tools and services provide information about the benefits to students in future language learning endeavors. All resources were designed to work well on mobile devices, so as to integrate into devices functioning today as students' daily companions (see Godwin-Jones, 2017b). The curation project is intended to provide students with an opportunity to find language resources of personal or professional interest, with the goal that that process might motivate them towards further language study.

References

Boulton, A., & Cobb, T. (2017). Corpus use in language learning: a meta-analysis. *Language Learning, 67*(2), 348-393. https://doi.org/10.1111/lang.12224

Gilmore, A. (2007). Authentic materials and authenticity in foreign language learning. *Language teaching, 40*(2), 97-118. https://doi.org/10.1017/S0261444807004144

Godwin-Jones, R. (2017a). Designing an intermediate level language textbook for mobile access and learner autonomy. *Folio, 17*(2), 4-11.

Godwin-Jones, R. (2017b). Smartphones and language learning. *Language Learning & Technology, 21*(2), 3-17.

Hilton, J. (2016). Open educational resources and college textbook choices: a review of research on efficacy and perceptions. *Educational Technology Research and Development, 64*(4), 573-590. https://doi.org/10.1007/s11423-016-9434-9

Hubbard, P. (2013). Making a case for learner training in technology enhanced language learning environments. *CALICO Journal, 30*(2), 163-178. https://doi.org/10.11139/cj.30.2.163-178

Tomlinson, B. (Ed.) (2016). *SLA Research and Materials Development for Language Learning*. Routledge.

Zuber-Skerrit, O. (2002). A model for designing action learning and action research programs. *The Learning Organisation, 9*(4), 143-149. https://doi.org/10.1108/09696470210428868

Southampton

Teacher perspectives on the integration of mobile-assisted language learning

Jennica Grimshaw[1], Walcir Cardoso[2], and Laura Collins[3]

Abstract. Mobile-Assisted Language Learning (MALL) provides second language (L2) learners and teachers with resources to enhance the learning experience, including its anytime, anywhere accessibility (Traxler, 2007). However, factors such as lack of confidence with technology (Son, 2014) and time limitations (Godwin-Jones, 2015) may prevent teachers from implementing MALL successfully. To better understand the barriers to using MALL, this pilot study investigated the perspectives of 21 L2 English teachers at secondary schools and colleges in Quebec (Canada). An online questionnaire, requiring 15-30 minutes to complete, consisted of six-point Likert scales, short answers, multiple-choice questions, and probed teachers' current practices, willingness to engage with different tools, and factors influencing their implementation (e.g. time restraints, lack of training). Results suggest that while most language teachers appear to be open to engaging their students in MALL, limitations and concerns regarding distractions, cheating, school policy, class disruption, and time pressures remain.

Keywords: MALL, teacher perspectives.

1. Introduction

MALL provides L2 learners and teachers with innumerable resources to enhance the learning experience. With MALL, not only can each student have L2 resources available at the literal tips of their fingers, but these resources can be accessed regardless of time or place (Traxler, 2007). However, the implementation of MALL in language curricula raises concerns, especially in schools where mobile devices are banned. Concerns include student distraction, academic misconduct, and privacy issues. Although González-Lloret and Ortega (2014, p. 1) argue that the

---

1. Concordia University, Montreal, Canada; jennica.grimshaw@concordia.ca
2. Concordia University, Montreal, Canada; walcir.cardoso@concordia.ca
3. Concordia University, Montreal, Canada; laura.collins@concordia.ca

How to cite this article: Grimshaw, J., Cardoso, W., & Collins, L. (2017). Teacher perspectives on the integration of mobile-assisted language learning. In K. Borthwick, L. Bradley & S. Thouësny (Eds), *CALL in a climate of change: adapting to turbulent global conditions – short papers from EUROCALL 2017* (pp. 135-139). Research-publishing.net. https://doi.org/10.14705/rpnet.2017.eurocall2017.702

pedagogical potential of technology is generally recognized and no longer disputed, instructors may be accustomed to more traditional forms of teaching. Many teachers also lack integrative training in computer-assisted language learning (Jalkanen, 2015) and may encounter barriers such as budgeting constraints, infrastructure issues, teacher overload, and individual factors such as teacher attitudes (Godwin-Jones, 2015), which can be influenced by their personal interest and confidence in using technology (Tour, 2015).

In this study, we probed teacher desires and concerns with respect to the implementation of MALL, simultaneously while conducting a study investigating the impact of MALL on student learning. The first step, reported here, was the piloting of an online mixed-item questionnaire; this pilot stage will enable us to refine questionnaire items before a planned distribution to a wider teacher population. This study addressed the following research questions:

- How are teachers currently using MALL in L2 teaching?

- What are their beliefs and attitudes towards MALL? What limitations and barriers do they face?

2. Method

An online mixed-item questionnaire (hosted on SurveyGizmo), consisting of six-point Likert scales and multiple-choice and short answer questions, was distributed via social media and emailed to professional contacts in the field. The questionnaire took 15-30 minutes to complete. Participants were 14 secondary and seven college (pre-university) English as a second language teachers ($M=7$, $F=14$; age range: 25-50) living and working in Quebec. The Likert scale questions were analyzed using descriptive statistics and multiple-choice questions were summarized via response counts. Short-answer questions were used to complement questionnaire results. Participants were not able to skip question items, but skip logic was used to automatically eliminate irrelevant sections for each respondent.

3. Results and discussion

Of the 21 participants, 11 had received formal training in using technology (eight in teaching training and three in professional development workshops) while five expressed that they were self-taught. In terms of personal technology use, all but one participant owned a smartphone or tablet. Mobile devices were ranked high in use: eight teachers ranked smartphones as their most-used device, two ranking it as their second most-used, and three as their third most-used. Overall, teachers were comfortable using technology (M=5.29, SD=0.78; additional Likert scale items are summarized in Table 1). Some participants (via short answers) attributed their high level of comfort to frequency and ease of use. One teacher who expressed less comfort suggested that there was simply "not enough time to invest in learning new technologies".

In terms of MALL, 13 teachers were familiar with using language learning applications (apps, e.g. Duolingo, Memrize) and ten had access to classroom sets of tablets or laptops. While only two had previously been trained on using apps for language teaching, 14 said they would recommend language learning apps to students, and nine expressed that they had either told their students about these apps or trained them how to use them.

Teachers were divided on how often they allow students to use mobile devices in the classroom, with responses ranging from 'never' to 'very frequently' (M=4.10, SD=1.70). Mobile devices were used in classrooms for activities such as looking up words or definitions (n=15), searching the web (n=14), taking notes (n=8), and playing language games (n=5). Other less frequently reported uses included downloading course content, reading texts, and using other apps (e.g. video editing applications). One participant commented that mobile devices were incorporated because "banning phones is a losing battle".

Table 1.   Relevant items from the online questionnaire

	Mean	Standard deviation
How would you rate your current level of comfort with technology outside the classroom?	5.29	0.78
I allow students to use their mobile devices in English class.	4.10	1.70
I train my students to use mobile apps to practice English.	4.05	1.50
In class, we use language learning apps.	2.50	1.36
I would like my students to use language learning apps to practise English outside the classroom.	4.86	1.01
Technology helps to engage students in the lesson or task rather than distract them.	4.29	0.85
The use of technology in class brings up many privacy issues.	3.86	1.59

Regarding the barriers influencing MALL implementation, only 6 participants reported the following reasons: distraction (n=4), academic misconduct via cheating (n=4), school policies (n=3), class disruption (n=2), and time limitations (n=2). Participants volunteered additional barriers to using technology in general via a short answer question, expressing that planning time, budgeting, and lack of training played significant roles, echoing Godwin-Jones's (2015) findings. Another participant commented that he "was classically trained as a student, so I tend to replicate that behavior as a teacher. It's hard to envision myself teaching in a different way than how I was taught even though I know it is possible".

In summary, the teachers surveyed appear to be open to the idea of using MALL with learners (as seen in Park, 2014), but there are several factors that continue to limit implementation. In addition to the training and planning issues outlined by Godwin-Jones (2015), we see that school policy and concerns regarding distraction, classroom disruption, and possible cheating may also influence a teacher's decision to allow the use of mobile devices in the classroom. It is important to acknowledge and address these issues in future teacher training, and researchers also need to take them into consideration when designing tools and technology-mediated tasks.

4. Conclusions

As this was a pilot project, the participant pool is small and the results therefore cannot be generalized to a larger population. Participants were recruited via social media and email, indicating a potential bias towards users of technology. For future recruitment, we will seek a larger sample of teachers via their institutions.

This pilot study will allow us to further refine the questionnaire for use with a larger participant pool; for example, some of the short answers provided by participants will be added to multiple-choice questions to provide future participants with more insightful choices. When implemented, the study will constitute phase one of a multi-phase project which aims to develop MALL resources that can be used outside the classroom to extend students' interaction with the target language while also complementing what they learn in class (e.g. by relating the out-of-class experience to work done inside the classroom). The results of the survey will be used in conjunction with a survey of student perspectives of technology for language learning (Collins & Cardoso, 2017), as successful implementation of any novel approach requires that BOTH student and instructor opinions be taken into consideration.

5. Acknowledgements

We would like to thank our teacher participants and, for their insightful feedback, Teresa Hernandez-Gonzales, Clinton Hendry, June Ruivivar, Lauren Strachen, and Kym Taylor.

References

Collins, L., & Cardoso, W. (2017, April). *Whose tasks? Whose context?* Paper presented at the Task-Based Language Teaching conference, University of Barcelona, Spain.

Godwin-Jones, R. (2015). The evolving roles of language teachers: trained coders, local researchers, global citizens. *Language Learning & Technology, 19*(1), 10-22.

González-Lloret, M., & Ortega, L. (2014). Towards technology-mediated TBLT: an introduction. In M. González-Lloret & L. Ortega (Eds), *Technology-mediated TBLT: researching technology and tasks* (pp. 1-22). John Benjamins.

Jalkanen, J. (2015). Future language teachers' pedagogical landscapes during their subject studies. *Nordic Journal of Digital Literacy, 9*(2), 84-101.

Park, M. (2014). A task-based needs analysis for mobile-assisted language learning in college ESL contexts. In J. B. Son (Ed.), *Computer-assisted language learning: learners, teachers and tools* (pp. 47-68). Cambridge Scholars Publishing.

Son, J. B. (2014). Moving beyond basics: from CALL coursework to classroom practice and professional development. In J. B. Son (Ed.), *Computer-assisted language learning: learners, teachers and tools* (pp. 122-149). Cambridge Scholars Publishing.

Tour, E. (2015). Digital mindsets: teachers' technology use in personal life and teaching. *Language Learning & Technology, 19*(3), 124-139.

Traxler, J. (2007). Defining, discussing and evaluating mobile learning: the moving finger writes and having writ... *The International Review of Research in Open and Distributed Learning, 8*(2). https://doi.org/10.19173/irrodl.v8i2.346

Online study: postgraduate student perceptions of core skills development

Patricia E. Grounds[1] and Caroline Moore[2]

Abstract. In this qualitative study, we analyze postgraduate students' perceptions of strategic behaviors they developed during their online studies and their ability to extend this behavior to their own praxis. Findings suggest that strategic behavior centers around the development of four core skills: engaging in self-directed thinking; fostering effective communication; fostering leadership and shared responsibility; and using technology to reinforce, extend, and deepen learning. Through a dialogic process, where the presence of a supportive online community of practice plays a central role, participants appear to use these skills to engage in a process of un-learning and re-learning. The asynchronous modality of the online medium, allowing delayed rather than immediate responses, appeared to facilitate deeper, more considered constructions of new understandings. Ultimately, this online modality appears propitious in building self-confidence, thus empowering participants to act in their professional domain.

Keywords: 21st century skills, online professional development, dialogic, community of practice.

1. Introduction

This paper explores how six teachers of English as a second or other language, graduates of a UK university's online Master of Arts (MA) in English Language Teaching (ELT), perceive their strategic development during their studies. Volunteer participants were working and studying simultaneously, allowing researchers to probe their perceptions of skills they used for mastering postgraduate course content and for application to professional activities.

---

1. The British Council, Mexico City, Mexico; p.grounds@soton.ac.uk
2. University of Guadalajara Cucosta, Puerto Vallarta, Mexico; caro_moore@yahoo.com

How to cite this article: Grounds, P. E., & Moore, C. (2017). Online study: postgraduate student perceptions of core skills development. In K. Borthwick, L. Bradley & S. Thouësny (Eds), *CALL in a climate of change: adapting to turbulent global conditions – short papers from EUROCALL 2017* (pp. 140-145). Research-publishing.net. https://doi.org/10.14705/rpnet.2017.eurocall2017.703

For learners and users of English as a second or other language, the development of strategic behaviors has been a priority since the 'four skills approach' emerged in English language teaching and learning.

Recently, studies into skills and strategies have expanded beyond the second language classroom, moving into the wider framework of skills which meet the demands of the day-and-age. Generally labeled '21st century skills', they favor the development of strategies for more effective behaviors in study, at work, and for life. Skills for effective problem solving, critical and creative thinking, collaboration and social action, and accessing new knowledge all figure in a 21st century skills framework; although definitions are various (Bellanca & Brandt, 2010), its visibility in current educational policy-making justifies further exploration.

In our role as online MA tutors, we had noticed during forum interaction the development of particular strategic behaviors in course participants. Since these behaviors resonated with core skills categories from the British Council's (2016) 'core skills for learning and society', we adopted this framework to scaffold our study.

Drawing on Fullan and Langworthy (2013), among others, the British Council framework proposes the skills categories of critical thinking and problem Solving, collaboration and communication, creativity and imagination, citizenship, digital literacy, student leadership, and personal development. For our study, we narrowed the scope to the four highest resonating categories, adding some further glossing (Table 1). These categories underpinned the design of our data collection instrument.

Table 1. The core skills framework for the study (abridged)

Core Skill 1 Engaging in self-directed thinking	Core Skill 2 Fostering effective communication
Skills involve critical thinking and problem solving: processes are essentially self-initiated, self-monitored, and self-corrective.	Skills for collaborative and constructive dialogue include clarity of thinking, empathy, and respect.
Core Skill 3 Fostering leadership and shared responsibility	Core skill 4 Using technology to reinforce, extend, and deepen learning
Skills include knowing when and how to assume the lead and/or sharing responsibility with others.	Skills involve discovering, mastering, and communicating knowledge and information to a global community.

The guiding research questions for the study were:

> Q1. Which key skills do participants perceive that they effectively develop during postgraduate study?
>
> Q2. How do these skills enable participants to interpret their understanding of the wider issues in their local ELT contexts?

2. Method

Adopting a qualitative interpretative approach (Mackey & Gass, 2005) to investigate participant perceptions of their skills development online, we approached potential participants online, delivering a questionnaire via individual emails and using individual Skype interviews for validity checking of our interpretations of participants' words and to reconfirm permission to quote anonymously. Centered around the core skills framework (Figure 1), questionnaire items prompted introspections and probed reflections on strategic behaviors related to participants' online studies and to the application of skills and knowledge to their professional contexts.

Figure 1. Data analysis process: core skills, themes, and higher order categories

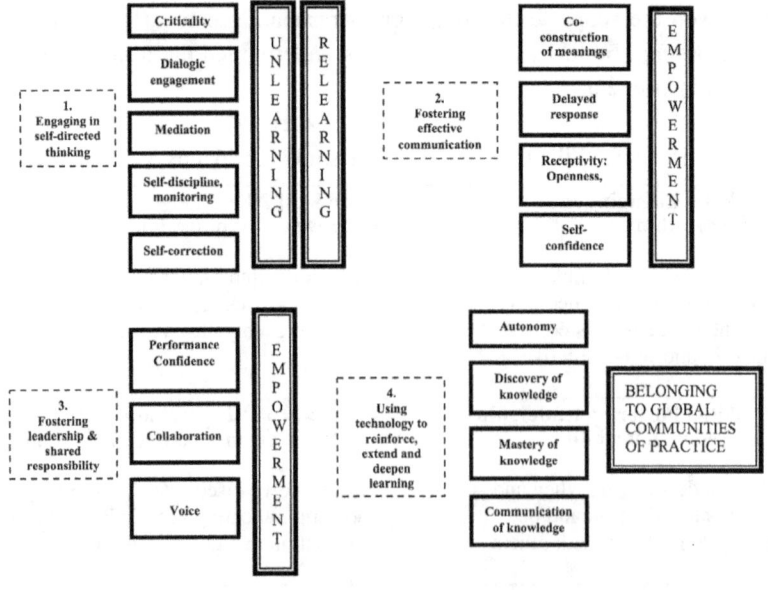

We applied a layered approach to data analysis, using a three-stage thematic analysis (Guest, MacQueen, & Namey, 2012). First, researchers identified and grouped prominent themes emerging from the data; next, data under each of these themes were re-analyzed and redistributed, using the core skills framework (Figure 1), to ascertain links between skills development and online learning (Research Question 1). In relation to Research Question 2, patterns were sought in the data and a more holistic underlying framework was suggested, consisting of three higher-order categories: un-learning/–re-learning, empowerment, and belonging to global communities of practice (Figure 1).

3. Discussion

Our analysis provided insights on the kinds of skills-building which participants perceive as facilitated by their online postgraduate study. Participants describe how such Core Skills (CSs) can be usefully applied to the tasks of teacher-learning and professional practice, as these data extracts suggest:

> "The skills I developed to analyze critically research from other countries, helped me analyzed [sic] my own context to provide more effective guidance for my students in their acquisition of the language" (CS1).

> "Now I am able to share my points of view with others, to propose solutions and also to defend the ideas that I think must be taken into consideration to improve the different areas of my teaching context" (CS2).

> "The programme provided me with a vision of [...] the numerous phenomena in ELT [...] that has helped me to think of possible research studies that might be carried out in order to contribute to improve the results in my teaching context and in other teaching contexts" (CS3).

> "I need technology in order to have access to the sources of information that will allow me to continue growing professionally and also to develop or choose material that my students can use to improve [...] their command of English" (CS4).

This and other data suggests that the four core skills in Figure 1 function in an essentially dialogic fashion, whereby strategic behaviors that participants perceived they had developed during online study then fed into participants' professional practice, mediating between the two domains of learning and praxis in the form of both external and internal dialogue. Additionally, data suggests that learning for professional development involves a process of challenging current beliefs and practices, followed by the dismantling of old habits or axioms, before learners can move forward toward more effective practice (un-learning/re-learning):

> "The discussion forums raised my level of awareness by reading for information, asking and answering questions or self-directed learning, i.e. finding out by reading to understand, at the same time assimilating and processing colleagues' knowledge to add to my own, before responding".

As this and other data suggest, it appears that an asynchronous modality of communication, allowing reflection time and delayed response, is a powerful tool in this process of un-learning and re-learning. Not only might it facilitate self-directed thinking, but it may also contribute to the building of self-confidence, the construction of voice, and eventually lead to willingness to assume leadership roles in local arenae. Similar findings are echoed in a selection of papers in Tomei (2006).

4. Conclusions

Our analysis leads us to conclude that un-learning and re-learning is facilitated when space is created for teachers to re-think in collaboration with others; an asynchronous medium allowing delayed, more considered, responses, appears to be propitious for this. A supportive community of learning can generate individual growth and self-confidence, with an empowering effect on its members, as they enable each other to find their voice. Membership of a global ELT discourse community seems to generate the confidence to assume leadership in local ELT practice.

In answer to our research questions, (1) through the medium of international online study, cognitive and attitudinal space can be created, favoring more critical learning and specific key skills development, and (2) the strategic behaviors which learners see themselves as having developed through their online studies are also perceived as having transfer-value to local contexts.

5. Acknowledgements

Sincere thanks to our participants, and the British Council, Mexico, for supporting the dissemination of our findings.

References

Bellanca, J., & Brandt, R. (2010). *21st century skills: rethinking how students learn.* Solution Tree Press.

British Council. (2016). *Unlocking a world of potential: core skills for learning, work and society.* https://www.britishcouncil.org.lb/sites/default/files/g139_core_skills_brochure_en_high_res_for_web.pdf

Fullan, M., & Langworthy, M. (2013). *Towards a new end: new pedagogies for deep learning.* Collaborative Impact. www.newpedagogies.nl/images/towards_a_new_end.pdf

Guest, G., MacQueen, K. M., Namey, E. E. (2012). *Applied thematic analysis.* Sage. https://doi.org/10.4135/9781483384436

Mackey, A., & Gass, S. M. (2005). *Second language research: methodology and design, chapter 6.* Lawrence Erlbaum Associates.

Tomei, L. (Ed.). (2006). *Integrating information & communications technologies into the classroom.* Information Science Publishing.

Evaluating lexical coverage in Simple English Wikipedia articles: a corpus-driven study

Clinton Hendry[1] and Emily Sheepy[2]

Abstract. Simple English Wikipedia is a user-contributed online encyclopedia intended for young readers and readers whose first language is not English. We compiled a corpus of the entirety of Simple English Wikipedia as of June 20th, 2017. We used lexical frequency profiling tools to investigate the vocabulary size needed to comprehend Simple English Wikipedia texts. We hypothesized that if the texts are indeed simple, learners should need to know far fewer than 8000 words. Our findings indicate that the texts are not as simple as the creators of the authoring guidelines intended. We suggest that authors of simplified texts be encouraged to provide plain language explanations of low-frequency technical terms either in-text or in glossary form. We will discuss implications for researching the pedagogical usefulness of the Simple English Wikipedia.

Keywords: simplified texts, corpus-driven research, lexical frequency, reading comprehension.

1. Introduction

The user-contributed online encyclopedia Simple English Wikipedia (SEW) is intended for young readers and readers whose first language is not English. Simplified reference materials could be of great use in English as a second language (ESL) or English as a foreign language instruction, particularly for learners pursuing advanced studies, but have a controversial place in pedagogy (e.g. Boulton & Cobb, 2017). Because text simplification is often accomplished using formulaic and mechanical methods (e.g. based on readability indices), simplified texts are often viewed as inauthentic and more difficult to comprehend than the originals (Crossley, Louwerse, McCarthy, & McNamara, 2007). Simple

---

1. Concordia University, Montreal, Canada; clinton.hendry@concordia.ca
2. Concordia University, Montreal, Canada; emily.sheepy@concordia.ca

How to cite this article: Hendry, C., & Sheepy, E. (2017). Evaluating lexical coverage in Simple English Wikipedia articles: a corpus-driven study. In K. Borthwick, L. Bradley & S. Thouësny (Eds), *CALL in a climate of change: adapting to turbulent global conditions – short papers from EUROCALL 2017* (pp. 146-150). Research-publishing.net. https://doi.org/10.14705/rpnet.2017.eurocall2017.704

English Wikipedia, however, is simplified by human authors following a style guide. Authors are advised to avoid overly complex sentence structures where possible, and to use Ogden's (1930) 850-word Basic English word List (OBEL). Our paper focuses on the lexical characteristics of Simple English Wikipedia texts.

Our study is guided by reading comprehension studies that consistently show that English learners need to know 98% of the running words that occur in a reading passage – 8000 to 9000 word families – in order to understand it adequately (Nation, 2006). Our aim is to estimate the vocabulary size needed to comprehend Simple English Wikipedia texts at the 98% coverage level. We hypothesize that if the texts are indeed simple, learners should need to know far fewer than 8000 words.

OBEL (Ogden, 1930) was created in 1930 as a functional ESL primer of 850 words. The website referenced by the SEW authoring guide states "we find that 90% of the concepts in [the Oxford Pocket English Dictionary] can be achieved with 850 words". However, we argue that this list lacks the coverage necessary for today's English learner. As Nation (2006) points out, the 2000 most common word families (often called the General Service List) in English cover about 80% of English writing; at 850 words, OBEL seems both short and outdated. Using the VocabProfiler on Lextutor.ca, which uses the BNC-COCA corpus to identify word frequency, we found that 117 words in OBEL are seen in the 3-K band or above, meaning that many of the OBEL words are not frequent in contemporary English (e.g. 'fowl', 'basin', and 'cork').

2. Method

2.1. Creating the SEW corpus

Our corpus-based study uses lexical frequency profiling tools to describe the lexical characteristics of SEW. We first created a corpus encompassing the entirety of its website as of June 20th, 2017. The corpus was created by compiling Simple English Wikipedia's content into a single text file that excluded most extraneous information (e.g. content lists, footnotes). We then removed as much superfluous coding information left over from the content dump as possible (e.g. <doc> tags). This left a corpus of approximately 17 million words: the Simple English Wikipedia Corpus and Concordia (SEWCC).

For our analysis, we used the corpus profiling program AntConc to make word lists based on frequency, and to measure coverage for OBEL and Baumann and Culligan's (1995) version of West's (1953, see www.lextutor.ca/freq/lists_download) General Service List (GSL). To estimate coverage, we created word lists that exclude OBEL and GSL word families from the SEW texts. We then calculated the percentage of tokens removed from the SEW list by this process.

2.2. Lexical profiling

For comparison, we applied OBEL and the GSL to two corpora: our SEWCC, and the Concordia Corpus of Wikipedia (ConCoW). ConCoW is a corpus of more than one million words divided over 12 thematic categories. It reflects the content available in the English version of Wikipedia at the time of its creation, February, 2016. It was designed to be representative of Wikipedia's approximately 2.9 billion words of English content, and to be used specifically for corpus analysis.

We first evaluated whether OBEL saw more coverage in the SEW than in ConCoW. Whether OBEL is a good metric for "simplicity" aside, it should see significantly more coverage in the SEW if people are following the SEW 2016 guidelines. Our results can be seen in Table 1.

Table 1.   SEWCC and ConCoW coverage results

Corpus	OBEL Coverage	GSL Coverage
SEWCC (17,592,204 tokens)	10,169,257 tokens (57.8%)	13,406,727 tokens (76.2%)
ConCoW (1,055,794 tokens)	790,598 tokens (74.9%)	778,887 tokens (73.8%)

Note. The GSL should see approx. 80% coverage in most English writing (Hsu, 2014; Nation, 2006).

Despite the SEW authoring guidelines, we can see that OBEL is not particularly representative of the vocabulary within SEWCC. According to Zipf's law, the 100 most common words in English should account for approximately 50% of English writing (Zipf, 1935). At 58% coverage, Ogden's 850-word list does not appear to offer much advantage. From a learner's point of view, neither OBEL nor the 100 most common words in English would adequately prepare readers to comprehend texts from SEWCC. The GSL fares better, with 76% coverage – within expectations for unsimplified English texts. As mentioned earlier, the GSL should see approximately 80% coverage in most unsimplified English writing (Hsu, 2014; Nation, 2006). However, if the SEWCC were simplified English, the GSL should have seen higher coverage than the above (e.g. Cobb, 2007; Nation, 2006).

Unexpectedly, ConCoW texts conform more closely to the SEW authoring guidelines than SEWCC texts. In ConCoW, OBEL sees about as much coverage as the GSL, at 74.9% and 73.8%, respectively. It appears that having receptive knowledge of OBEL might actually be an efficient way to boost one's vocabulary coverage for reading standard Wikipedia, however OBEL is poorly represented in the SEWCC.

3. Discussion

Our findings indicate that SEW articles require surprisingly large vocabularies to comprehend, comparable to that required to read standard Wikipedia articles. A major limitation of our analysis is that it does not account for other comprehensibility indices (e.g. syntactic complexity). SEW authors may rely more heavily on reduction of syntactic complexity or elaboration strategies in developing simplified articles rather than following the authoring guidelines. Authors may wish to avoid introducing ambiguity when describing technical topics and so avoid strictly controlling their vocabulary, perhaps by defining difficult terms instead of replacing them with less specialized vocabulary. Follow-up studies should examine whether articles with technical content differ from others. However, given that Tweissi (1998) found that texts simplified using a controlled lexicon supported greater comprehension gains than other methods of text simplification, we encourage SEW authors to provide plain language explanations of low-frequency technical terms either in-text or in glossary form, as recommended by Nation (2013).

Two key findings from our results are that OBEL is not being used much in SEW, with only 57.8% coverage, and that SEW is not using appreciably more simplified vocabulary than Wikipedia proper. Both encyclopaedias have similar coverage from the 2000 most frequently used word families in English (76.2% and 73.8%). From a pedagogical perspective, ESL learners will not find the SEW easier to read than the normal Wikipedia. Based on our results, unless the teacher prefers the shorter SEW texts (Hendry, 2016), there is little advantage to choosing SEW over standard Wikipedia texts for ESL learning.

4. Conclusions

Previous research (e.g. Cobb, 2007; Nation, 2006) argues strongly for the use of simplified texts for ESL learning, and there is a dearth of simplified English texts for adults. SEW could easily fill the need for simplified texts, providing teachers and ESL students with nigh-infinite interesting content across disciplines. However, the results from our study indicate it has a long way to go before it could rightfully be called simplified.

References

Baumann, J., & Culligan, B. (1995). *General service list*. http://jbauman.com/aboutgsl.html

Boulton, A., & Cobb, B. (2017). Corpus use in language learning: a meta-analysis. *Language Learning, 67*(2), 348-393. https://doi.org/10.1111/lang.12224

Cobb, T. (2007). Computing the vocabulary demands of L2 reading. *Language Learning & Technology, 11*(3), 38-63.

Crossley, S. A., Louwerse, M. M., McCarthy, P. M., & McNamara, D. S. (2007). A linguistic analysis of simplified and authentic texts. *The Modern Language Journal, 91*(1), 15-30. https://doi.org/10.1111/j.1540-4781.2007.00507.x

Hendry, C. (2016). *Wikipedia as a graded reader suitability analysis*. Unpublished work.

Hsu, W. (2014). Measuring the vocabulary load of engineering textbooks for EFL undergraduates. *English for Specific Purposes, 33*, 54-65. https://doi.org/10.1016/j.esp.2013.07.001

Nation, I. (2006). How large a vocabulary is needed for reading and listening? *Canadian Modern Language Review, 63*(1), 59-82. https://doi.org/10.3138/cmlr.63.1.59

Nation, I. S. P. (2013). *Learning vocabulary in another language*. Cambridge University Press.

Ogden, C. K. (1930). *Basic English: a general introduction with rules and grammar*. Kegan Paul.

Tweissi, A. I. (1998). The effects of the amount and type of simplification on foreign language reading comprehension. *Reading in a foreign language, 11*(2), 191-204.

West, M. (1953). *A general service list of English words*. Longman.

Zipf, G. K. (1935). *The psychology of language*. Houghton-Mifflin.

A chatbot for a dialogue-based second language learning system

Jin-Xia Huang[1], Kyung-Soon Lee[2], Oh-Woog Kwon[3], and Young-Kil Kim[4]

Abstract. This paper presents a chatbot for a Dialogue-Based Computer-Assisted second Language Learning (DB-CALL) system. A DB-CALL system normally leads dialogues by asking questions according to given scenarios. User utterances outside the scenarios are normally considered as semantically improper and simply rejected. In this paper, we assume that raising the freedom of dialogue can stimulate the user's interest in learning. For this, a chatbot based on a search engine with a dialogue corpus has been developed to deal with conversations out of the scenarios. We evaluate the chatbot separately in two different cases: as an independent bot and as an auxiliary system. The results showed that, unlike the independent chatbot system, the chatbot as an auxiliary system showed a much lower turn success ratio.

Keywords: chatbot, computer-assisted second-language learning system, dialogue-based CALL, dialogue system.

1. Introduction

Dialogues between a user and a DB-CALL system normally need to follow given scenarios on chosen topics. It is a system that leads dialogues by asking questions. The language learner needs to answer the questions (Lee et al., 2011). The system evaluates the answers to see if they are appropriate for the given question (Kwon et al., 2015). Such evaluation is totally based on the given scenarios and so utterances outside the scenarios would be considered as semantically improper

---

1. Electronics and Telecommunications Research Institute/Chonbuk National University, Daejeon, Korea; hgh@etri.re.kr
2. Chonbuk National University, Jeonju, Korea; selfsolee@chonbuk.ac.kr
3. Electronics and Telecommunications Research Institute, Daejeon, Korea; ohwoog@etri.re.kr
4. Electronics and Telecommunications Research Institute, Daejeon, Korea; kimyk@etri.re.kr

How to cite this article: Huang, J.-X., Lee, K.-S., Kwon, O.-W., & Kim. Y.-K. (2017). A chatbot for a dialogue-based second language learning system. In K. Borthwick, L. Bradley & S. Thouësny (Eds), *CALL in a climate of change: adapting to turbulent global conditions – short papers from EUROCALL 2017* (pp. 151-156). Research-publishing.net. https://doi.org/10.14705/rpnet.2017.eurocall2017.705

and rejected by the system. This means that even meaningful conversations are perceived as errors.

In this paper, we present a DB-CALL system which adopts a chatbot to enable free conversations between the learner and the system. We also investigate what preparation a chatbot needs to assist a DB-CALL system.

2. GenieTutor – a task-oriented dialogue system for second-language learning

We developed GenieTutor, a DB-CALL system for English learners in Korea several years ago. At first, it was a role-play dialogue system for second language learners (Kwon et al., 2015). After that, an upgraded version of GenieTutor was developed. Our goal was to increase the freedom of the user's conversation so that it would become more like a conversation between people. In order to achieve this, topics were considered as tasks, which could be separated into several smaller subtasks; the execution of some of the subtasks could, in turn, be independent of the orders. As a result, a certain degree of freedom in the order of utterances was allowed (Choi, Kwon, Kim, & Lee, 2016; Kwon, Kim, & Lee, 2016). For example, for a task of 'ordering food', which consisted of subtasks '[greeting] >> choose main dishes > choose side dishes > pay the bill >> [greeting]', the sub-task [greeting] can be skipped, and the user can choose side dishes with the main dishes at once and then just ask for the bill.

Despite a greater degree of freedom, user utterances could still be rejected – the reason might be a lack of keywords which are necessary for the user utterances, or the utterances might be outside the scenarios. In either case, the system would treat them as "unknown utterances", and ask the user to re-utter their responses again. Here is an example - the system simply repeats its previous utterance of "Your total comes to 160 dollars", when the user answers with "I don't have money" which is an utterance outside the scenario:

> System: Your total comes to 160 dollars.
>
> User: I don't have money.
>
> System: Your total comes to 160 dollars.
>
> User: Here you go.

We performed a user evaluation on this system, where a question was asked: "Do you think the out of topic conversation (free talking) function is necessary for a DB-CALL system?". About 66.7% of 30 participants answered with "necessary" or "very necessary". This percentage increases to 86.7% for intermediate level learners. Considering only 46.7% of the elementary level learners were positive, higher level learners prefer to learn language through free dialogue (Table 1).

Table 1. User evaluation on GenieTutor: "Is out of topic conversation necessary?"

Answer	Elementary level learners	Percentage	Intermediate Level learners	Percentage	In total
5: Very necessary	5	33.3%	5	33.3%	33.3%
4: Necessary	2	13.3%	8	53.3%	33.3%
3: Not sure	3	20%	0	0%	10.0%
2: Not necessary	3	20%	2	13.3%	16.7%
1: Very unnecessary	2	13.3%	0	0%	6.7%
In Total	15	100%	15	100%	100%

3. GenieTutor Plus – allows free conversations with chatbot

To meet the user needs shown in Table 1, a chatbot was considered necessary for the DB-CALL system. A search-based chatbot was developed to assist GenieTutor to allow users to have free conversations with the system. The dialogue is still mainly based on scenarios. However, if the semantic correctness evaluation module determines that the user utterance cannot be classified to any predefined dialogue acts, it would be considered as an out-of-task utterance, and responded to as such by the chatbot.

The main purpose of the DB-CALL system is to help learners practice given dialogues. To fulfill this purpose, right after the chatbot response, the system would induce the user to return to the topic conversation by speaking in accordance with the scenario. For example, when a user presents "I have no money", the system will utter "What a pity!" with the chatbot, and then repeat "Your total comes to 160 dollars" according to the scenario (Figure 1). The sentences presented by the chatbot are highlighted in red.

Figure 1. GenieTutor with chatbot

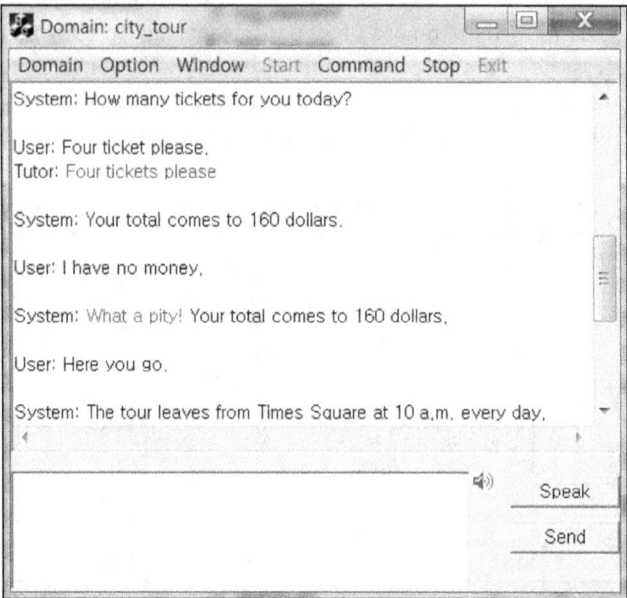

The search engine Indri (Strohman, Metzler, Turtle, & Croft, 2005) was adopted to retrieve the most similar dialogue examples from a dialogue corpus. Each dialogue example contains two utterances, called a turn in the dialogue system: a query uttered with a reply. As most of the dialogues consist of short sentences (which is different from document retrieval), a rescoring function was adopted to re-rank similar examples. In the case of a lack of a similar example, an utterance was randomly output to the user, which was supposed to be similar to a topic change in human conversation.

About 410,000 turns are contained in the corpus, of which 18,000 were developed by human developers, 237,000 were extracted from the MovieDic corpus (Banchs, 2012), and another 155,000 were collected from various educational or traveling materials, which have been developed over the recent decades for dialogue machine translation purposes.

4. User evaluation

Firstly, the chatbot was evaluated as an assistant module of GenieTutor Plus. The learners were required to have conversations with the system. The users were allowed to enjoy free talking with the system (non-topic related conversation), while all subtasks had to be finished to achieve the task. The turn success ratio was evaluated as the ratio of system responses which were evaluated as 'proper' to user utterances. Twenty English learners participated in the evaluation on topics including 'buying city-tour tickets' and 'ordering food'. An evaluation on the independent chatbot was also performed. The users were required to chat with the chatbot freely, with at least twenty turns being uttered.

Table 2. User evaluation on the chatbot as an auxiliary system of DB-CALL versus as an independent system

Topic	Turn success ratio (topic and non-topic)	Non-topic user utterances	Turn success ratio (non-topic)
Chatbot for GenieTutor Plus	71.30%	8.38%	33.33%
Independent chatbot	-	100%	52.78%

From Table 2, we can see that, compared with an independent bot, the chatbot has a lower success ratio as an assistant bot for a DB-CALL system. The reason is that users tended to evaluate a non-topic response in the context of the topic conversation on a more stringent basis. For example, the following system utterances would be acceptable if they were uttered by an independent chatbot, but would be considered as improper if they happened during a food ordering task, in which the DB-CALL system acted in the role of waiter:

System: Would you like something to drink?

User: Nothing.

System: It is a damned ugly nothing.

5. Conclusion

In this paper we introduced a chatbot to a DB-CALL system to deal with out of topic user utterances, so that the conversation could be more natural, like a conversation between people. However, the turn success ratio of such free-talking in a DB-CALL system was lower than with an independent chatbot. We would like to continue our research to extract small but more suitable dialogue corpus for each topic in the DB-CALL system.

6. Acknowledgements

This work was supported by the Institute for Information & communications Technology Promotion (IITP) grant funded by the Korea government (MSIT) (R0126-15-1117, core technology development of the spontaneous speech dialogue processing for language learning), and Electronics and Telecommunications Research Institute (ETRI) grant funded by the Korea government (17, strengthening competitiveness of automatic translation industry for realising a language barrier-free Korea).

References

Banchs, R. E. (2012). MovieDic: a movie dialogue corpus for research and development. *Proceedings of ACL* (pp. 203-207).

Choi, S.-K., Kwon, O.-W., Kim Y.-K., & Lee, Y. (2016). Using a dialogue system based on dialogue maps for computer assisted second language learning. In S. Papadima-Sophocleous, L. Bradley & S. Thouësny (Eds), *CALL communities and culture – short papers from EUROCALL 2016* (pp. 106-112). Research-publishing.net. https://doi.org/10.14705/rpnet.2016.eurocall2016.546

Kwon, O.-W., Kim, Y.-K., & Lee, Y. (2016). Task-oriented spoken dialog system for second-language learning. In S. Papadima-Sophocleous, L. Bradley & S. Thouësny (Eds), *CALL communities and culture – short papers from EUROCALL 2016* (pp. 237-242). Research-publishing.net. https://doi.org/10.14705/rpnet.2016.eurocall2016.568

Kwon, O.-W., Lee, K., Roh, Y. H., Huang, J. X., Choi, S. K., Kim, Y. K., Jeon, H. B., Oh, Y. R., Lee, Y. K., Kang, B. O., Chung, E., Park, J. G., & Lee, Y. (2015). GenieTutor: a computer assisted second-language learning system based on spoken language understanding. *Proceedings of the 2015 International Workshop on Spoken Dialogue Systems* (pp 257-262). https://doi.org/10.1007/978-3-319-19291-8_26

Lee, S., Noh, H., Lee, J., Lee, K., Lee, G. G., Sagong, S., & Kim, M. (2011). On the effectiveness of robot-assisted language learning. *ReCALL, 23*(1), 25-58. https://doi.org/10.1017/S0958344010000273

Strohman T., Metzler, D., Turtle, H., & Croft, W. B. (2005). Indri: a language model-based search engine for complex queries. *Proceedings of the International Conference on Intelligence Analysis*.

Motivational factors in telecollaborative exchanges among teenagers

Kristi Jauregi[1] and Sabela Melchor-Couto[2]

Abstract. Motivational factors play an important role in (language) learning processes and research indicates that this is also true for telecollaboration exchanges (Jauregi, de Graaff, van den Bergh, & Kriz, 2012; Melchor-Couto, 2017; in press). This short paper will introduce a study into how motivational factors play a role in telecollaboration exchanges by teenagers depending on the interaction constellation, the tools being used, and the telecollaborative experience. A total of 202 foreign language learners from different European countries took part in telecollaboration activities. All participants carried out an average of four telecollaborative sessions either by written chat or by video communication. Data from a survey measuring motivational factors, including self-efficacy beliefs, motivation, and anxiety, was gathered after every session. A small number of pupils were also interviewed on aspects related to motivation and anxiety. The results show: (1) a significant decrease in anxiety across conditions as sessions progress, especially for those communicating in Lingua Franca (LF) constellations using chat; (2) that pupils interacting with Native Speakers (NSs) seem to be the most confident concerning their perception of competence; and (3) that those communicating with NSs were significantly more positive about the learning potential of communicating with NSs.

Keywords: telecollaboration, motivation, self-efficacy, anxiety, video communication, chat.

1. Introduction

Motivational factors play an important role in (language) learning processes (Bandura, 1997; Dörnyei, MacIntyre, & Henry, 2016; Ryan & Deci, 2000) and

---

1. University of Utrecht, Utrecht, The Netherlands; k.jauregi@uu.nl
2. University of Roehampton, London, United Kingdom; s.melchor-couto@roehampton.ac.uk

How to cite this article: Jauregi, K., & Melchor-Couto, S. (2017). Motivational factors in telecollaborative exchanges among teenagers. In K. Borthwick, L. Bradley & S. Thouësny (Eds), *CALL in a climate of change: adapting to turbulent global conditions – short papers from EUROCALL 2017* (pp. 157-162). Research-publishing.net. https://doi.org/10.14705/rpnet.2017. eurocall2017.706

research indicates that this is also true for telecollaboration exchanges (Jauregi et al., 2012; Melchor-Couto, 2017, in press). Telecollaboration or online intercultural exchange is an "internet-based intercultural exchange between groups of learners of different cultural/national backgrounds set up in an institutional blended-learning context with the aim of developing both language skills and intercultural communicative competence" (Guth & Helm, 2012, p. 42).

Most of the studies addressing telecollaboration to date have focused on university students. This study addresses the motivational dimension of telecollaboration among teenagers, a much neglected target group in studies addressing online intercultural exchanges.

This study intends to analyse the motivational dimension involved in telecollaboration by looking at pupils' self-efficacy and anxiety levels as well as their attitudes towards interactions with Native Speakers (NSs) and Non Native Speakers (NNSs). Interaction was in the foreign language either via the chat application in Moodle or via video communication (BigBlueButton (BBB) in Moodle), and with or without a webcam.

2. Method

A total of 202 foreign language learners from Spain, France, the Netherlands, Germany and the UK were recruited for telecollaboration activities within this project, which was funded as part of the European TILA project (Telecollaboration for Intercultural Language Acquisition)[3]. All participants carried out an average of four telecollaborative sessions either by written chat or by video communication. They worked in either Lingua Franca (LF), Tandem (T), or Mixed constellations (M).

A survey measuring motivational factors, including self-efficacy beliefs, motivation, and anxiety was circulated to all participants after every session. Three pupils were also interviewed on aspects related to motivation and anxiety.

2.1. Instructional context

Every pupil was paired with a peer from another country in order to carry out regular telecollaboration sessions during class time. A total of 44% of the survey

---

[3]. http://www.tilaproject.eu/

responses came from pupils telecollaborating in a LF constellation (interactions between NNSs of the target language), and 17% of the reactions correspond to pupils interacting in T constellations (with NSs of their target language, who were in turn learning their partner's mother tongue). Finally, 39% used a mixed approach (tandem with lingua franca).

2.2. Data collection

A questionnaire measuring self-efficacy beliefs, attitudes toward NS and NNS interaction and anxiety was adapted from Jauregi et al. (2012) and distributed among learners to be completed after every session. Most items were to be scored by participants on a five-point Likert scale (1='strongly disagree'; 5='strongly agree').

Questionnaires were devised in English and translated into Dutch, French, German, and Spanish. They were circulated electronically via SurveyMonkey. Three students from Colexio Apóstol Santiago (Vigo, Spain), all at the B1 proficiency level, were randomly chosen to be interviewed for this study.

2.3. Data analysis

The quantitative data collected was coded for analysis and mean values were calculated. The qualitative data was analysed by identifying different coding categories (Bogdan & Biklen, 2006) related to the topics being researched in the present study.

3. Results

The first part of this section will present the survey analysis per category and the second part will focus on the interview findings.

3.1. Self-efficacy

Pupils participating in Colexio Apóstol Santiago T exchanges showed the highest mean scores for language competence and expressing themselves correctly (3.8), closely followed by the LF group (3.7), see Table 1.

As for the last item, the LF group showed the highest mean scores (4.6), followed by the T group (3.8). The pupils participating in M constellations got the lowest mean values across sessions for the three items (3.1; 2.9; 2.9).

Table 1. Mean values for self-efficacy according to language constellation (LF, T, & M) and environments (chat & video communication (VC)) used in telecollaboration

Item	LF	T	M	Chat	VC
I think that my foreign language competence is good enough to communicate with native speakers.	3.7	3.8	3.1	3.6	3.3
I can express myself correctly in the foreign language.	3.7	3.8	2.9	3.6	3.3
I understand (almost) everything that my partner says in the foreign language.	4.6	3.8	2.9	4.5	3.4

Regarding the differences in use of tools, pupils collaborating in chat were much more confident about being able to express themselves correctly (3.6) and particularly about understanding the partner (4.5) compared to those interacting by video communication (3.3; 3.4, respectively). As to the differences across sessions for the last item (understanding the interaction partner), in the first session the item scored average (3.5), while in the sixth session the mean values reached 4.2.

3.2. Willingness to communicate

Pupils communicating with NSs in the telecollaboration exchanges got much higher mean scores for the first item (4.1) than M constellations (3.4), while the LF group obtained the lowest mean values of all (3.1) (see Table 2). The pupils performing in BBB video communication thought they had learned a lot by communicating with NSs (3.5) compared to the chat group (3.1).

3.3. Anxiety with communication

Anxiety diminished as pupils got more familiar with telecollaboration. For instance, for the first item (I get nervous when I communicate), the first session got a mean score of 3.1, while the sixth session obtained a mean score of 1.5. The same tendency was observed for worrying about making mistakes (2.9>1.7) or getting nervous about a lack of understanding (2.7>1.7).

As to the language constellation, the LF group showed the lowest anxiety scores and the M group the highest ones. Regarding the tool being used for the exchanges, chat showed much lower anxiety scores than those communicating by VC.

Table 2. Mean values for anxiety comparing language constellations (LF, T, & M) and the environments (chat & VC) used in telecollaboration

Item	LF	T	M	Chat	VC
I get nervous when I communicate in the foreign language.	2.1	2.3	2.6	x	x
I worry a lot if I make mistakes when I communicate in the foreign language.	1.8	2.4	2.7	1.6	2.4
I get nervous when I don't understand every word that my exchange partner says.	1.6	2.4	2.6	1.6	2.4

3.4. Interview outcomes

The TILA activities undertaken were highly valued by the pupils, who rate them nine out of ten for enjoyment. What they valued the most was being able to get to know someone their age from a different country who is also learning English. They were interested in learning about how other people from different countries speak English. One of them pointed out that this is very important because in real life they will not always have the opportunity to interact with NNSs of English. None of the pupils expressed a preference towards NS interaction. Video communication seemed to be more appealing to them, although they preferred to start with written chat.

4. Conclusions

The present study shows results regarding motivational issues related to self-efficacy, interactions with NSs/NNSs, and anxiety.

Regarding the self-efficacy items, pupils interacting with NSs seem to be the most confident as far as their perception of competence (communicate and express correctly) is concerned, closely followed by the LF group, while the LF group outperformed the other groups regarding their perception of understanding the speech partner. The confidence on their competence seems to be higher by those engaging in chat sessions.

As far as willingness to communicate is concerned, those communicating in T constellations with NSs are significantly more positive about the learning potential of communicating with NSs than the other groups, and so are the pupils communicating in BBB.

A significant decrease was noticed as sessions progressed across conditions. Pupils engaging in LF constellations showed the lowest anxiety levels while the M constellation group showed the highest ones. The chat group showed lower anxiety scores than pupils performing in BBB.

5. Acknowledgements

We would like to thank the pupils participating in the exchanges, their teachers and the TILA team.

References

Bandura, A. (1997). *Self-efficacy: the exercise of control.* W. H. Freeman.

Bogdan, R. C., & Biklen, S. K. (2006). Qualitative research for education: an introduction to theories and methods. Pearson Education Group.

Dörnyei, Z., MacIntyre, P., & Henry, A. (Eds) (2015). *Motivational dynamics in language learning.* Multilingual Matters.

Guth, S., & Helm, F. (Eds). (2012). *Telecollaboration 2.0. language literacies and intercultural learning in the 21st century.* Peter Lang.

Jauregi, K., de Graaff, R., van den Bergh, H., & Kriz, M. (2012). Native non-native speaker interactions through video-web communication, a clue for enhancing motivation. *Computer Assisted Language Learning Journal, 25*(1), 1-19. https://doi.org/10.1080/09588221.2011.582587

Melchor-Couto, S. (2017). Foreign language anxiety levels in Second Life oral interaction. *ReCALL Journal, 29*(1), 99-119. Cambridge University Press. https://doi.org/10.1017/S0958344016000185

Melchor-Couto, S. (in press). Virtual world anonymity and foreign language oral interaction. In S. Nocci, S. Panichi, R. Sadler, & C. Wigham (in press), *ReCALL, Special Issue "Interactions for language learning in and around virtual worlds".* Cambridge University Press.

Ryan, R., & Deci, E. (2000). Self-determination theory and the facilitation of intrinsic motivation, social development, and well-being. *American Psychologist, 55*(1), 68-78. https://doi.org/10.1037/0003-066X.55.1.68

The TeCoLa project: pedagogical differentiation through telecollaboration and gaming for intercultural and content integrated language teaching

Kristi Jauregi[1] and Sabela Melchor-Couto[2]

> **Abstract.** The Erasmus+ TeCoLa project (2016-2019) aims to develop and test innovative gamified telecollaboration approaches for secondary schools that address issues of learning diversity in intercultural and Content Integrated Language Learning (CLIL) and teaching. Authentic task-based transnational interactions among peers from different socio-cultural, educational and language backgrounds are at the very heart of the learning process, using telecollaboration as a way to communicate and collaborate. In this paper we will shortly describe the project's foci and will elaborate on the teacher training programme that has been designed on the basis of the teachers' needs and on a sound conceptualisation of telecollaboration tasks that are useful, enjoyable, and meaningful.
>
> **Keywords**: telecollaboration, gamification, intercultural communicative competence, CLIL, teacher training.

1. Introduction

Experts in the fields of foreign language education, intercultural telecollaboration, teacher education, and technology-mediated pedagogy from six countries (Belgium, France, Germany, the Netherlands, Spain, and UK)[3] collaborate in the TeCoLa project[4] with the aim of developing and validating innovative gamified telecollaboration approaches for secondary schools. The main project focus

---

1. Utrecht University, Utrecht, The Netherlands; k.jauregi@uu.nl
2. University of Roehampton, London, United Kingdom; s.melchor-couto@roehampton.ac.uk
3. Project partners are: Utrecht University, LINK, University of Roehampton, University of Antwerp, University of Valencia, Transit Lingua, and 3DLES.
4. https://sites.google.com/site/tecolaproject/

How to cite this article: Jauregi, K., & Melchor-Couto, S. (2017). The TeCoLa project: pedagogical differentiation through telecollaboration and gaming for intercultural and content integrated language teaching. In K. Borthwick, L. Bradley & S. Thouësny (Eds), *CALL in a climate of change: adapting to turbulent global conditions – short papers from EUROCALL 2017* (pp. 163-169). Research-publishing.net. https://doi.org/10.14705/rpnet.2017.eurocall2017.707

is to address issues of learning diversity in intercultural and content integrated language learning and teaching. At the very heart of the pedagogical process are authentic task-based telecollaborations among peers from different socio-cultural, educational, and language backgrounds.

As described below there are several aims and objectives of this collaborative, international project:

(1) To empower pre- and in-service teachers to use telecollaboration and gamification, in order to:

- facilitate the development of intercultural communicative competence as a prime objective of foreign language learning and European citizenship-building;

- create conditions for real-life communication in a foreign language in lingua franca or tandem constellations;

- foster autonomous collaboration and authenticity as key principles of task-based learning;

- strengthen personalised learning and learner agency as part of a differentiated pedagogy approach.

(2) To internationalise education by integrating telecollaboration at schools to innovate, enrich, and make language teaching programmes more meaningful and effective.

(3) To contribute to the integration of all pupils regardless of their background by promoting intercultural dialogue in telecollaboration events among diverse populations of pupils from secondary schools across Europe.

(4) To exploit the possibilities that web 2.0 applications, virtual worlds, serious games, and gamification offer with a view of diversifying teaching and facilitating CLIL alongside intercultural dialogue and play in telecollaboration encounters.

2. Project activities

In the first project year we have:

- gathered relevant information on teachers' experience and perceived needs by conducting surveys and focus groups in relation to TeCoLa's foci: enhancing authentic intercultural communication among peers, promoting CLIL, addressing diversity, and digitalising education favouring internationalisation and EU citizenship building;

- created teacher training modules on gamified telecollaboration based on the information gathered on teachers' specific needs;

- developed a task design model and the first task prototypes for telecollaboration.

2.1. Measuring teachers' experiences and perceived needs

2.1.1. Method

A survey with 36 closed items was created to gather teachers' experiences and perceived needs. The survey covered: (1) background information; (2) the teachers' experience and perceived training needs regarding the use of digital communication tools and their perceptions of the usefulness of these across four parameters: learning challenges, intercultural awareness, communicative competence and CLIL; and (3) information about the context in which teachers work.

A five-point Likert scale (1=strongly disagree, 5=strongly agree) was employed with additional space to provide open-ended comments for each section. The survey was distributed by email via SurveyMonkey to teachers in Belgium, France, Germany, the Netherlands, Spain, and the UK. A total of 177 responses were received.

Additionally, six focus groups (semi-structured group interviews) were carried out in all project countries either face-to-face or via Skype with a total of 29 teachers to gain more focused and in-depth information on the issues addressed in the survey.

2.1.2. Results

Table 1 below shows the mean score of each construct. The diversity and learning challenge results showed a mean score of 3.9, intercultural awareness and competence was 4.1, and communicative competence was 4.5. Both were relevant or extremely relevant to the teacher's teaching practice. On the contrary, CLIL did not seem to be as relevant to the teachers (3.0). One possible reason for this outcome could be that most teachers who completed the survey may not be familiar with this methodology.

Table 1. Relevance items for language teaching

To what extent are the following issues RELEVANT in your teaching practice? (1=not at all relevant, 5=extremely relevant)		
	Mean	St. Dev.
Diversity and learning challenges	3.9	0.9
Intercultural awareness and competence	4.1	0.8
Communicative competence	4.5	0.7
To support CLIL	3.0	1.4

Regarding the issues that are problematic for their teaching experience, promoting communicative competence is perceived by teachers to be a difficulty (Table 2).

Table 2. Problematic issues in language teaching

To what extent are the following issues PROBLEMATIC in your teaching practice? (1 = not at all problematic, 5 = extremely problematic)		
	Mean	St. Dev.
Diversity and learning challenges	2.7	1.0
Intercultural awareness and competence	2.2	0.9
Communicative competence	3.5	1.1
To support CLIL	2.3	1.3

In terms of teachers' experience with TeCoLa's main digital tools, teachers have little experience with all the tools mentioned (video communication mean 2.3 and online games mean 2.12) but particularly little with virtual worlds (mean 1.4).

As to the perceived usefulness of these tools to deal with diversity, promote intercultural awareness and communicative competence, results show that teachers identify video communication as the most valuable (Table 3). This might be linked to familiarity issues with the tool.

Table 4 shows how much training teachers believe that they require to be able to use each tool, which is higher for the more unknown virtual worlds (mean 3.8).

Table 3. Teacher beliefs on tool affordances

Do you think the following tools in international school collaboration would help ... (1 = not at all, 5 = a lot)		
	Mean	St. Dev
to better deal with LEARNING CHALLENGES due to cultural, cognitive, or social DIVERSITY among your students?		
Video communication	3.8	1.1
Online games	3.1	1.2
Virtual worlds	3.0	1.2
to promote your students' INTERCULTURAL AWARENESS and COMPETENCE?		
Video communication	4.2	0.9
Online games	3.0	1.2
Virtual worlds	3.1	1.2
to promote your students' COMMUNICATIVE COMPETENCE?		
Video communication	4.3	0.9
Online games	3.3	1.2
Virtual worlds	3.2	1.3
to support CLIL		
Video communication	3.6	1.2
Online games	3.0	1.2
Virtual worlds	2.7	1.2

Table 4. Perceived training needs

How much TRAINING do you think you would need to be able to use the following tools as a teaching resource? (1 = none, 5 = a lot)		
	Mean	St. Dev.
Video communication	3	1.1
Online games	3	1.2
Virtual worlds	3.8	1.2

With regards to the focus groups, responses showed that the participating teachers value telecollaboration as a way to provide their students with much needed opportunities for authentic interactions. Such interactions can have a strong motivational effect on learners and also improve their intercultural competence. They also commented on the differentiation possibilities that can be demonstrated by having a range of tools to choose from. Teachers acknowledged, however, a number of barriers that will need to be overcome. Several teachers indicated that they lacked the technical equipment for these practices, and also the time to organise them in their busy schedules, as they are increasingly burdened with administrative duties. They also highlighted issues around fitting them in the curriculum.

2.2. Teacher training modules

Based on the information gained from the teachers' experiences and needs survey, and from the focus groups, teacher training modules have been developed. The main topics addressed are:

- general introduction to telecollaboration and gamification for foreign language learning;

- telecollaboration and gamification for intercultural communication development and European citizenship building;

- telecollaboration and gamification for subject integrated and vocational language learning;

- telecollaboration and gamification for differentiated pedagogical practices;

- learner preparation for pedagogical telecollaboration and gamification;

- gamified telecollaboration and assessment.

These modules will be used for teacher training in the second project year and will be available on the project's site in due course.

2.3. Task design model and task prototypes

TeCoLa's task design model is underpinned by different theories and pedagogical experiences, in particular, task based language teaching (González-Lloret & Ortega, 2014), motivational theories (Deci & Ryan, 2000; Dörnyei & Ushioda, 2009), and knowledge gained through previous European projects (TILA[5] and NIFLAR[6]). A main concern in task design relates to the need to address learners' interests and motivation in order to be able to create meaningful, enjoyable, and usable telecollaboration tasks while addressing diversity in the language classroom. Based on this design concept, some task prototyping templates for task examples have been created and will be validated in future studies.

---

5. http://www.tilaproject.eu/
6. http://niflar.eu/

3. Conclusions

In the initial year of this TeCoLa project, we have established the basis for the creation of teacher training programmes and a model for the elaboration of meaningful gamified telecollaborative tasks that address diversity in different educational contexts. In the second and third years, this model will be validated in several case studies and online pedagogical guides created for stakeholders interested in integrating gamified telecollaboration in their teaching. All materials will be available at the TeCoLa's Open Educational Resources Pool.

4. Acknowledgements

We would like to thank all TeCoLa partners for their joint efforts in making TeCoLa a reality.

References

Deci, E. L., & Ryan, R. M. (2000). The "what" and "why" of goal pursuits: human needs and the self-determination of behavior. *Psychological Inquiry, 11*, 227-268. https://doi.org/10.1207/S15327965PLI1104_01

Dörnyei, Z., & Ushioda, E. (Eds). (2009). *Motivation, language identity and the L2 self*. Multilingual Matters.

González-Lloret, M., & Ortega, L. (2014). *Technology-mediated TBLT: researching technology and tasks*. John Benjamins. https://doi.org/10.1075/tblt.6

Students' views on the helpfulness of multimedia components of digital flashcards in mobile-assisted vocabulary learning

Regina Kaplan-Rakowski[1] and Barbara Loranc-Paszylk[2]

Abstract. This study examines learners' perceptions of the helpfulness of various multimedia components embedded in digital flashcards for explicit, informal foreign language vocabulary learning. Advanced learners of English (N=59) studied 48 new words using digital flashcards on smartphones. After ten days, the learners completed perception surveys. The goal of this study was to investigate which flashcard components were perceived as most helpful in learning vocabulary. The results of nonparametric statistical tests revealed that students perceive Foreign Language (FL) definitions to be significantly less helpful compared to other flashcard components. Moreover, when given a choice between having access to translation or pronunciation, translation was perceived as significantly more helpful in vocabulary learning. These findings have practical implications for the development of multimedia digital flashcards in mobile-assisted language learning applications.

Keywords: digital flashcards, mobile-assisted language learning, foreign language vocabulary.

1. Introduction

In the context of mobile-assisted language learning, the use of flashcards for studying vocabulary has attracted considerable research interest (Byrd & Lansing, 2016). In a large-sample study (N=247) by Wissman, Rawson, and Pyc (2012), over 80% of students pointed to vocabulary learning as the main area where they

---

1. Independent researcher, Dallas, Texas, United States of America; rkaplan@siu.edu
2. University of Bielsko-Biala, Bielsko-Biala, Poland; bloranc@ath.edu.pl

How to cite this article: Kaplan-Rakowski, R., & Loranc-Paszylk, B. (2017). Students' views on the helpfulness of multimedia components of digital flashcards in mobile-assisted vocabulary learning. In K. Borthwick, L. Bradley & S. Thouësny (Eds), *CALL in a climate of change: adapting to turbulent global conditions – short papers from EUROCALL 2017* (pp. 170-176). Research-publishing.net. https://doi.org/10.14705/rpnet.2017.eurocall2017.708

used flashcards. Apart from a growing body of studies testing the effect of mobile devices on vocabulary learning, researchers have explored students' experiences and preferences within this learning environment.

Previous studies showed that students perceived learning vocabulary on their mobile phones as engaging (Azabdaftari & Mozaheb, 2012), effective, and entertaining (Başoğlu & Akdemir, 2010). Hung (2015) further identified participants' positive attitudes towards the use of flashcards in such categories as perceived usefulness, perceived ease of use, and intention to use.

Various studies exploring the use of mobile phones in vocabulary learning focused on multimedia components. For example, Lin and Yu (2017) used four different modes (i.e. components) of vocabulary presentation on mobile phones: text only (translation and example sentences), text plus image, text plus sound, and all the modes combined. The majority of subjects (N=32) perceived the vocabulary presentation as motivating (81.3%), effective (93.8%), and beneficial (96.9%). Over 90% of subjects considered each of the presentation components as necessary for learning new words. However, it was beyond the scope of that study to precisely test how each of the presentation components was perceived relative to the others.

Our study fills this research gap by comparing learners' perceptions of the helpfulness of different presentation modes/components for learning new vocabulary with flashcards. Our research question was: *"Which flashcard components do students perceive as helpful in explicit vocabulary learning?"*. We then looked into a more detailed question examining to what degree each of the components were perceived to be helpful.

2. Method

2.1. Participants

The 59 participants were all native speakers of Polish studying English at an advanced level. The subjects were sent 48 digital flashcards containing English nouns. The learning process took place on the students' personal smartphones using the *AnkiDroid* app. After ten days, the learners completed a survey measuring their perceptions of the helpfulness of flashcard components for learning new vocabulary.

2.2. The survey

We report on two survey questions:

- *Which flashcard components did you find most helpful?*: For this multiple-choice question, we calculated the percentage of subjects who reported each flashcard component as being helpful.

- *To what degree did you find each of the flashcard components helpful?*: For this Likert scale question (1='not helpful at all' and 5='very helpful'), we conducted a nonparametric Friedman test, followed by pairwise Wilcoxon signed-rank tests.

2.3. Flashcard design

Each flashcard had a front and back side (see Figure 1). The front side contained the target word. The back side presented a relevant image representing the target word, the FL definition, and the Polish translation. There were also flashcards with the pronunciation of the target word, the sound effect associated with the target word, or the combination of the two audio enhancements. Consequently, flashcards had the following components: the target word, the FL definition, the Polish translation, the image, the pronunciation, the sound effect, and the combination of pronunciation plus sound effect.

Figure 1. An example of the front side (left) and the back side (right) of a flashcard

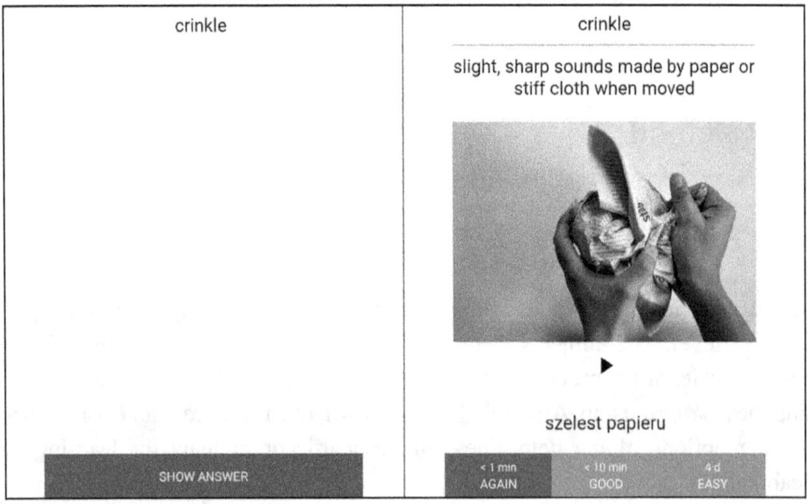

3. Results

Out of the 59 participants who completed the survey, 66% reported using the flashcards about three times in ten days. Most learners (58%) reported feeling that studying vocabulary with the flashcards was effective and 51% of them reported that they found it engaging.

3.1. Flashcard components perceived as helpful in learning vocabulary

One of the questions was *"Which components of the flashcards did you find helpful in vocabulary learning?"*. As Table 1 shows, the highest percentage of students reported the image (74.58%), followed by the translation (61.02%), as most helpful in learning.

Table 1. Flashcard components and percentages of students reporting the components as helpful

Flashcard components	%
Image	74.58%
Translation	61.02%
Sound effects	44.07%
Sound effects + pronunciation	42.37%
Pronunciation	32.20%
Translation + FL definition	20.34%
No sound	1.69%

3.2. Degree of the helpfulness of flashcard components

Our other question of interest was: *"To what degree were the flashcard components helpful?"*. As seen in Table 2, the median values reported for translation and for image were the highest, while the median value reported for FL definition was the lowest.

Table 2. Medians and mean ranks of flashcard components

Flashcard components	Median	Mean ranks
Polish translation	5	4.27
Image	5	4.02
Sound effects + pronunciation	4	3.81
Sound effects	4	3.60
Pronunciation	4	3.16
FL definition	3	2.14

The analysis of the Friedman test procedure revealed the mean rank to be the highest for translation ($M=4.27$), followed by images ($M=4.02$), with FL definitions being the lowest ($M=2.14$). The test showed a statistically significant difference between the components: $\chi^2(df=5, N=59) = 64.04$, $p<0.001$. To establish which flashcard components were perceived to be more helpful, we conducted post hoc analysis with Wilcoxon signed-rank tests, reported in Table 3. The Bonferroni correction (for 15 possible pairwise combinations) resulted in a significance level set at $p<0.0033$. Pairwise comparison tests revealed that FL definitions were perceived as less helpful compared with any other components. Further, when pronunciation and translation were compared, pronunciation was perceived as significantly less helpful than translation.

Table 3. Wilcoxon sign-rank test statistics

	Z	Sig.
image vs definition	4.75	<0.01*
image vs translation	0.72	0.47
image vs pronunciation	2.90	<0.01
image vs sound effects	1.69	0.09
image vs (pronunciation and sound effects)	1.27	0.20
definition vs translation	5.43	<0.01*
definition vs pronunciation	3.23	<0.01*
definition vs sound effects	3.91	<0.01*
definition vs (pronunciation and sound effects)	4.87	<0.01*
translation vs pronunciation	4.05	<0.01*
translation vs sound effects	2.48	0.01
translation vs (pronunciation and sound effects)	2.18	0.03
pronunciation vs sound effects	1.66	0.10
pronunciation vs (pronunciation and sound effects)	2.15	0.03
sound effects vs (pronunciation and sound effects)	0.70	0.49
* Indicates significance at the 95% level with the Bonferroni correction		

4. Discussion

Our analysis provided us with two major outcomes. First, students did not find FL definitions helpful on flashcards compared with other flashcard components. On the one hand, this is somewhat surprising because advanced language learners are more likely to read more challenging FL definitions in the target language than novice language learners. On the other hand, this is consistent with translations and images being sufficient, with no additional need for FL definitions. In fact, it is possible that definitions occupy too much space on already small smartphone screens, causing cognitive overload, which is disadvantageous for learning (Sweller, 1994).

Our second main finding is that when students are given a choice between having pronunciation and translation as a component of their flashcard, translation is perceived as significantly more helpful than pronunciation. We may assume that students prefer translations because they are carriers of semantic information and explain the meaning of new words. At the beginning of the learning process, the meaning-form link is probably most important (Schmitt, 1998).

5. Conclusions

This study investigated students' perceptions of multimedia flashcard components studied on smartphones for explicit vocabulary learning. Overall, most learners expressed positive feedback regarding the perceived effectiveness and engagement towards the flashcards. Our statistical analyses provided evidence that FL definitions are not perceived to be helpful compared to other flashcard components, such as translation, image, pronunciation, sound effects, or pronunciation plus sound effects. Furthermore, pronunciation recordings are not perceived as significantly more helpful than translations. Flashcard designers (whether they are teachers, instructional designers, or students themselves) can benefit from these findings by including or excluding those components in their flashcard creation.

References

Azabdaftari, B., & Mozaheb, M. A. (2012). Comparing vocabulary learning of EFL learners by using two different strategies: mobile learning vs. flashcards. *The Eurocall Review, 20*(2), 47-59.

Başoğlu, E. B., & Akdemir, Ö. (2010). A comparison of undergraduate students' English vocabulary learning: using mobile phones and flashcards. *TOJET: The Turkish Online Journal of Educational Technology, 9*(3), 1-7.

Byrd, D. R., & Lansing, B. (2016). Electronic flashcards inside the classroom: practical and effective. *The Journal of Language Teaching and Learning, 6*(2), 1-13.

Hung, H. T. (2015). Intentional vocabulary learning using digital flashcards. *English Language Teaching, 8*(10), 107-112. https://doi.org/10.5539/elt.v8n10p107

Lin, C. C., & Yu, Y. C. (2017). Effects of presentation modes on mobile-assisted vocabulary learning and cognitive load. *Interactive Learning Environments, 25*(4), 528-542. https://doi.org/10.1080/10494820.2016.1155160

Schmitt, N. (1998). Tracking the incidental acquisition of second language vocabulary: a longitudinal study. *Language Learning, 48*(2), 281-317. https://doi.org/10.1111/1467-9922.00042

Sweller, J. (1994). Cognitive load theory, learning difficulty, and instructional design. *Learning and Instruction, 4*(4), 295-312. https://doi.org/10.1016/0959-4752(94)90003-5

Wissman, K. T., Rawson, K. A., & Pyc, M. A. (2012). How and when do students use flashcards? *Memory, 20*(6), 568-579. https://doi.org/10.1080/09658211.2012.687052

The comparison of the impact of storytelling and digital storytelling assignments on students' motivations for learning

Naoko Kasami[1]

Abstract. The purpose of this study was to explore how a Digital StoryTelling (DST) assignment affected and changed students' motivations for learning English as a Foreign Language (EFL) in comparison with a StoryTelling (ST) assignment. A course entitled 'Information English' was held for Japanese university students at a faculty of information and communications in the fall term of 2014. The study goal of the course was to acquire skills and knowledge to present ideas and messages effectively with the use of Information and Communications Technology (ICT) and English. Students conducted ST tasks in the class as a midterm assignment, then created digital stories and peer-reviewed them as a final assignment. The impact of the DST assignment on students' motivations was analyzed by means of midterm and post-assessment questionnaires based on Keller's ARCS model (four categories of which are attention, relevance, confidence, and satisfaction) and compared to data collected for the ST assignment. The findings showed that most students were more motivated for learning with the DST assignment than the ST assignment.

Keywords: digital storytelling, motivation, EFL, ICT.

1. Introduction

The purpose of this study was to investigate how a DST assignment affected non-English Major students' motivations for learning English in comparison with a traditional (non-digital) ST assignment. Advances in technologies are changing

---

1. J. F. Oberlin University, Tokyo, Japan; naoko.kasami@gmail.com

How to cite this article: Kasami, N. (2017). The comparison of the impact of storytelling and digital storytelling assignments on students' motivations for learning. In K. Borthwick, L. Bradley & S. Thouësny (Eds), *CALL in a climate of change: adapting to turbulent global conditions – short papers from EUROCALL 2017* (pp. 177-183). Research-publishing.net. https://doi.org/10.14705/rpnet.2017.eurocall2017.709

learning activities, and DST is one of these new learning activities. DST and ST assignments were conducted in a course entitled 'Information English', held for Japanese university students at a faculty of information and communications over a period of 15 weeks. Numerous researchers have pointed out the effectiveness of DST in EFL education (Abdel-Hack & Helwa, 2014). Kasami (2014) focused on the comparison of the impact of essay writing and DST assignments on students' motivations for learning and Kasami (2016) attempted to examine the impact of DST assignments on students' perceptions of learning effectiveness.

In the research described here, the impact of the DST assignment was analyzed in terms of motivation for learning based on Keller's (2010) ARCS model and then compared with similar results from a (non-digital) ST assignment. The following research questions were proposed:

- Does the DST assignment enhance motivation for learning more than the ST assignment?

- Does the DST assignment enhance motivation for learning in terms of aspects of ARCS when compared with the ST assignment?

- In what way does the DST assignment enhance motivation for learning more than the ST assignment?

2. Method

This study focuses on the practices of a course entitled 'Information English' for students at a faculty of information and communications in a university in Japan. The course was held during the fall term of 2014 (September 2014 to January 2015). The study goal was to acquire skills and knowledge to present ideas and messages effectively with the use of ICT and English. Seventy-six students participated in three courses, and two assignments were conducted at different points in the course (Figure 1).

In this course, as a midterm assignment, students were required to conduct the ST assignment in small groups. The general theme of the ST assignment was to introduce the student's favorite object. As a final assignment, they were encouraged to create digital stories by recording their voices using software such as Windows Movie Maker and PowerPoint. The general theme of the DST assignment was 'Tips for Better Understanding Japanese Culture' (Figure 2).

Figure 1. The process of the two assignments

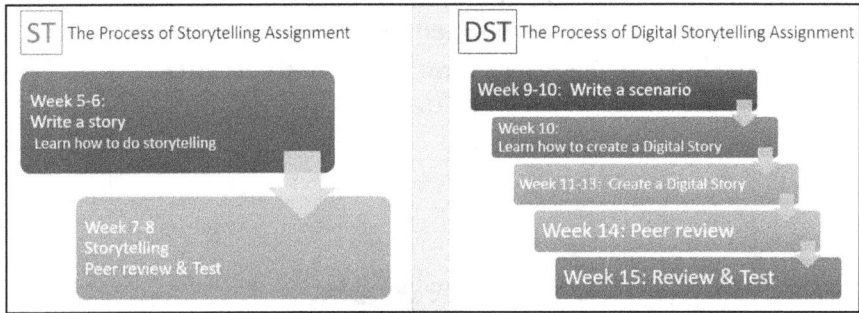

Figure 2. The images of the classroom situations during the two assignments

Data was collected from midterm and post-assessment questionnaires administered using Google Drive (in Week 8 and Week 15). The study comprised 63 students in three courses who had answered all (pre, midterm and post) of the questionnaires and who had taken two (midterm and final) tests.

3. Results

The results of the analysis regarding the three research questions are presented.

First, the students were asked to compare the two assignments. The first research question was 'does the DST assignment enhance motivation for learning more than the ST assignment?'. The questionnaire was answered with a five point Likert scale (1=Strongly Negative to 5=Strongly Positive). As a result, 77.77% (49 students) of all students answered 4 (positive) or 5 (strongly positive) and 7.94 % (5 students) of all students answered 2 (negative); see Figure 3.

Figure 3. The comparison of the two assignments

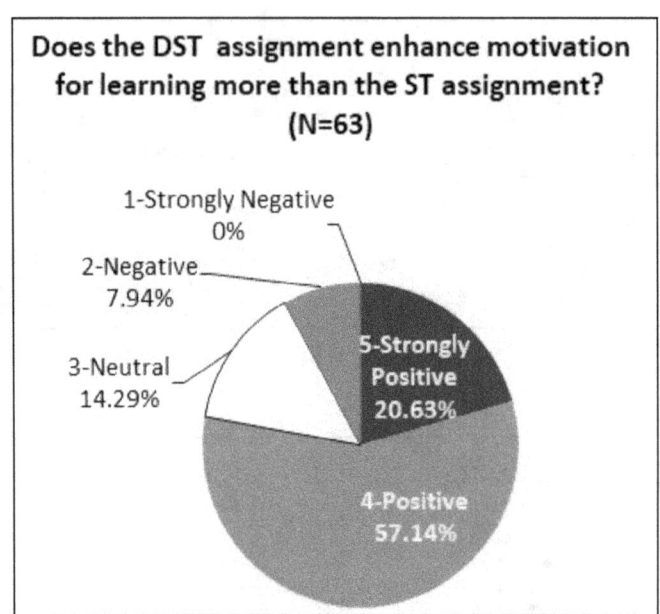

Second, the students were asked to rate both assignments (scores ranging from one to nine, where the greater numerical value represented a stronger motivating factor). The questionnaire questions were set according to 12 sub-categorical question items using a semantic differential scheme by asking how much the student felt about the assignment by placing a mark in between two adjectives opposite each other on the web (e.g. objectives were 'vague' vs. 'clear'), as referred to in the research by Suzuki, Nishibuchi, Yamamoto, and Keller (2004) and based on Keller's ARCS model. The middle score (five) means a neutral response (e.g. 1=strongly vague, 5=neutral, 9=strongly clear).

The result of a paired-sample t-test analyzed by IBM SPSS Statistics Version 22 showed that the mean difference between the two assignments was significant ($p<0.05$, or the DST assignment had significantly higher mean scores than the ST assignment) in aspects of 'A2: Inquiry Arousal', 'A3: Variability', 'R1: Goal Orientation', 'R3: Familiarity', 'C1: Learning Requirements', 'C3: Personal Control', 'S2: Positive Consequences', and 'S3: Equity'. Significant differences were not recognized in aspects of 'A1: Perceptual Arousal', 'R2: Motive Matching', 'C2: Success Opportunities', and 'S1: Natural Consequences'. The greatest mean difference was 0.98, observed in 'A3: Variability' between the DST assignment ($M=6.98$, $SD=1.26$) and the ST assignment ($M=6.00$, $SD=1.49$) at the level of significance (*t*=4.731, *df*=62, *p*<0.0001, two-tailed) (Figure 4). (The result of a Wilcoxon signed-rank test also indicated that there were significant differences (*p*<0.05) in the same aspects. The greatest difference was observed in 'A3: Variability' (*z*=4.090, *N*-Ties=46, *p*<0.001, two-tailed).

Figure 4. The comparison of the two assignments in terms of aspects of Keller's ARCS model

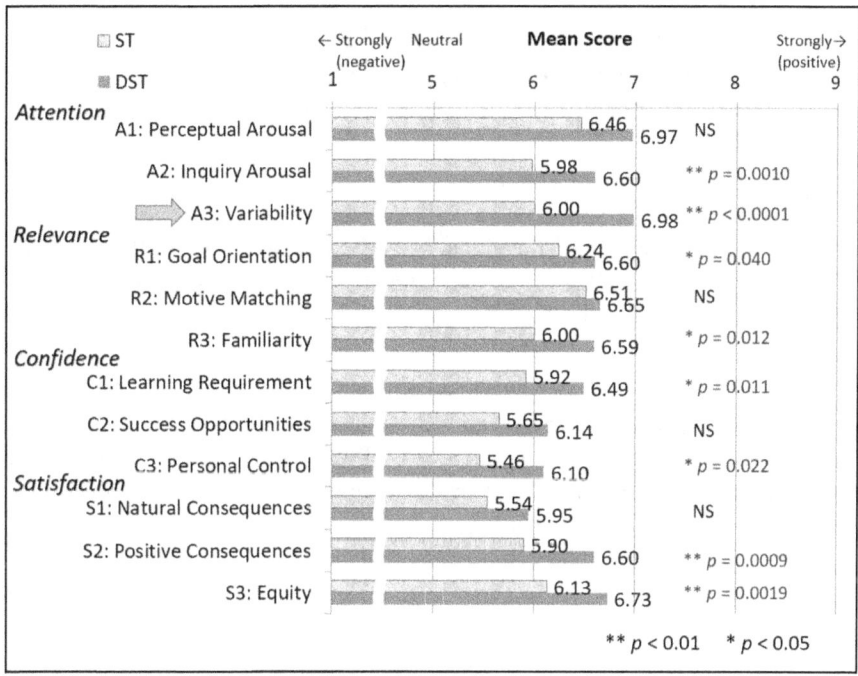

Third, the open-ended question was presented at the end of the course. Students were asked to write down the reason why they answered so in the question of 'Does the DST assignment enhance motivation for learning more than the ST assignment?'. Comments were given by 52 students. From all of the comments, the author and another collaborative researcher collected keywords. The following keywords had a frequency of more than five:

- enjoy/fun (ten times);

- movie (eight times);

- variability/new (seven times);

- creativity/creatively (five times);

- present my work (five times);

- self-efficacy/achievement (five times);

An example of a positive comment:

> "It was a new experience for me and I enjoyed learning by creating a movie file with my narration and creating my original work as it was an unusual opportunity".

One negative comment was noted:

> "When I heard about the digital storytelling assignment for the first time, I thought it was hard to create a digital story using movie or image data with background music".

Thus, though some students who were not familiar with using ICT might have negative first impressions, DST assignments enhanced learning motivations. This might be because many students felt that DST was new and stimulating. While they enjoyed DST by making and presenting their own work creatively, it also gave some students a sense of achievement.

4. Conclusions

The purpose of this study was to investigate the impacts of the DST assignment in terms of motivation for learning in comparison with the ST assignment. The answers to the research questions are stated below. First, according to the questionnaire results, it was revealed that 77.77% of all students were more motivated for learning with the DST assignment than with the ST assignment. Second, the DST assignment had significantly higher mean scores than the ST assignment in eight aspects of ARCS. There was the greatest difference (improvement) with the DST assignment shown in 'A3: Variability'. Third, the most frequently used keywords included 'enjoy', 'movie', 'variability', 'creativity', 'present my work', and 'self-efficacy'.

It is inferred that the DST assignment gave most students more chances to enjoy variability and it enhanced students' motivations for learning more than the ST assignments. The limitations of this study should be highlighted. In this course, as the theme, timing, and time spent for DST and ST assignments differed, there are possibilities that those factors might have had an impact on the results.

5. Acknowledgements

I would like to thank Dr. Julian Lewis for his advice on my paper.

References

Abdel-Hack, E. M., & Helwa, H. S. A.-H. A. (2014). Using digital storytelling and weblogs instruction to enhance EFL narrative writing and critical thinking skills among EFL majors at faculty of education. *Educational Research, 5*(1), 8-41.

Kasami, N. (2014). The impacts of a digital storytelling assignment on non-english-major-students' motivation for learning English in a Japanese university. In L. Liu & D. Gibson (Eds), *Research highlights in technology and teacher education 2014* (pp. 91-100). AACE.

Kasami, N. (2016). The impact of a digital storytelling assignment on students' perception of learning effectiveness compared to a storytelling assignment. *Proceedings of Global Learn*, 420-429.

Keller, J. M. (2010). *Motivational design for learning and performance: the ARCS model approach.* Springer. https://doi.org/10.1007/978-1-4419-1250-3

Suzuki, K., Nishibuchi, A., Yamamoto, M., & Keller, J. M. (2004). Development and evaluation of website to check instructional design based on the ARCS motivation model. *Information and Systems in Education, 2*(1), 63-69.

A Facebook project for pre-service language teachers

Liliia Khalitova[1], Gulnara Gimaletdinova[2], Gulnara Sadykova[3], and Albina Kayumova[4]

Abstract. This report is based on an action research study conducted in an English language course with a group of low-residency students of a teacher education master's program: *Multilingual Technologies of Early Childhood Education*, at Kazan Federal University. A Social Networking Site (SNS), Facebook, was used as a platform for practising and developing the students' teaching skills. The purpose of the study was to show the students the potential educational value of Facebook in teaching English to preschool children. The data sources include pre- and post-project questionnaires, interviews with students, field notes, and the reflective diary of the instructor-researcher. The results show that while designing an educational page on Facebook, the students changed their attitude towards the educational value of SNSs and acquired knowledge and skills necessary for implementing SNSs into their teaching practices. The research findings will be of interest to English language educators, especially foreign language teachers involved in early childhood education, and to Computer Assisted Language Learning (CALL) practitioners.

Keywords: CALL, Facebook, SNS, pre-service teacher training.

1. Introduction

Recent studies demonstrate that social networking sites (SNS) can be effectively integrated into a foreign language curriculum (Harrison, 2013; Leier & Cunningham, 2016). Facebook, as one of the most popular SNSs, can serve as a tool to help students improve motivation, social interaction, and language learning skills (Blattner & Lomicka, 2012; Promnitz-Hayashi, 2011). Still, some teachers are skeptical about the educational value of SNSs and see them as a social/

---

1. Kazan Federal University, Kazan, Russia; lilia_khalitova@mail.ru
2. Kazan Federal University, Kazan, Russia; gim-nar@yandex.ru
3. Kazan Federal University, Kazan, Russia; gsadykova2015@mail.ru
4. Kazan Federal University, Kazan, Russia; alb1980@yandex.ru

How to cite this article: Khalitova, L., Gimaletdinova, G., Sadykova, G., & Kayumova, A. (2017). A Facebook project for pre-service language teachers. In K. Borthwick, L. Bradley & S. Thouësny (Eds), *CALL in a climate of change: adapting to turbulent global conditions – short papers from EUROCALL 2017* (pp. 184-188). Research-publishing.net. https://doi.org/10.14705/rpnet.2017.eurocall2017.710

entertainment tool (Peeters, 2015). As our pre-project questionnaire revealed, students of a teacher education master's program (age group under 30 years old) use Facebook and other SNSs only for their everyday personal interactions and never in their teaching practice. Student-teachers need examples and models of how SNSs can be used in education successfully (Venkatesh, Thong, & Xu, 2012).

Teachers' unwillingness to integrate SNSs in the language classroom is often rooted in inadequate teacher-training. Unfortunately, not all teacher-training programs include courses that focus specifically on how to use social networks and other CALL tools for teaching languages. Still, such training could be provided within other courses (Leier & Cunningham, 2016). This report describes action research in progress that focuses on the efforts of one instructor to change the attitudes of her pre-service foreign language teachers towards the educational value of Facebook in an English language course. Students were given a choice of any SNS, but they chose Facebook due to its informal character and worldwide popularity.

2. Method

The study involved an instructor and her low-residency students (N=14) of a teacher education master's program offered in Kazan Federal University in the winter-spring 2017 semester. The purpose of the research was to examine and evaluate the effects of a Facebook-related project that the instructor integrated into her English language course to attempt to change the attitudes of students towards the use of Facebook as an educational tool. We formulated the following research questions:

- What are the students' attitudes towards SNSs as an educational tool?

- Do the students feel they have gained knowledge and skills to implement an educational page on Facebook in their teaching practice?

Data was collected from project activities: the students completed a pre-project questionnaire, wrote a report, developed their project on Facebook, and completed a final self-reflection questionnaire. Data sources also included field notes and the reflective diary of the instructor-researcher.

The pre-test consisted of (1) a questionnaire on students' attitudes to social networking and (2) a written report on the possible effects of SNSs on students with reference to their involvement in social activities and academic performance. The following task was given:

You have been asked to write a report on the effects of social networking sites on students, with reference to their involvement in social activities and their academic performance. You should make recommendations for addressing problem areas. Write your report in 250-300 words.

Then the students were asked to create an educational page on Facebook named "Kid Family English" (https://www.facebook.com/Kid-Family-English-510355809352691/?fref=ts). They worked in small groups of two and three to create short lessons for kids and their parents. During this Facebook-related project, the students were asked to complete post-project questionnaires (a final self-reflection questionnaire) and interviews.

3.   Discussion

The pre-project questionnaire showed that all students have accounts in SNSs (Facebook, Vkontakte, and WhatsApp) and six students have had accounts in Twitter and Instagram for more than three years. They use these SNSs to participate in social events, chat with friends, connect with relatives, and share photos/videos. Most of the students (N=10) said that they use Facebook to keep in touch with friends from other countries. The pre-project report written by students at the beginning of the Facebook project revealed that all students (N=14) admitted the positive influence of social networking on everyday life, but most of them (N=12) did not see SNSs as valuable tools for language learning and teaching. Only two students wrote that SNSs "might improve academic performance if planned well" or could be used for "arranging online conferences".

While designing an educational page, "Kid Family English", and developing the content, the students collaborated with peers and the instructor. Each lesson they posted on Facebook was discussed during the class when students shared experiences, concerns, and reported about the progress.

The post-project questionnaires and interviews with the students revealed two major challenges. First, students found it difficult to upload video/audio as well as to shoot the appropriate video-lesson, thus showing their inadequate technical skills. Second, the students demonstrated low engagement and motivation that could be attributed to the fact that they were not graded on this assignment and their Facebook projects were not a part of their overall course evaluation. Similar findings linking motivation to grading policies are reported elsewhere (see, for example, Cao & Hong, 2011).

In the final self-reflection questionnaire, the students were asked to answer the questions concerning:

- their attitude towards Facebook as an educational tool;
- their feelings as teachers while designing "Kid Family English";
- their plans for using SNSs in their future teaching practice;
- benefits of "Kid Family English" for young learners and teachers;
- their thoughts about integrating SNSs in the English language classroom.

With the help of a student-oriented project focused on designing a language learning page on Facebook, the results show that students have changed their attitude and see SNSs as valuable tools for language learning and teaching. This is indicated by findings from their final self-reflection questionnaire:

> "Now I think that Facebook can be used by teachers as an educational tool. Prior to the lesson preparation, I did a lot of research and it was a surprise to me that so many teachers actually use Facebook as an educational tool".

> "Before participating in this Project I used Facebook only as a social networking [site] in order to communicate with my friends from another countries [sic]. Now I see that [with] the help of Facebook we really can teach and learn".

> "To tell the truth, I didn't expect any emotions from this Project. And I was surprised when I enjoyed participating in such kind of work [sic]. You feel satisfied if everything goes in the way you wanted. Now I think that it is interesting kind of work. And this project give me [sic] a great opportunity to do what I have not done before".

4. Conclusions

The research indicates that the students of the teacher education master's program *Multilingual Technologies of Early Childhood Education*, acquired understanding of the educational value of Facebook, learned how to develop the content and design the page, as well as how to collaborate with peers, followers, and the instructor. The results suggest the need to integrate a Facebook project assessment into the overall evaluation of the course, which may compensate for the lack of external motivation. Instructors could be recommended to create their own pages to demonstrate the potential of SNSs and model the final product. The research findings will help to inform language practitioners and developers of language teacher training programs. They reveal the importance of teaching training in the use of SNSs.

5. Acknowledgements

We would like to thank the low-residency students of the teacher education master's program *Multilingual Technologies of Early Childhood Education* at Kazan Federal University who contributed to this research.

References

Blattner, G., & Lomicka, L. (2012). Facebook-ing and the social generation: a new era of language learning. *Alsic, 15*(1). https://alsic.revues.org/2413

Cao, Y., & Hong, P., (2011). Antecedents and consequences of social media utilization in college teaching: a proposed model with mixed methods investigation. *On the Horizon, 19*(4), 297-306. https://doi.org/10.1108/10748121111179420

Harrison, R. (2013). Profiles in social networking sites for language learning – livemocha revisited. In M.-N. Lamy & K. Zourou (Eds), *Social networking for language education* (pp. 100-116). Palgrave Macmillan. https://doi.org/10.1057/9781137023384_6

Leier, V., & Cunningham, U. (2016). 'Just facebook me': a study on the integration of Facebook into a German language curriculum. In S. Papadima-Sophocleous, L. Bradley & S. Thouësny (Eds), *CALL communities and culture – short papers from EUROCALL 2016* (pp. 260-264). Research-publishing.net. https://doi.org/10.14705/rpnet.2016.eurocall2016.572

Peeters, W. (2015). Tapping into the educational potential of Facebook: encouraging out-of-class peer collaboration in foreign language learning. *Studies in Self-Access Learning Journal, 6*(2), 176-190.

Promnitz-Hayashi, L. (2011). A learning success story using Facebook. *Studies in Self-Access Learning Journal, 2*(4), 309-316.

Venkatesh, V., Thong, J., & Xu, X. (2012). Consumer acceptance and use of information technology: extending the unified theory of acceptance and use of technology. *MIS Quarterly, 36*(1), 157-178.

Using a learning management system to enhance an extensive reading program

Cory J. Koby[1]

Abstract. The Extensive Reading (ER) approach to second language acquisition is increasingly one of the methods of choice amongst English as a Foreign Language (EFL) educators around the world. This method requires learners to read a large volume of easily comprehensible text, and teachers to track and manage their students' progress in some manner. There are several different ways to monitor and assess student compliance with, and participation in an ER program, and this paper highlights the features and benefits of the world's only purpose-built Learning Management System (LMS) and integrated digital library designed specifically for ER students and practitioners. Participants (n=146) in the ER program for which the LMS is employed are first- and second-year Japanese university students majoring in English literature or linguistics. This ER program currently requires all participants to read a minimum of 540,000 words over the two years. An efficient method of managing this somewhat challenging requirement is provided by the LMS described in the following article.

Keywords: extensive reading, LMS, EFL.

1. Introduction

ER has, in recent years, garnered the increasing interest and attention of language educators worldwide (Yamashita, 2015). Japan, particularly, has seen a proliferation of ER programs at the tertiary level, and in recent years even the secondary school level. The benefits of ER, including overall second language acquisition, expanded vocabulary, increased reading speed, and elevated scores on achievement tests such as the Test Of English for International Communication (TOEIC) have been well documented (Nishizawa, Yoshioka, & Fukada, 2010).

---

1. Miyagi Gakuin Women's University, Sendai, Japan; corykoby@gmail.com

How to cite this article: Koby, C. J. (2017). Using a learning management system to enhance an extensive reading program. In K. Borthwick, L. Bradley & S. Thouësny (Eds), *CALL in a climate of change: adapting to turbulent global conditions – short papers from EUROCALL 2017* (pp. 189-193). Research-publishing.net. https://doi.org/10.14705/rpnet.2017.eurocall2017.711

As part of a curriculum overhaul in the English Department at Miyagi Gakuin Women's University (MGU) that came into effect in April 2016, ER was assigned a central role in the new program. MGU is a private 4-year liberal arts university in northern Japan, with a total of 3000 students enrolled in a number of undergraduate programs. All first- and second-year students (n=79 and n=67, respectively) in the English Studies Department are required to participate in the ER program. ER performance is typically measured in terms of the number of books, pages, or, most frequently, words that students read in a given period of time. ER reading volume targets or requirements vary widely amongst the many different ER programs available, often depending on the amount of in-class and out-of-class time teachers expect their students to spend reading. Successful completion of the ER program at MGU is mandatory for graduation, and one weekly class of 90 minutes for the first four 15-week semesters, is allocated as class time for ER. With this in mind, it was decided that somewhat ambitious reading volume targets would be set throughout each of the semesters. Now in its second year, the program currently requires students to read 90,000, 120,000, 150,000, and 180,000 words in semester one through four respectively. To track and manage what will amount to at least 540,000, and for some students certainly exceed 1,000,000 words of reading, it was decided that an LMS would be employed.

Investigation by our program administrator into the availability of suitable LMS options revealed that there were only two ready-made platforms specifically designed for ER program management. The first, *MReader*, is a fee-free platform available to ER practitioners worldwide that includes a bank of short comprehension quizzes for nearly 6,000 books (often referred to as *graded readers*) common to many ER programs. The second (fee-bearing) option, *Xreading*, includes all of the features of *MReader*, which allows students to read from a physical library of graded readers of up to 6,000 different titles, with the additional benefit of a digital library of over 800 graded reader e-books which students can access anywhere, anytime. Because of the large volume of reading students are required to complete in the MGU program, access to books was a key issue for our program administrator, so *Xreading* was selected to best serve our students' needs.

2. Features of Xreading

2.1. Reading achievement of paper books: the tests

Assessing students engaged in ER is a topic of some debate (Brierley, 2009). However, as this particular program is situated in a university context, and credit towards graduation is earned in the ER classes, it was felt that some level of verification beyond student self-reporting, which is common in many ER programs, was essential for our program. With this in mind, it was decided that the short comprehension quizzes provided by *Mreader* would be employed. While not necessarily perfect (Brierley, 2009), with a passing score set at just 50%, these multiple-choice quizzes afford at least some level of validity that the students have, in fact, read the books they are claiming.

Beginning in April of 2016, *Xreading* (Figure 1) incorporated the *Mreader* bank of over 6,000 graded reader quizzes into its platform. Actual quiz data is still situated within the *Mreader* system, and when students search on *Xreading* for available book titles, the data is retrieved from the *Mreader* site. Quiz items vary in their construction, and include multiple choice, true or false, and chronological sequencing of events included in the books. Each quiz contains ten questions, but draws from a pool of up to 25 items, thus each time a quiz is created it varies from the last, therefore reducing the chances of students cheating on the quizzes. Conveniently, these quizzes can be taken on mobile devices as well as desktop computers.

Figure 1.   Screenshot of Xreading teacher's dashboard

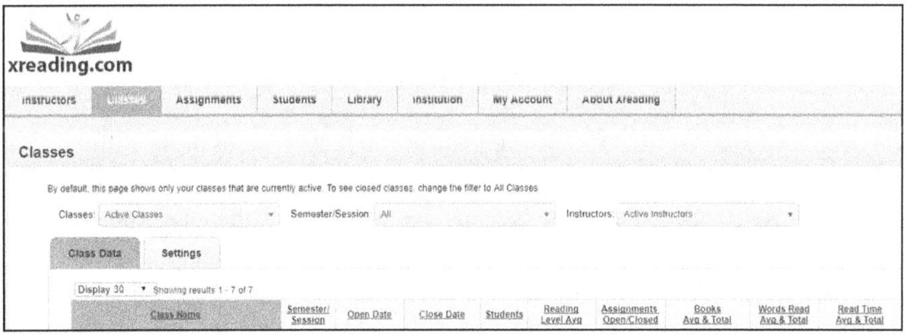

2.2. The digital library

One of the fundamental objectives of this particular ER program is to provide our students with freedom and choice. While we do have over 5,000 printed books in our extensive reading library, the fact that there are only single copies of most of the titles, coupled with the limited time that students have access to the books, were viewed as potential impediments to students' reading. The digital library of over 800 titles provided by *Xreading* solves this problem of access. Students can simultaneously read the same title, and read as many of the e-books as they find interesting.

Instructors have the ability to limit access to the digital library by student, class reading level, genre, or individual title. For the MGU ER program, we have allowed all first-year students access to approximately 250 titles at the lower reading level, while second-year students can access the lower 500 titles in the first semester, and have unrestricted access to the entire collection in semester. This is in keeping with our graduated ER program structure described in detail in Koby (2017).

2.3. Data collection for the administrator

Xreading provides instructors with a wealth of data about their students' reading. Data related to books, student activity, and test scores, are sortable within seconds and readily available and downloadable in .csv format. This data can be used for assessment, analysis, and identifying possible attempts by students to cheat. Same-title books entered by multiple students can be identified in seconds, which can help instructors in managing and reducing potentially dishonest behavior amongst the students. In addition, individual student reading level and volume can be monitored, and lack of participation can be easily identified. Our particular ER program guidelines suggest that students should read regularly (ideally daily), and this activity can be monitored on an instructor's mobile device or computer in seconds.

3. Using Xreading in the ER classroom

Students involved in MGU's ER program use *Xreading* thousands of times each semester. While both first- and second-year students have demonstrated a clear preference for paper books, there is a significant difference that has been observed between the two grades. Of the 9,350 books read in first semester by first-year students, just 1,193 (12.75%) were e-books. However, second-year students read 31.95% of their books in the digital format. While the exact reasons for this shift have yet to be firmly identified, it is clear that the choice of *Xreading* has been beneficial overall to contributing to our students' success.

Results from the first semester of 2017 indicate that overall reading volume met the targets set by the instructors. First-year students, who are required to read a minimum of 90,000 words to pass, read an average of 148,500 words. In comparison, second-year students (who are on an older incarnation of the ER program), were required to read 115,000 words to pass and ended up reading an average of 149,100 words. This would have been much more difficult to monitor and manage without *Xreading* in use.

4. Conclusions

Xreading is a learning management partner that allows ER instructors to administer their ER programs efficiently and effectively. The ER program briefly described in this article relies heavily on the use of the *Xreading* LMS, and it is believed that through the use of *Xreading*, students' motivation and participation were substantially enhanced.

References

Brierley, M. (2009). Assessing extensive reading through written responses and comprehension tests. In E. Skier & T. Newfields (Eds), *Infinite possibilities – expanding limited opportunities in language education: proceedings of the 8th annual JALT Pan-SIG Conference* (pp. 45-53). JALT.

Koby, C. (2017). The anatomy of an extensive reading syllabus. In P. Clements, A. Krause, & H. Brown (Eds), *Transformation in language education*. JALT.

Nishizawa, H., Yoshioka, T., & Fukada, M. (2010). The impact of a 4-year extensive reading program. In A. M. Stoke (Ed.), *JALT2009 Conference Proceedings* (pp. 632-640). JALT.

Yamashita, J. (2015). In search of the nature of extensive reading in L2: cognitive, affective, and pedagogical perspectives. *Reading in a Foreign Language, 27*(1), 168-181.

Exploring meaning negotiation patterns in synchronous audio and video conferencing English classes in China

Chenxi (Cecilia) Li[1], Ligao Wu[2], Chen Li[3], and Jinlan Tang[4]

Abstract. This work-in-progress doctoral research project aims to identify meaning negotiation patterns in synchronous audio and video Computer-Mediated Communication (CMC) environments based on the model of CMC text chat proposed by Smith (2003). The study was conducted in the Institute of Online Education at Beijing Foreign Studies University. Four dyads each performed four information gap tasks through synchronous audio/video CMC environments. Target lexical items were especially 'embedded' in the tasks to elicit negotiated interactions within dyads. The online classes were screen recorded as multimodal data for analysis. Then, participants took a face-to-face, one-to-one video stimulated recall interview to recall their thoughts during the negotiated interactions and to share their attitudes towards Task-Based Language Teaching (TBLT) in synchronous audio/video CMC environments. Negotiated interactions have been transcribed and are being analyzed based on Smith's (2003) model first, but new patterns may be identified from further analysis.

Keywords: meaning negotiation, CMC, synchronous audio and video conferencing, TBLT, China.

---

1. The Open University, Milton Keynes, United Kingdom; cecilia.li@open.ac.uk
2. Beijing Foreign Studies University, Beijing, China; wuligao@beiwaionline.com
3. Beijing Foreign Studies University, Beijing, China; lichen@beiwaionline.com
4. Beijing Foreign Studies University, Beijing, China; tangjinlan@beiwaionline.com

How to cite this article: Li, C., Wu, L., Li, C., & Tang, J. (2017). Exploring meaning negotiation patterns in synchronous audio and video conferencing English classes in China. In K. Borthwick, L. Bradley & S. Thouësny (Eds), *CALL in a climate of change: adapting to turbulent global conditions – short papers from EUROCALL 2017* (pp. 194-199). Research-publishing.net. https://doi.org/10.14705/rpnet.2017.eurocall2017.712

1. Introduction

Varonis and Gass (1985) define meaning negotiation episodes as responses to instances of non-understanding, and propose a model summarizing meaning negotiation patterns between non-native speakers. Their model consists of four steps: T→I→R→RR. A *Trigger* (T), is an utterance that causes non-understanding for the hearer. Then, the hearer signals non-understanding through an *Indicator* (I). A *Response* (R) phase is when the speaker fixes the non-understanding. Finally, the hearer makes a *Reaction to the Response* (RR). Based on Varonis and Gass (1985) and other studies on meaning negotiation patterns, Smith (2003) summarizes the possible subcategories of each stage of a meaning negotiation routine (Table 1), which have been widely used for analyzing meaning negotiation patterns in different CMC contexts.

Table 1. Subcategories of negotiation routine stages

Trigger	Indicator	Response	Reaction to Response
Lexical	Global	Minimal	Minimal
Syntactic	Local	RT + Lexical	Metalinguistic talk
Discourse	Inferential	Rephrase/	Task appropriate response
Content		Elaboration	Testing Deductions

Smith (2003) also expands Varonis and Gass's (1985) model by adding two more possible stages: *Confirmation* (C) and *ReConfirmation* (RC), and listing several possible pathways for a negotiation routine. These stages occur very often in computer-mediated negotiation interaction due to learners' particular demand for explicit acknowledgements of the understanding/non-understanding in CMC text chat environments.

As technology and CALL developed, synchronous audio and video CMC have become widely used for online language teaching. However, oral and visual interactions are very different from written interactions in terms of modality, language use, and participants' emotions and attitudes, all of which may lead to different ways of communicating and of language learning. Therefore, it is necessary to examine how meaning is negotiated in these new online learning environments.

Building on Smith's (2003) model, this study aims to contribute to the development of a more suitable framework for meaning negotiation patterns in synchronous audio/video CMC environments and hopefully gain insights into how languages can be learned through online peer interactions.

2. Method

2.1. Context

This study was conducted in the Institute of Online Education (also called 'BeiwaiOnline') at Beijing Foreign Studies University, a prestigious higher education institution specialized in teaching foreign languages. BeiwaiOnline provides both independent online language courses and qualification courses at undergraduate and postgraduate levels. Students at BeiwaiOnline are usually full time employed adult learners and study online in their spare time to gain a better degree, expand their knowledge, and improve their language ability.

This project was designed by the first author as her doctoral research project. It was provided as a free online speaking course and students' performances were not related to their assessment at the school. The coauthor (Jinlan Tang) organized a team for carrying out the project, while the two other co-authors (Ligao Wu and Chen Li) were responsible for the delivery of this online course. Their role in this study was to give task instructions, facilitate task interactions when needed, and offer post-task feedback to participants.

All eight participants were recruited from BeiwaiOnline and all have at least half a year online language learning experience. They are all female adult learners with proficiency levels of around B2.

Figure 1. BeiwaiOnline video conferencing system

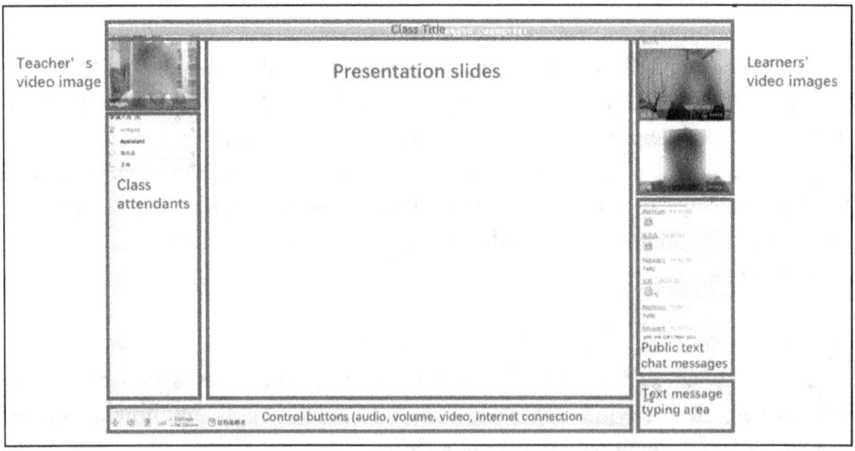

The BeiwaiOnline video conferencing system (Figure 1) consists of presentation slides, online teacher's video image, class attendants' information, students' video images, students' text chat area, and some control buttons. The online teacher has the overall control of the system. He/She can give access to audio/video channels to certain students for verbal or multimodal interactions with online teachers and peers.

2.2. Procedures

The data were collected in three stages (Table 2). The first stage was designed to familiarize participants with their peers and with audio/video peer interaction, and to test their general English proficiency and their knowledge of target lexical items. Then, each dyad performed two types of tasks (spot-the-difference tasks and problem solving tasks) in both audio and video mode respectively. In each dyad, two participants had different task sheets. They were asked to describe the pictures or items in their own task sheet to each other and together work out the differences or make decisions.

Table 2. Research procedures

Stages	Session	Content	Data
Stage 1: Preparation	SCMC Session 1	Introduction, pairing, ice-breaking; pre-task vocabulary test (video only)	Not used for analysis.
	SCMC Session 2	Mock IELTS speaking test; opinion gap tasks (audio & video)	
Stage 2: Main tasks	SCMC Session 3	Spot-the-difference tasks (1 in audio & 1 in video)	8 hours of screen video recordings
	SCMC Session 4	Problem solving tasks (1 in audio & in video)	
Stage 3: Interviews	Face-to-face interview	a) Video stimulated recall interview about negotiated interactions b) Normal interview on students' opinions and background	12 hours of audio recordings

The target lexical items were 'embedded' into the tasks so that students had to negotiate the meaning of these words to complete the tasks. Their performances were recorded as the main data for analyzing meaning negotiation patterns in audio/video Synchronous CMC (SCMC) classrooms. After each task session, the researcher watched the recordings, identified meaning negotiation stances, and prepared related questions for the video stimulated recall interview. The interview aimed to gain more information about students' thoughts during negotiated interactions, their previous language learning experience, and their opinions about peer audio/visual interaction and task-based language learning. The interview was necessary because why students performed the way they did is as, if not more, important than how they performed in negotiated interactions in this environment.

3. Preliminary observations and conclusions

According to interview data, all participants preferred video interactions to audio when there were no technical issues. Although none of them had done video or audio peer interactions in online classes before this project, they had done audio/video chat in daily life through social networking tools, so they were able to fit in with this form of communication quickly. Many students think visual elements including gaze, hand gestures, and body movements (nodding, shaking head) can offer important information in negotiated interactions, from which they were able to tell their peers' (non)understanding. However, two students indicated that even in the video mode, they didn't often look at the screen because they had to completely focus on how to express themselves clearly in English. It seems that video mode was better than audio for them because it offers them the availability to see visual elements from their peers, but whether to use this function is a choice they make consciously, according to specific circumstances. Some students also complained there were more technical issues in video than in audio mode. In summary, for students to negotiate meaning smoothly in SCMC, being able to talk to and hear each other clearly is their priority. Non-verbal elements in video mode can offer them important additional information which can facilitate the meaning negotiation process.

Another finding is that students held contradictory attitudes towards meaning negotiation. While most students were happy and able to negotiate the meaning of new lexical items, some showed strong resistance to it. For example, when one student came across something she did not understand, she began looking it up in an online dictionary even when her peer was actually explaining the meaning of the word to her. During the interview, these students emphasized that they didn't feel embarrassed but they wanted to take responsibility for their own learning. Interestingly, there is no strong correlation between learners' English proficiency and their attitudes towards and their ability in meaning negotiation. Those who were resistant seemed to view English as a subject that needs serious learning, whereas those who were good at meaning negotiation tended to hold the view that English is a tool for communication that can be acquired through oral interactions.

Building on Smith (2003), further analysis will be done to uncover if there are any new meaning negotiation patterns in SCMC audio and video environments, and what the differences are in meaning negotiation patterns between the two modes.

4. Acknowledgements

Chenxi (Cecilia) Li, a Ph.D. student at the Open University, is thankful to the funding from the university, and the guidance from her supervisors: Dr. Tim Lewis, Dr. Uwe Baumann, and Dr. Lijing Shi. We are grateful to the outstanding teachers, staff, and student participants from BeiwaiOnline involved in this project.

References

Smith, B. (2003). Computer–mediated negotiated interaction: an expanded model. *The Modern Language Journal*, *87*(1), 38-57. https://doi.org/10.1111/1540-4781.00177

Varonis, E. M., & Gass, S. (1985). Non-native/non-native conversations: a model for negotiation of meaning. *Applied linguistics*, *6*(1), 71-90. https://doi.org/10.1093/applin/6.1.71

Re-mediating postmillennial posters

Paul A. Lyddon[1] and Jaime Selwood[2]

Abstract. While modern conference papers have evolved almost universally to exploit the potential of digital technologies to enhance the effectiveness of their presentation, academic posters still largely ignore the novel affordances of digital tools and media, rather continuing to operate almost entirely within the constraints of their traditional material format. This paper offers an explanation of this anachronism and suggests a more dynamic vision of poster presentations. First, it distinguishes posters as a unique genre of academic presentation with its own set of communicative purposes. Next, with these purposes in mind, it identifies key considerations in effective poster design. Finally, it offers a practical proposal for leveraging the novel affordances of digital technologies to enrich this design, such as by integrating rollover text, audio, and video links into posters that can be downloaded through QR codes to permit local user control.

Keywords: poster presentations, genre, multimodal communication, user autonomy.

1. Introduction

The proliferation of multimedia technologies in the Digital Age has produced profound changes in the ways people present and process information, in academia as elsewhere. In most scholarly fields today, conference presenters are expected to complement their oral message with some sort of visual support, at a minimum. However, whereas oral presentations have now evolved to incorporate such digital resources as slideshows with audio-visual elements and hyperlinks, poster presentations, with rare exception, tend to rely mainly on the paper or cloth medium on which they are printed. While technology should never be implemented merely for its own sake, here we wish to examine this discrepancy and suggest a

---

1. Osaka Jogakuin College, Osaka, Japan; lyddon@wilmina.ac.jp
2. Hiroshima University, Hiroshima, Japan; jselwood@hiroshima-u.ac.jp

How to cite this article: Lyddon, P. A., & Selwood, J. (2017). Re-mediating postmillennial posters. In K. Borthwick, L. Bradley & S. Thouësny (Eds), *CALL in a climate of change: adapting to turbulent global conditions – short papers from EUROCALL 2017* (pp. 200-204). Research-publishing.net. https://doi.org/10.14705/rpnet.2017.eurocall2017.713

re-mediation of posters to capitalize on some of the digital resources that would render them more effective.

2. Background

Given the limited number of time slots and meeting rooms at most conferences, vetting for paper acceptance is often highly competitive, and otherwise worthy papers, regrettably, cannot always be included in the program. To mitigate this unfortunate situation, conference organizers generally prioritize large-scale, completed research projects, which are expected to have wider appeal than other efforts, such as pilot studies or works-in-progress. They also expand opportunities for conference participation through the option of logistically less demanding poster presentations.

While calls for papers are gradually changing, poster invitations have traditionally been offered to paper proposals that were rejected for oral presentations. As such, posters have a reputation as being lower in prestige, their acceptance being seen as a consolation prize for a second-rate paper (MacIntosh-Murray, 2007). Sadly, many posters inadvertently reinforce this notion by merely condensing and reformatting what was originally conceived as a formal talk. However, posters are not simply short papers, and to view them as such would be analogous to a magazine editor asking a short story author to resubmit his or her contribution as a poem so as to take up less space and require less reading time. In short, posters constitute their own genre of academic presentation and need to be treated as such.

Swales (1990) defines 'genre' as "a class of communicative events, the members of which share some set of communicative purposes" (p. 58). Moreover, he notes that it is recognition of these distinct purposes that informs the conventions that define them, not the reverse, although the latter still influence the former. In other words, the mode and medium of expression should be appropriate to the intended communicative purpose, in what Kress (2010) has come to call "aptness" (p. 156).

Although electronic posters have existed in some form since the turn of the century (e.g. De Simone et al., 2001) and their evolution continues to this day (D'Angelo, 2012), at present they generally entail displaying a document on a large LCD screen, sometimes with the option of giving a short introductory speech and the possibility of changing the projected image in the same manner as slides. In short, it appears that these e-posters are trying ever harder to imitate formal talks, whereas it is our contention that posters will never truly rise from their second-class status so long as they do not come to terms with their identity as a genre of their own.

So what exactly are the communicative purposes of posters? And how can digital technologies best be used to advance them?

3. Discussion

Whereas oral presentations may be characterized as one-to-many, largely top-down communications with interaction mostly limited to a brief question-and-answer session at the end, poster presentations may rather be seen as one-to-few, bottom-up encounters initiated by an audience that is drawn to a physical artifact. As such, posters must take into consideration the attractiveness of their visual design in order to compete for visitor attention in a way that oral presentations do not. As posters are limited in shape, size, and orientation, however, they must also employ their semiotic resources judiciously so as not to sacrifice content for form.

Another important consideration for posters is the nature of the intended interaction. Unlike oral presentations, which control the flow of information in a linear fashion, posters display their entire content at once, thus risking redundancy on the part of the presenter. As most posters are indeed the products of either pilot studies or works-in-progress, the presenter should ideally seek to engage the audience not for the purpose of making broad knowledge claims but rather soliciting comments and questions from interested peers. As such, although the poster design should be logical, it should also allow the viewer to peruse its contents independently at his or her own pace in any order, much like a restaurant menu.

A final consideration is that poster presentations do not involve captive audiences. Though the number and depth of interactions between presenters and their audience may be more substantial with posters than with oral presentations, poster visitors should be free to come and go as they please and not feel pressured to stay for a certain length of time as they do during a formal talk. In short, the poster should be designed not only to elicit engagement but to naturally sustain it as well.

Taking these three main considerations into account, below is a proposal for how electronic poster sessions might evolve to make full use of current digital technologies.

First, digital posters should be created as webpages rather than as conventional electronic documents (e.g. PDFs) to be printed and hung or displayed on a monitor. This would allow visitors to view them on the device of their choice. As to the question of how to keep the presentation focused when the viewer can potentially link deeper and deeper into the web page, our suggested solution is to use an in-image interaction tool, such as ThingLink, which allows users to link text, audio, and video as rollovers on a fixed background. In short, these links can essentially be viewed without navigating away from the homepage. In fact, Rowe and Ilic (2009) came up with a similar idea, namely incorporating interactive elements into a static image. However, they were constrained to the use of a single laptop, thus limiting local control to only one user at a time.

Next, we suggest that QR codes should be included in conference programs along with the presentation titles and abstracts. In this way, conference participants can scan the codes and preview the posters to help them decide which ones to visit. Moreover, with the poster contents now resident on their devices, participants can truly navigate the material at their own pace in their own manner. Depending on the software, visitors might even be given permission to clone these posters so as to make modifications and, thus, personalize the content. As such permission generally requires a code from the poster creator, it also provides an additional incentive for personal interaction.

Finally, actual paper or cloth posters would still need to be made. However, their function would shift more toward helping pre-interested parties locate the presenters and to attracting incidental visitors.

4. Conclusion

Though conference paper presentations have successfully managed to take advantage of new digital technologies, academic posters seem comparatively stifled in their development. A major hindrance has been a pervasive view of them as second-rate papers, which has resulted in a failure to acknowledge them as a unique genre of academic presentation with their own communicative purposes. To raise the professional profile of posters, we need to become explicitly aware of these distinct purposes and take them into account in our poster design. Only then can we truly begin to take advantage of the novel affordances of the Digital Age.

In short:

> A poster is more
>
> Than a slideshow on paper.
>
> Let's keep this in mind.

References

D'Angelo, L. (2012). From posters to e-posters: the evolution of a genre. In L. J. O'Brien & D. S. Giannoni (Eds), *University of reading language studies working papers, vol. 4* (pp. 46-54).

De Simone, R., Rodrian, J., Osswald, B., Sack, F.-U., De Simone, E., & Hagl, S. (2001). Initial experience with a new communication tool: the 'digital interactive poster presentation' [Letter to the editor]. *European Journal of Cardio-thoracic Surgery, 19*, 953-955. https://doi.org/10.1016/S1010-7940(01)00694-7

Kress, G. (2010). *Multimodality: a social semiotic approach to contemporary communication*. Routledge.

MacIntosh-Murray, A. (2007). Poster presentations as a genre in knowledge communication: a case study of forms, norms, and values. *Science Communication, 28*, 247-376. https://doi.org/10.1177/1075547006298251

Rowe, N., & Ilic, D. (2009). What impact do posters have on academic knowledge transfer? A pilot survey on author attitudes and experiences. *BMC Medical Education, 9*(71). https://doi.org/10.1186/1472-6920-9-71

Swales, J. M. (1990). *Genre analysis: English in academic and research settings*. Cambridge University Press.

Designing and developing a blended course: toward best practices for Japanese learners

Parisa Mehran[1], Mehrasa Alizadeh[2], Ichiro Koguchi[3], and Haruo Takemura[4]

Abstract. This paper outlines the iterative stages involved in designing and developing a blended course of English for General Academic Purposes (EGAP) at Osaka University. First, the basic Successive Approximation Model (SAM 1) is introduced as the guiding instructional design model upon which the course was created. Afterward, the stages of design and development of the blended course are explained with a focus upon assessing Japanese students' English language needs and their e-learning readiness. Additional points discussed include the way in which the iteration process has allowed for the discovery of some opportunities and problems at the early phases of the blended course design and development, and the refinements that were made to enhance opportunities and to mitigate the difficulties.

Keywords: blended course design and development, successive approximation model, quality assurance.

1. Introduction

In response to the government's drive to increase the use of technology in education, such as 'i-Japan Strategy 2015', and as a commitment to meeting the 21st century needs of students, such as flexibility and autonomy, an increasing number of Japanese universities have gained pace in adopting online and blended learning in recent years. With regard to English Language Teaching (ELT), a range of online English courses, from fully online to blended, have been recently offered at higher education institutions in Japan. As distance learning grows in popularity,

---

1. Osaka University, Osaka, Japan; mehran.parisa@lab.ime.cmc.osaka-u.ac.jp
2. Osaka University, Osaka, Japan; alizadeh.mehrasa@lab.ime.cmc.osaka-u.ac.jp
3. Osaka University, Osaka, Japan; ikoguchi@lang.osaka-u.ac.jp
4. Osaka University, Osaka, Japan; takemura@cmc.osaka-u.ac.jp

How to cite this article: Mehran, P., Alizadeh, M., Koguchi, I., & Takemura, H. (2017). Designing and developing a blended course: toward best practices for Japanese learners. In K. Borthwick, L. Bradley & S. Thouësny (Eds), *CALL in a climate of change: adapting to turbulent global conditions – short papers from EUROCALL 2017* (pp. 205-210). Research-publishing.net. https://doi.org/10.14705/rpnet.2017.eurocall2017.714

quality assurance becomes more paramount. In order to offer successful online/blended courses, it is necessary to know how to ensure the quality of the course through careful planning and ongoing evaluation in the process of online/blended learning design and development. Following SAM 1, the purpose of this paper is thus to outline the iterative stages involved in designing and developing a blended course for Japanese learners of English and to serve as a practical model for future online instructional designers.

2. Osaka University Global English Online (OUGEO)

Under the project title of OUGEO, a blended course of EGAP was designed and developed at Osaka University targeting second-year undergraduate students from the Faculties of Law, Economics, and Letters for a period of 15 weeks, during which ten sessions were purely online and five were face-to-face.

3. SAM 1

SAM 1, proposed by Allen (2012), was selected as the guiding instructional design model upon which the course was created. The first reason we opted for this model was that it is an improvement over earlier models of instructional design, such as the ADDIE model (Branson et al., 1975). The latter consists of five discrete stages of Analysis, Design, Development, Implementation, and Evaluation sequenced in a linear fashion and described as a waterfall approach (Allen, 2012), whereas SAM 1 not only allows for, but also necessitates, iteration. In addition, it is a more appropriate choice for smaller projects where an individual or a small team are involved in the process of instructional design. Figure 1 depicts the basic iterative process in SAM 1.

Figure 1. SAM 1

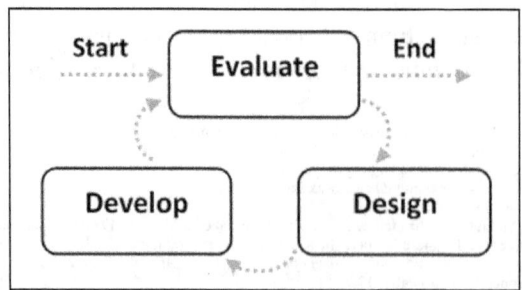

4. Designing and developing OUGEO using SAM 1

In the following, the agile process of designing and developing OUGEO based on SAM 1 is described. It is worth emphasizing that the design and development process was iterative, and frequent course corrections and modifications were conducted on the basis of ongoing evaluation.

4.1. Start

The first step in this process was to conduct a meticulous review of standard checklists for online course design and development. One useful resource was the checklist provided by Vai and Sosulski (2011, pp. 189-195), which is a reader-friendly guide on the basics of online course design and includes a detailed list of criteria to consider when designing and developing an online course. The second major resource used was the Higher Ed Course Design Rubric developed by Quality Matters, which can be used for the design of fully online and blended courses. We also created a Google Site for OUGEO (https://sites.google.com/view/ougeo) where we could document everything and keep track of all the procedures involved in course design and development.

4.2. Evaluate

At this stage, we carried out a detailed analysis of the situation by identifying the prospective learners, their overall language skills, their difficulties, needs and wants, as well as their level of computer literacy and e-learning readiness. In order to delve into learner needs, wants, and difficulties, we conducted a language needs analysis study with a sample of 278 Japanese undergraduate students and with 12 English instructors (Alizadeh, Mehran, Koguchi, & Takemura, 2017). The results of this survey study indicated that Japanese learners struggled the most with English pronunciation, listening, and speaking; thus, the aforementioned skills need to be further emphasized in the OUGEO course. Furthermore, some students wished to improve their conversational English whereas others aimed at developing their academic English skills. Consequently, the initial hypothesis that the course had to be offered at more than one level was confirmed. Therefore, we set out to offer the course at three levels (from B1 up to C1, according to Common European Framework of Reference for languages (CEFR) to accommodate varying proficiency levels.

In another attempt to evaluate the e-learning readiness of the target group of learners, an e-readiness assessment study was conducted where the participants were asked to self-report their skills in performing basic to advanced user tasks when using computers and mobile devices (Mehran, Alizadeh, Koguchi, & Takemura, 2017). The findings of this study showed that some students needed training with certain aspects of technology use. Therefore, we decided to create tutorials which would help the less tech-savvy students with fulfilling the technological requirements of the course.

4.3. Design

Based on the results of the initial evaluation and with consideration of Japan's current efforts at globalization, the course's overall goals, learning objectives, and learning outcomes were determined, and a multidimensional syllabus, i.e. an amalgamation of skill-based syllabus and task-based syllabus (available at https://sites.google.com/view/ougeo/syllabus), was designed with the aim of increasing motivation and global awareness among Japanese learners of English.

For materials development, copyright issues had to first be addressed. Hence, through educational portals such as MERLOT, Open Educational Resources (OERs) for ELT were found, and a number of them were selected (e.g. http://elllo.org for listening and English Kickstart for pronunciation). Permission was taken from the owner of Breaking News English (http://www.breakingnewsenglish.com/) to use reading lessons from the website.

Other resources (e.g. TED Talks) were cited appropriately and linked back to their websites. The course calendar for all the online and face-to-face sessions (available at https://sites.google.com/view/ougeo/course-calendar) was then written in detail, and afterwards course tasks, activities, quizzes, tutorials, and rubrics for writing and speaking assignments were prepared.

It is worth mentioning that the speaking and writing tasks were designed to foster global understanding, critical thinking, collaboration, communication, and creativity by the use of online affordances, and the term project (i.e. poster presentation, delivered face-to-face) was defined as a group activity through which the students could broaden their global perspectives as well as their digital literacy by exploring augmented reality technology.

4.4. Develop

At the development stage, the sketches created at the design phase were prototyped. Several e-learning content authoring tools (e.g. Adobe Captivate) were used to digitize the instructional materials, and a sample week was demoed at a Faculty Development (FD) seminar at the English Department of Osaka University. Meanwhile, the stage for online course delivery was set by uploading the course content on Collaboration and Learning Environment (CLE), the commercial learning management system Blackboard to which Osaka University has subscribed since 2005 (see Figure 2). The test delivery was also done to check the quality of the content on Blackboard mobile applications (Blackboard Mobile Learn™ and Bb Student).

Figure 2. A screenshot of OUGEO on CLE

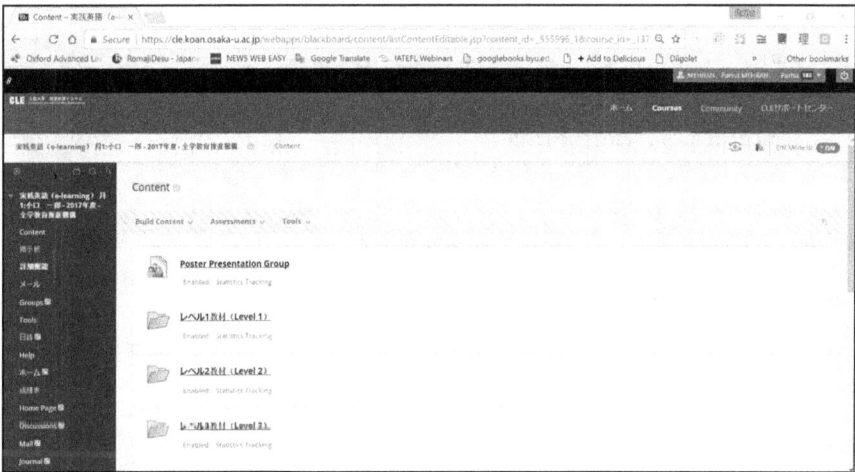

This stage involved iterative review cycles to evaluate, refine, and modify the previous process. For instance, course labeling decisions were changed from 'week by week' to 'level by level'. Due to incompatibility, it was decided to upload the instructional materials on CLE without digitizing them via e-authoring tools. Based on the feedback from the FD seminar demonstration, some modifications were also made to the course learning objectives and the related materials and tasks by adding global issues.

4.5. End

After prototyping and applying the changes, OUGEO was implemented in the spring semester of 2017 (April–July). The iterative evaluation continued, and some minor modifications were applied during the implementation phase, such as adding Japanese translations to the course instructions.

5. Conclusion

As a pioneering attempt at the in-house design and development of a blended course of EGAP at Osaka University, adopting SAM 1 as our instructional design model aided us in smoothly moving along the iterative cycle of evaluation, design, and development while leaving room throughout the entire process for the consideration of context-relevant factors and the characteristics particular to Japanese learners of English.

References

Alizadeh, M., Mehran, P., Koguchi, I., & Takemura, H. (2017). *Language needs analysis and internationalization of higher education: the unaddressed factor in Japan.* Unpublished manuscript submitted for publication.

Allen, M. (2012). *Leaving ADDIE for SAM: an agile model for developing the best learning experiences.* ASTD Press.

Branson, R. K., Rayner, G. T., Cox, J. L., Furman, J. P., King, F. J., & Hannum, W. H. (1975). *Interservice procedures for instructional systems development* (5 vols). U.S. Army Training and Doctrine Command.

Mehran, P., Alizadeh, M., Koguchi, I., & Takemura, H. (2017). Are Japanese digital natives ready for learning English online? A preliminary case study at Osaka University. *International Journal of Educational Technology in Higher Education, 14*(8), 1-17. https://doi.org/10.1186/s41239-017-0047-0

Vai, M., & Sosulski, K. (2011). *Essentials of online course design: a standards-based guide.* Routledge.

Listening difficulty detection to foster second language listening with a partial and synchronized caption system

Maryam Sadat Mirzaei[1], Kourosh Meshgi[2], and Tatsuya Kawahara[3]

Abstract. This study proposes a method to detect problematic speech segments automatically for second language (L2) listeners, considering both lexical and acoustic aspects. It introduces a tool, Partial and Synchronized Caption (PSC), which provides assistance for language learners and fosters L2 listening skills. PSC presents purposively selected words along with a video in the form of synchronized text-to-speech captions. It uses corpus-based information and conducts speech-data analysis to detect difficulties in speech, thus achieving effective word selection. To this end, PSC uses an Automatic Speech Recognition (ASR) system as a model for L2 listeners to elucidate speech difficulties for these learners. In this method, misrecognized words by the ASR system are analyzed to find useful patterns that could signal problematic speech segments for L2 listeners. The identified patterns were evaluated by experiments to ensure that they cause difficulties for L2 listeners in the same way that they impede ASR performance. Experimental findings confirm that adding these instances to PSC significantly improves learners' recognition of the respective segments.

Keywords: L2 listening, partial and synchronized caption, automatic speech recognition, error analysis.

1. Introduction

L2 listening is a transient process which entails sophisticated skills to recognize speech and achieve comprehension (Rost, 2013). While L2 listeners need to process

---

1. Kyoto University, Kyoto, Japan; maryam@sap.ist.i.kyoto-u.ac.jp
2. Kyoto University, Kyoto, Japan; meshgi-k@sys.i.kyoto-u.ac.jp
3. Kyoto University, Kyoto, Japan; kawahara@i.kyoto-u.ac.jp

How to cite this article: Mirzaei, M. S., Meshgi, K., & Kawahara, T. (2017). Listening difficulty detection to foster second language listening with a partial and synchronized caption system. In K. Borthwick, L. Bradley & S. Thouësny (Eds), *CALL in a climate of change: adapting to turbulent global conditions – short papers from EUROCALL 2017* (pp. 211-216). Research-publishing.net. https://doi.org/10.14705/rpnet.2017.eurocall2017.715

input attentively and utilize skills adeptly to gain adequate comprehension, some factors associated with the speech input itself can impede their listening (Bloomfield et al., 2010). The lexical units used in speech and the ambiguities involved in articulation, such as uncertain word boundaries, can lead to difficulties for many learners (Field, 2008). Despite many studies focusing on L2 listening difficulties, analyzing the nature of speech and identifying problematic speech segments for individual L2 listeners has not been systematically investigated. This highlights the need for a tool that can predict speech-related difficulties for language learners and provide a learner-specific scaffold to assist in learner comprehension. This paper describes an attempt to achieve this goal by using ASR errors as a source of information to indicate difficult speech segments for L2 listeners.

ASR systems process speech signals to generate a transcript of an audio track. This process often involves some errors, which are often (but not always) the product of intrinsic speech difficulties (Meyer, Brand, & Kollmeier, 2011). Through a comparison between ASR errors and L2 speech recognition mistakes, we found specific patterns of ASR errors such as homophones, minimal pairs, negative cases, and breached boundaries. These kinds of errors cause similar problems in comprehension for both for ASR and L2 learners (Mirzaei, Meshgi, & Kawahara, 2016). The study described here focuses on the automatic detection of such ASR error patterns and how they can be embedded in PSC to provide better assistance to language learners.

Figure 1. Screenshot of a TED talk with PSC (Original sentence: "Orion facing the roaring bull")

PSC anticipates learners' listening difficulties when using authentic materials by detecting difficult-to-recognize words/phrases and presenting them in the caption to provide assistance to the learner (Figure 1). To this end, it draws on features that impede L2 listening comprehension, based on L2 studies of areas of difficulty. The baseline PSC system is based on a heuristic approach, mainly using lexical features that influence L2 listening, such as word frequency and specificity (Webb, 2010). The only speech-related factor used in the baseline system is the speech rate; it overlooks other patterns. We regard ASR errors as a source to provide other useful cases for PSC. Moreover, as the system strives to serve individual learners, it adjusts word selection to the proficiency levels of the learners. However, for PSC to be more effective, its parameters need to be better tuned.

2. Method

Using TED talks as the material for PSC, we employed an ASR system to generate a transcript and make word-level synchronization. Next, we compared it with the human-annotated transcript, provided by TED, to detect the mismatches (ASR errors). These errors were further analyzed to extract useful instances for speech difficulties. Meanwhile, lexical features were assessed to unveil useful words/phrases for L2 listeners. Based on the outcome of this process, coupled with the assessment of the learners' proficiency levels, the system can automatically decide on the words/phrases that impede listening. To prioritize the most useful instances, we enhanced the baseline system selection by using the ASR error clues.

2.1. Automatic detection of useful ASR errors

We mark a word as (1) a homophone (e.g. "rain" /R EY N/ and "reign" /R EY N/) if the Levenshtein distance between the phonetic sequences of the ASR erroneous phrase and its corresponding transcript is zero, and (2) a minimal pair (e.g. "pin" /P IH N/ and "bin" /B IH N/) if the distance is one. Negative cases are detected by considering the negative particle "not", plus prefixes and suffixes that form negation (e.g. "legal" and "illegal"). To detect breached boundaries, we checked for the following patterns based on L2 studies (Cutler, 2005; Field, 2008):

- Strong-syllable strategy: learners tend to insert word boundaries when they encounter a strong syllable and set it as the beginning of the word (e.g. "disguise" heard as "the skies"). In addition, learners tend to delete the boundary before a weak syllable and thus merge the words (e.g. "ten-to-two" heard as "twenty to").

- Assimilation rule: learners have difficulty in setting the right word boundaries due to the common phonological process which alters a word ending sound in expectation of the following sound (e.g. "right you are" as "rye chew are").

- Frequency rule: learners have a general tendency to insert word boundaries to perceive more frequent words than the actual word (e.g. "achieve her" heard as "a cheaper").

- Resyllabification: resyllabification happens when the final consonant of a word attaches to the following syllable (e.g. "made out" heard as "may doubt").

2.2. Enhancing PSC using ASR clues

The baseline PSC system is enhanced not only by embedding the detected cases, but also by improving the word selection through refining the system thresholds (Figure 2). If the learner prefers to receive more words, we may simply add ASR erroneous cases to the baseline system to provide more choices that relate to speech difficulty. However, if the learner prefers minimal, but targeted assistance, the system trims the number of cases by refining the thresholds based on ASR erroneous cases. Therefore, if ASR has difficulty in recognizing a word, the system prioritizes that word to those deemed difficult by the baseline.

Figure 2. Enhanced PSC using ASR clues

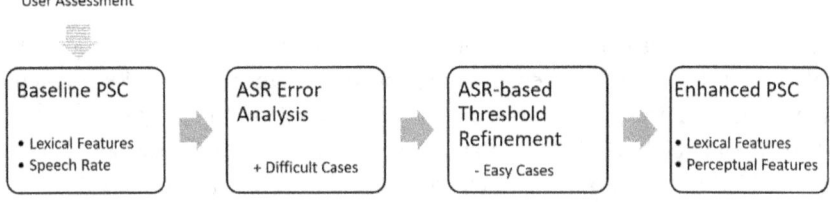

3. Experimental evaluations

Enhanced PSC was compared with the no-caption as well as baseline PSC in experiments with L2 learners of English. In the first experiment (enhanced PSC vs. no-caption), 18 learners of English with TOEIC scores above 750 listened to TED talks of about three minutes long, either with enhanced PSC or without captions. After each video, the participants were asked to answer the comprehension questions and the listening cloze tests that followed (videos were rotated among participants). Figure 3 Left, shows the participants' scores on no-caption versus enhanced PSC condition. As the figure demonstrates, learners' scores were significantly higher when they received enhanced PSC as opposed to no captions ($p<.001$).

In the second experiment, 38 intermediate-level learners were divided into two groups and watched a series of short video segments either with baseline PSC or with enhanced PSC, followed by several paraphrasing questions. The numbers of shown words to both groups were controlled to be the same, while the choices of words in the baseline and enhanced versions were different. The results are shown in Figure 3 Right, which suggests using the enhanced version led to a significant increase in participants' paraphrasing scores.

Figure 3. Experimental results of enhanced PSC

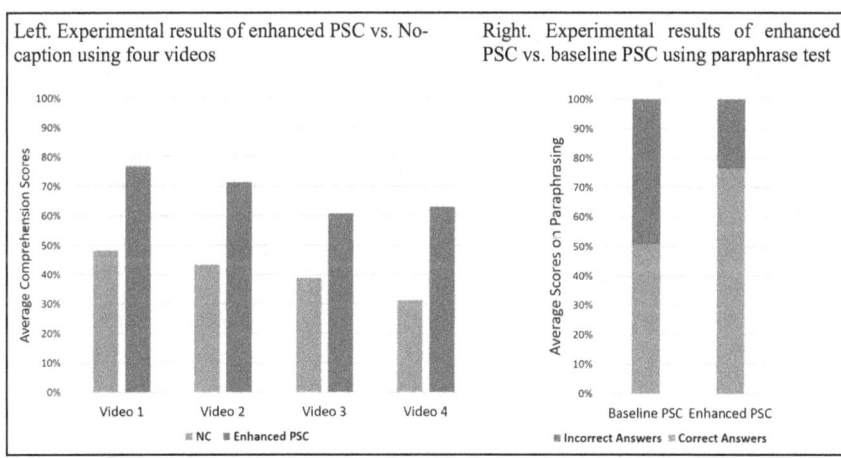

4. Conclusions

In this study, we focused on the detection of speech-related difficulties for L2 learners and proposed the use of ASR errors as indicators of such difficulties. Compared with other studies, which consider ASR errors as a drawback of these systems, in this study we tried to make use of these errors and considered them as indicators of speech difficulties. To this end, useful cases of ASR errors for L2 listeners are automatically detected and embedded into the PSC system to provide better assistance. Moreover, we prioritized PSC choices based on the ASR clues. Experimental results showed increased recognition with the use of enhanced PSC over no captions or the baseline. However, more experiments are needed to reflect PSC's learner-specific adjustments for varying levels of language proficiency. PSC aims to promote learner autonomy in developing L2 listening skills by allowing learners to adjust the number of shown words through the course of study and to customize the system's features based on their preference. This method can be used easily for an ample number of listening materials to provide learners with an adjustable amount of scaffolding and allow teachers to recognize learners' listening difficulties.

References

Bloomfield, A., Wayland, S. C., Rhoades, E., Blodgett, A., Linck, J., & Ross, S. (2010). *What makes listening difficult? Factors affecting second language listening comprehension.* University of Maryland. https://doi.org/10.21236/ADA550176

Cutler, A. (2005). The lexical statistics of word recognition problems caused by L2 phonetic confusion. *Interspeech Lisboa 2005: 9th European Conference on Speech Communication and Technology, September 4-8*, 413-416. Causal Productions.

Field, J. (2008). Bricks or mortar: which parts of the input does a second language listener rely on? *TESOL quarterly, 42*(3), 411-432. https://doi.org/10.1002/j.1545-7249.2008.tb00139.x

Meyer, B. T., Brand, T., & Kollmeier, B. (2011). Effect of speech-intrinsic variations on human and automatic recognition of spoken phonemes. *The Journal of the Acoustical Society of America, 129*(1), 388-403. https://doi.org/10.1121/1.3514525

Mirzaei, M. S., Meshgi, K., & Kawahara, T. (2016). Leveraging automatic speech recognition errors to detect challenging speech segments in TED talks. In S. Papadima-Sophocleous, L. Bradley & S. Thouësny (Eds), *CALL communities and culture – short papers from EUROCALL 2016* (pp. 313-318). Research-publishing.net. https://doi.org/10.14705/rpnet.2016.eurocall2016.581

Rost, M. (2013). *Teaching and researching: listening* (2nd ed.). Routledge.

Webb, S. (2010). Using glossaries to increase the lexical coverage of television programs. *Reading in a Foreign Language, 22*(1), 201-221.

Can you understand me?
Speaking robots and accented speech

Souheila Moussalli[1] and Walcir Cardoso[2]

Abstract. The results of our previous research on the pedagogical use of Speaking Robots (SRs) revealed positive effects on motivating students to practice their oral skills in a stress-free environment. However, our findings indicated that the SR was sometimes unable to understand students' foreign accented speech. In this paper, we report the results of a study that investigated the ability of an SR to recognize and process non-native English speech from different levels of accentedness. The analysis is based on how the SR handled the participants' speech in terms of accuracy, the number and types of communication breakdowns observed, and how the participants behaved to solve the interaction problems that they experienced with the SR. Based on the study's surveys, interviews, and observations of users' interactions with the device, the results emphasize SRs' potential to recognize different types of accented L2 speech and their use as pedagogical tools.

Keywords: personal assistants, speaking robots, L2 accented speech.

1. Introduction

In the past few years, our reliance on voice commands in our daily interactions (e.g. voice-activated searches on smartphones) has increased dramatically. Despite this trend, the recognition accuracy of accented speech remains problematic for certain accents (Moussalli & Cardoso, 2016). Moussalli and Cardoso's (2016) study investigated learners' perceptions of the pedagogical use of a speaking robot (Amazon Echo and its associated app, Alexa) as cylinder speaker that provides oral answers to any questions asked. The results showed that the SR can extend the reach of the classroom, promote self-learning, and motivate oral practice in a stress-free environment. The results also showed that Echo offered helpful

---

1. Concordia University, Montreal, Canada; souheilamoussally@hotmail.com
2. Concordia University, Montreal, Canada; walcir.cardoso@concordia.ca

How to cite this article: Moussalli, S., & Cardoso, W. (2017). Can you understand me? Speaking robots and accented speech. In K. Borthwick, L. Bradley & S. Thouësny (Eds), *CALL in a climate of change: adapting to turbulent global conditions – short papers from EUROCALL 2017* (pp. 217-221). Research-publishing.net. https://doi.org/10.14705/rpnet.2017.eurocall2017.716

negative feedback and, more importantly, its use was perceived as an effective and efficient L2 learning tool. However, the results suggested that heavily-accented beginner learners experienced difficulties understanding and being understood by Echo, as has been observed in studies involving speech recognition (Coniam, 1999; Derwing, Munro, & Carbonaro, 2000).

Interestingly, human-to-human interactions involving speakers with accented L2 speech reveals that, in this context, effective and efficient communication is possible and is not always hampered by accented speech (Derwing & Munro, 2009). Following Derwing and Munro (2009), we define accented speech as "the way in which speech differs from the local variety of [that speech] and the impact of that difference on speakers and listeners" (p. 476). The concept of accentedness includes two sub-components: intelligibility (how much a listener can understand an utterance) and comprehensibility (the listener's perception of the degree of difficulty in understanding the interlocutor). To address this discrepancy between human-human and human-SR interactions with L2-accented speech and to address one of the limitations of SR use reported above, this study aims to answer the following research questions:

- How much can Echo understand the L2-accented speech of English learners?

- How do Echo and raters (English as a second language teachers) compare in their ability to understand L2-accented speech?

- When Echo-human communication fails, what strategies do learners use to resolve it (types and numbers of Communication Breakdowns (CBs) and resolutions)?

2. Method

2.1. Participants and design

Eleven L2-accented participants (five males, six females; ages: 19-30) from seven different language backgrounds (French, Cantonese, Mandarin, Arabic, Hindi, Tulu, and Marathi-Gujarati) and proficiency levels (low-intermediate to advanced) interacted with Echo for approximately 30 minutes by asking the SR a pre-established set of requests and other personal questions (total=30). They were also asked to fill out a language background questionnaire, and two surveys using a five-point Likert scale (1=strongly disagree and 5=strongly agree). The first survey consisted of 17 items to quantify their responses regarding several statements about their perceptions regarding their experience using the SR (e.g. 'Echo is able to understand me'). The second included two items for rating Echo's speech globally (to test comprehensibility), and one item that asked participants to transcribe what they heard after asking Echo a question (to test intelligibility). After the surveys, participants engaged in semi-structured interviews where they articulated their experience with the SR.

The judges and transcribers were two native English speakers who were asked to rate 15 randomly selected speech samples that represented different types of interactions from the participants using a five-point Likert scale on accentedness and intelligibility. They were also asked to transcribe participants' speech to determine their intelligibility.

3. Analysis and results

Means and standard deviations were calculated for each survey item. As illustrated in Table 1, contrary to our previous study, participants found that Echo is able to understand them relatively easily (3.55/5) and they can understand it without difficulties (4.18/5). Overall, the results also revealed that participants felt comfortable interacting with Echo (3.36/5), would consider it to learn other languages (4/5), and enjoyed using it (4.45/5).

Table 1. Mean and standard deviation: survey statements

Statements	Mean	SD
Echo can understand me.	3.55	0.934
I can understand Echo.	4.18	0.751
I felt more comfortable speaking English using Echo than I would in other types of classroom activities (e.g. role-playing, group work).	3.36	1.629
I would like to use Echo to learn other languages.	4.00	0.894
Overall, I enjoyed using Echo in this project.	4.45	0.934

CBs were assessed by two native English-speaking judges (inter-rater reliability: Accentedness: ICC=0.588; Comprehensibility: ICC=0.576; Intelligibility – via transcriptions: 84.6% – Cohen's kappa κ=0.567, suggesting a moderate level of reliability). Of the 1000 interactions between Echo and the participants, the number of CBs was 177, which were mainly caused by pronunciation issues (94/177= 53.11%; indicated by *), as summarized in Table 2.

Table 2. Types of communication breakdown

Type	Example	Total/177
*Pronunciation error: segments	How many cups in a liter ([lajtər])?	40
*Hesitations	um... could you... help me with pronouncing b.i.t...s?	37
Incorrect sentence structure	From Montreal and Quebec, what is the distance between?	33
Atypical demand	Can you shout for me?!	28
Phrases not requiring a response	Wow, that's great!	11
Complex questions	I'm thinking what to have for lunch; suggest something which is Mexican cuisine.	11
*Extremely fast speech	N/A	10
*Extremely slow speech	N/A	7

The results of the CB analysis are provided in Table 3. As CBs occurred, participants behaved differently from each other in terms of resolving the interaction problems with Echo, which was indicated via a follow-up question, silence, or an incorrect response. Participants tended to repeat their questions, abandon them altogether, or re-phrase them, as the following exchange illustrates:

> Participant: Alexa, where is located Niagara Falls?
>
> Echo: I can't find the answer to the question I heard.
>
> Participant: Alexa, where is Niagara Falls located?
>
> Echo: Niagara Falls, New York, is a waterfall in ...

Table 3. Communication breakdowns and resolutions

Type of Behavior	Mean	Standard deviation
Repetition	7	5.514
Rephrasing	3.45	3.984
Abandonment	4.91	4.592

Finally, an analysis of the transcribed interviews indicated that participants found Echo convenient to use and it provided speaking and listening language practice: "I think it's great tool because there are [...] so many nationalities not fluent in English, they could just sit and practice"; "it's difficult to have a conversation with a person if your English is weak, you [...] wouldn't feel comfortable. But if you talk with Echo, you can always practice at your own pace". The participants also commented that the SR accommodated and helped them understand where and why their communication failed: "when I was asking the question what she was thinking about, the first time, she didn't understand, […] I think I said everything, but maybe she didn't hear something". However, the results also revealed that participants wanted specific feedback "as I was asking my questions she didn't get what I wanted to say, but I didn't know what she didn't understand".

4. Discussion and conclusions

This study investigated an SR's ability to understand oral English as spoken by accented L2 learners and also be understood by the same speakers, without incurring human-SR communication breakdowns. Our findings indicate that, contrary to what was reported in a previous study on learners' perceptions of the pedagogical use of SRs (Moussalli & Cardoso, 2016), Echo's ability to understand and be understood by L2 learners and vice-versa is relatively unproblematic from both quantitative and qualitative standpoints. Future studies could look at learning gains at the segmental and prosodic levels, as well as the effects of SRs on fluency development. Despite the number of obvious limitations (small sample size, limited time-on-task), we conclude that SRs are ready to be considered for English L2 instruction due to their pedagogical potential, particularly their ability to motivate students to practice their aural listening and speaking skills (including pronunciation) in a stress-free environment.

References

Coniam, D. (1999). Voice recognition software accuracy with second language speakers of English, *System, 27*(1), 49-64. https://doi.org/10.1016/S0346-251X(98)00049-9

Derwing, T. M., & Munro, M. J. (2009). Putting accent in its place: rethinking obstacles to communication. *Language Teaching, 42(*4), 276-490. https://doi.org/10.1017/S026144480800551X

Derwing, T. M., Munro, M. J., & Carbonaro, M. (2000). Does popular speech recognition software work with ESL speech? *TESOL Quarterly, 34*(3), 592-603. https://doi.org/10.2307/3587748

Moussalli, S., & Cardoso, W. (2016). Are commercial 'personal robots' ready for language learning? Focus on second language speech. In S. Papadima-Sophocleous, L. Bradley & S. Thouësny (Eds), *CALL communities and culture – short papers from EUROCALL 2016* (pp. 325–329). Research-publishing.net. https://doi.org/10.14705/rpnet.2016.eurocall2016.583

Improving expressive writing in EFL through blogging

Rana Namouz[1], Hagit Misher-Tal[2], and Orly Sela[3]

Abstract. The purpose of this study was to investigate the effect of integrating blogging into the English as a Foreign Language (EFL) curriculum on students' performance in expressive writing. Previous studies have shown that integrating blogging into EFL learning raises students' motivation and develops their linguistic and social skills as a result of the interaction between the blogger and his/her readers. In the present study, 22 high school Israeli-Arab students were asked to post guided essays to personal blogs and comment on each other's posts. The blogs were analyzed and the students' errors categorized, counted, and recorded over a four-month period. In addition, the students filled out a questionnaire at the end of the study period aimed at understanding their attitudes towards the process and the blogging experience. The results of the study showed a significant improvement in writing quality and a decrease in the amount of student errors. Moreover, the students expressed a positive attitude towards using blogs as a platform for developing writing skills.

Keywords: EFL, expressive writing, linguistic development, blogging.

1. Introduction

Expressive writing in EFL has been emphasized in the last few years, particularly in relation to technological development and information and communications technology. Therefore, EFL students face the challenge of learning expressive writing, especially when the linguistic rules of their mother tongue are different from those of the target language (Ismail, 2011). A number of approaches to teaching writing in EFL have been discussed over the last two decades, with a combination of the process approach and the genre approach being considered the most effective. Both these approaches emphasize writing as a cognitive process

1. Oranim College, Kiryat Tiv'on, Israel; rana.n3456@gmail.com
2. Holon Institute of Technology, Holon, Israel; Hagitmt@hit.ac.il
3. Oranim College, Kiryat Tiv'on, Israel; orlysela@oranim.ac.il

How to cite this article: Namouz, R., Misher-Tal, H., & Sela, O. (2017). Improving expressive writing in EFL through blogging. In K. Borthwick, L. Bradley & S. Thouësny (Eds), *CALL in a climate of change: adapting to turbulent global conditions – short papers from EUROCALL 2017* (pp. 222-228). Research-publishing.net. https://doi.org/10.14705/rpnet.2017.eurocall2017.717

requiring planning, gathering information from different resources, and receiving feedback which enhances self-reflection and revision (Badger & White, 2000; Daskalogiannaki, 2012; Silva, 1990; Tangpermpoon, 2008; Zen, 2005).

Recent research has shown that the integration of social networking into learning has benefits in exposing students to a wide range of information resources and connecting the learner with a large number of learning partners. Research has demonstrated that weblogs positively affect students' writing, raise their motivation to learn, and develop their social skills. Having the possibility of collaborating with others and receiving feedback makes weblogs a suitable tool for elevating the writer's expressive ability. The negotiation of meaning between the writer and his/her audience assists him/her in the process of developing their ideas and improving their writing (Gedera, 2012; Hashemi & Najafi, 2011; Trajtemberg & Yiakoumetti, 2011). Research has also shown that blogging improves EFL skills. Blogging by its nature enhances the expansion of the learners' lexical and grammatical knowledge, since they constantly search for complex structures to express themselves clearly (Hashemi & Najafi, 2011; Yunus et al., 2013).

Based on the ample evidence of the qualities of blogging in promoting the writing process, a research question concerning the practice of blogging was formulated: In what ways does blogging affect the writing skills of EFL high-school learners?

2. Method

Twenty-two high school students from an Arab school in Israel took part in an action research project. The research group studied four weekly English classes as part of the school curriculum, and according to the Israeli Ministry of Education requirements.

In the beginning of the study, each of the participants established a personal blog through https://www.blogger.com. Before receiving each writing task, the participants prepared for it through different in-class activities, such as brainstorming and learning the relevant grammar. The participants were then asked to upload their essays to their personal blogs within two days. Eight writing assignments yielded 178 posts which were collected and analyzed. The analysis included error counting and classification.

In order to comprehend the efficiency of blogging in promoting writing, four main parameters were examined: grammar errors, vocabulary errors, spelling errors, and the general grading each assignment received. A repeated-measures ANOVA test and a post-hoc test were conducted to reveal the significance of differences among the assignments. In addition, a teacher's log was kept, where the in-class and log activities were recorded. Furthermore, a satisfaction questionnaire, using Likert scale questions and one open-ended question, was given to the participants at the end of the study period, in an attempt to support the numerical data and understand the participants' perception of blogging.

3. Results

The results show a significant decrease in the amount of errors of all types detected in the students' posts throughout the research period.

3.1. The number of errors of all types

The study yielded 1557 errors. The results show that the average number of errors of all types dropped from 13.52 errors in the first writing assignment to 5.27 errors in the eighth assignment. The ANOVA test revealed a significant difference between the assignments ($F(2,20)=40.64$, $p<0.001$). Figure 1 illustrates the results of the average number of errors.

Figure 1. The average number of errors

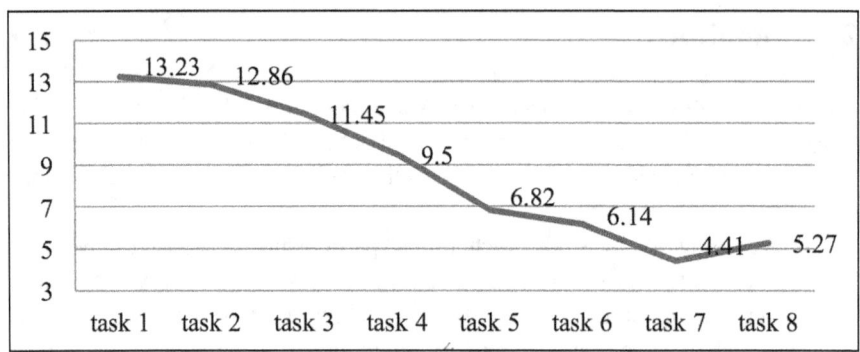

3.2. Grammatical errors

The grammatical errors classification included the following error types: errors of tenses, word order in a sentence, adding/omitting an unnecessary auxiliary, omitting articles, errors in capitalization, adding unnecessary pronouns, run-on sentences/fragment sentences, and wrong use of apostrophes.

The results show that there was a significant decrease in the number of grammatical errors made by the participants throughout the eight assignments, and the ANOVA repeated measures test showed a significant difference between the tasks ($F(2,20)=57.32$, $p<0.001$). Figure 2 exhibits the averages of grammatical errors in each of the eight tasks.

Figure 2. The average number of grammatical errors

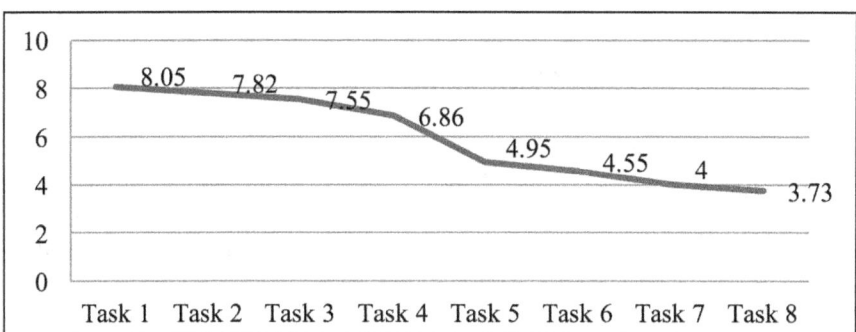

3.3. Vocabulary errors

After counting the vocabulary errors, the results demonstrate a significant decline in the average number of vocabulary errors. The ANOVA repeated measures test showed a significant difference between the tasks ($F(2,20)=4.57$, $p<0.001$). Figure 3 illustrates the decline in the average number of errors.

Figure 3. The average number of vocabulary errors

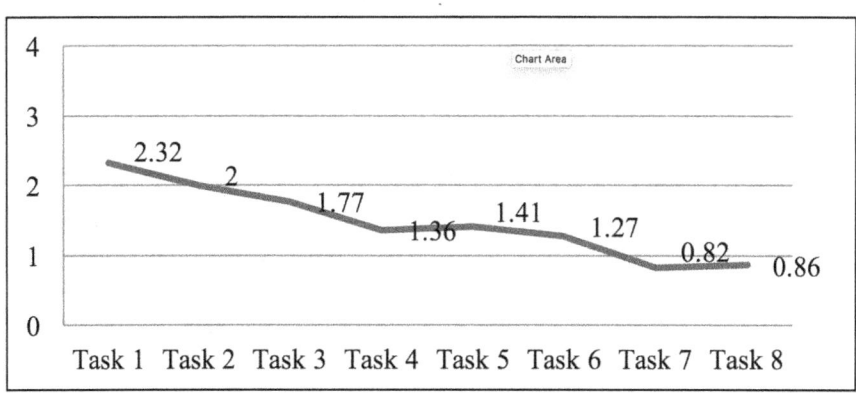

3.4. Spelling errors

The results also revealed a decline in the average number of spelling errors throughout the research period. While the average number of spelling errors in the first task was 2.86 errors, it declined gradually from task to task and an average of 0.68 errors was detected in the last task. The ANOVA repeated measures test also indicated a significant difference between the different tasks ($F(2,20)=7.12$, $p<0.001$).

3.5. The average grading of tasks

The results indicate a 16 point increase in the average grading each task received according to the rubric of the Israeli Ministry of Education for assessing written presentations at this level. The difference between tasks was significant ($F(2,20)=65.03$, $p<0.001$). Figure 4 indicates the increase in the average grading of the tasks.

Figure 4. The average grades of the tasks

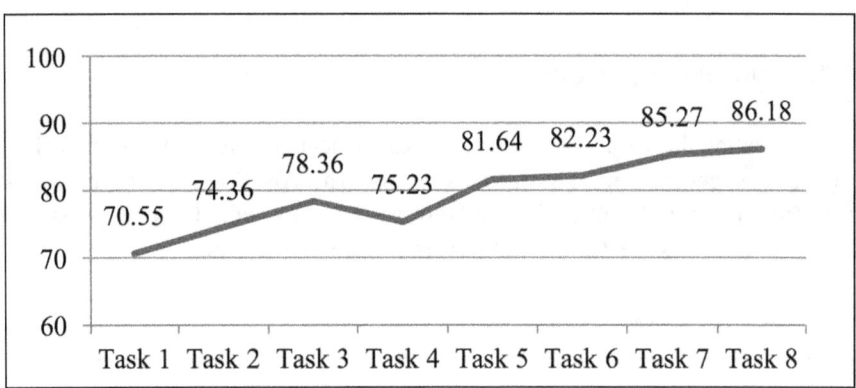

3.6. The questionnaire results

The questionnaire results reveal a positive attitude towards the blogging experience. Most students felt that the integration of blogs improved their expressive writing skills significantly. Most of the participants agreed that the feedback they received from their peers contributed to their development in writing in EFL, as well as elevating their sense of responsibility towards their learning.

4. Discussion and conclusion

The results of the present study have demonstrated the efficiency of blogging in promoting expressive writing in EFL. Blogging and massive peer feedback empower learners' use of language. The results also indicate that blogging enriches lexis and develops the use of correct grammatical structures. The results of the grading indicate that the quality of writing has increased significantly as a result of the reduction of errors; it seems that the students have become more aware of their writing and noticed their mistakes, which enabled them to correct them and avoid repeating them. The results of the present study enforce other studies' findings regarding the efficacy of blogging (Gedera, 2012; Hashemi & Najafi, 2011; Trajtemberg & Yiakoumetti, 2011; Yunus et al., 2013).

The implications of the study are that an emphasis must be put on the process of writing through blogging; i.e. the process has to include explicit and implicit teaching of logistic skills, in addition to preparing the students for correspondence in a blog, such as methods for providing constructive feedback and responding to it. Moreover, the choice of tasks affects students' improvement; tasks which arouse discussion and debate are preferable for developing writing skills.

In conclusion, the engagement of blogging in teaching EFL writing is effective for K-12 learners, on condition that it is accompanied by conventional methods of teaching and much guidance throughout the process on using technology properly.

5. Acknowledgements

I would like to thank my instructors and co-writers, Dr. Hagit Misher-Tal and Dr. Orly Sela, for their tremendous contribution and efficient guidance throughout the implementation of this study.

References

Badger, R., & White, G. (2000). A process genre approach to teaching writing. *ELT Journal*, *54*(2), 153-160.

Daskalogiannaki, E. (2012). Developing and assessing EFL students' writing skills via a class-blog. *Research Papers in Language Teaching & Learning*, *3*(1), 269-293.

Gedera, D. (2012). The dynamics of blog peer feedback in ESL classroom. *Teaching English with Technology*, *12*(4), 16-30.

Hashemi, M., & Najafi, V. (2011). Using blogs in English language writing classes. *International Journal of Academic Research, 3*(4), 599-604.

Ismail, S. A. A. (2011). Exploring students' perceptions of ESL writing. *English Language Teaching, 4*(2), 73-83. https://doi.org/10.5539/elt.v4n2p73

Silva, T. (1990). Second language composition instruction: developments, issues, and directions in ESL. In B. Kroll (Ed.), *Second language writing: research insights for the classroom* (pp. 11-23). Cambridge University Press. https://doi.org/10.1017/CBO9781139524551.005

Tangpermpoon, T. (2008). Integrated approaches to improve students writing skills for English major students. *ABAC Journal, 28*(2), 1-9.

Trajtemberg, C., & Yiakoumetti, A. (2011). Weblogs: a tool for EFL interaction, expression, and self-evaluation. *ELT journal, 65*(4), 437-445. https://doi.org/10.1093/elt/ccr015

Yunus, M. M., Nordin, N., Salehi, H., Embi, M. A., & Salehi, Z. (2013). The use of information and communication technology (ICT) in teaching ESL writing skills. *English Language Teaching, 6*(7), 1-7. https://doi.org/10.5539/elt.v6n7p1

Zen, D. (2005). Teaching ESL/EFL writing beyond language skills. A paper presented at the 3rd International Annual LATEFL China Conference, Tonghua, China.

Criteria for evaluating a game-based CALL platform

Neasa Ní Chiaráin[1] and Ailbhe Ní Chasaide[2]

Abstract. Game-based Computer-Assisted Language Learning (CALL) is an area that currently warrants attention, as task-based, interactive, multimodal games increasingly show promise for language learning. This area is inherently multidisciplinary – theories from second language acquisition, games, and psychology must be explored and relevant concepts from each drawn together. Based on extensive research in these three areas and on subsequent evaluation in the context of a newly developed immersive language learning game (*Digichaint*), this paper proposes nine criteria that should be taken into account both at the design and evaluation stages of game-based CALL platforms.

Keywords: games, CALL, design, evaluation.

1. Introduction

Formal evaluation systems have received relatively little attention in CALL literature, with some notable exceptions (McMurry et al., 2016). Reliable measures of learning outcomes are scarce in relation to all types of CALL platforms (Burston, 2015). Computer gaming as a CALL activity has increased in importance over the past decade and is a promising area of study for future years. Initial studies suggested that simulations and games are indeed beneficial for language acquisition (Peterson, 2010).

The present paper examines the factors which make good CALL games and suggests criteria for the evaluation of such games.

---

1. Trinity College, Dublin, Ireland; neasa.nichiarain@tcd.ie
2. Trinity College, Dublin, Ireland; anichsid@tcd.ie

How to cite this article: Ní Chiaráin, N., & Ní Chasaide, A. (2017). Criteria for evaluating a game-based CALL platform. In K. Borthwick, L. Bradley & S. Thouësny (Eds), *CALL in a climate of change: adapting to turbulent global conditions – short papers from EUROCALL 2017* (pp. 229-234). Research-publishing.net. https://doi.org/10.14705/rpnet.2017.eurocall2017.718

2. Games as a CALL activity

Gee (2005) saw the potential for computer games to enhance learning since they could potentially mimic *interaction* in real-life situations and create virtual worlds. CALL games are essentially task-based activities where the participant is given a specific achievable goal together with clear directions on how this goal may be achieved. While this concept is very closely aligned with the pedagogical concept of task-based language learning (Prabhu, 1987), nevertheless, gaming as a language teaching methodology has not achieved a huge popularity in CALL literature. Steel and Levy (2013) note that language students are yet to be convinced of the value of such technology.

In the evaluation of CALL games, theory from a number of distinct disciplines, including Second Language Acquisition (SLA), psychology, and games must be taken into account. These theories form the basis for the nine criteria set out below which have been used to evaluate the *Digichaint* game (see Ní Chiaráin & Ní Chasaide, 2016). While each of the criteria are somewhat cross-disciplinary, they draw primarily from one or other discipline but are contextualised specifically for CALL games. The criteria are not set in any form of priority. Due to the limitations of the present paper each has but a short comment, although each one may be considered a serious study in of itself.

3. Game-based CALL evaluation criteria

- **The game should be task-based with a focus on meaning and on the use of the target language**

This criterion is based on the work of SLA theorists who subscribe to communicative language teaching and to task-based language learning in particular.

- **Learners should have the opportunity to develop metalinguistic awareness through having the language difficulty set at an appropriate level**

This criterion is based on Chapelle's (2001) claims on language difficulty level or language fit so that the learner can focus on the meaning being conveyed. This will depend on the learner's tolerance of failure such that a balance can be achieved between the metalinguistic development of the learner and the demands of the successful negotiation of the game (Franciosi, 2011).

- **The game should be enjoyable and have a playful spirit**

Learners with gaming experience expect that enjoyment should be associated with the concept of a game, whether this has a purely entertainment value or some educational value. Purushotma, Thorne, and Wheatley (2009) emphasise that all elements of a game should have a playful spirit. Sweetser and Wyeth (2005) distinguish between playfulness and enjoyment, and suggest enjoyment can be an intrinsic part of all elements of a game, including concentration, skills, and challenges, etc.

- **The game should have a clear plot with helpful aids such as a hypertext dictionary**

Effective general computer games share the characteristics of establishing clear goals for the game, rules for playing the game, task feasibility, self-governance, and immediate feedback (Peirce & Wade, 2010). The use of a hypertext dictionary may be helpful (see Chapelle, 2001, 'meaning focus').

- **The game should have a logical structure with appropriate cues for maneuvering through it successfully**

Cues give feedback to the learner on the usefulness or otherwise of particular moves. The player should be aware of his/her level of success in achieving his/her target. Instant feedback can encourage active learning and provide the necessary motivation for the player to continue (Mitchell & Savill-Smith, 2004).

- **The game should promote an appropriate intensity of engagement**

The concept of "flow", introduced by psychologist Csíkszentmihályi (1988), refers to the degree to which players are physically and mentally immersed in the world of the game. Errors in game design or the need for irrational solutions to problems take from the flow of the game.

- **The game should be visually attractive and have appropriate aural material**

There is an aesthetic need for good graphics, visual effects, and appropriate music and sound effects (Greitzer, Kuchar, & Huston, 2007). The ideal game combines entertainment and learning in such a way that the player does not experience the learning part as something external to the game (Breuer & Bente, 2010).

- **The game narrative should have a cultural legitimacy**

A successful game needs to have a credible narrative, be purposeful, have concrete goals, and have a quantifiable scoring system (Mitgutsch & Alvarado, 2012; Peirce & Wade, 2010). Platforms need to be personalised to the needs and characteristics of the target groups of learners (Ní Chiaráin, 2014).

- **There should be clarity in screen layout with no unnecessary distracting features**

This criterion is based on psychology and cognitive load theory in particular, which assumes that human working memory is very limited and that overload occurs when too many distractors are present. This causes significant delays in problem solving, failure to apply correct rules, and ultimately a breakdown of participation in the task (VanLehn, 1999).

4. Discussion and conclusion

CALL games are very diverse in nature and format, ranging from games played by individuals in isolation to games played as a collaborative activity. The design and evaluation of CALL games is a cross disciplinary exercise drawing from fields of SLA, game theory, as well as emerging general CALL theories. The criteria outlined above are drawn from a literature review of these areas and applied to the *Digichaint* game (Ní Chiaráin & Ní Chasaide, 2016). Initial analyses of the results add support to the importance of each of the criteria.

5. Acknowledgements

We are grateful to *The Department of Arts, Heritage and the Gaeltacht* for their support.

References

Breuer, J., & Bente, G. (2010). Why so serious ? On the relation of serious games and learning. *Eludamos. Journal for Computer Game Culture, 4*(1), 7-24.

Burston, J. (2015). Twenty years of MALL project implementation: a meta-analysis of learning outcomes. *ReCALL, 27*(1), 4-20. https://doi.org/10.1017/S0958344014000159

Chapelle, C. (2001). *Computer applications in second language acquisition: foundations for teaching, testing, and research*. Cambridge University Press. https://doi.org/10.1017/CBO9781139524681

Csíkszentmihályi, M. (1988). The flow experience and its significance for human psychology. In M. Csíkszentmihalyi & I. S. Csíkszentmihalyi (Eds), *Optimal experience: psychological studies of flow in consciousness* (pp. 15-35). Cambridge University Press. https://doi.org/10.1017/CBO9780511621956.002

Franciosi, S. J. (2011). A comparison of computer game and language-learning task design using flow theory. *CALL-EJ, 12*(1), 11-25.

Gee, J. P. (2005). Why are video games good for learning? http://www.academiccolab.org/resources/documents/MacArthur.pdf

Greitzer, F., Kuchar, O., & Huston, K. (2007). Cognitive science implications for enhancing training effectiveness in a serious gaming context. *Journal on Educational Resources in Computing, 7*, 1-16. https://doi.org/10.1145/1281320.1281322

McMurry, B., West, R., Rich, P., Williams, D., Anderson, N., & Hartshorn, J. (2016). An evaluation framework for CALL. *TESL-EJ Teaching English as a Second or Foreign Language, 20*(2).

Mitchell, A., & Savill-Smith, C. (2004). *The use of computer and video games for learning: a review of the literature*. Learning and Skills Development Agency.

Mitgutsch, K., & Alvarado, N. (2012). Purposeful by design? A serious game design assessment framework. In *Proceedings of the International Conference on the Foundations of Digital Games* (pp. 121-128). ACM.

Ní Chiaráin, N. (2014). *Text-to-speech synthesis in computer-assisted language learning for Irish: development and evaluation.* Doctoral thesis, CLCS, Trinity College, Dublin.

Ní Chiaráin, N., & Ní Chasaide, A. (2016). The Digichaint interactive game as a virtual learning environment for Irish. In S. Papadima-Sophocleous, L. Bradley & S. Thouësny (Eds), *CALL communities and culture – short papers from EUROCALL 2016* (pp. 330-336). Research-publishing.net. https://doi.org/10.14705/rpnet.2016.eurocall2016.584

Peirce, N., & Wade, V. (2010). Personalised learning for casual games: the "Language Trap" online language learning. In *Proceedings of the Fourth European Conference on Game Based Learning* (pp. 306-315). Bente Meyer.

Peterson, M. (2010). Computerized games and simulations in computer-assisted language learning: a meta-analysis of research. *Simulation & Gaming, 41*, 71-93. https://doi.org/10.1177/1046878109355684

Prabhu, N. S. (1987). *Second language pedagogy*. Oxford University Press.

Purushotma, R., Thorne, S., & Wheatley, J. (2009). 10 key principles for designing video games for foreign language learning. http://lingualgames.wordpress.com/article/10-key-principles-for-designing-video-27mkxqba7b13d-2/

Steel, C., & Levy, M. (2013). Language students and their technologies: charting the evolution 2006-2011. *ReCALL, 25*(3), 306-320. https://doi.org/10.1017/S0958344013000128

Sweetser, P., & Wyeth, P. (2005). GameFlow: a model for evaluating player enjoyment in games. *Computers in Entertainment - Theoretical and Practical Computer Applications in Entertainment, 3*(3), 1-24. https://doi.org/10.1145/1077246.1077253

VanLehn, K. (1999). Rule-learning events in the acquisition of a complex skill: an evaluation of Cascade. *The Journal of the Learning Sciences, 8*, 71-125. https://doi.org/10.1207/s15327809jls0801_3

Designing for ab initio blended learning environments: identifying systemic contradictions

Oisín Ó Doinn[1]

Abstract. In recent years, Computer Assisted Language Learning (CALL) has become more accessible than ever before. This is largely due to the proliferation of mobile computing devices and the growth of open online language-learning resources. Additionally, since the beginning of the millennium there has been massive growth in the number of students studying a foreign language in the European Union (Eurostat, 2012). Unfortunately, according to the Education and Training Monitor 2016[2], within formal education at all levels, there is a lack of guidance regarding the integration of CALL tools with face-to-face classroom instruction. This is particularly in relation to lower-level language instruction. This paper presents some preliminary findings of the author's doctoral research project that addresses the question: what contradictions and tensions emerge in ab initio blended language learning courses? Capturing the development of human activity in complex learning environments and the difficulties that manifest themselves therein is a challenging methodological task. This paper proposes that Cultural-Historical Activity Theory (CHAT) is a useful conceptual tool for Blended Learning (BL) researchers in identifying emerging contradictions with complex learning environments.

Keywords: blended learning, ab initio language learning, cultural-historical activity theory.

1. Introduction

The majority of the European Union (EU) has seen continuous growth in the number of people studying a foreign language since the start of the millennium

---

1. Dublin City University, Dublin, Ireland; odoinn@gmail.com
2. https://ec.europa.eu/education/sites/education/files/monitor2016_en.pdf

How to cite this article: Ó Doinn, O. (2017). Designing for ab initio blended learning environments: identifying systemic contradictions. In K. Borthwick, L. Bradley & S. Thouësny (Eds), *CALL in a climate of change: adapting to turbulent global conditions – short papers from EUROCALL 2017* (pp. 235-241). Research-publishing.net. https://doi.org/10.14705/rpnet.2017.eurocall2017.719

(Eurostat, 2012). This is as a result of shifts in students' foreign language choices and the expansion of the EU in 2004. As a consequence of increasing student numbers, Member States are facing increasing pressures to provide quality language education to their students. These pressures relate to increasing class sizes and demand for additional appropriately qualified teaching staff familiar with the Common European Framework of References for languages (CEFR).

Currently, CALL resources are more available to the general public than ever. Massive Open Online Courses (MOOCs) for language learning (LMOOCs) such as those offered by Coursera and language learning apps such as Duolingo, offer learners the opportunity to interact with target languages independently. The users of these platforms can number in tens of millions. Across Europe, the importance of integrating information communication technology (blended learning) into education has been acknowledged. Unfortunately, there is a lack of pedagogical guidance in relation to how this can be achieved (European Commission, 2014).

BL formats offer many advantages to both the student and the teacher over traditional classrooms. BL is often described as the best of both traditional teaching methods and CALL (Marsh, 2012). Some of the main benefits of BL noted by researchers are increased student autonomy, increased student engagement with the target language, and the development of metacognitive strategies (Blin & Jalkanen, 2014; Scida & Saury, 2013). Unfortunately, research in this sphere of BL is limited with regard to the study of language learners at different levels, particularly with respect to levels defined by the CEFR.

The research presented here is based upon a preliminary analysis of data collected as a part of the author's doctoral study. The author sought to address the research question: 'What contradictions and tensions emerge in an ab initio BL course?'. To investigate this question, the author conducted a study of ab initio language learners' activities over the duration of a six-week introductory Irish language course at Carnegie Mellon University, Pittsburgh, USA. Initially, the learning objectives of the course were defined using the CEFR, namely the topics laid out from level A1 to A2. The design of the course was heavily influenced by recommendations from researchers in the field of CHAT, CALL, BL, and by the participants' motivations for taking the course (Blin & Jalkanen, 2014; Chapelle, 2009; Jonassen & Rohrer-Murphy, 1999; Neumeier, 2005).

Table 1 below provides a brief outline of the BL course's weekly topics and assignments.

Table 1. BL course breakdown

Week	Topic	CEFR level	End-of-week Assignments
1	Meeting people and talking about your background	A1	CALL assignment (grammar, listening tasks, vocabulary)
2	Your background and where you live	A1	CALL and speaking assignment
3	Your family	A1/A2	CALL assignment
4	Your pastimes	A2	CALL and speaking assignment
5	Daily life	A2	CALL and speaking assignment
6	Daily life and review	A2	CALL assignment

CHAT offers researchers a method to understand and describe interactions between individuals and their environment (Yamagata-Lynch, 2010). To study something from a cultural historical perspective is to study something in the process of change (Blin, 2005). CHAT provides qualitative researchers with a powerful conceptual tool with which to understand collective human activity within a complex BL environment (Yamagata-Lynch, 2010). CHAT is also well suited to the identification of contradictions in BL environments. It must be understood that contradictions do not manifest as problems exclusively.

> "Contradictions reveal themselves as breakdowns, conflicts, problems, tensions, or misfits between elements of an activity or between activities" (De Souza & Redmiles, 2003, p. 3).

Figure 1. Engeström's triangles (Burry, 2012)

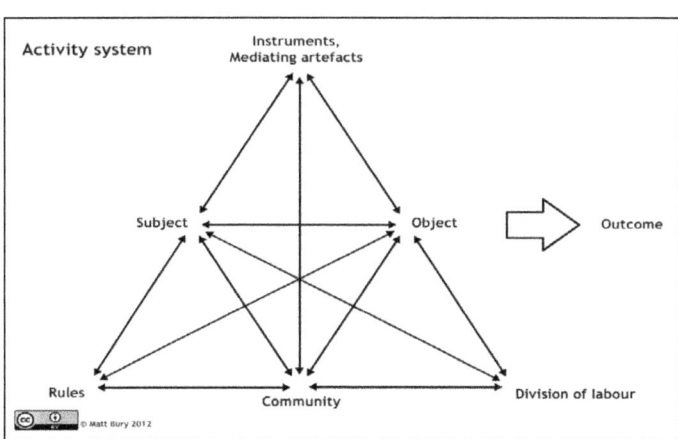

According to Engeström (1987), an Activity System (AS) is comprised of six interrelated elements. These elements are: (1) the object or goal of the AS; (2) the subject (in this study the student/participant); (3) the community; (4) the tools or artefacts; (5) the rules; and (6) the division of labour. Contradictions can occur between each of these elements and other activity systems. Figure 1 above illustrates the relationship between these elements.

2. Method

2.1. Participants and method

Eleven participants were recruited for this study. These participants came from a variety of educational and professional backgrounds, and ranged in age from 18 to 54. Importantly for the study, each participant was an ab initio Irish learner. Over the six weeks, 12 one-hour face-to-face classes were held. Students were introduced to the CALL tools gradually. The main technologies that constituted the courses were: Duolingo's Irish course, Anki Intelligent Flashcards, SpeakApps, and SoundCloud. The researcher used several research instruments to pursue the research question. The primary instruments used were a background questionnaire, CHAT structured observation sheets (Figure 3), and weekly student feedback sheets (Figure 2). A group interview was also conducted at the conclusion of the study.

Figure 2.   Student feedback sheet

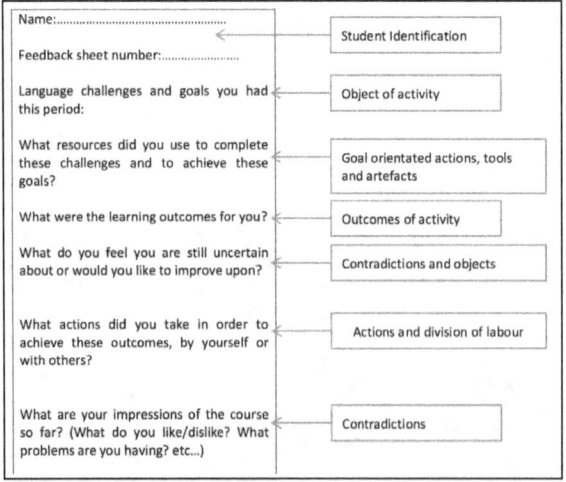

Figure 3. CHAT structured observation sheets

Object of activity
Tools and Artefacts
Teacher:
Students:
Actions observed
Prior to class (online):
In class observations:
Division of Labour (DOL)
DOL prior to class:
Teacher DOL in-class:
Student DOL in-class:
DOL After class:
Rules
Observed Difficulties/Problems
Outcomes

2.2. Empirical analysis

To analyse the data, the researcher engaged in data triangulation and adopted a CHAT-based coding scheme designed to identify contradictions in the language courses (Blin, 2005).

3. Results and discussion

Eight participants successfully completed the course. Three participants were unable to complete the course due to other commitments. These participant 'dropped out' in the third and fourth weeks of the course respectively. Six of the eight participants who completed the course participated in an optional recorded conversation with the course's teacher at the end of the study. These recordings were later sent for analysis by an Irish language educator and specialist in the CEFR. Her analysis revealed a mismatch between students' perceived ability in the language and their actual ability. Students overestimated their language ability to be at a B1 level when in fact their actual level was at A1.

In order to pursue the research question, the author applied Blin's (2005) CHAT coding scheme to the study's data to construct a model of the course's inter-related AS elements. Preliminary analysis reveals that contradictions emerged at various level within the AS as defined by Engeström (1987). One notable contradiction is the impact that the online and face-to-face activities had on participants' use of the target language with members of their wider social community. The openness and usability of the tools coupled with classroom activity reinforcements appear to have given the participants the confidence to engage others about the target language that were not a part of their formal community of learners.

4. Conclusions

Though the findings of this study are still preliminary, this paper showcases the affordance of CHAT to identify relationships between elements that constitute a complex learning environment such as a BL course. The findings of the study will be published in the researcher's doctoral thesis in the coming year.

5. Acknowledgements

I would like to thank my supervisors for their support. I would also like to thank the Irish Research Council for funding this research.

References

Blin, F. (2005). *CALL and the development of learner autonomy: an activity theoretical study.* Doctoral thesis. The Open University.
Blin, F., & Jalkanen, J. (2014). Designing for language learning: agency and languaging in hybrid environments. *Apples - Journal of Applied Language Studies, 8*(1), 147-170.
Burry, M. (2012). *Engestrom's triangles.* http://en.wikipedia.org/wiki/Activity_theory#mediaviewer/File:Activity_system.png

Chapelle, C. A. (2009). The relationship between second language acquisition theory and computer assited language learning. *The Modern Language Journal, 93*(1), 741-753. https://doi.org/10.1111/j.1540-4781.2009.00970.x

De Souza, C. R., & Redmiles, D. F. (2003). Using activity theory to understand contradictions in collaborative software development. *Automated Software Engineering, Montreal, CA, IEEE Press.*

Engeström, Y. (1987). Learning by expanding: an activity-theoretical approach to developmental research. Orienta Konsultit.

European Commission. (2014). *Improving the effectiveness of language learning: CLIL and computer assisted language learning.* http://ec.europa.eu/dgs/education_culture/repository/languages/library/studies/clil-call_en.pdf

Eurostat (2012). *Foreign language learning.* http://appsso.eurostat.ec.europa.eu/nui/show.do?dataset=educ_thfrlan&lang=en

Jonassen, D. H., & Rohrer-Murphy, L. (1999). Activity theory as a framework for designing constructivist learning environments. *Educational Technology Research and Development, 47*(1), 61-79. https://doi.org/10.1007/BF02299477

Marsh, D. (2012). *Blended learning: creating learning opportunities for language learners.* Cambridge University Press.

Neumeier, P. (2005). A closer look at blended learning—parameters for designing a blended learning environment for language teaching and learning. *ReCALL, 17*(2), 163-178. https://doi.org/10.1017/S0958344005000224

Scida, E. E., & Saury, R. E. (2013). Hybrid courses and their impact on student and classroom performance: a case study at the University of Virginia. *CALICO Journal, 23*(3), 517-531.

Yamagata-Lynch, L. C. (2010). *Activity systems analysis methods: understanding complex learning environments.* Springer Science & Business Media. https://doi.org/10.1007/978-1-4419-6321-5

How "blended" should "blended learning" be?

Boguslaw Ostrowski[1], Scott Windeatt[2], and Jill Clark[3]

Abstract. Concerns about progression rates of international students enrolled in an academic English course to prepare them for university studies led to the addition of an online teaching component, including both synchronous and asynchronous elements. Due to what appeared to be inconsistent student engagement with the online element, this study was initiated to investigate students' approaches to the new aspects of the course. Students were asked to rank the principal elements of the course according to their importance using diamond ranking, a critical thinking tool, and to make comments to explain their reasons for the rankings produced. What seems to emerge quite clearly from the initial data is (1) the need for closer coordination between the teachers who deliver the online course elements and students who are expected to engage in Blended Learning (BL), and (2) for them to have a clearer understanding of both the potential and the limitations of blended learning and teaching.

Keywords: blended learning, English for academic purposes, students' views, diamond ranking.

1. Introduction

The use of web-based materials and computer-mediated communication as part of classroom-based courses is so widespread now that almost any language course that is not delivered entirely online will include such an element alongside the face-to-face (f2f) classroom teaching, and could therefore be described as adopting a 'blended learning' approach. BL is adopted and implemented in models of teaching which reside somewhere on the continuum between traditional classroom delivery involving f2f interaction and completely online courses with no classroom f2f tuition. Where there is no reduction in f2f teaching time, the term 'technology

---

1. Newcastle University, Newcastle-upon-Tyne, United Kingdom; boguslaw.ostrowski@newcastle.ac.uk
2. Newcastle University, Newcastle-upon-Tyne, United Kingdom; scott.windeatt@newcastle.ac.uk
3. Newcastle University, Newcastle-upon-Tyne, United Kingdom; jill.clark@newcastle.ac.uk

How to cite this article: Ostrowski, B., Windeatt, S., & Clark, J. (2017). How "blended" should "blended learning" be? In K. Borthwick, L. Bradley & S. Thouësny (Eds), *CALL in a climate of change: adapting to turbulent global conditions – short papers from EUROCALL 2017* (pp. 242-247). Research-publishing.net. https://doi.org/10.14705/rpnet.2017.eurocall2017.720

enhanced learning' has been applied (Graham, Woodfield, & Harrison, 2013). The range of possibilities afforded by the use of technology potentially presents the teacher and course designer not only with opportunities, but also with additional responsibilities.

This presentation is concerned with the evaluation of a BL course where the classroom and online elements were designed separately, and in which the f2f and online teaching were mostly carried out by different teachers, that is, most of the teachers were responsible for either the online or the f2f teaching, but not both. This has raised questions about the relative effectiveness of the two elements of the course, the way in which the two elements are coordinated, and whether the nature of the coordination is linked to the effectiveness of each element and to the overall course.

2. Method and context

A cohort of 86 international students, divided into five groups, enrolled in an English language programme to prepare them for university undergraduate (UG) or postgraduate (PG) studies, were asked to give their views on the different elements of a BL course. The principal investigator had direct access to four of the five groups (74 students), spread across three proficiency levels, via classes held to deliver one of the elements of the BL course, meeting each of the groups on three occasions each week for 10 weeks. One of the data collection tools (diamond ranking), selected to provide both quantitative and qualitative data, was tested on all four groups, and the initial results are presented.

Diamond ranking is a critical thinking skills tool (Clark, 2009) which has been used in a variety of contexts, including in higher education, where its potential use across the curriculum has been investigated (Ostrowski, 2013). Interactive diamond ranking grids were emailed to students asking them to rank nine options, each representing one element of the BL course. The grid allows students to 'drag & drop' each option into a position indicating its relative importance, or value, to them personally as a constituent part of the programme (Figure 1). The five-tier grid permits nine options to be ranked: the top-most position (1) represents the most important choice, the bottom-most position (5) represents the least important choice, and three intermediate levels (2, 3, and 4), allowing co-ranking of options, indicate decreasing levels of importance. The students' choice of ranking for each option on the grid is justified with their own explanations by writing in 'drag & drop' comment balloons.

Figure 1. Level 6 (IELTS 5.0 – 5.5) students' diamond ranking and comments

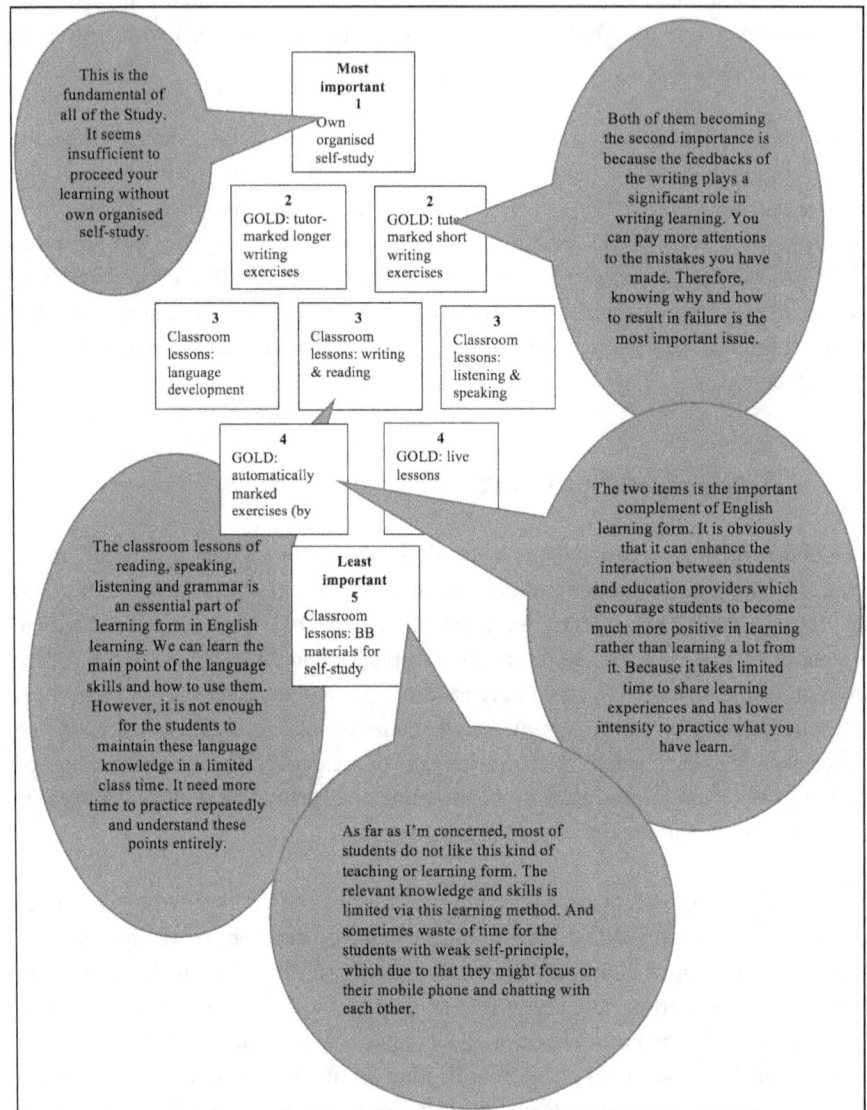

3. Discussion

These initial results are from a single iteration of the course only, and were obtained from students using diamond ranking activities. The preliminary results suggest that elements of the course which were taught in the classroom were viewed with greater positivity across four different levels of English language ability (Figure 2) than were several different components of the online course. Most respondents, across all groups, placed the classroom-taught elements of the BL course in the upper tiers of the diamond ranking grid, whilst the online components of the course tended to occupy the lower (less valued) tiers of the grid. Comments made to justify the rankings (Figure 3) further indicate that students' perceptions of the latter are received with lower positivity than the f2f elements.

Since this data was collected, however, the online course has been re-designed, and two further iterations to provide further data are planned. One of the principal significant changes made is that classroom teachers now deliver the online element of the BL course, and are free to decide how tasks in the four main skills areas (reading, writing, listening, and speaking) are released to the classes which they teach, hence increasing the possibility of integrating the online and classroom elements of the BL course.

Figure 2. Diamond ranking frequency distribution of blended learning course elements for all four groups

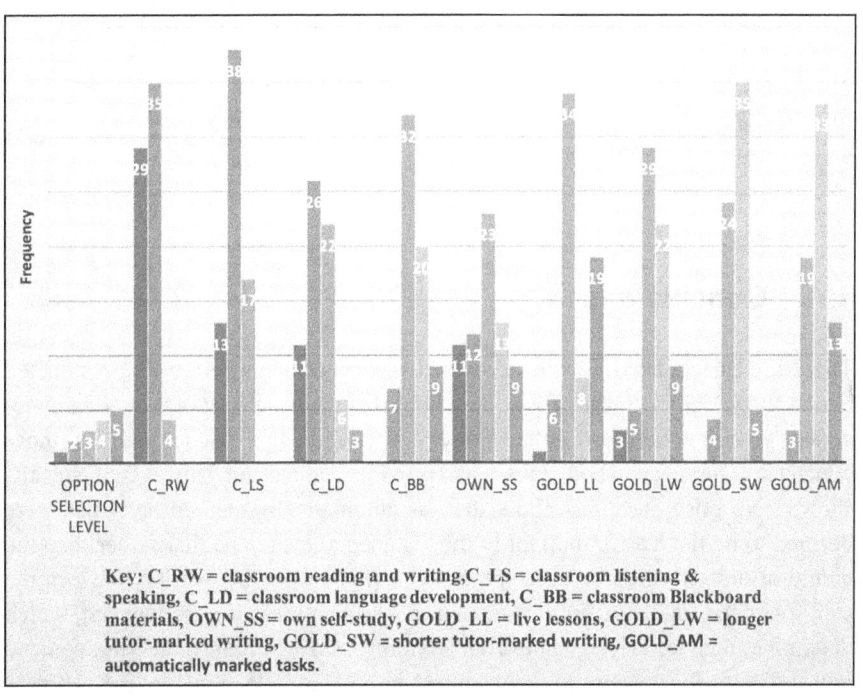

Key: C_RW = classroom reading and writing, C_LS = classroom listening & speaking, C_LD = classroom language development, C_BB = classroom Blackboard materials, OWN_SS = own self-study, GOLD_LL = live lessons, GOLD_LW = longer tutor-marked writing, GOLD_SW = shorter tutor-marked writing, GOLD_AM = automatically marked tasks.

Figure 3. Comments indicating positive or negative attitudes towards specific course components: GOLD live lessons, Level 4 group (IELTS ~4.0). Numbers in brackets equate to position on diamond ranking grid

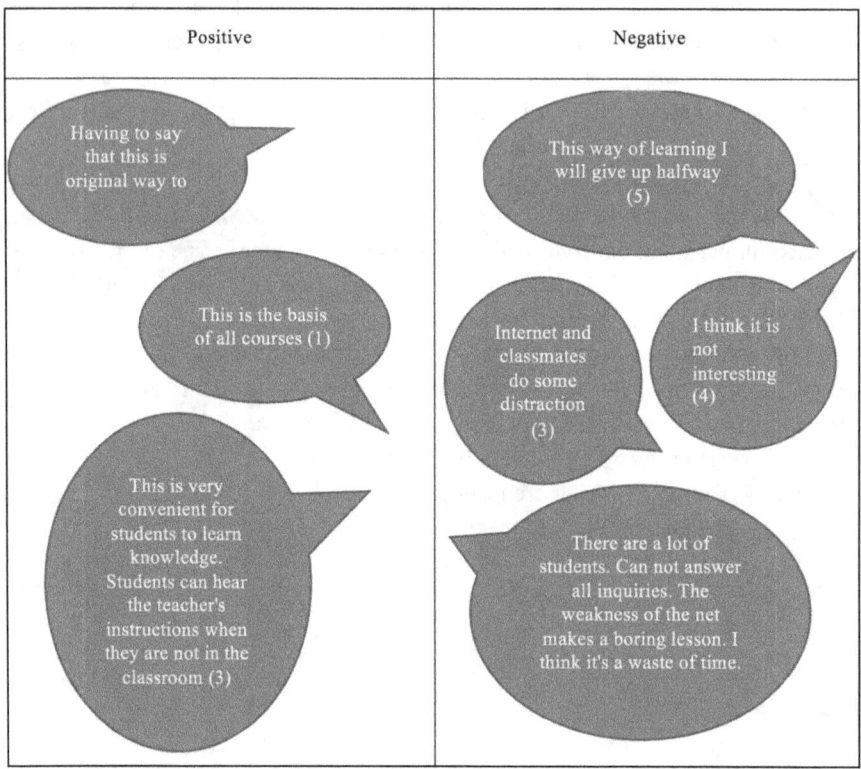

4. Conclusions

There is clearly a need to consider which aspects of a course are best conducted online and which in the classroom. It may be that there are certain types of activity which are better suited to online presentation, without a teacher, such as those which the computer can both deliver and provide feedback on. However, the results shown here raise questions about that, as automatically marked activities were deemed to be the least important to most students. It may be that rather than the nature of the activities, or even the content, it could be the overlap between the classroom and online tasks, or the manner in which the tasks are blended, which determines their perceived value. That is, simply making online materials available is insufficient for meaningful engagement in a blended learning course, whereas reasoned integration of the two elements may fulfil students' potential abilities for greater independence in their studies.

References

Clark, J. (2009). Exploring the use of diamond ranking activities as a visual methods research tool. In *1st International Visual Methods Conference, University of Leeds.*

Graham, C. R., Woodfield, W., & Harrison, J. B. (2013). A framework for institutional adoption and implementation of blended learning in higher education. *Internet and Higher Education, 18*, 4-14. https://doi.org/10.1016/j.iheduc.2012.09.003

Ostrowski, B. (2013). Are intercultural communication and intercultural competence teachable/learnable in the university context? *British Association for Applied Linguistics Special Interest Group on Intercultural Communication in Higher Education Seminar, Newcastle University, 16-17 May 2013.* https://baalicsig.wordpress.com/activities/icsig-seminar2013/seminar-presentations/paper-7-ostrowski/

'L2 assessment and testing' teacher education: an exploration of alternative assessment approaches using new technologies

Salomi Papadima-Sophocleous[1]

Abstract. Most Second Language (L2) Teacher Training Assessment and Testing courses focus on testing. Through the development of a Master of Arts (MA) in a computer assisted language learning module (based on a constructivist and 'practise what you preach' approach, entailing that the teachers experience firsthand the assessment types they were asked to develop), the instructor/researcher aimed to provide Computer Assisted Language Assessment and Testing (CALAT) teacher education, focusing on classroom assessment. The module was based on (1) current theories and practices; (2) participants' earlier assessment and testing background experiences as school students, and their assessment and testing experiences and current practices as L2 teachers; (3) participants' assessment experiences not as L2 teachers but as students of the MA assessment and testing module; (4) participants' L2 CALAT practising needs; and (5) problem-solving by constructing assessments suitable for their practising needs. This article draws on a small-scale questionnaire, participant in- and on-action reflective journal entries, and webinar chat notes to examine the extent to which these goals were achieved. Data analysis and discussion reveals that, the hands-on, technology-based, constructivist, and reflective approach applied enhanced participants' knowledge, skills and experiences in CALAT in general and in L2 classroom assessment in particular.

Keywords: computer assisted language assessment and testing, CALAT, teacher education, learner perceptions.

---

1. Cyprus University of Technology Language Centre, Limassol, Cyprus; salomi.papadima@cut.ac.cy

How to cite this article: Papadima-Sophocleous, S. (2017). 'L2 assessment and testing' teacher education: an exploration of alternative assessment approaches using new technologies. In K. Borthwick, L. Bradley & S. Thouësny (Eds), *CALL in a climate of change: adapting to turbulent global conditions – short papers from EUROCALL 2017* (pp. 248-253). Research-publishing.net. https://doi.org/10.14705/rpnet.2017.eurocall2017.721

1. Introduction

When students and teachers think of assessment and testing, they usually recall moments of stress and anxiety. This is because very often tests or high-stakes examinations drive second language (L2) learning (Cheng, 2013) and teaching. Often, results reflect the ability to pass an exam and not language competence. However, because society and educational systems traditionally believe in tests and examinations as evidence of learning, emphasis is given to them not only in the learning and teaching process, but in teacher training as well.

Most L2 assessment and testing teacher education programmes still focus mainly on testing and high-stakes examinations. This limits trainees' ability to develop their L2 assessment knowledge, skills and experiences, particularly for formative classroom assessment and its washback effect, and to be adequately equipped for an L2 language assessment and testing practice that would, to a considerable extent, involve classroom assessment and reflect real-life language competence.

At the same time, language assessment literacy (Fulcher, 2012; Inbar-Lourie, 2013) is a relatively new field, "as far as theoretical and empirical research is concerned" (Taylor, 2013).

According to the language assessment and testing literature, assessment literacy began around 2003. L2 assessment literacy requires special teacher training. Different researchers have investigated various aspects of L2 assessment literacy, such as language assessment course content (Jeong, 2013) and the effect of language assessment training on pre-service teachers (Lam, 2015). However, as research in teachers' classroom assessment practices is just emerging (Cheng, 2013), more research is needed in the area.

2. Method

This action-research study investigated the development of an MA in a CALAT module, focusing on classroom/formative assessment for L2 practitioners. The 14-week module was based on a constructivist approach, which supports learning through construction, sharing, collaboration, and interactivity. It was also based on the post-communicative era teaching methods, current theories and practices in L2 assessment and testing, and problem-solving by constructing assessments suitable for their L2 practising assessment needs. The question was to what extent and how successfully the module achieved such training.

The study was conducted during autumn 2016. The 12 participants were pre-primary, primary and secondary practising teachers from different countries, teaching different languages. Participants were assisted in constructing L2 assessment and testing knowledge, skills and experiences through hands-on tasks. They participated synchronously (Skype, Messenger) and asynchronously (Moodle, Google Drive and Document, Facebook, Messenger, email) to access the course materials and to interact, collaborate, construct, and share knowledge, skills and experiences on a weekly basis. Participants actively engaged in weekly tasks, the construction of ten artifacts and an in- and on-action reflective journal (Schön, 1983), all showcased in participants' ePortfolios.

The study adopted a qualitative and quantitative approach. Data were collected from a small-scale questionnaire, self-assessment grids, participants' in- and on-action reflective journals, and final webinar participants' reflective chats.

3. Findings

According to the questionnaire data, all students had a favourable overview of their learning experience. They all strongly agreed that the content learning outcomes were clearly set, and content and assignments reflected the learning outcomes.

3.1. Practise what you preach

Students learned about formative assessment (Bennett, 2011) through the way they experienced it as learners of the module, with the use of technologies. All participants systematically completed weekly self-assessment grids, where most students expressed that they achieved the expected outcomes successfully (most responses ranged from 'excellent' to 'very well'). They also had hands-on experience as students of rubrics, as each artifact was accompanied by one. Students acknowledged rubrics' importance and felt they helped them in both the construction and the evaluation of each artifact. Another assessment type participants experienced as learners and appreciated was the end-of-the-module 'can do' list. The following summed up the importance found in it by most participants:

> "The flashback of the weeks was completed with the fill in of the 'Can Do List'. I was impressed when I saw the amount of knowledge gained through this course summarised in that document, and I really feel that this 'journey' made me grow as a teacher. I feel benefited and I believe

that I improved my testing and assessment methods with the use of technology" (Student 4).

Participants also found great value in the in- and on-action reflective journal, as it helped them establish what they brought into the module from earlier experience, learned during the module and needed to develop in the future.

Peer feedback, instructor feedback, and ePortfolios were three more types of formative assessment participants found helpful as learners. The following comments are indicative:

> "I understood that peer-assessment and reflections are vital in making students feel involved in their learning and promoting learner autonomy" (Student 1).

> "Indeed, when we visited each other's portfolio at the end of week 13, we were afforded the opportunity to remark students' evidence of learning and exchange feedback with each other" (Student 2).

3.2. Collaboration, sharing and formative assessments construction

Students also enriched their assessment practices by learning about formative assessment through creating related artifacts with the use of technologies. The following comment is indicative of how most participants felt about the 'timeline':

> "While creating the L2 Assessment & Testing Historical Background Timeline, not only I was informed on the different [historical] stages of L2 assessment and testing, I have also discovered how to use a software different from PowerPoint" (Student 3).

Participants also appreciated their engagement in collaboration and sharing:

> "The collaborative annotated assessment pool was a unique experience because we worked as a community" (Student 4).

> "We navigated through the internet to find rubrics assessing different skills and included them in a collaborative rubric data base. This process aided us in constructing our own rubrics" (Student 2).

In addition, students learned about classroom assessment through constructing classroom assessment tasks, thus evidencing ability to construct such types of assessment tasks for their L2 assessment practice needs:

> "The artifact this week was a unique and maybe the most valuable experience I had since this master programme started. It was really useful and challenging... I created two Computer Based Tests (CBTs); the one is traditional and the other one communicative. Through this experience I have realised that creating a communicative CBT is not only motivational for the students but for the teacher who creates it as well!" (Student 5).

> "This task made me think how I could turn at least formative authentic-like assessment tasks into more engaging activities for my students. I would definitely try to employ similar assessment tasks in the future" (Student 7).

> "I have to admit that [developing our own rubrics for four different activities] was very challenging and engaging to choose the appropriate criteria for each rubric and make correlations with the [common European framework of reference for languages] criteria" (Student 12).

4. Discussion and conclusion

Literature indicated that there is lack of sufficient training in teacher education programmes on L2 Formative Assessment. This article has given some insights into the extent to which the provision of a CALAT teacher education focusing on classroom assessment was achieved, in an attempt to share ways in which and to what extent such training can occur. The study of the different data revealed that participants felt they benefited from the experiences they had of formative assessment as trainees, from the 'practise what you preach' type of teacher training and from the constructivist, hands-on approach applied, which included alternative assessment construction. The whole process enabled the participants to build a sound understanding of alternative assessment. Additional research in the area would further explore and enrich this domain.

References

Bennett, R. E. (2011). Formative assessment: a critical review. *Assessment in Education, 18*(1), 5-25.

Cheng, L. (2013). *Language classroom assessment*. TESOL International Association.

Fulcher, G. (2012). Assessment literacy for the language classroom. *Language Assessment Quarterly, 9*(2), 113-132. https://doi.org/10.1080/15434303.2011.642041

Inbar-Lourie, O. (2013). Guest editorial to the special issue on language assessment literacy. *Language Testing, 30*(3), 301-307. https://doi.org/10.1177/0265532213480126

Jeong, H. (2013). Defining assessment literacy: is it different for language testers and non-language testers? *Language Testing, 30*(3), 345-362. https://doi.org/10.1177/0265532213480334

Lam, R. (2015). Language assessment training in Hong Kong: implications for language assessment literacy. *Language Testing, 32*(2), 169-197. https://doi.org/10.1177/0265532214554321

Schön, D. (1983). *The reflective practitioner: how professionals think in action*. Temple Smith.

Taylor, L. (2013). Communicating the theory, practice and principles of language testing to test stakeholders: some reflections. *Language Testing, 30*(3), 403-412. https://doi.org/10.1177/0265532213480338

MALL with WordBricks – building correct sentences brick by brick

Marina Purgina[1], Maxim Mozgovoy[2], and Monica Ward[3]

Abstract. Mobile-Assisted Language Learning (MALL) use is increasing and it is good to be able to provide language learners with new resources to enhance their language learning experience. One such resource is WordBricks, a non-commercial, educational app that facilitates the learning and reinforcement of grammar rules. It uses bricks and connectors of different colours and shapes for different parts of speech, and the learner can (only) form grammatically correct sentences. Learners can choose to form sentences from examples or create their own original sentences. Originally, WordBricks was designed for personalised, individual, out-of-classroom learning for English language learners. This paper provides an overview of research on the original WordBricks app for English. A version of WordBricks has been developed for Irish and adapted for use in the primary school setting. There are very few interactive resources available for Irish and the Irish WordBricks app is a new addition to the Irish Computer-Assisted Language Learning (CALL) cannon. This paper reports on how the Irish WordBricks app was used by teachers and students in a primary school and the feedback received on the app.

Keywords: MALL, WordBricks, mobile app, Irish, grammar.

1. Introduction

MALL is one of the newer aspects of CALL and may become more prevalent (Stockwell, 2010) and normalised in the future. WordBricks (Mozgovoy & Efimov, 2013) is a MALL resource that enables learners to construct grammatically correct sentences. Learners have to join the appropriate words together to make a sentence. WordBricks leverages visual learning techniques in order to facilitate

---

1. University of Aizu, Aizu, Japan; mapurgina@gmail.com
2. University of Aizu, Aizu, Japan; mozgovoy@u-aizu.ac.jp
3. Dublin City University, Dublin, Ireland; monica.ward@dcu.ie

How to cite this article: Purgina, M., Mozgovoy, M., & Ward, M. (2017). MALL with WordBricks – building correct sentences brick by brick. In K. Borthwick, L. Bradley & S. Thouësny (Eds), *CALL in a climate of change: adapting to turbulent global conditions – short papers from EUROCALL 2017* (pp. 254-259). Research-publishing.net. https://doi.org/10.14705/rpnet.2017.eurocall2017.722

the language learning process. Language learners can use WordBricks to reinforce topics covered in a traditional classroom, while independent learners can use the WordBricks app to check their own understanding of grammar. WordBricks can be integrated into a traditional classroom setting, as it enables teachers to make in-class learning experiences more interactive and engaging for learners.

The WordBricks engine/template is language independent and appeals to learners of all ages. It was originally designed as a MALL app for adult learners who may wish to revisit a previously learnt language or who are learning a new one. It is appropriate for young learners as the construction of sentences using blocks of different colours and shapes (corresponding to different parts of speech) appeals to them and is akin to constructing items using Lego or light-touch programming with the visual programming environment, Scratch.

This paper shows how WordBricks has been used for two different languages (English and Irish) in two different contexts (university and primary school) and provides feedback on the use of this visual sentence construction tool from teachers and learners.

2. Method

2.1. Overview of WordBricks

The WordBricks system is based on a traditional approach to grammar learning using a system of rules to combine words into sentences. Learners can test themselves with a set of predefined exercises, but they do not have the opportunity to try out different words and rules. WordBricks enables learners to construct grammatically correct sentences and it can provide feedback on which rules have been violated if the learner tries to construct an incorrect sentence. WordBricks is influenced by the visual programming language, Scratch (Resnick et al., 2009). WordBricks uses shaped blocks and connectors which the learner can combine into sentences.

2.2. Overview of English WordBricks

The first WordBricks app was for English. The target users were L2 English language learners. The words of a sentence are jumbled up and the bricks have different colours and shapes based on their grammatical category (see Figure 1).

Figure 1. Screenshot of the English WordBricks

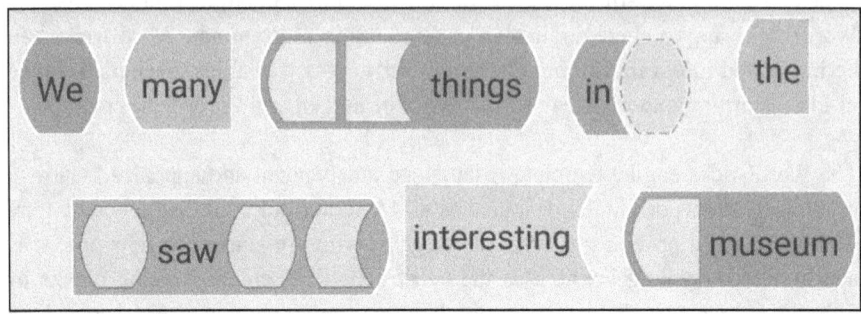

An experimental study using the English WordBricks app was carried out with computer science students in Japan (n=21) on an elective English grammar course (Park, Purgina, & Mozgovoy, 2016). The control group (G1) studied two grammar topics using a traditional textbook (Murphy, 2012) and the test group (G2) used WordBricks exclusively to understand the rules of English grammar by experimenting and playing with the bricks.

G2 showed a greater improvement for both topics, based on comparing pre-test and post-test results. G1's scores increased from 15.18 to 21.0 (out of 30), while G2's scores increased from 15.90 to 24.20. A second experimental study showed slightly different results. There were 16 students and in this study the control group's scores improved from 17.13 to 20.70, while the test group had a smaller increase from 17.94 to 20.31 (see Park et al., 2016, for details).

Qualitative data was also collected from the students and while some reported their preference for using a book, many of the students reported that they enjoyed using the app for learning.

2.3. Overview of Irish WordBricks

Irish is a Verb-Subject-Object (VSO) language, which can make sentence construction challenging for students, the vast majority of whom have English as their L1. Sometimes, students try to use two verbs at the beginning of a sentence.

They also have problems with Irish spellings as the Irish orthography is not very transparent to learners. WordBricks can help to overcome these issues as students can only construct grammatically correct sentences and they do not have to spell words as they are already written on the bricks (Figure 2).

Figure 2. Screenshot of Irish WordBricks

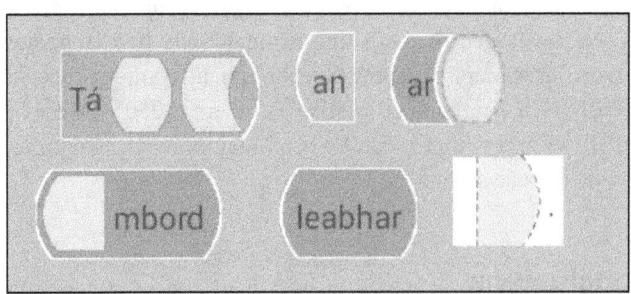

WordBricks was originally intended for use by adults, but it can be used by learners of all ages as it is colourful and has an easy-to-use interface. It was not possible to use a mobile device in the primary school classroom, so an alternative approach was adopted. The classroom laptop was used and the Irish WordBricks app was displayed for all students to see. The teacher had covered the topics in advance and used the Irish WordBricks app as a tool for review. A study was conducted in a (typical) primary school in Ireland, with 5 different classes. There were two cohorts: the first had two classes (C1, C2) of students aged 10-11, and the second had three classes (C3, C4, C5) of students aged 8-9. All classes covered the first three topics, while C2 covered four topics and C1 covered six topics.

The aim of the study was to see if the Irish WordBricks app could be used successfully in the classroom. The feedback from the teachers and the students shows that the app can be used without any major problems. The feedback from Cohort 1 indicates that the majority of students said (1) they enjoyed the app, (2) it was easy to use, (3) they thought it helped them to learn Irish, and (4) they would like their teacher to use the app again in class. Just over half of the students would like to use the app at home. Further analysis is being carried out on the feedback from Cohort 2, but the initial indications are that both the students and the teachers are also positive about the Irish WordBricks app. They have made several useful suggested for future improvements to the app.

3. Discussion

Educational apps must have a pedagogical focus and sometimes the focus is very narrow and the app may not be very practical. In the past, some edutainment apps adopted a 'chocolate covered broccoli' approach, which still exists today (Chen, 2016). Sweetser and Wyeth (2005) note the individual fun factors that contribute to the overall enjoyability of an app. The WordBricks app aims to provide a fun educational app that covers a specific grammar topic. WordBricks apps have been developed for both English and Irish, two languages that have a different word order and different morphological complexities, Irish being a morphologically rich language (Christian Brothers, 1980). One of the benefits of the WordBricks app is that it can be used inside the classroom as well as by learners outside the classroom.

4. Conclusions

MALL is not going to be a silver bullet for language learning as some may assume (Stockwell, 2012). However, MALL does have the potential to enhance the language learning process and this study shows that MALL resources, such as WordBricks, can be used effectively by learners and also adapted and used in the classroom setting. The key is to adopt a user-centred and collaborative design approach. It is important that the pedagogical motivations are clearly understood and implemented and that the students' needs are at the centre of the design process.

5. Acknowledgements

This publication has emanated from research conducted with the financial support of Science Foundation Ireland under the International Strategic Cooperation Award Grant Number SFI/13/ISCA/2846.

References

Chen, S. (2016). Facing edutainment's dark legacy. http://www.gamesandlearning.org/2016/01/25/facing-edutainments-dark-legacy/

Christian Brothers. (1980). *New Irish Grammar*. Irish Book Center.

Mozgovoy, M., & Efimov, R. (2013). WordBricks: a virtual language lab inspired by Scratch environment and dependency grammars. *Human-centric Computing and Information Sciences 3*(1), 1-9. https://doi.org/10.1186/2192-1962-3-5

Murphy, R. (2012). *English grammar in use*. Ernst Klett Sprachen.

Park, M., Purgina, M., & Mozgovoy, M. (2016). Learning English grammar with WordBricks: classroom experience. *Proceedings of the 2016 IEEE International Conference on Teaching and Learning in Education*.

Resnick, M., Maloney, J., Monroy-Hernández, A., Rusk, N., Eastmond, E., Brennan, K., & Kafai, Y. (2009). Scratch: programming for all. *Communications of the ACM, 52*(11), 60-67. https://doi.org/10.1145/1592761.1592779

Stockwell, G. (2010). Using mobile phones for vocabulary activities: examining the effect of the platform. *Language Learning & Technology, 12*(2), 95-110.

Stockwell, G. (2012). Mobile-assisted language learning. *Contemporary computer-assisted language learning, 16*(3), 24-31.

Sweetser, P., & Wyeth, P. (2005). GameFlow: a model for evaluating player enjoyment in games. *Computers in Entertainment, 3*(3), 3-3. https://doi.org/10.1145/1077246.1077253

Collective designing and sharing of open educational resources: a study of the French CARTOUN platform

Nolwenn Quere[1]

Abstract. Designing and sharing Open Educational Resources (OERs) requires teachers to develop new competences, in particular with digital resources. In this paper, the case of a language resource production group is introduced. Due to the centrality of the OERs in their collective activity, I show that the documents they produce are essential to the group's work. The theoretical framework of the Documentational Approach (DA) is used in order to analyse their design of resources, the development of their resource system, and how it is linked with professional development.

Keywords : OER, collective teacher work, professional development.

1. Introduction

The availability of OERs has introduced drastic changes in education (European Commission, 2013) regarding both the nature of resources and teachers' interactions with such resources, as *users* as well as *designers*. Designing and using an OER, in particular OERs like lesson plans incorporating the use of software, requires new competences. Using OERs is likely to contribute to teachers' professional development and more specifically the development of new practices with digital resources. Collective teacher work can support this integration. The example of lesson studies in Japan (Miyakawa & Winsløw, 2009) highlights the benefits of collective work (construction of a lesson) for professional development. In this paper, the aim is to analyse how collective designing of OERs, and exchanging such resources on a distant platform can contribute to teachers' professional development. The elements presented are the results of an ongoing study on language teachers; members of a group supported by the regional local authorities.

---

1. Université de Bretagne Occidentale, Brest, France; nol.quere@gmail.com

How to cite this article: Quere, N. (2017). Collective designing and sharing of open educational resources: a study of the French CARTOUN platform. In K. Borthwick, L. Bradley & S. Thouësny (Eds), *CALL in a climate of change: adapting to turbulent global conditions – short papers from EUROCALL 2017* (pp. 260-264). Research-publishing.net. https://doi.org/10.14705/rpnet.2017.eurocall2017.723

2. Theoretical framework

To conduct the analysis, the theoretical framework of the DA (Gueudet & Trouche, 2009) is used. This approach has been developed to study the interactions between teachers and resources; when using these resources, teachers develop schemes of use (Vergnaud, 1998). The mixed entity composed of resources and schemes of use is called a document.

The scheme is a stable structure associated with an aim of the activity, comprising several components, in particular Operational Invariants (OIs). The OIs are divided in theorem-in-action, considered as true by the subject when he/she acts, or concept-in-action, and considered as relevant to categorise and select information. The OIs are interpreted as professional knowledge.

Gueudet and Trouche (2009) argue that resources influence the teacher's activity (instrumentation, i.e. the modification of the subject's schemes of action). The teacher acts on his/her resources in return by adapting them (instrumentalisation, i.e. the creation of new functions of the artifact by the subject) during documentational genesis to generate a document. Teachers develop resources and document systems. Their professional development is directly linked with the development of these systems. In this paper, the following research questions are addressed:

- Do the members' group really integrate the resources of the community in their own resources' system?

- Do their participation in the group make their OIs evolve?

3. Data collection methods and analysis

The group of pedagogical integration of the uses of digital technology (GIPUN) is the name of the collective followed. The group is composed of seven language teachers (four English, two Spanish, and one German teacher). The collective concentrates part of its activity on designing resources for a platform named CARTOUN. The latter offers a collaborative geo-positioning service listing pedagogical activities designed and uploaded by teachers and for teachers in Brittany.

The data introduced is extracted from the annual meeting of the group. They use a mailing list during the rest of the year for their exchanges. The study is based on a qualitative methodology. Observed, in particular, is how resources are designed by the members. I do not interact with the members during their work. The audio of the exchanges is recorded and reduced into a synopsis. From there some specific episodes are selected which can illustrate the work of the members on their documents. Finally, these episodes are transcribed in order to identify OIs in members' speeches.

4. Results and discussion

4.1. Introduction of a new resource into the community resources' system

The group has an activity devoted to technological watch focussed on digital resources. This activity leads the members to discover and experiment with new resources. During the meeting, the group facilitator and English teacher (with 14 years teaching experience) presents the BRNE (digital library for schools). This database currently offers resources in English and German to help teachers set up differentiated pathways in class. Following a presentation, the group facilitator asks the members to test this new resource and to provide some feedback by producing an activity document[2] on CARTOUN.

To conduct the analysis, elements in the members' accounts on the possibilities of compatibility of the BRNE with their resources are identified. The time constraint associated with the discovery of new resources is mentioned in the discussion by one of the members. A member explains about her work that "it's more time consuming when I use an unfamiliar digital tool I need to test […]. I needed at least 2 hours of personal involvement". From this extract, the following OI (theorem-in-action) is inferred: "discovering a new digital tool takes time". Another member highlights her interest in the resource as it allows differentiation: "It's good to help those who do not get there, it always saddens me to see those who are bored". The following OIs are defined in this regard: "the weaker students are bored in class if something specific is not prepared for them". These examples suggest that the BRNE is a resource whose appropriation is time-consuming and facilitates the implementation of differentiation in the classroom. These first elements do not seem to contradict the members' OIs. Therefore, I assume that the resource can be introduced into an individual member's resource system.

---

2. To share their OER online, the teachers have to fill a form with specific items (class, subject, hardware/software).

4.2. Discussing new aims: a way to help OIs evolve

After having worked on the design of resources, the members wish to support their management in order to favour its appropriation and dissemination. To do this, they move towards setting up what they call 'functional help'. When a teacher designs the document, he/she inputs the information he/she judges necessary for the implementation of the session/sequence. This suggests that a teacher who is not a member of the group but only a *user* of the documents must have a certain amount of knowledge, notably on technological resources, to master this resource. However, the teachers' knowledge outside the community is not necessarily the same as the members' group knowledge. That's why the latter want to facilitate the users' appropriation of these resources. Another English teacher, with teaching experience of more than seven years, points out this difficulty and starts the discussion. She has already animated webinars[3]. Also, she is familiar with questions on ownership, explaining that "doing basic training on Audacity, Plickers, and Windows Movie Maker would not be a bad idea". She also says that it is "crucial that those who present their successful project also discuss their difficulties". From these examples, two OIs are inferred. The first is that it is necessary to ensure basic knowledge of softwares. The second highlights that the difficulties encountered in the design and/or implementation must be shared. It can be assumed that sharing this knowledge will have two effects on the teachers' work. Firstly, the discussion about resources should lead to transformation/modification of the document forms (instrumentalisation) by the members trying to incorporate these new points. Secondly, in these exchanges, the teacher brings elements of her professional knowledge that could change the members' interactions with their resources by modifying their design work. She is likely to influence the development of the document systems of all members.

5. Conclusion

In this paper the aim was to show how collective work with OERs can contribute to evolutions in the resources and document systems of teachers and to their professional development. Analysing the data collected, this study shows that a new resource is integrated into the resource's system if this resource is compatible with one of the teacher's OIs. Also, OIs, as elements of knowledge, are likely to evolve during the discussion between members in a collective. Teachers' OIs will be studied over a long period in order to analyse the central role of the

---

3. Webinar: various types of online collaborative services and peer-level web meetings.

documents in the resources' system of the community. These documents allow the double process of instrumentation-instrumentalisation that supports professional development (Gueudet & Trouche, 2009).

6. Acknowledgements

I would like to thank the group of teachers who allowed me to follow them, and the Brittany region for funding my research.

References

European Commission (2013). *Analysis and mapping of innovative teaching and learning for all through new technologies and open educational resources in Europe.* http://eur-lex.europa.eu/LexUriServ/LexUriServ.do?uri=SWD:2013:0341:FIN:EN:PDF

Gueudet, G., & Trouche, L. (2009). Towards new documentary systems for mathematics teachers. *Educational Studies in Mathematics, 71*(3), 199-218. https://doi.org/10.1007/s10649-008-9159-8

Miyakawa, T., & Winsløw, C. (2009). Un dispositif japonais pour le travail en équipe d'enseignants: étude collective d'une leçon. *Education & Didactique, 3*(1), 77-90. https://doi.org/10.4000/educationdidactique.420

Vergnaud, G. (1998). Toward a cognitive theory of practice. In A. Sierpinska & J. Kilpatrick (Eds), *Mathematics education as a research domain: a search for identity* (pp. 227-241). Kluwer Academic Publisher.

University of Southampton

Harnessing the power of informal learning: using WeChat, the semi-synchronous group chat, to enhance spoken fluency in Chinese learners

Marion Sadoux[1]

Abstract. This research is an exploratory study that seeks to evaluate the potentials of the Chinese app WeChat to enhance the spoken fluency of learners of French in China, who report having limited and insufficient opportunities to practice speaking in their daily life. WeChat is an extremely popular instant messenger facilitating communication through a media rich environment that can be used synchronously, asynchronously or semi-synchronously with voice or text messages. WeChat is widely used in China and a growing number of informal highly autonomous language learners join or form WeChat groups to learn and practice speaking languages in personal networks of learning. The study sought to bring together French learners and expert users to give them increased opportunities to practise their spoken French on a daily basis for a period of three months to support the development of spoken fluency.

Keywords: semi-synchronous computer mediated communication, fluency development, autonomy, language learning strategies.

1. Introduction

The digital age has brought along a plethora of new exciting avenues to learn, teach, and practice a foreign language: from the access to seemingly unlimited authentic multimedia resources in almost any target language, to the availability anywhere anytime, at the click of a button, of a native speaker with whom one may communicate for free, in writing or virtually face-to-face (or voice-to-voice). Formal instructed language learning continues to occupy the central stage, yet it is clear that the affordances and strategies of self-instructed language learning

---

1. University of Nottingham Ningbo China, Ningbo, China; sadouxm@gmail.com

How to cite this article: Sadoux, M. (2017). Harnessing the power of informal learning: using WeChat, the semi-synchronous group chat, to enhance spoken fluency in Chinese learners. In K. Borthwick, L. Bradley & S. Thouësny (Eds), *CALL in a climate of change: adapting to turbulent global conditions – short papers from EUROCALL 2017* (pp. 265-270). Research-publishing.net. https://doi.org/10.14705/rpnet.2017.eurocall2017.724

through the internet could be transforming the language learning landscape and that fully autonomous language learners are increasingly numerous and able to reach high levels of competence without or beyond formal instruction (Cole & Vanderplank, 2016).

This study stems from the desire to explore the possibility of harnessing some of the affordances and learning strategies of successful users of social networking apps and sites for language learning (such as Hello Talk, Busuu, High Natives), as well as communities of Chinese user groups on WeChat, to support the development of speaking fluency among learners of French at the University of Nottingham Ningbo China (UNNC). This research initially seeks to validate the hypothesis that the affordances of WeChat can facilitate informal engagement and practice in the target language in a way that may support fluency development. It also seeks to examine whether learners in instructed contexts can embrace strategies for best practice from their interaction with fully autonomous expert users.

Figure 1. WeChat to French fluency interface and functions

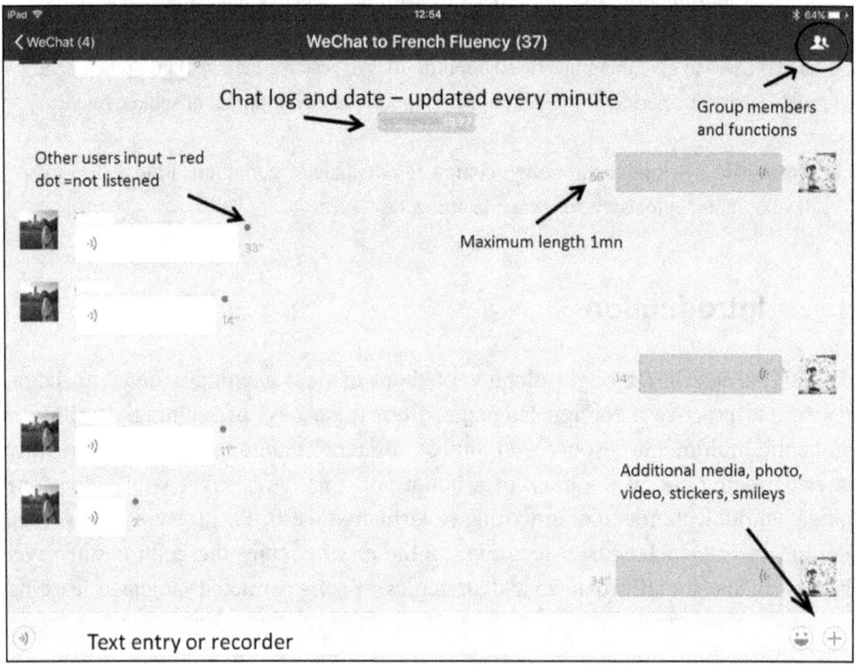

WeChat is an everyday feature of Chinese life, its use ranging far beyond social networking to banking and daily wireless transactions, apps within apps, and all aspects of required connectivity. It is also widely used for learning and numerous 'public' accounts are set up to provide pushed learning objects towards communities of learners (see Hujiang, http://www.hujiang.com/app). Most students at UNNC, both Chinese and international, are well versed in the use of WeChat. Critically, this app offers the possibility of setting up media rich semi-synchronous interaction through voice or text messaging with a minimum time lag. Studies on Semi-Synchronous Computer Mediated Communication (SSCMC) have shown that these can support the development of spoken fluency. Two key features are that these "conversations in slow motion" (Beauvois, 1992, p. 455) generally permit greater participation (Kern, 1995) and offer a highly beneficial short time lag, giving learners an opportunity to plan and repair their communication. Studies have shown that SSCMC leads to uses of language that manifest both higher complexity and wider lexical diversity (Smith, 2005).

The instructional intervention in this exploratory study follows principles of sociocultural theory and microgenesis (Ford, Johnston, Mitchell, & Myles, 2004) and took place between April and June 2017. There were a total of 32 participants and three facilitators[2]. These were all volunteers and included non-specialist students at UNNC on level A2-B1 French courses (the target participants) along with specialist students on a joint honours Bachelor of Arts in French and Chinese from the University of Nottingham in the UK (level C1, the more proficient peers) and experienced users of WeChat from informal learning groups (B2-C1, the fully autonomous expert users of WeChat). The WeChat group also included three French native speaker facilitators with different roles and relations to the target participant group.

2. Methodology

2.1. The intervention

During a period of three months, students were invited to participate to informal discussions in French on WeChat using its semi-synchronous voice facilities. Although the students were invited to make predominant use of the voice messaging function, texting was also encouraged. The facilitation operated with three different aims[3]:

---

2. See supplement, part 1, for more details: https://research-publishing.box.com/s/od48ywuqbcwl72cp2cu6li3jqg9hb1kd
3. See supplement, part 2, for detailed examples: https://research-publishing.box.com/s/od48ywuqbcwl72cp2cu6li3jqg9hb1kd

- to initiate or take part in conversations with occasional corrective feedback to keep communication going;

- to propose warm up activities or topics for discussion;

- to boost engagement with focussed activities and materials timed according to assessment points in the life of the modules the target participants were taking.

There was no set time to participate and participants were totally free to talk about anything – protocols were established from the start in terms of ways to enter and leave the chat through appropriate signals and using basic courtesy.

2.2. Methods

This investigation, which was exploratory in intent, followed mixed research methods focussing on a wide range of potential issues. The WeChat group logs constituted the main data to explore and this was done using both a transcription and coding of some key events – longer and more sustained exchanges or voice input from highly active participants – as well as the chat data available in WeChat (time and duration of voice output). Questionnaires and semi-structured interviews of participants were also used. The table in the supplementary materials[4] summarises the data collection and findings.

3. Results and discussion

The initial findings point to positive outcomes for learners with a high level of regular participation. The chat log clearly shows learners using verbal and non-verbal strategies to produce their messages, but also making use of structural features of the app to maintain a focus on meaning and produce and refine messages: the semi-synchronous nature of the app allows for segmentation, which in turn supports the proceduralisation of more complex messages and the instant deleting of messages by participants also provides an initial safety net enabling learners to feel more able to speak spontaneously, as they can withdraw any message they wish to recall. These latter features are not possible in face-to-face communications and may be one of the reasons why learners indicated feeling less anxious to speak through online tools such as WeChat, which they reported in the

---

4. See supplement, part 3, for more details: https://research-publishing.box.com/s/od48ywuqbcwl72cp2cu6li3jqg9hb1kd

interview as convenient, easy to use, and reducing their fear of making mistakes. This hypothesis is confirmed by the data from questionnaires and semi-structured interviews with target participants.

As an illustrative example, the detailed analysis of the chat log of one highly active participant shows instances of deleted voice messages totally disappearing from the log after a month, an increasing use of verbal fillers as opposed to onomatopoeia ("comment dire..." as opposed to "heu..."), and a decreasing number of short mid-sentence interruptions to produce a complete output. In parallel, there is a small gain in fluency measured as syllables per second.

In relation to the exploration of how to bring practice from expert successful autonomous learners who are expert users, a very low level of uptake of regular chatting activity among the group of target participants (non experts) suggests that this possibly requires a particular type of didactic intervention or embedding into the syllabus which did not occur in this study.

The semi-structured interviews between low participation target participants and expert users showed clear differences: the target participants were less sophisticated in their critical evaluation of learning tools and showed lower levels of willingness to participate relating to both their fear of making mistakes as well as the lesser value they attributed to social interaction in language learning.

4. Conclusions

The results of this study suggest that familiar social media tools enabling semi-synchronous communication and the creation of a mixed network of participants can enhance language learning. However, learners in formal instructed contexts may require further guidance, including a focus on learning how to learn a language. Not surprisingly perhaps, in a Chinese context, the fear of making mistakes, often perceived by learners as 'shyness', proved to be both the biggest obstacle to participation and the biggest gain and liberation among those who did chat.

5. Acknowledgements

I would like to thank Michel, everyone on the Français Facile 2 WeChat Group, and all the participants at UNNC.

References

Beauvois, M. H. (1992). Computer assisted classroom discussion in the foreign language classroom: conversations in slow motion. *Foreign language Annals, 25*, 455-464. https://doi.org/10.1111/j.1944-9720.1992.tb01128.x

Cole, J., & Vanderplank, R. (2016). Comparing autonomous and class-based learners in Brazil: evidence for present-day advantages of informal, out-of-class learning. *System, 61*, 31-42. https://doi.org/10.1016/j.system.2016.07.007

Ford, P., Johnston, B., Mitchell, R., & Myles, F. (2004). Social work education and criticality: some thoughts from research. *Social Work Education, 23*(2), 185-198. https://doi.org/10.1080/0261547042000209198

Kern, R. G. (1995). Restructuring classroom interaction with networked computers: effects on quantity and quality of language production. *The Modern Language Journal, 79*, 457-6. https://doi.org/10.1111/j.1540-4781.1995.tb05445.x

Smith, B. (2005). The relationship between negotiated interaction, learner uptake and lexical acquisition in task-based computer mediated communication. *TESOL Quarterly, 39*(1), 33-58. https://doi.org/10.2307/3588451

ESL learners' online research and comprehension strategies

Noridah Sain[1], Andy Bown[2], Andrew Fluck[3], and Paul Kebble[4]

Abstract. In order to enhance second language (L2) acquisition, English as a Second Language (ESL) students are encouraged to exploit the abundant information and opportunities for authentic language use afforded by the Internet. This study investigated the online research and comprehension strategies employed by ESL learners in a public university in Malaysia. The study was descriptive and the data was collected via the Qualtrics survey system. Data analysis demonstrated the most and least frequently used online research and comprehension strategies of 74 ESL undergraduates and uncovered an overview of the ESL undergraduates' existing online research and comprehension strategies. The findings suggest that explicit training in the area of online research and comprehension processes is worth pursuing in the development of online study skills. This study also presents validation of a survey instrument used within the study to assess ESL learners' online research and comprehension strategies.

Keywords: online research strategies, digital literacies, ESL learners, Asia.

1. Introduction

The Internet has become an important, if not indispensable, tool for communication, information retrieval, transaction processing, and problem solving in all aspects of our lives. In classroom contexts, learners today rely heavily on the Internet as a source of information, rendering the ability to comprehend what is read during online research and learning even more crucial to knowledge-based societies (Goldman et al., 2012). "The plethora of information available online, coupled

---

1. University of Tasmania, Launceston, Australia; noridah.sain@utas.edu.au
2. University of Tasmania, Launceston, Australia; andy.bown@utas.edu.au
3. University of Tasmania, Launceston, Australia; andrew.fluck@utas.edu.au
4. University of Tasmania, Launceston, Australia; paul.kebble@utas.edu.au

How to cite this article: Sain, N., Bown, A., Fluck, A., & Kebble, P. (2017). ESL learners' online research and comprehension strategies. In K. Borthwick, L. Bradley & S. Thouësny (Eds), *CALL in a climate of change: adapting to turbulent global conditions – short papers from EUROCALL 2017* (pp. 271-276). Research-publishing.net. https://doi.org/10.14705/rpnet.2017.eurocall2017.725

with heavy reliance on the Internet by information seekers raise issues of the credibility or quality of information found online" (Metzger, 2007).

To make effective use of new technologies in their academic and future endeavors, Malaysian undergraduates need to be aware of the skills required to autonomously use the Internet for academic purposes. Located within the ESL context in a public university in Malaysia, this study aimed to explore the use of the Internet when undergraduates conduct online research and comprehension activities in order to provide practitioners with data about the use of the Internet to better assist their students.

2. Method

Seventy-four undergraduates (21 male and 53 female) from a public university in Malaysia were identified using convenience sampling to participate in this study. They were around the age of 19 to 21 years old. These 74 students were second and third semester ESL students from various courses.

The instrument developed for this study is the Online Research And Comprehension Strategies (ORACS) survey. The ORACS survey consisted of 37 items. Sixteen items were based on the five processes involved in online research and comprehension activities suggested by the new literacies of online research and comprehension perspectives (Kingsley & Tancock, 2014) while the other 21 items were taken from the Online Survey of Online Reading Strategies (OSORS) by Anderson (2003). OSORS made use of a five point Likert scale and each item in the ORACS survey used a similar scaling option. To date, OSORS (Anderson, 2003) has been widely used to assess students' strategies when reading online and comprehending online information.

However, this popular survey instrument lacks the navigational aspect, which is important in assessing online research and comprehension strategies. The ORACS survey instrument included the navigational aspect, which was missing in OSORS. The Cronbach's alpha for the ORACS was found to be .97. The survey was administered in a computer laboratory during a formal weekly meeting.

The ORACS survey link was uploaded to the e-learning platform used by the academic staff and students of the chosen public university. Prior to filling out the ORACS survey, participants were first led to the online informed consent on which they were required to indicate their willingness to participate in the study.

3. Results

Table 1 summarizes the top five online research and comprehension strategies among the total 37 items in the ORACS survey.

Table 1. Five online research and comprehension strategies most frequently used by ESL undergraduates

Online Research and Comprehension Strategies	Never	Rarely	Sometimes	Often	Always	Mean*	Std. Deviation
I read the article closely after I have identified specific information within webpages when conducting online research.	0	6 (8.1%)	17 (23.0%)	40 (54.1%)	11 (14.9%)	3.76	.808
I re-read online text to increase my understanding when online text becomes difficult.	1 (1.4%)	4 (5.4%)	20 (27%)	33 (44.6%)	16 (21.6%)	3.80	.891
Online Research and Comprehension Strategies	**Never**	**Rarely**	**Sometimes**	**Often**	**Always**	**Mean***	**Std. Deviation**
I use reference material (e.g. an online dictionary) to help me understand what I read online.	1 (1.4%)	2 (2.7%)	23 (31.1%)	23 (31.1%)	25 (33.8%)	3.93	.941
I use keyword search and phrase searching strategies when conducting online research.	0	3 (4.1%)	24 (32.4%)	35 (47.3%)	12 (16.2%)	3.76	.773
I click on links or hyperlinks that are useful for my task within webpages that I find when conducting online research.	0	5 (6.8%)	23 (31.1%)	35 (47.3%)	11 (14.9%)	3.70	.806

*Never=1, Rarely=2, Sometimes=3, Often =4, Always=5

Table 2 lists the five online research and comprehension strategies that the ESL undergraduates would use the least when conducting online research based on the ORACS survey.

Table 2. Five least frequently used online research and comprehension strategies by ESL undergraduates

Online Research and Comprehension Strategies	Never	Rarely	Sometimes	Often	Always	Mean*	Std. Deviation
I differentiate the author's tone and purpose in the sources that I find on the Internet when conducting online research.	0	8 (10.8%)	41 (55.4%)	19 (25.7%)	6 (8.1%)	3.31	.775
I use Google Scholar when conducting online research.	8 (10.8%)	18 (24.3%)	22 (29.7%)	17 (23.0%)	9 (12.2%)	3.01	1.19
I use Google Advanced Search or Yahoo! Advanced Web Search to narrow down my search results when conducting online research.	3 (4.1%)	18 (24.3%)	26 (35.1%)	14 (18.9%)	13 (17.6%)	3.22	1.13
I print out a hard copy of the online text then underline or circle the information to help me remember it.	1 (1.4%)	21 (28.4%)	21 (28.4%)	21 (28.4%)	10 (13.5%)	3.24	1.06
Online Research and Comprehension Strategies	Never	Rarely	Sometimes	Often	Always	Mean*	Std. Deviation
I read aloud to help me understand what I read when online text becomes difficult.	4 (5.4%)	16 (21.6%)	23 (31.1%)	21 (28.4%)	10 (13.5%)	3.23	1.11

*Never=1, Rarely=2, Sometimes=3, Often =4, Always=5

4. Discussion

The results from this study revealed that the ESL undergraduates would often or always use strategies that help them understand the online information when conducting online research. They do this by reading carefully, re-reading, and using online tools such as an online dictionary when trying to comprehend the online information. They would also often or always use keyword and phrase searching strategies followed by clicking on links or hyperlinks that they perceived to be useful for their task within the webpages that they found when conducting online research. These strategies are related to one of the five processing practices that occur during online research and comprehension activity: locating online information. The other four processing practices are defining important questions, evaluating online information, synthesizing online information, and communicating online information (Kingsley & Tancock, 2014). From Table 2, it is found that one of the strategies that these ESL undergraduates would rarely or never use is connected to the practice of evaluating online information (differentiating the author's tone and purpose in online sources). Such low frequencies of the practice of critically evaluating online information imply that the participants lack awareness with regard to the issue of reliability and credibility of online information. Other less frequently used strategies point to the participants' insufficient exposure to several online tools (Google Scholar, Google Advanced Search, and Yahoo! Advanced Web Search) that may assist them in locating online information more effectively during online research. Overall, the findings showed that the ESL undergraduates did not use all of the strategies investigated in the ORACS survey and the way they used the strategies was centered on a particular, or presumably, limited number of strategies.

5. Conclusion

The findings from this research substantiate the growing concern among educators about the ability of current students to successfully conduct online research and critically evaluate online information sources for academic purposes (Sain, Md. Nawi, Mustafa, & Kadir, 2014). However, the small sample size obtained from a single university limits the external validity of this study. Future research should also compare the students' self-reported strategies with their actual online research and comprehension performance. Nevertheless, it is hoped that the findings from this research will further assist language practitioners and policymakers to put forward approaches to boost the online research and comprehension skills among students in Malaysia so that these students may utilize their skills and strategies for their future needs.

6. Acknowledgements

This work was supported by the University of Tasmania, Australia.

References

Anderson, N. (2003). Scrolling, clicking, and reading English: online reading strategies in a second/foreign language. *The Reading Matrix, 3*(3), 1-33. http://citeseerx.ist.psu.edu/viewdoc/download?doi=10.1.1.110.2782&rep=rep1&type=pdf

Goldman, S. R., Braasch, J. L. G., Wiley, J., Graesser, A. C., & Brodowinska, K. (2012). Comprehending and learning from internet sources: processing patterns of better and poorer learners. *Reading Research Quarterly, 47*(4), 356-381.

Kingsley, T., & Tancock, S. (2014). Internet inquiry. *The Reading Teacher, 67*(5), 389-399. https://doi.org/10.1002/trtr.1223

Metzger, M. J. (2007). Making sense of credibility on the web: models for evaluating online information and recommendations for future research. *Journal of the American Society for Information Science and Technology, 58*(13), 2078-2091. https://doi.org/10.1002/asi.20672

Sain, N., Md. Nawi, S., Mustafa, H., Kadir, H. (2014). Investigating the needs for innovative online-based research practices in the ESL classrooms. In C. Fook et al. (Eds). *7th International Conference on University Learning and Teaching (InCULT 2014) Proceedings.* Springer. https://doi.org/10.1007/978-981-287-664-5_52

Combining formal and informal learning: the use of an application to enhance information gathering and sharing competence in a foreign language

Yukiko Sato[1], Irene Erlyn Wina Rachmawan[2], Stefan Brückner[3], Ikumi Waragai[4], and Yasushi Kiyoki[5]

Abstract. This study aims to enhance foreign language learners' language competence by integrating formal and informal learning environments and considers how they can improve their grammatical and lexical skills through the gathering (comprehension) and sharing (writing) of information in the foreign language. Experiments with German learners at a Japanese university preparing to study in Germany were conducted. An application to archive newspaper articles was created, indexing current German coverage. A worksheet was provided, where learners were asked to select, read, and summarize articles via the application. Feedback was given to their summary. Participants were divided into two groups, learners that studied only in an informal setting, and those that were also instructed in a formal setting. Interviews were conducted with the participants in order to evaluate how the activities affected their language skills. Results showed that the practice affected their reading methods and heightened their motivation for further language learning in general. Students participating in activities in and outside the classroom showed improvements in their lexical knowledge, and better understanding of subtle nuances in written texts, which positively affected their writing skills and their speaking ability.

Keywords: second language learning, news article material, formal and informal learning, language competence.

---

1. Keio University, Tokyo, Japan; ysato0724@gmail.com
2. Keio University, Tokyo, Japan; ireneerl@sfc.keio.ac.jp
3. Keio University, Tokyo, Japan; bruckner@sfc.keio.ac.jp
4. Keio University, Tokyo, Japan; ikumi@sfc.keio.ac.jp
5. Keio University, Tokyo, Japan; kiyoki@sfc.keio.ac.jp

How to cite this article: Sato, Y., Wina Rachmawan, I. E., Brückner, S., Waragai, I., & Kiyoki, Y. (2017). Combining formal and informal learning: the use of an application to enhance information gathering and sharing competence in a foreign language. In K. Borthwick, L. Bradley & S. Thouësny (Eds), *CALL in a climate of change: adapting to turbulent global conditions – short papers from EUROCALL 2017* (pp. 277-282). Research-publishing.net. https://doi.org/10.14705/rpnet.2017.eurocall2017.726

1. Introduction

In recent years, the importance of practising communicative language learning competence has been highlighted in foreign language learning and teaching, together with an increased use of current technological means to facilitate communication skills. According to a study by Burston and Arispe (2016), 81% of computer assisted language studies focus on 'writing' skills of foreign language learners. While the learners' grammatical and communicational abilities could be enhanced, few studies have been focusing on the learners' enhancement of their reading, grammatical, and lexical competence. Previous studies investigated the effects of reading in language learning. Al Ghazali (2016) and Lee and Pulido (2016) examined the acquisition of vocabulary from reading English texts in the classroom. Wang (2017) studied the impact of mobile learning on reading comprehension. Fenner (2006) advocates a learner centered language teaching environment. Meskill (2009) examines the possibilities that online venues for individual informal learning, integrated with face-to-face instruction, hold for higher education language learning. Panichi (2015) highlights the benefits of the use of social media for several learning activities, while Krashen (2016) states "that the crucial elements for success, for both literacy and cognitive development, are self-selected reading and engaging in problem-solving in an area of intense personal interest" (p. 2). This research focuses on the question of how students can expand their grammatical and lexical knowledge through the gathering (comprehension) and sharing (writing) of information in a foreign language. It attempts to contribute to solving this problem by creating an application that archives newspaper articles, focusing on a specific theme collected in the learned foreign language. It is postulated that learners will enhance their lexical and grammatical knowledge through the application when combined with formal learning (in class) and informal learning (outside the classroom).

This study was carried out with Japanese students in the German learning course (Level A2 to B1) at the Shonan Fujisawa Campus (SFC) of Keio University (Japan), who are preparing to study abroad in Germany. The German department at SFC has developed their own original textbook for beginners in order to develop a 'communication-based' language learning environment, in which students are only confronted with limited grammar and vocabulary through their textbooks.

2. Method

Four students were separated into two groups: Group A (Participant A and B) and Group B (Participant C and D). Group A consisted of students participating in a preparatory course for carrying out fieldwork in Germany, in order to study the effects of combining formal and informal learning environments. Students in Group B did not participate in class and studied in an informal setting during their free time.

For this study, the following steps were carried out: (1) a survey study with the Japanese students in order to determine what kind of media they tend to use to obtain information about Germany; (2) construction of the newspaper article database and application; (3) handing out worksheets to the participants, asking them to write summaries of the articles they read; (4) lectures and feedback in class (Group A); and (5) evaluation of the submitted worksheet and follow-up interviews with the learners (Figure 1). The results from the survey, worksheet, and interview with the students were analyzed through a content analysis, paying special attention to how students improved their skills in gathering and sharing information relating to Germany, as well as their grammatical and lexical skills.

Figure 1. Structure of the study

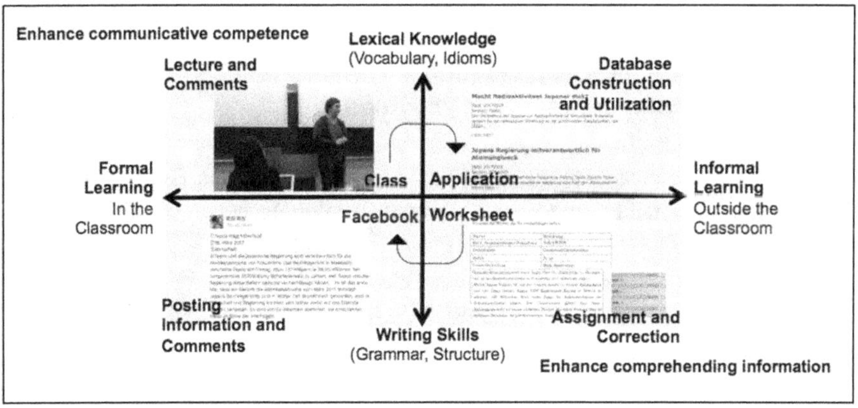

3. Discussion

3.1. Database and application design

For the application, newspaper articles from the web version of the German newspapers *Frankfurter Allgemeine Zeitung* and *Süddeutsche Zeitung*, relating to the theme of the Big Earthquake, Tsunami, and nuclear disaster in Japan 2011, were collected. The topic was selected based on its continued societal importance, both in Germany and Japan. An original German newspaper archive application was created so students could choose to read articles according to their own interests (Figure 2).

Figure 2. The newspaper archive application

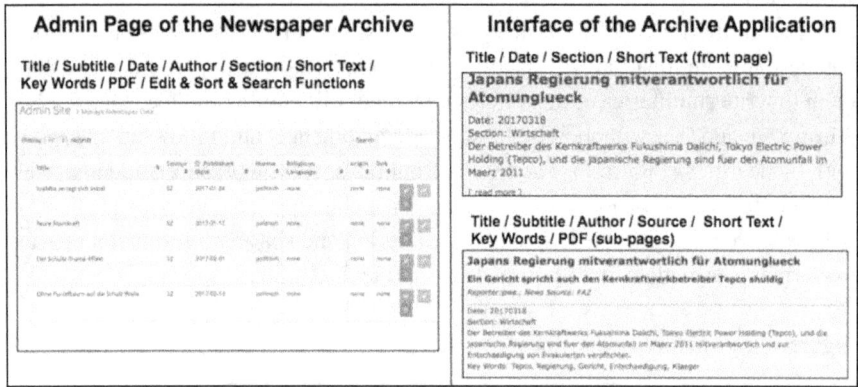

3.2. Use of the news application and reading news article activities

The survey made clear that all participants regularly accessed German language information by attempting to read German articles accessed via Facebook or Twitter. However, none of the students read the articles completely. Instead, they routinely relied on supplementing the articles with English language sources, or translated them into English or Japanese by using Google Translator. Results from the interview showed that the use of the application and the task of summarizing the article improved the participants' reading skills by looking up new vocabulary in dictionaries, while trying to comprehend the text in the original German. Students participating using the developed application showed improvements in their language skills.

Participant A learned technical terms and the subtle nuances of prepositions (such as 'da', 'bis', 'ein') because of the frequent use of the words 'bisher' (until now) and 'daher' (because) in the newspaper article. Participant B reported that the exercise influenced her result during the oral German examination at the end of the semester, as she remembered words such as "Gefahr" (danger) from the articles she read. This shows that this learning method combining the reading of newspaper articles of a related or specific theme, with writing exercises and feedback, also proved to have a positive influence on the long-term retention of learned words (Figure 3).

Figure 3. Activities and results

4. Conclusions

Students in Group A showed an enhancement in several aspects by: (1) noticing new lexical elements through reading; (2) better understanding the nuances of the vocabulary through writing exercises and direct feedback; and (3) enhancing their competence to convey the obtained information orally. In general, participation in the experiment positively influenced students' motivation to learn German. It also influenced the learning style of the participants, encouraging them to try to comprehend the meaning of the article in the foreign language. The aim in constructing this learning system was to positively affect the lexical and grammatical skills of foreign language learners and to enhance their skills to gather and share the information obtained in a foreign language, by utilizing an original newspaper archive system. Results showed that combining exercises with the German article archive system positively affected their reading comprehension and ability to convey information literally and orally. However, this study was conducted in a short term with a limited number of participants. A long-term study with a greater number of participants is important in order to determine the effects of the proposed system.

References

Al Ghazali, F. (2016). *Extensive reading strategies in EFL classrooms: a practical overview for enhancing reading comprehension*. Lambert Academic Publishing.

Burston, J., & Arispe, K. (2016). The contribution of CALL to advanced-level foreign/second language instruction. In S. Papadima-Sophocleous, L. Bradley & S. Thouësny (Eds), *CALL communities and culture – short papers from EUROCALL 2016* (pp. 61-68). Research-publishing.net. https://doi.org/10.14705/rpnet.2016.eurocall2016.539

Fenner, A.-B. (2006). Learner autonomy – one of the most widely touted terms in recent discussion of language teaching? In A.-B. Fenner & D. Newby (Eds), *Coherence of principles, cohesion of competences: exploring theories and designing materials for teacher education* (pp. 27-39). Council of Europe.

Krashen, S. (2016). Compelling reading and problem-solving: the easy way (and the only way) to high levels of language, literacy and life competence. In L. Yiu-nam (Ed.), *Epoch making in English language teaching and learning. Twenty-fifth international symposium on English teaching* (pp. 115-125). English Teachers' Association. http://www.sdkrashen.com/content/articles/2016_krashen_eta_compelling_reading_and_ps.pdf

Lee, S., & Pulido, D. (2016). The impact of topic interest, L2 proficiency, and gender on EFL incidental vocabulary acquisition through reading. *Language Teaching Research, 21*(1), 118-135. https://doi.org/10.1177/1362168816637381

Meskill, C. (2009). CMC in language teacher education: learning with and through instructional conversation. *Innovation in Language Learning and Teaching, 3*(1), 51-63. https://doi.org/10.1080/17501220802655474

Panichi, L. (2015). The employment of social networking for language learning and teaching: insights and issues. In R. Hernandez & P. Rankin, *Higher education and second language learning: promoting self-directed learning in new technological and educational contexts* (pp. 159-179). Peter Lang.

Wang, Y. H. (2017). Integrating self-paced mobile learning into language instruction: impact on reading comprehension and learner satisfaction. *Interactive Learning Environments. 25*(3), 397-411. https://doi.org/10.1080/10494820.2015.1131170

An open-sourced and interactive ebook development program for minority languages

Emily Sheepy[1], Ross Sundberg[2], and Anne Laurie[3]

Abstract. According to Long (2014), genuine task-based pedagogy is centered around the real-world activities that learners need to complete using the target language. We are developing the OurStories mobile application to support learners and instructors of minority languages in the development of personally relevant, task-based learning resources. The initial prototype, which we are inviting community organizations to use and adapt to their needs, takes the form of an audio-enabled ebook as well as the software and a series of templates used for developing future materials. We introduce the OurStories software, its interactive features, and the research-based development process. We also discuss plans to expand the project into a program directed by in-group members of Indigenous language communities who wish to continue the development of pedagogically sound technologies.

Keywords: language revitalization, task-based language learning, computer-assisted language learning, open educational resources.

1. Introduction

We are developing a prototype mobile application (app) for collecting spoken language samples as part of a larger research program in technology-supported language revitalization for Indigenous and other minority language communities. The app is to be used in conjunction with a community-centered ebook production process to create audio-enabled Task-Based Language Learning (TBLL) resources. Here, we present the development of our production process and the creation of templates for creating future open-sourced materials.

---

1. Concordia University, Montreal, Canada; emily.sheepy@concordia.ca
2. Concordia University, Montreal, Canada; ross.sundberg@concordia.ca
3. Concordia University, Montreal, Canada; anne.laurie142@hotmail.com

How to cite this article: Sheepy, E., Sundberg, R., & Laurie, A. (2017). An open-sourced and interactive ebook development program for minority languages. In K. Borthwick, L. Bradley & S. Thouësny (Eds), *CALL in a climate of change: adapting to turbulent global conditions – short papers from EUROCALL 2017* (pp. 283-288). Research-publishing.net. https://doi.org/10.14705/rpnet.2017.eurocall2017.727

1.1. Motivation for the project

Today, all Canadian Indigenous languages are endangered (Battiste, 2013). Consequently, Indigenous children are growing up speaking languages other than their heritage language as their dominant language (Norris, 2006). In an effort to revitalize Indigenous languages in North America, organizations such as Native Languages of the Americas (native-languages.org) accumulate resources to be used in teaching or preserving endangered languages. To aid in the creation of locally relevant learning materials, we set out to develop a community-centered ebook production process to serve as a platform for generating open-sourced TBLL resources.

Research has suggested that adding audio for texts used in language revitalization curricula is valuable to vocabulary and phonological development (Grgurović & Hegelheimer, 2007). Additionally, there is a need for language education materials (that will address the needs of parents or other community members who are not proficient in a heritage language) to facilitate heritage language literacy development in children who are solely fluent in colonial languages (Nettle & Romaine, 2000). Recording everyday language use for use in the development of communicative language teaching programs and TBLL resources could be of great use for Indigenous communities, but also for other heritage language communities. Developing tools that are easy to use and adopt will empower community members to exercise their right to independently revitalize their language without the need for ongoing intervention from external researchers or generic textbooks, which are not tailored to reflect local and personal learner needs.

1.2. Task-based learning

According to Long (2014), genuine task-based pedagogy concerns real-world activities that learners need to complete using a new language. An example of a TBLL activity is conducting a mock interview in the target language, as the student's goal is to apply for jobs (Long, 2014). A common practice in second language teaching is to select a task according to the linguistic elements required to complete it (e.g. conducting interviews to practise asking questions) rather than selecting tasks on the basis of students' goals (Long, 2014).

Our open-sourced tool is designed so that communities can select tasks important to their needs and then incorporate the language forms required to complete such tasks. Therefore, a needs analysis forms the foundation for the TBLL syllabus specific to the community involved because the target tasks are chosen by the learners.

1.3. Learning with OurStories

OurStories is intended to facilitate exchanges between the learner and an experienced speaker of the target language. The learner can adapt existing interview guides with questions or prompts, then record a speaker's responses. The recorded segments can then be used in learning activities, and metadata tags added to audio files can help learners revisit vocabulary in context. The completed application will enable the learners to publish their interviews with labelled audio files as interactive audio-enabled web pages, either as integrated narratives or in question-and-answer formats (Figure 1).

Figure 1.   Sample screens from the OurStories prototype

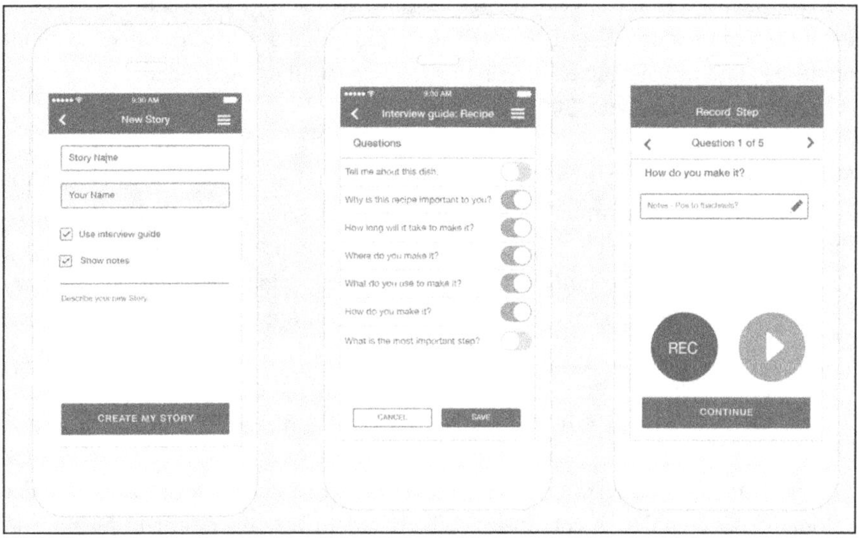

2. Method and design principles

The following principles guided our design for the prototype application.

2.1. Providing a constructivist learning environment

According to Oliver and McLoughlin (1999), constructivist learning experiences are characterized by the use of learning tasks that are relevant and authentic, embedded in social experiences, and encourage learner voice and ownership in the learning process.

In pragmatics field research, structured elicitation techniques are often used in interviews to elicit personal narratives, where the topic of discussion and interview guide is designed to elicit the speech events or features of interest. Researchers applying ethnographic methodologies may present previously elicited personal narratives to third parties to elicit further commentary about those narratives (Oliver & McLoughlin, 1999). Our tool provides the learners with structured elicitation interview guides that enable them to elicit learning materials for themselves in a personally relevant social interaction.

2.2. Supporting communicative language teaching

Gatbonton and Segalowitz (2005) argue for a model of communicative language teaching that places the development of automatic fluency as its central goal. They define automatic fluency as a "smooth and rapid production of utterances, without undue hesitations and pauses, that results from constant use and repetitive practice" (Gatbonton & Segalowitz, 2005, p. 326).

Specifically, they propose the ACCESS instructional approach, which stands for Automatization in Communicative Contexts of Essential Speech Segments. In this instructional approach, lessons are structured around target sets of utterances, called essential speech segments, that learners are expected to acquire and practice. Our app is intended to provide structured elicitation opportunities to collect such target utterances.

2.3. Supporting fluency development with advanced planning

Second language learners' speech production varies in characteristic ways under different task completion conditions. When learners are given time to plan ahead of a production task, they produce more fluent and lexically varied language, and when learners are required to plan online, they produce more grammatically accurate but less lexically rich speech (Yuan & Ellis, 2003). To support learners' development with respect to fluency, complexity, and accuracy, our application and associated instructional materials are intended to facilitate activity completion under varied conditions following TBLL conventions (e.g. Robinson, 2005).

2.4. Scaffolding learner development

By providing adaptable elicitation scripts for use in the application, we aim to support learning activities that require varied levels of learner independence (for a few examples, see Figure 2).

Figure 2. Examples of learning activities with different levels of learner support

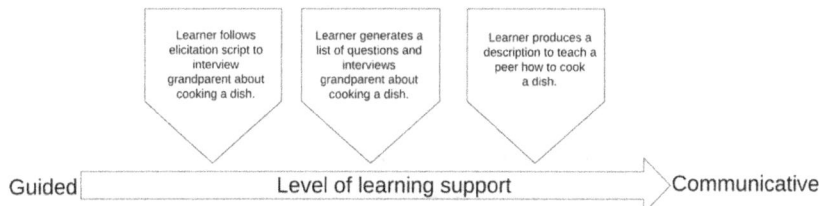

Though TBLL is task-based, guided activities that provide focus on form are seen as being better able to drive accurate proceduralization of L2 skills (Celce-Murcia, Brinton, & Goodwin, 2010; Foster & Skehan, 1996). We propose alternating guided and communicative activities with the focus tending toward more communicative activities as learners' fluency levels increase (see Figure 3). Activity variations afforded by the application are described in the user guide currently under development.

Figure 3. Balancing guided and communicative activities in relation to learner fluency

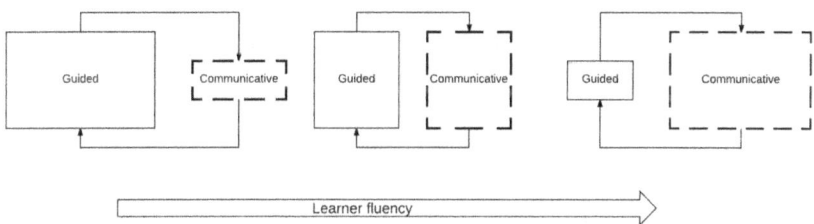

3. Future directions and conclusions

The OurStories application addresses a need for tools supporting rapid development of task-based learning materials for minority language learners. It has not been tested in a learning environment, which would allow us to explore its potential for integration into curricula.

We hope to explore how visual aids might be integrated into elicitation scripts and incorporated into complementary study aids, such as multimedia quizzes and audio-enabled flashcards. Further research could explore the usefulness of the application for learners of different languages, and for learners of different ages.

4. Acknowledgements

This project is supported by seed funding from the Centre for the Study of Learning and Performance (http://www.concordia.ca/research/learning-performance.html).

References

Battiste, M. (2013). *Decolonizing education: nourishing the learning spirit.* Purich Publishing.

Celce-Murcia, M., Brinton, D. M., & Goodwin, J. M. (2010). *Teaching pronunciation: a course book and reference guide* (2nd ed.). Cambridge University Press.

Foster, P., & Skehan, P. (1996). The influence of planning and task type on second language performance. *Studies in Second language acquisition, 18*(3), 299-323. https://doi.org/10.1017/S0272263100015047

Gatbonton, E., & Segalowitz, N. (2005). Rethinking communicative language teaching: a focus on access to fluency. *Canadian Modern Language Review, 61*(3), 325-353. https://doi.org/10.3138/cmlr.61.3.325

Grgurović, M., & Hegelheimer, V. (2007). Help options and multimedia listening: students' use of subtitles and the transcript. *Language Learning & Technology, 11*(1), 45-66.

Long, M. (2014). *Second language acquisition and task-based language teaching.* John Wiley & Sons.

Nettle, D., & Romaine, S. (2000). *Vanishing voices: the extinction of the world's languages.* Oxford University Press.

Norris, M. J. (2006). *Aboriginal languages in Canada: trends and perspectives on maintenance and revitalization.* Aboriginal Policy Research Consortium International (APRCi). Paper 122. http://ir.lib.uwo.ca/aprci/122

Oliver, R., & McLoughlin, C. (1999). Curriculum and learning-resources issues arising from the use of web-based course support systems. *International Journal of Educational Telecommunications, 5*(4), 419-435.

Robinson, P. (2005). Cognitive complexity and task sequencing: studies in a componential framework for second language task design. *International Review of Applied Linguistics in Language Teaching, 43*(1), 1-32. https://doi.org/10.1515/iral.2005.43.1.1

Yuan, F., & Ellis, R. (2003). The effects of pre-task planning and on-line planning on fluency, complexity and accuracy in L2 monologic oral production. *Applied Linguistics, 24*(1), 1-27. https://doi.org/10.1093/applin/24.1.1

Reception of Japanese captions: a comparative study of visual attention between native speakers and language learners of Japanese

Eline C. Sikkema[1]

Abstract. Nowadays, television programmes are not only accessed through a conventional TV set; they can be viewed through streaming services on the internet, smartphones, and tablets to name but a few media. For language learners, this development has opened up opportunities for accessing authentic materials in foreign languages outside of the classroom. Studies have shown that the simultaneous presentation of aural and visual information in captioned audiovisuals in a foreign language has the potential to improve language learners' listening skills (Mitterer & McQueen, 2009). Recent research has prompted extension of this discussion to online language learning behaviour and to analyses of what information learners attend to while watching captioned programmes (Vanderplank, 2015). This doctoral research seeks to contribute to this new perspective and explores actual viewing behaviour of native speakers and language learners of Japanese while watching a captioned Japanese variety show through the use of eye-tracking and questionnaires. This paper discusses the context and methodology of this study as the data analysis is in its initial phase. It is hoped that the results will deepen our understanding of language learners' reception of Japanese captions and make suggestions as to how such authentic material can complement Japanese language learning.

Keywords: captions, Japanese language learning, eye-tracking, visual attention.

1. Introduction

Learning materials that contain AudioVisual (AV) input, such as television programmes, have been a topic of particular discussion in research that explores the

---

1. Dublin City University, Dublin, Ireland; eline.sikkema2@mail.dcu.ie

How to cite this article: Sikkema, E. C. (2017). Reception of Japanese captions: a comparative study of visual attention between native speakers and language learners of Japanese. In K. Borthwick, L. Bradley & S. Thouësny (Eds), *CALL in a climate of change: adapting to turbulent global conditions – short papers from EUROCALL 2017* (pp. 289-293). Research-publishing.net. https://doi.org/10.14705/rpnet.2017.eurocall2017.728

use of leisure-oriented media products in Foreign Language (FL) learning. Studies have shown that the simultaneous presentation of aural and visual information in an FL through the use of same-language text on screen has the potential to improve language learners' listening skills and ability to segment speech, recognise word boundaries, and retune perceptual processing (Charles & Trenkic, 2015; Mitterer & McQueen, 2009). This shows the potential of such same-language text as an aid to learners for visualising FL aural input. Building on studies that examined the effects of same-language text on screen, recent research has increasingly focussed on what language learners do and which information learners attend to while watching videos with such text (Vanderplank, 2015). Additionally, recent CALL research (O'Rourke et al., 2016) has analysed online learning behaviour in Synchronous Computer-Mediated Communication (SCMC) through the application of eye-tracking technology and principles in Second Language Acquisition (SLA).

This doctoral study is no exception to this trend, in that the focus is on the reception of authentic AV material. However, it expands the discussion to online viewing behaviour of Japanese Language Learners (JLLs) while watching a Japanese variety show with same-language text on screen. This study is part of a larger project run at Dublin City University (DCU) that focuses on the reception of this particular media product by different viewer groups. What makes Japanese variety shows different from other types of captioned authentic material studied in SLA research is the integrated text on screen. Rather than incorporating white text that covers the imagery as little as possible, it is common to see same-language text placed on almost half of the television screen in bright colours, a variety of typefaces, and accompanied with different sound effects. A good grasp of how such material is received by JLLs helps to effectively complement the Japanese language classroom with its use. This paper discusses the methodology of this doctoral research as the data analysis is still underway.

2. Context of this study

2.1. Main objectives

Two main objectives form the basis of this research. The general overarching aim of this study is to gain insights into focal attention and online viewing behaviour of JLLs while watching a Japanese variety show with same-language text on screen. A second, more specific goal is to investigate the visual attentional shifts of JLLs against the audio track of the media product in order to gain insights into vision-sound matching or speech monitoring practices of JLLs. It is expected that the findings of this study will contribute towards a better understanding of the subconscious language learning process that precedes the improvement of FL listening skills as has been observed in research on the effects of captions (Charles & Trenkic, 2015; Mitterer & McQueen, 2009).

2.2. Participants and data collection

Data has been collected from 45 JLLs who were at different stages of their Japanese language study at DCU at the time of data collection (three first-years, 15 second-years, 20 third-years, and seven fourth-year students). Data has also been gathered from seven native Japanese speakers who function as a reference group with which learner behaviour is compared. The eye-tracking experiments were conducted in an experimental setting in both Ireland and Japan with a portable Tobii X2-60 eye-tracker attached to a laptop.

3. Methodology

3.1. Methods

A Mixed Methods Research (MMR) design has been developed in order to address the objectives of this study as well as possible. Whereas the first aim requires a largely quantitative approach for searching trends in focal attention and online viewing behaviour of JLLs; the second objective calls for the researcher to zoom in on individual viewing experiences of participants in order to uncover how JLLs monitor speech and attend different types of input. The abundance of highly contextualised information emitted from television programmes gives FL learners the opportunity to attend or select, whether consciously or subconsciously, input that fits their capabilities and supplements their personal learning journeys (Gilmore, 2007). Quantitative and qualitative approaches combined can therefore help explore such processes more thoroughly and inform a better judgement of the appropriate use of captioned television programmes by JLLs.

This research collated data gathered from eye-tracking technology and questionnaires. The data generated by eye movements allows for both a quantitative and qualitative assessment of focal attention based on numerical fixation data within particular Areas Of Interest (AOIs) in the video stimulus and by overlaying the video stimulus with a replay of the gaze of participants. As research on same-language textual inserts in screen-based media have shown that such text on screen fosters learners' listening skills, data on eye movements is approached with a multimodal lens. AOIs are defined based on the type of resemblance identified between the textual inserts and corresponding dialogue (e.g. identical, similar or different representations). The questionnaire responses contain information on factors that may have influenced participants' focal attention such as demographics, experience with Japanese television, and opinions on the text on screen. Furthermore, during the debriefing at the end of each experiment session, participants provided some additional insights into their thoughts on the experiment.

3.2. Data analysis phases

For the purposes of this study it was decided to divide the data analysis into three phases. These phases are defined as follows:

- Identification of resemblance types in the video stimulus

- Generation of numerical eye movement data for each resemblance type and selection of a select number of gaze replay segments

- Interpretational analysis of gaze replay segments

A nested model is applied in order to facilitate the shift in focus for the eye-tracking data analysis from a quantitative into a qualitative approach. This means that a smaller, representative sample is further explored for the qualitative analysis. Although this overview primarily describes how the eye-tracking data is analysed, field notes and questionnaire responses are consulted throughout this process.

4. Potential implications of findings and conclusion

FL learning through authentic material generally emphasises instruction that is not focused on the linguistic aspects of a language; rather, it is based on language in use and often accompanied with awareness-raising tasks (Gilmore, 2007). This implies different teaching formats, instruction styles, and consideration for ways in which technology can enhance the language classroom. Although this doctoral research is foremost a study of language learning behaviour, insights into focal attention and feedback from JLLs on the use of captioned AV material at different academic stages can help deepen our understanding of how to raise Japanese language awareness and the appropriate time to use this type of language learning material. It is expected that the findings of this study will show that different types of resemblance between same-language text on screen and dialogue is accompanied with different speech monitoring practices.

5. Acknowledgements

I would like to thank Dr Joss Moorkens and Prof Françoise Blin for their comments and feedback on this paper. I would also like to thank the School of Applied Language and Intercultural Studies for the travel grant to present my paper at EUROCALL 2017.

References

Charles, T., & Trenkic, D. (2015). Speech segmentation in a second language: the role of bi-modal input. In A. Caimi, Y. Gambier & C. Mariotti (Eds), *Subtitles and language learning: principles, strategies and practical principles* (pp. 173-197). Peter Lang.

Gilmore, A. (2007). Authentic materials and authenticity in foreign language learning. *Language teaching, 40*(2), 97-118. https://doi.org/10.1017/S0261444807004144

Mitterer, H., & McQueen, J. M. (2009). Foreign subtitles help but native-language subtitles harm foreign speech perception. *PLoS one, 4*(11), e7785. https://doi.org/10.1371/journal.pone.0007785

O'Rourke, B., Prendergast, C., Shi, L., Smith, B., & Stickler, U. (2016). Eyetracking in CALL – present and future. In A. Gimeno, M. Levy, F. Blin & D. Barr (Eds), *WorldCALL: sustainability and computer-assisted language learning* (pp. 285-298). Bloomsbury Academic.

Vanderplank, R. (2015). Thirty years of research into captions/same language subtitles and second/foreign language learning: distinguishing between 'effects of' subtitles and 'effects with' subtitles for future research. In A. Caimi, Y. Gambier & C. Mariotti (Eds), *Subtitles and language learning: principles, strategies and practical principles* (pp. 19-40). Peter Lang.

The potential of automated corrective feedback to remediate cohesion problems in advanced students' writing

Carola Strobl[1]

Abstract. This study explores the potential of a feedback environment using simple string-based pattern matching technology for the provision of automated corrective feedback on cohesion problems. Thirty-eight high-frequent problems, including non-target like use of connectives and co-references were addressed providing both direct and indirect feedback. Advanced students of German as a foreign language (L2) (n=36) received this feedback on summary writing in three subsequent sessions. Their revision activities were analysed for a ratio per 100 words and success rate, and their attitudes towards the feedback were investigated using questionnaires. The results show that automated feedback based on pattern matching has the potential to remedy over- and under-use of connectives and co-reference devices. Furthermore, although participants preferred direct feedback, the revision rate was higher with indirect metacognitive feedback providing grammar explanations.

Keywords: automated feedback, advanced writing, cohesion, human computer interaction.

1. Introduction

Cohesion in written learner language is an important, yet under-researched area of investigation. L2 learners struggle with cohesion even at advanced levels of mastery. Cohesion can be expressed through a broad range of lexico-grammatical devices (Halliday & Hasan, 1976). Different lexico-grammatical preferences between the L2 and their mother tongue (L1) can cause L2 writers to make non-target like choices of cohesive features. Furthermore, the pedagogical approach

---

1. Ghent University, Ghent, Belgium; carola.strobl@ugent.be

How to cite this article: Strobl, C. (2017). The potential of automated corrective feedback to remediate cohesion problems in advanced students' writing. In K. Borthwick, L. Bradley & S. Thouësny (Eds), *CALL in a climate of change: adapting to turbulent global conditions – short papers from EUROCALL 2017* (pp. 294-299). Research-publishing.net. https://doi.org/10.14705/rpnet.2017.eurocall2017.729

towards cohesion in L2 textbooks has been identified as harmful, as it is frequently characterised by a focus on grammatical accuracy, rather than on stylistic appropriateness (Cho & Shin, 2014). It is therefore timely to develop pedagogic support that addresses cohesion problems in learner writing in a more appropriate way.

Automated feedback on L2 writing has long been applied mainly to address grammar, lexical, and/or mechanical issues in lower-level instruction. It is only recently that automated writing evaluation systems for English have adopted technologies that allow for a more sophisticated analysis of, and feedback on, learner writing with regard to cohesion (Crossley, Kyle, & McNamara, 2016). For German, no such tool has been developed yet.

This explorative study investigates the potential of a tool using simple pattern matching technology for the provision of corrective feedback on cohesion problems. It also adds to the debate about the effectiveness of written corrective feedback in electronic writing environments (Bitchener, 2012; Ene & Upton, 2014). It was driven by the following research questions: (1) Can cohesion problems successfully be addressed through automated feedback based on pattern-matching technology? (2) Does direct or indirect feedback trigger a higher amount of (successful) revisions? (3) What are students' attitudes towards this feedback?

2. Method

2.1. Feedback creation

The environment used for this study was developed at Ghent University (Belgium) for electronic teacher feedback. Among other features, this tool allows for the automated lookup of words and utterances in predefined lists, highlighting matches in students' texts. By hovering over the highlighted words, additional information can be visualised. This feature was used in the study to provide automated feedback regarding potential non-target like use of cohesion devices. As cohesion is context bound by its very nature, the absence of context-sensitive lookup options and of Natural Language Processing (NLP) technologies for linguistic analysis posed a major challenge. Therefore, the feedback messages were formulated as non-directive suggestions inviting students to reflect their choice of cohesive devices.

To establish a list of potential cohesion problems in summary writing (the assignment used), a corpus of 72 summaries written by a comparable cohort of students to the participants in the study was scrutinised. Thirty-eight high-frequent problems emerged that can be identified through string-based pattern-matching. They mainly concern the non-target like use of connectives and co-reference devices. To target those 38 problems, 125 list entries were created covering morphological and lexical variations of the words or utterances involved. Three lists were produced, each conveying a different type of feedback: (1) direct feedback providing a suggestion for correction of the potential problem (DF), (2) indirect metacognitive feedback providing a grammar explanation (IF1), and (3) indirect feedback providing example utterances (IF2).

2.2. Study design and data collected

Thirty-six students of an intact writing class took part in the experiment. All participants have Dutch as their L1 and major in German L2, with a medium advanced writing proficiency level[2]. Prior to the experiment, they received instruction on summary writing, with a focus on the use of cohesive devices. They also had one session to familiarise with the feedback tool.

The participants received automated feedback on three summaries. On the first occasion, DF was provided, followed by indirect feedback in the two subsequent occasions. To avoid a sequencing effect, half of the group received first IF1 and then IF2[3], and the other half vice-versa. Quantitative data of the revision activities were obtained through comparison of drafts before and after self-correction, and changes were coded according to successfulness. Furthermore, two questionnaires were administered to evaluate participants' attitudes.

3. Results and discussion

3.1. Revision rate and success by feedback type

Figure 1 displays the quantitative results of the revision analysis. To account for differences in word count in the three conditions, revisions per 100 words were calculated. IF1 triggered most revisions by far, totalling two and two and a half times the amount of DF and IF2, respectively. Furthermore, the success rate of

---
2. B2-C1 on the common european framework of reference for languages scale
3. See feedback examples: https://research-publishing.box.com/s/4ebxytqv1crnxml85ij5ilboc9ubv53q

revisions was higher following IF2 (74% of all changes induced by this feedback type) than following DF (64%) and IF1 (61%)[4]. These findings are not in line with the results of earlier studies on electronic (human) feedback on complex L2 writing that ascribed a higher success rate to direct, explicit feedback (c.f. Ene & Upton, 2014, p. 89).

Figure 1. Revision rate and success by feedback type

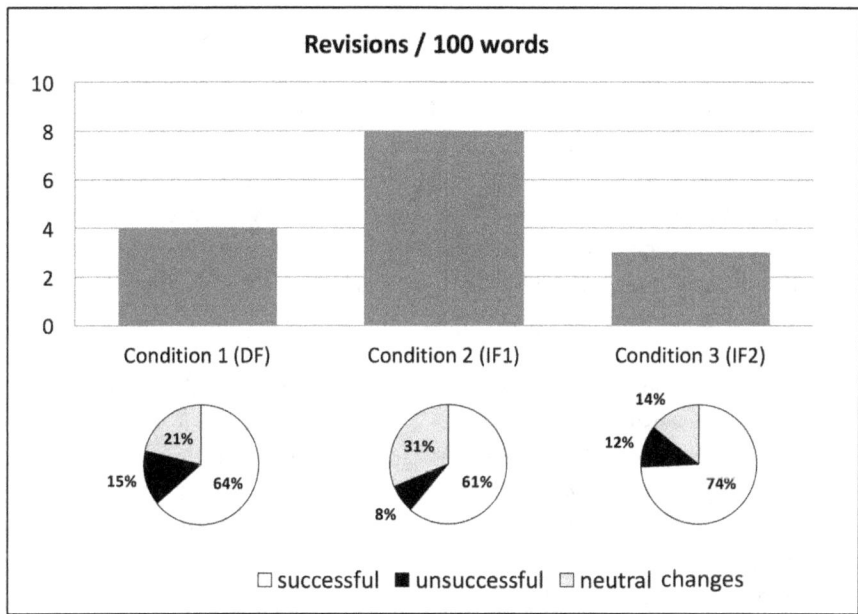

3.2.   Students' attitudes towards the feedback

Three results obtained from the questionnaires will be discussed here. They concern (1) preferences for feedback type, (2) overall attitudes towards usefulness of the automated feedback, and (3) attitudes with regard to the unnecessary feedback created due to lack of sophisticated technology.

(1) Contrary to expectations based on the amount of revisions, students did not prefer indirect feedback based on grammar explanations, which actually received the lowest preference score (28%), followed by indirect feedback based on

---

4. See revision examples: https://research-publishing.box.com/s/4ebxytqv1crnxml85ij5ilboc9ubv53q

examples (31%). Students' comments comparing the two indirect feedback can be interpreted as windows to their preferred learning styles, i.e. inductive learning ("I like to deduce rules from examples; grammar explanations are tedious") versus deductive learning ("I prefer an explanation because I want to know why things are wrong"). The majority of students, however, preferred direct feedback (41%).

(2) Overall, students were positive with regard to the feedback received, rating the usefulness for self-correction in the concrete assignment 3 (50%) or 4 (41%) on a Likert scale of 5 (1= not useful, 5 = very useful). Furthermore, 71% of the students declared they would like to use the tool in self-directed study mode to revise their bachelor papers. Regarding the usefulness of the feedback as a tool to raise awareness for potential problems in their writing in general, the satisfaction scores were even higher: 3 (24%), 4 (53%), and 5 (15%). Indeed, students declared to look at their written texts "with different eyes" after having received automated feedback on cohesion three times in a row. This suggests that the feedback was helpful to increase their noticing ability (Schmidt, 1990), which is important for the development of learner autonomy.

(3) As mentioned above, one of the main challenges in the study design was the lack of context-sensitive lookups which lead to a high amount of unnecessary highlighting of words and utterances that actually were well formulated. As this might have a potentially overwhelming effect, it was important to elicit students' attitudes about this aspect. Interestingly, only 6% of the students rated the unnecessary feedback annoying (4 on a Likert scale ranging from 1=not annoying at all to 5=very annoying), while 15% felt not annoyed at all (1 on Likert scale). The majority rated their degree of annoyance as 3 (47%) or 2 (35%).

4. Conclusions

This explorative study provided evidence that cohesion problems can successfully be addressed through automated feedback. Simple pattern-matching technologies in combination with tentatively formulated suggestions can help students to remediate over- and under-use of connectives and co-reference devices. While students preferred direct feedback, indirect feedback proved to be more successful for revision, with grammar explanations triggering a higher amount of revisions, and example utterances leading to a higher rate of successful revisions. These findings add to our understanding about the effectiveness of written corrective feedback, adding non-directive automated feedback as a new, under-researched setting. Perhaps even more important than revision success, students reported that the repeated provision of feedback through highlighting potentially problematic words and utterances increased their noticing. These promising results indicate that automated feedback on cohesion is a path worth further exploration. For future tool development, implementing NLP for linguistic and semantic analysis should be considered. This way, the range of cohesive devices to be addressed can be expanded and unnecessary feedback can be avoided.

References

Bitchener, J. (2012). A reflection on 'the language learning potential' of written CF. *Journal of Second Language Writing, 21*(4), 348-363. https://doi.org/10.1016/j.jslw.2012.09.006

Cho, H. Y., & Shin, J.-A. (2014). Cohesive devices in English writing textbooks and Korean learners' English writings. *English Teaching, 69*(1), 41-59.

Crossley, S. A., Kyle, K., & McNamara, D. (2016). The tool for the automatic analysis of text cohesion (TAACO): automatic assessment of local, global, and text cohesion. *Behavior Research Methods, 48*(4), 1227-1237. https://doi.org/10.3758/s13428-015-0651-7

Ene, E., & Upton, T. A. (2014). Learner uptake of teacher electronic feedback in ESL composition. *System, 46*, 80-95. https://doi.org/10.1016/j.system.2014.07.011

Halliday, M. A. K., & Hasan, R. (1976). *Cohesion in English.* Longman.

Schmidt, R. (1990). The role of consciousness in second language learning. *Applied Linguistics, 11*, 129-158.

A dynamic online system
for translation learning and testing

Yan Tian[1]

Abstract. Translation is one of the items tested in many national English proficiency tests for non-English majors in China because translation competence is regarded as one of the productive language skills which could be used to assess learners' language proficiency. However, the feedback on translation exercises and self-tests are usually provided by human raters. As a result, students cannot have instant feedback after they finish their translation exercises or self-tests out of class, which would lead to the students' low motivation in practising translation by themselves. This paper reports on the process of the development of a dynamic online system with automated scoring and intelligent feedback for non-English majors' translation exercises and self-tests. It also discusses the obstacles encountered from a technical perspective.

Keywords: dynamic, online system, translation learning and testing, instant feedback.

1. Introduction

Generally, Chinese non-English majors are rather weak at translation, both from Chinese to English and English to Chinese. Due to limited time in class, teachers do not spend much time explaining translation techniques and analyzing students' translation errors. However, translation competence is required by the National English Syllabus for non-English majors. Therefore, there are two major national English tests for non-English majors in China in which students are required to participate, the National College English Test Band IV and the National College English Test Band VI. Both exams contain translation tests. Besides, the National Entrance Examination for Postgraduates also has translation items. Each year, millions of students participate in these exams. However, because of the lack of instant feedback, students do not practise translation adequately out of class. Consequently, they do not score high enough in translation.

---

1. Shanghai Jiao Tong University, Shanghai, China; tianyan@sjtu.edu.cn

How to cite this article: Tian, Y. (2017). A dynamic online system for translation learning and testing. In K. Borthwick, L. Bradley & S. Thouësny (Eds), *CALL in a climate of change: adapting to turbulent global conditions – short papers from EUROCALL 2017* (pp. 300-305). Research-publishing.net. https://doi.org/10.14705/rpnet.2017.eurocall2017.730

To motivate the students to practise translation out of class and to provide an online experiential learning (Kolb, 1984) environment, a dynamic online system for translation learning (English to Chinese and Chinese to English) and self-test of their translation competence has been designed. With this system, students can experience the translation tests and reflect on their translation errors with the aid of the automated scores and instant personal feedback provided by the system.

The concept of 'dynamic' means that a learner's learning behaviors and achievements are constantly changing, which can be reflected by the learner's multiple online behaviors, such as the time spent, the amount of exercises done, the frequencies to take the tests, and the scores obtained in the tests, etc. A dynamic online system is to capture the entire online behaviors of learners to help them improve their learning efficiency and achievements by providing them with adaptive exercises and tests to enhance self-directed use of technology (Lai, Shum, & Tian, 2016).

This paper reports on the development of such a system which is mainly composed of a scoring module and a feedback module. The scoring module, based on a machine learning approach, is capable of scoring students' translations instantly after they submit their translations. The feedback module, supported by a learner English-Chinese translation error corpus and a learner Chinese-English translation error corpus, adopts the rule-based approach which can identify the translation errors of the learners and provide personal feedback. Hopefully, this system could motivate non-English majors to practise translation by themselves with interest and joy.

2. Method

2.1. Construction of learner translation error corpora

The learner Chinese-English translation error corpus is constructed in three steps.

The first step is to collect the raw data of learners' translations. The online platform uses Wenjuanxing (www.sojump.com) which makes it possible for learners to do translation exercises online and for the teachers to download learners' translations.

The Chinese-English translation materials used for the construction of the learner translation error corpora are the authentic Chinese-English translation items in the National College English Test and the model tests for this test. Each item is a short paragraph of 140 to 160 Chinese characters about Chinese culture, such as Chinese holidays, Chinese cuisines, or Chinese tourist sites. The learners are asked to finish the tests online within 20 minutes.

The second step is to annotate learners' translations. The raw data were downloaded and annotated manually according to the criteria of annotation. After many experimental annotations, the errors were manually categorized by the postgraduates of Masters of Translation at Shanghai Jiao Tong University into 14 categories, such as improper dictions, improper collocations, and improper word order, etc. Besides, the corrections are also supplied so that the system can provide learners with the corrections as well as their scores. The construction of the learner English-Chinese translation error corpus follows the same steps as that of the construction of this corpus.

The third step is to transform these corpora into machine readable forms to enable the rating module and the feedback module to realize automated scoring and personalized feedback.

2.2. Development of automated scoring and feedback system

The dynamic online system for translation learning and testing should be able to track, store, and analyze the frequently changing data of learners. It should also be able to present the learners with the learning materials and tests based on the analyzed results of the data by the system. In other words, the system should be able to adapt to the dynamic state of learners' online learning and testing activities by providing them with the suitable materials and tests according to their dynamic translation scores.

The system is composed of a scoring system and a feedback system. The scoring system consists of a statistical-based scoring module which can score students' translations automatically and instantly after they submit their translations online. The feedback system, which is supported by the learner English-Chinese translation error corpus, the learner Chinese-English translation error corpus, and the standard translation database, is a rule-based module which can identify students' translation errors and provide personal feedback, such as the correct translations and the guidance for further learning.

2.3. Development of online platform

There are seven columns on the online platform (see Figure 1 left). A pretest of translation proficiency is the first test that students take (see Figure 1 right).

Figure 1.   Left: homepage of the online platform. Right: interface of pretest of translation proficiency

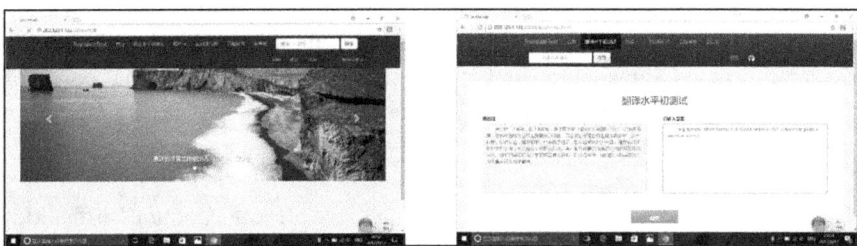

Their online behaviors (see Figure 2 left) and daily ranking of peers (see Figure 2 right) can be presented to them.

Figure 2.   Left: Students' online behaviors. Right: Daily ranking of peers

From the perspective of sociocultural theory (Lantolf & Thorne, 2007), peers could promote individual learning. Thus, the online platform is also designed to provide the rankings, the frequencies, and the progress of the peers who are taking the translation tests, hoping that peers' continuous progress can inspire learners to keep on doing the exercise and taking the test.

3.   Discussion

Feedback plays a key role in the process of learning. Instant feedback is essential to online foreign language learning and testing. It is a necessity to make an attempt to provide online feedback on translation exercises and self-tests for students in the context of online learning.

Due to different language proficiencies and translation skills, learners make different progress when learning and testing translation (Angelelli & Jacobson,

2009). An online system to assist translation learning and testing should be able to track the differences and then adapt to the individual differences by providing personal feedback. In this sense, the word 'dynamic' is used to describe the system. A dynamic online system for translation learning and testing as a way forward is the solution to individual needs for translation learning and testing in the context of online learning. It should feature intelligence and individuality, making it possible to realize the learner-system interaction without intervention from the teachers.

This dynamic system is only a pilot project. Up to the present, enormous difficulties concerning natural language processing have emerged (Amaral, Meurers, & Ziai, 2011). For example, finding a good algorithm for the feedback module to determine the type of translation errors poses a great challenge. Besides, the heavy workload of manual annotation, which is very time consuming, is another great difficulty.

4. Conclusions

It is believed that it is hard to achieve efficient language learning without the aid of personal guidance. Currently, online learning and testing systems generally do not have instant feedback and personal guidance, especially when the testing items involve subjective items, such as translation. The dynamic online system for translation learning and testing is an attempt to provide instant scoring and instant feedback for non-English majors after they submit their translation exercises and self-tests online. It is also an attempt to provide them with personal guidance according to the translation errors analyzed by the system. Besides, it is capable of providing learners with the learning activities and achievements of their online peers to encourage them to continue their online learning and testing.

5. Acknowledgements

We would like to thank the National Social Science Foundation of China (No. 16BYY081) for funding this project.

References

Amaral, L., Meurers, D., & Ziai, R. (2011). Analyzing learner language: towards a flexible natural language processing architecture for intelligent language tutors. *Computer Assisted Language Learning, 24*(1),1-16. https://doi.org/10.1080/09588221.2010.520674

Angelelli, C.V., & Jacobson, H. E. (2009). *Testing and assessment in translation and interpreting studies*. John Benjamins Publishing Company. https://doi.org/10.1075/ata.xiv

Kolb, D. (1984). *Experiential learning as the science of learning and development*. Prentice Hall.

Lai, C., Shum, M., & Tian, Y. (2016). Enhancing learners' self-directed use of technology for language learning: the effectiveness of an online training platform. *Computer Assisted Language Learning, 29*(1), 40-60. https://doi.org/10.1080/09588221.2014.889714

Lantolf, J., & Thorne, S. L. (2007). Sociocultural theory and second language learning. In B. van Patten & J. William (Eds), Theories in second language acquisition (pp. 201-224). Lawrence Erlbaum.

The use of MOOC as a means of creating a collaborative learning environment in a blended CLIL course

Svetlana Titova[1]

Abstract. The objective of this action research is to work out the possible ways of Massive Open Online Course (MOOC) integration in a blended Content and Language Integrated Learning (CLIL) course to create an authentic online collaborative community. The theoretical framework of the intervention is based on current MOOC theories, connectivism, and the Substitution, Augmentation, Modification, and Redefinition (SAMR) model by Puentedura for implementing new technologies and open educational resources into teaching. Thirty bachelor students from Moscow State University, enrolled in a Methodology of English Language Teaching blended course, participated in the first cycle of the research. The analysis based on the quantitative data (questionnaire) demonstrated the learners' positive attitude to this intervention due to the following possibilities: getting familiar with the theories and terminology on English as a Foreign Language (EFL) teaching, sharing experiences on the MOOC forums with the learners from all over the world and developing writing skills, etc.

Keywords: MOOC, CLIL, collaborative learning, interactive environment.

1. Introduction

Many educators argue today that MOOCs present new educational opportunities for face-to-face language classes. They enable instructors to create an authentic educational environment to develop learner communicative and digital skills by providing online interaction and high-quality online educational resources from top-ranking universities and colleges (Milligan, Littlejohn, & Margaryan, 2013).

---

1. Far Eastern Federal University, Vladivostok, Russia; stitova3@gmail.com

How to cite this article: Titova, S. (2017). The use of MOOC as a means of creating a collaborative learning environment in a blended CLIL course. In K. Borthwick, L. Bradley & S. Thouësny (Eds), *CALL in a climate of change: adapting to turbulent global conditions – short papers from EUROCALL 2017* (pp. 306-311). Research-publishing.net. https://doi.org/10.14705/rpnet.2017.eurocall2017.731

MOOCs foster high demand in digital age approaches, such as the general and the calibrated peer review, and collaborative enquiry-based and project-based methods (Dyer, 2014). They enhance learner motivation through prompt and timely feedback from course participants. Godwin-Jones (2014) outlined the three areas within language learning where MOOCs can be implemented efficiently: teaching English as a Second language (ESL), study of indigenous languages, and teaching Language for Special Purposes (LSP). The last area of integration is of particular interest for this study because MOOCs offer "a convenient vehicle for reaching professionals or trainees who need specialized language skills" (Godwin-Jones, 2014, p. 12). Unfortunately, limited research and empirical data were provided to support the effectiveness of such intervention in blended CLIL or language classrooms. The objective of this action research is twofold. First, to work out the possible ways of MOOC integration in a blended CLIL course to create an authentic online collaborative community, and second, to analyze students' perceptions of their MOOC experience as well as the pedagogical impact of this intervention on their motivation and learning outcomes.

2. Method

2.1. Research objectives

The most frequently described way of MOOC integration is their use for flipped learning or hybrid MOOC models (Bruff, Fisher, McEwen, & Smith, 2013). This study, which is based on current MOOC theories, connectivism and SAMR approaches, focuses on working out a methodological framework for MOOC implementation in a CLIL course to create an authentic interactive environment where students can collaborate with the participants from other countries and learn with authentic materials. Our model of instruction includes a blended CLIL course supported by the group blog and student participation in the MOOC forums. The MOOC is used in this model as additional learning resources for setting up an authentic online collaborative community. This educational model provides different focuses of perspective on the course content, exposes students to different ways of teaching content, and helps students develop their communicative skills.

The research includes the *enhancement* and *substitution* cycles (Puentedura, 2011). The key objective of the enhancement cycle is to analyze MOOC intervention from the perspective of students' engagement and their attitude to the intervention. The second cycle of this action research will focus mainly on learning outcomes. This paper is devoted to the analysis of the first cycle of research.

The first cycle target group consisted of 30 undergraduate students from Lomonosov Moscow State University enrolled in a blended CLIL 15-week course, Methodology of English Language Teaching. The language competence of the students was B2-C1 according to the common european framework of references for languages.

2.2. Data collection

The enhancement cycle took place from September 2016 to January 2017. The students were asked to enroll for the MOOC *Understanding language: Learning and Teaching* (Southampton University, UK) in October 2016. They had to fulfill MOOC activities and participate in the forums every week. Student participation in the MOOC was included into the course evaluation and was assessed on the basis of the e-portfolios that reflected their participation in the MOOC forums, and the course blog peer collaboration where they could comment on each other's contributions and experience. Survey data on student perception of the MOOC experience were collected using a post-intervention questionnaire. The post-intervention questionnaire contained ten questions, out of which five questions were in the format of a four-level Likert scale, three were multiple choice questions, and two were free-text comments aiming to get student views on their attitude to MOOC integration. The questionnaire was completed by 30 students (22 female, eight male).

3. Discussion

Our data analysis demonstrated the overall positive attitude (87%) of the learners to the MOOC integration. The students agreed that this integration helped them: develop writing skills (80%); develop collaborative skills and digital literacies (77%); share experiences and opinions with other learners and be a member of peer community learning (70%); and acquire some knowledge in ESL teaching and get ready for the tests and colloquium (67%); see Figure 1.

Some free-text comments provided additional insight into learner experiences and revealed their positive attitude to the MOOC intervention. Answering the question *What did you like best about taking part in the MOOC?*, almost 70% of the participants mentioned the opportunity to communicate with other people via forum discussions. There were other benefits resulting from the use of MOOCs:

43% of the students indicated the opportunity to learn more about teaching approaches, and 27% of the students liked the way video content was presented. Our findings suggest that the students place heavy emphasis on the value of the lectures showing and demonstrating some practical approaches.

Figure 1. Results of the post-study questionnaire

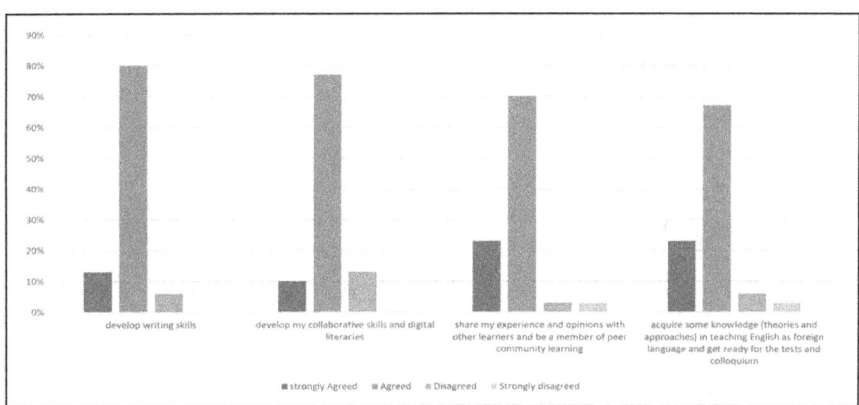

The most frequently mentioned negative impact on the MOOC experience identified by the students was the time requirement (33% of the students) and the overloaded schedule of the course (27% of the students) due to MOOC intervention (Figure 2). They complained that task completion required an extensive amount of time. This may be because some students did not have an appropriate language level, so they had to spend more time on listening and reading tasks, although none of the students mentioned that it had a negative impact on their experience. In order to solve the problems of the language barrier, the instructors have to adjust the content of on-campus language or CLIL courses to integrate MOOC materials in the learning process efficiently. Teachers have to provide language support through glossaries and tasks designed on MOOC materials. One more way to support knowledge development is through participant forums or blogs of on-campus courses, due to "a lack of familiarity among students with online learning and with the teaching and learning method used in a MOOC" (Godwin-Jones, 2014, p. 11). It is possible to "improve learners' performance by providing personalized planning, tips and hints for time management" (Gutiérrez-Rojas et al., 2017, p. 44, cited in Godwin-Jones, 2014, p. 11).

Surprisingly enough, although 70% of the students mentioned the opportunity to communicate with other people via forums as their positive experience, still, some (20%) argued that they did not like collaborative tasks where they had to give arguments or counter arguments. This can be explained by the lack of student experience with online discussion participation. It seems to have been the biggest challenge encountered by the students.

Figure 2. The negative impacts on the MOOC experience identified by the students

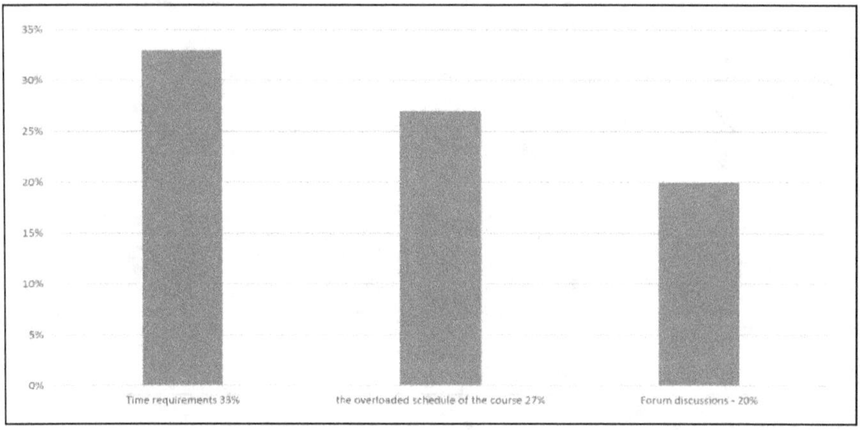

[Bar chart showing: Time requirements 33%, the overloaded schedule of the course 27%, Forum discussions – 20%]

4. Conclusions

MOOCs in education represent a new stage not only in distance learning and self-directed learning, as many authors assert, but also in a traditional face-to-face classroom (Israel, 2015).

Integration of the MOOC in the course syllabus helped the instructor enhance learner motivation by means of creating an authentic interactive online environment that enabled students to be engaged in collaborative activities and develop communication skills. The data analysis demonstrated that the learners' positive attitude to this integration may be due to the following possibilities: sharing ideas and experiences on the MOOC forums with learners from all over the world, getting familiar with the theories on EFL teaching and learning, improving EFL terminology knowledge, and developing writing skills.

Our future research steps will be devoted to the investigation of the relationships between the students' use of MOOC and their learning outcomes. During the fall semester 2017, we are going to compare the learning outcomes in the hybrid group and in the traditional face-to-face group.

5. Acknowledgements

I would like to thank Kate Borthwick and all the authors of the MOOC *Understanding language: learning and teaching* (Southampton University, UK) for making this research possible.

References

Bruff, D. O., Fisher, D. H., McEwen, K. E., & Smith, B. E. (2013). Wrapping a MOOC: student perceptions of an experiment in blended learning. *MERLOT Journal of Online Learning and Teaching, 9*(2). http://jolt.merlot.org/vol9no2/bruff_0613.htm

Dyer, R. A. D. (2014). Exploring the relevancy of massive open online courses (MOOCs): a Caribbean university approach. *Information Resources Management Journal, 27*(2), 61-77. https://doi.org/10.4018/irmj.2014040105

Godwin-Jones, R. (2014). Global reach and local practice: the promise of MOOCS. *Language Learning & Technology, 18*(3), 5-15. http://llt.msu.edu/issues/october2014/emerging.pdf

Gutiérrez-Rojas, I., Alario-Hoyos, C., Pérez-Sanagustín, M., Leony, D., & Delgado-Kloos, C. (2014). Scaffolding self-learning in MOOCs. In U. Cress & C. Kloos (Eds), *Proceedings of the European MOOC Stakeholder Summit 2014* (pp. 43-49). PAU Education. http://educate.gast.it.uc3m.es/wp-content/uploads/2014/02/Scaffolding_self-learning_in_MOOCs.pdf

Israel, M. J. (2015). Effectiveness of integrating MOOCs in traditional classrooms for undergraduate Students. *International Review of Research in Open and Distributed Learning 16*(5), 102-118. https://doi.org/10.19173/irrodl.v16i5.2222

Milligan, C., Littlejohn, A., & Margaryan, A. (2013). Patterns of engagement in connectivist MOOCs. *MERLOT Journal of Online Learning and Teaching, 9*(2), 149-159.

Puentedura, R. R. (2011). *A brief introduction to TPCK and SAMR.* http://hippasus.com/rrweblog/archives/2011/12/08/BriefIntroTPCKSAMR.pdf

Language students learning to manage complex pedagogic situations in a technology-rich environment

Riikka Tumelius[1] and Leena Kuure[2]

Abstract. Being a language teacher in the modern world requires sensitivity to complexity, which may pose challenges for student teachers and teachers in the field accustomed to classroom-based learning and teaching. This study examines how language students are managing complex pedagogic situations in a technology-rich environment while exploring new ways of being language teachers. The case context of the study is a university course, which entailed the students designing and carrying out an online English language project for fifth-graders in two Finnish schools. The project activities included online chat sessions, which the students and the course teacher administered from the teacher's office at the university. The office was an important site for the participants to negotiate and process pedagogic issues and practical matters that arose in the course of the work. The research approach draws on nexus analysis (Scollon & Scollon, 2004) and multimodal (inter)action analysis (Norris, 2004). Video recordings from the office as well as the researchers' participatory observations are the primary materials for the analysis. The study provides implications for developing language teacher education.

Keywords: language teacher education, sensemaking, complexity, nexus analysis.

1. Introduction

Despite the arrival of new technologies for the service of education, people still typically see language learning situated in the classroom. Language teachers have been guides for learners to proceed through activities arising from the thematic content of the textbook (Taalas, Kauppinen, Tarnanen, & Pöyhönen, 2008). Teaching practice as part of pedagogic studies has also largely concentrated on preparing students to handle classroom situations. However, educational authorities and

---

1. University of Oulu, Oulu, Finland; riikka.tumelius@oulu.fi
2. University of Oulu, Oulu, Finland; leena.kuure@oulu.fi

How to cite this article: Tumelius, R., & Kuure, L. (2017). Language students learning to manage complex pedagogic situations in a technology-rich environment. In K. Borthwick, L. Bradley & S. Thouësny (Eds), *CALL in a climate of change: adapting to turbulent global conditions – short papers from EUROCALL 2017* (pp. 312-316). Research-publishing.net. https://doi.org/10.14705/rpnet.2017.eurocall2017.732

strategic bodies have voiced the need to broaden the perspective from classrooms to learning in daily life. The sites for language learning are diverse, distributed across informal and formal settings in hybrid configurations (see Ryberg, Davidsen, & Hodgson, 2016). Language learning emerges from meaningful activities and social interaction where language intertwines with a range of other multimodal resources (Kramsch & Whiteside, 2008; Norris, 2004; van Lier, 2004).

In situations where people need to manage multiple, overlapping tasks, the coordination of the activities proceeds through distributing attention and engaging in sensemaking in different ways due to emerging needs (see Jones, 2005; Norris, 2004; Pirini, 2014). Team members monitor surreptitiously the situation and the behaviour of each other, which helps them in upholding a fluent workflow while information is communicated and diverse tasks and activities coordinated (Heath & Luff, 1992). The modal density of actions fluctuates from moment to moment the focus of attention moving between foreground, mid-ground, and background (Norris, 2004).

We will examine how language students appropriated new approaches to being teachers during a university course where the students designed and carried out an online learning project for young Finnish learners of English. The analysis focuses on the activities during tutoring sessions in the course teacher's office, and is conducted on video recordings with the support of other materials gathered throughout the project. Special attention is paid to how different issues and problems related to pedagogic issues, collaboration, and technology are negotiated and resolved by the participants and how this will reflect on the students' evolving identities as language teachers of the future. The research approach draws on nexus analysis (Scollon & Scollon, 2004) and multimodal (inter)action analysis (Norris, 2004). Research in the field is only emerging. The results have relevance for reconsidering the professional profiles, identities, and skills of language teachers in the changing field of language education.

2. Research materials and methodology

During the course (13 weeks), 15 language students created a four-week learning project for two schools (25 fifth-graders, 11–12 years of age). Project design advanced through face-to-face and online teamwork. During the school project, weekly synchronous chat sessions were organised with the pupils during their English lessons. To administer online chat, the students worked together with the course teacher in her office. Sometimes, an additional tutor from a distance location participated in the activities. During the sessions, the team practiced managing complex pedagogic situations, but also engaged in sensemaking about various aspects of learning and teaching together with the course teacher.

As for the affordances of technology in the sessions, one desktop and two laptop computers with webcams were available for the participants. The primary route for the pupils to enter the learning project environment was the workspace created on a virtual learning environment platform. Depending on the activities, the pupils used the materials and discussion lists there or used a link to proceed to another environment, such as the chat built within a desktop meeting system. The course teacher and the schoolteachers were using an instant messaging tool and mobile phones for exchanging information and negotiating about practical matters during the chat session. Two video cameras were used for recording the sessions.

The analysis started with the researchers viewing the materials and discussing their interpretations with respect to the aspects of social action according to nexus analysis (Scollon & Scollon, 2004, pp. 13-14), i.e. interaction order (relationships between participants), historical body (personal habits and experiences), and discourses in place (situationally foregrounded, relevant discourses). This supported reflection on the historical perspectives, e.g. what was being treated as belonging to the past, present or future. In viewing the video material, the focus was directed to what was being done, what were the discourses circulating *in situ*, and what kinds of multimodal means were used as resources in collaboration, problem solving, and sensemaking (Norris, 2004).

3. Findings

Figure 1 provides a synthesis of an online tutoring session in the teacher's office as a site of engagement (Jones, 2005). As the participants immersed themselves in managing a new pedagogic setting, diverse discourses were circulating in the situation, echoing accustomed practices and generating new ones.

The students and the teacher in the office were engaged in varied activities, e.g. distributing tasks and responsibilities as well as contemplating on course design. An intensive phase requiring various means for communication took place at the beginning of the chat session when the teacher was in contact with the schoolteachers (via mobile phone and messenger) and the tutoring students were engaged in a chat with the pupils through the video conferencing system. During work, topics related to pedagogic aspects either closely related to the work at hand or more general in nature emerged. In the discussion, the participants were reflecting on their experiences, exploring their relationship to being language teachers. Sometimes, the course teacher took more the role of an instructor, and sometimes she just participated in the joint activities as another team member. They all kept thinking aloud, wondering and solving issues together in a laid-back manner. The students were offering their views in the negotiation work and they assumed agency in the situation. Considering the traditional roles of learners and teachers, this setting provided new experiences for the participants.

Figure 1. Intersecting discourses during an online tutoring session

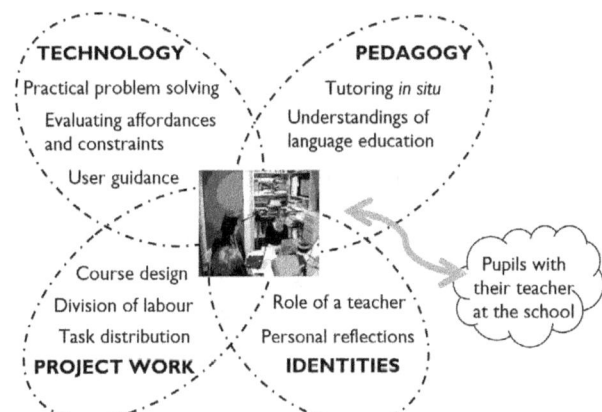

4. Conclusion

The analysis focused on what was going on when language students were designing and carrying out a learning project for schoolchildren. Special attention was given to managing complex pedagogic situations in a technology-rich environment. The historical bodies of the participants were being transformed in terms of language education as the participants were working in new roles, gaining new experiences and engaging in sensemaking about practical solutions and broader pedagogic issues to do with language learning. Such experiences involved novel configurations of interaction order as the students and the course teacher were collaboratively solving problems as equal members of the team while simultaneously connected with participants at a distance. The language teacher's work involved technology-mediated multitasking and continuously negotiating solutions related to the ongoing learning project. The video data from the office showed the students appropriating new practices as language teachers without any great difficulty. The discourses emerging during work also indicated that assuming new identities is a slow process. Nevertheless, the students gained valuable hands-on experience of technologically mediated language teaching, which helps them in constructing their vision of future working life.

5. Acknowledgements

We would like to thank the participating schools and the language students designing and implementing the school project for active participation in collaboration.

References

Heath, C., & Luff, P. (1992). Collaboration and control: crisis management and multimedia technology in London underground line control rooms. *Journal of Computer Supported Cooperative Work, 1*(1), 24-48. https://doi.org/10.1007/BF00752451

Jones, R. H. (2005). Sites of engagement as sites of attention: time, space and culture in electronic discourse. In S. Norris & R. Jones (Eds), *Discourse in action: introducing mediated discourse analysis* (pp. 144-154). Routledge.

Kramsch, C., & Whiteside, A. (2008). Language ecology in multilingual settings: towards a theory of symbolic competence. *Applied Linguistics, 29*(4), 645-671. https://doi.org/10.1093/applin/amn022

Norris, S. (2004). *Analyzing multimodal interaction. A methodological framework*. Routledge.

Pirini, J. (2014). Producing shared attention/awareness in high school tutoring. *Multimodal Communication, 3*(2), 163-179.

Ryberg, T., Davidsen, J., & Hodgson, V. (2016). Problem and project based learning in hybrid spaces: nomads and artisans. In S. Cranmer, N. Bonderup Dohn, M. de Laat, T. Ryberg, & J.-A. Sime (Eds), *Proceedings of the 10th International Conference on Networked Learning 2016* (pp. 200-209). Lancaster University.

Scollon, R., & Scollon, S. W. (2004). *Nexus analysis: discourse and the emerging internet*. Routledge.

Taalas, P., Kauppinen, M., Tarnanen, M., & Pöyhönen, S. (2008). Media landscapes in school and in free time – two parallel realities? *Digital Kompetanse – Nordic Journal of Digital Literacy, 3*(4), 240-256.

Van Lier, L. (2004). *The ecology and semiotics of language learning: a sociocultural perspective*. Kluwer Academic. https://doi.org/10.1007/1-4020-7912-5

Exploring AI language assistants with primary EFL students

Joshua Underwood[1]

> **Abstract**. The main objective of this study was to identify ways to incorporate voice-driven Artificial Intelligence (AI) effectively in classroom language learning. This nine month teacher-led design research study employed technology probes (Amazon's Alexa, Apple's Siri, Google voice search) and co-design methods with a class of primary age English as a Foreign Language (EFL) students to explore and develop ideas for classroom activities using AI language assistants. Speaking to AI assistants was considered highly engaging by all students. Students were observed to speak more English when using AI assistants in group work, and to spontaneously reformulate, self-correct, and joyfully and playfully persist with speaking English in their attempts to get AI assistants to do what they wanted them to do.
>
> **Keywords**: AI, voice recognition, learning experience design, language learning.

1. Introduction

Uses of AI technologies and robots to support language learning, particularly with children, have been explored for several years (Han, 2012). Drivers for such research include the desire to give individual students more attention in large classes and the observation that children often enjoy talking to robots and are more relaxed about using a foreign language to speak with machines than with humans (Han, 2012). In short, AI has the potential to provide more, and more motivating, opportunities for children to engage in spoken interaction in the target language. However, it is only recently that increased affordability and reliability of AI technologies have made exploring this vision in everyday classrooms practical; voice interaction has improved more in the last 30 or so months than it did in its first 30 years, "word error rate for voice-recognition systems [...] is now on par with humans" (Nordrum, 2017, n.p.).

---

1. British Council, Bilbao, Spain; josh.underwood@gmail.com

How to cite this article: Underwood, J. (2017). Exploring AI language assistants with primary EFL students. In K. Borthwick, L. Bradley & S. Thouësny (Eds), *CALL in a climate of change: adapting to turbulent global conditions – short papers from EUROCALL 2017* (pp. 317-321). Research-publishing.net. https://doi.org/10.14705/rpnet.2017.eurocall2017.733

For some, the idea of affordable AI in the classroom raises concerns about the role of teachers, teacher replacement, and loss of human values. Others emphasise ways AI and teachers may work together and even 'humanise' classes, for example by removing the need for standardised testing (Luckin & Holmes, 2017). Interestingly, the idea of robot teachers doing away with the need for tests, though very differently conceived, is also present in some children's visions of robot-assisted learning (Underwood, 2016). Essentially, the enthusiastic argument expressed in one student's essay is that, as robot teachers will have a complete record of all interaction with the student, they will be able to generate an accurate assessment of competence without the need for tests. While conscious of concerns, as a teacher I personally view AI assistants as potentially engaging and useful and it is in this spirit that this study was conducted.

The study reported here is teacher-led research motivated by the desire to address classroom challenges encountered on returning to teaching primary age students, a specific example being the need to simultaneously answer spontaneous questions from several children at once (e.g. "How do you say… in English? How do you spell…? What does… mean? Etc.) and the observation that many of those questions might easily and satisfactorily be answered by currently available AI technologies. The study addresses two questions: (1) Can currently available AI technologies provide children with satisfactory answers to some of the questions that are very common in language classrooms?; and (2) How might we exploit AI to get children speaking in the target language?

Further objectives of this study are to provide insights into: ways of supporting children in developing appropriate AI-assisted task designs; classroom management issues when working with AI classroom assistants; and other practicalities such as coping with inaccurate voice-recognition.

2. Method

The 'in the wild' design approach (Rogers, 2011) adopted in this study employed existing AI technologies as probes to stimulate children and teachers to think about current and future opportunities for using AI in natural classroom settings over a period of nine months so as to address issues of novelty and ecological validity as well as revealing practical issues. During the study, the author/teacher and a class of 11 primary-age EFL students made frequent use of various AI technologies (a single Amazon Alexa; Siri on a class set of iPads: Google voice search on the teacher's mobile phone and iPads) to support various classroom activities. Example uses included: student-directed 'free' language use in research for project work (e.g. "Alexa, how much does an Osprey weigh?"); teacher-directed controlled practice of hard to distinguish sounds (e.g. "Ok Google, show me a picture of a ship/sheep"); and challenges like "Which group can get Alexa to answer the most complicated question?". Over time we gradually moved from teacher-designed to student-designed tasks and more spontaneous integrated uses, e.g. students saying "Why don't we ask Google?".

As in Underwood (2014), I employed co-design strategies (e.g. Arnold, Lee, & Yip, 2016) to support children in reflecting on these experiences and help them develop and communicate their own ideas about what AI language assistants might be like and how they might be used. Co-design activities included developing play-doh models of 'English Helpers', describing what they could do, and designing posters and short presentations about "robot teachers" with peer feedback. As we shall see, these methods influence the kind of results obtained and will be revised in future studies (Figure 1).

Figure 1. Primary children's play-doh representations of 'My English Helper'

3. Results and discussion

Can currently available AI technologies provide children with satisfactory answers to some of the questions that are very common in language classrooms? The answer to this varied depending on which AI was used. *How do you spell* was mostly answered correctly but often too fast and is far easier for students to make use of when they both see and hear the spelling (e.g. Siri and Google). *What does [...] mean* was often answered correctly but frequently not in ways that were easily understood by primary-age EFL learners. *How do you say [...] in English* was rarely understood but occasionally correctly answered, for Spanish words, by Google. Generally students quickly learnt what was not likely to get a satisfactory answer and how to phrase questions in ways that were more likely to be answered. Despite current generally poor performance on these kinds of questions, it seems highly-likely that this could be greatly enhanced through voice interaction designs specific for language classrooms and particular first language backgrounds.

How can we exploit AI to get children speaking in the target language? The children in this study were intrigued by what any particular implementation of AI was capable of and highly motivated to test their ideas through trial and error, thus engaging in extensive interactive target language speaking whilst developing potentially valuable 21st century skills for working with AI. Speaking to AIs engaged these children's natural curiosity, largely in order to explore what the AIs were and were not capable of. For these children, asking questions, giving commands (e.g. "play some music"), and getting a response appears to have made speaking English meaningful and often joyful, even when they were not understood they often tried again, reformulated, and persisted. However, activities resulting in linked utterances, students' responding to AIs utterances, and conversations were far harder, though some Alexa skills such as 'Guess the animal' worked to some extent.

How can we support children in developing appropriate AI-assisted task designs? These students tended to design AI language helpers that were anthropomorphic and more like friends that would play with them. However, the activities they would like AI assistants to engage in with them (e.g. "be my friend", "play video games with me") were under-described probably because the co-design methods employed did not sufficiently scaffold the development of such ideas. In future studies, I aim to use storyboards, scripting of skills to implement as programmes, and peer evaluation to help children design AI-assisted tasks.

What are classroom management issues when working with AI classroom assistants? Inaccurate voice-recognition can result in inappropriate search results, so ensure safe-search is on. Voice-recognition works poorly when students speak simultaneously so they need to develop turn-taking. Students engage so enthusiastically that you need to develop good strategies for stopping activity and getting attention.

4. Acknowledgements

I would like to thank all my students who so enthusiastically engaged with the various technologies we tried out and so generously shared their ideas.

References

Arnold, L., Lee, K. J., & Yip, J. C. (2016). Co-designing with children: an approach to social robot design. In *Proceedings 2nd Workshop on Evaluating Child Robot Interaction at HRI 2016*. https://childrobotinteraction.org/proceedings-2nd-workshop-hri-2016/

Han, J. (2012). Emerging technologies: robot assisted language learning. *Language Learning & Technology, 16*(3), 1-9. http://llt.msu.edu/issues/october2012/emerging.pdf

Luckin, R., & Holmes, W. (2017, January 04). *A.I. is the new T.A. in the classroom – how we get to next*. https://howwegettonext.com/a-i-is-the-new-t-a-in-the-classroom-dedbe5b99e9e

Nordrum, A. (2017, January 04). CES 2017: the year of voice recognition. http://spectrum.ieee.org/tech-talk/consumer-electronics/gadgets/ces-2017-the-year-of-voice-recognition

Rogers, Y. (2011). Interaction design gone wild. *Interactions, 18*(4), 58. https://doi.org/10.1145/1978822.1978834

Underwood, J. (2014). Using iPads to help teens design their own activities. In S. Jager, L. Bradley, E. J. Meima & S. Thouësny (Eds), *CALL design: principles and practice - proceedings of the 2014 EUROCALL conference, Groningen, The Netherlands* (pp. 385-390). Research-publishing.net. https://doi.org/10.14705/rpnet.2014.000250

Underwood, J. (2016). *Recurrent themes in 80 young learners' essays about their ideal future language learning classes*. Unpublished report. British Council.

Construction and evaluation of an integrated formal/informal learning environment for foreign language learning across real and virtual spaces

Ikumi Waragai[1], Tatsuya Ohta[2], Shuichi Kurabayashi[3], Yasushi Kiyoki[4], Yukiko Sato[5], and Stefan Brückner[6]

Abstract. This paper presents the prototype of a foreign language learning space, based on the construction of an integrated formal/informal learning environment. Before the background of the continued innovation of information technology that places conventional learning styles and educational methods into new contexts based on new value-standards, environment models of foreign language learning constantly face the necessity to change. A structured environment for foreign language learning can be created only when the learning environment in the real space, which is constructed in many forms outside the classroom, constantly connects with the formal learning environment inside the classroom. This study assumes two axes of a learning environment – formal/informal and real/cyber space – and attempts to integrate them to create a circulating four-dimensional model. Integrating formal and informal environments connects real space, which depends on the physical location and situation, with cyber space, which does not. In this study, sentences written in a foreign language by language learners will be auto-collected and analyzed in cyber space, which plays a great role in students' daily lives. Thus, a 4D foreign language learning environment, which automatically delivers practical knowledge to the learner by a comprehensive analysis of formal and informal learning between real and cyber space, will be constructed.

Keywords: informal learning, foreign language learning, 4D foreign language learning environment.

1. Keio University, Tokyo, Japan; ikumi@sfc.keio.ac.jp
2. Nanzan University, Nagoya, Japan; FZE00305@nifty.ne.jp
3. Cygames Inc., Tokyo, Japan; kurabayashi_shuichi@cygames.co.jp
4. Keio University, Tokyo, Japan; kiyoki@sfc.keio.ac.jp
5. Keio University, Tokyo, Japan; ysato0724@gmail.com
6. Keio University, Tokyo, Japan; stebru89@googlemail.com

How to cite this article: Waragai, I., Ohta, T., Kurabayashi, S., Kiyoki, Y., Sato, Y., & Brückner, S. (2017). Construction and evaluation of an integrated formal/informal learning environment for foreign language learning across real and virtual spaces. In K. Borthwick, L. Bradley & S. Thouësny (Eds), *CALL in a climate of change: adapting to turbulent global conditions – short papers from EUROCALL 2017* (pp. 322-327). Research-publishing.net. https://doi.org/10.14705/rpnet.2017.eurocall2017.734

1. Introduction

In the field of foreign language education, the important issue is, how to bridge the gap between learning activities inside the classroom and learning activities outside of it. Foreign language learning environments are constantly changing together within the learners' daily lives, increasing the need not only to revise the formal learning space, but also the whole structure of the learning environment. From the perspective of foreign language learning, practice in the field is the most important space for linguistic 'output'. Therefore, it is necessary to examine the daily situation of learners – in 'real' space as well as in 'cyber' space.

The relevance of bridging both spaces is pointed out in studies on mobile learning, where it has been shown that connecting the formal learning in the classroom with learners' real-life experiences can be supported with smartphones detecting the learners' locations and supplying them with multimedia content that matches their real-time situation (Waragai, Kurabayashi, Ohta, & Raindl, 2012).

This study is carried out before the long-term background of our continuous experiments. At the Keio University Shonan Fujisawa Campus (Japan), researchers and educators have been working on designing computer-based language learning environments to provide language learners (mainly of German) with learning opportunities outside the classroom that are linked to classroom content (Waragai, Ohta, Raindl, & Kurabayashi, 2013; Waragai et al., 2014).

Figure 1. 4D foreign language learning environment

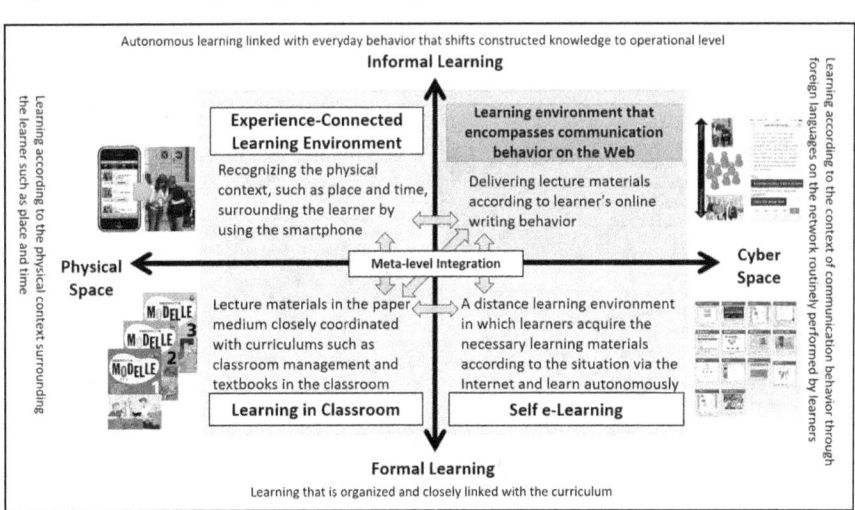

This paper is focused especially on writing activity in a foreign language. It is often argued that mobile learning has the potential to connect formal learning and informal learning experiences (Kukulska-Hulme & Sharples, 2016). Also, the prototype of a Mobile Language Learning Environment (MLLE) shows that "the use of the loci method mapping with mobile devices might lead to changes in learning awareness and an expansion of strategy knowledge" (Waragai, Raindl, Ohta, & Miyasaka, 2016, p. 462). Results from a recent study show that handwritten feedback is more effective compared to e-feedback (Elwood & Bode, 2014). In this study we locate the writing dimension in cyber space among the four dimensional spaces (Figure 1).

2. System design

A recent study presented a software which enables the recording of writing processes by gathering keystroke data (Kusanagi, Abe, Fukuta, & Kawaguchi, 2015). Our approach introduces a smart foreign language writing editor that integrates paper-based classroom learning and digital device-based independent learning. We have developed a foreign language learning system as a smartphone web application. This learning environment offers a novel image-based learning support mechanism that associates the knowledge acquired in a classroom with the current context of writing text. This system analyzes statistical features of the text to calculate the similarity between the current text and the previously reviewed writing assignments, showing the most relevant material in order to assist learners in ways that increase their language learning awareness.

Figure 2.   Image of the system design

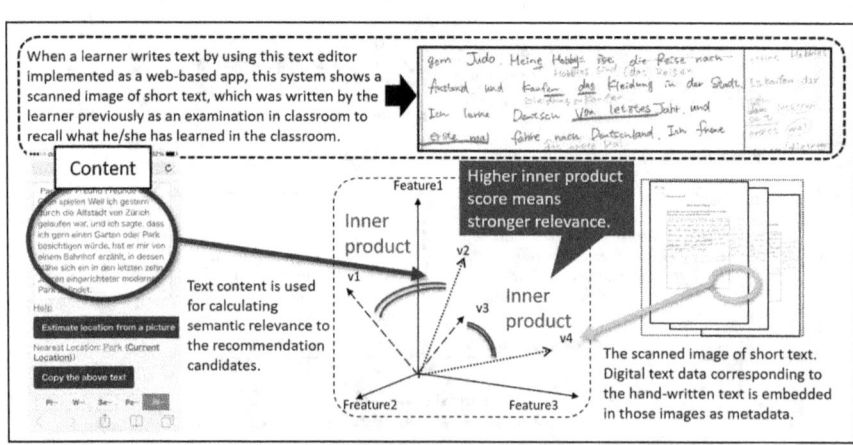

Figure 2 shows an architectural overview of our system. When a learner writes using this system, he/she is shown a scanned image of short texts which were previously hand-written by the learner during class, in order to recall what he/she has learned in the classroom. The scanned images of the short texts include metadata that contain digital text data corresponding to the hand-written text. The system calculates semantic relevance between the typed text and the scanned images by using this metadata. This system consists of two modules: (1) a text analysis module and (2) a semantic relevance calculation module. The text analysis module generates n-gram text statistics, which is a contiguous sequence of *n*-items from a text. For example, 2-gram sequence of the text 'apple' is 'ap', 'pp', 'pl', and 'le'. This sequence represents a statistical feature of 'apple' by decomposing the text into primitive sequences. The semantic relevance calculation module measures how words, sentences, paragraphs are appropriate to a user by calculating content-based similarity between the currently inputting text and the scanned images. We can calculate the relevance of two texts by using n-gram as follows:

$$\text{relevance}(q, t) := \sum_{i=0}^{n} (q_i \cdot t_i)$$

Where *q* and *t* denotes n-gram statistics of given text, qi denotes i-th primitive of n-gram of text *q*, and t_i denotes i-th primitive of n-gram of text *t*. The system shows the most relevant scanned image by using the calculated score. This context-aware recommendation helps the learner to express his/her daily-life experiences in a foreign language. In addition, this system gives special weight to the last word, referring to the word that the user entered last, and the current word, referring to the as yet incomplete word that the user is just typing.

3. Discussion

This project is targeting three participants of a German skill course at Keio University. None of them have any experience of staying abroad for an extended period of time. All of them have learned English as second language. The experiment for this pre-survey carried out in a class focused practicing of writing skills. Figure 3 shows the process of the experiment focusing on the writing process (left) and the interview data of the three participants in order to evaluate the process (right). In total they have written four essays (one per week) on four different topics. Each essay was corrected with comments and rewritten by the learners during class. After this four week process, we have interviewed the participants. The questions were focused on how they have memorized the mistakes they corrected.

Figure 3. Experiment and evaluation of the writing process

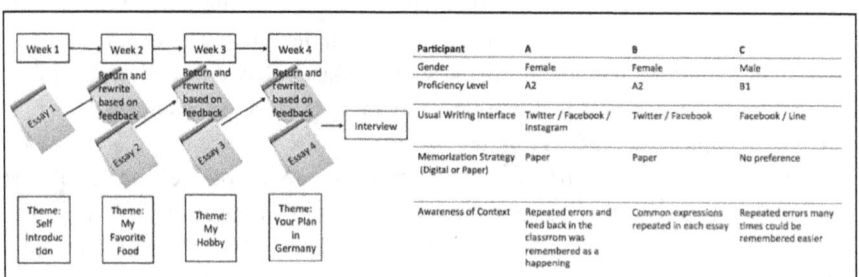

4. Conclusion

The interviews showed that learners' memories are connected not only with the memories about their grammar or expression errors, but more closely with what happened in the classroom (Participant A and B). This relates mostly to the communication with the educator according to the feedback during class. Participant C paid more attention to the errors, which he felt he had repeated many times. For the three participants, the handwritten error-correction of the essay was more impressionable than digital correction by Microsoft Word. It could be seen that errors are easier to remember when shown visually. When writing an essay, the memory of prior mistakes seemed to remain in visual form rather than as knowledge. The conclusions that can be drawn from the experiment and the interview data of only three subjects are certainly limited. However, this study could be continued by the following steps: a test run with the developed system and consideration of the method of how we can provide a holistic systemized learning environment for language learners.

References

Elwood, J. A., & Bode, J. (2014). Student preferences vis-à-vis teacher feedback in university EFL writing classes in Japan. *System*, *42*, 333-343. https://doi.org/10.1016/j.system.2013.12.023

Kukulska-Hulme, A., & Sharples, M. (2016). Waypoints along learning journeys in a mobile world. In W. Ng & T. M. Cumming (Eds), *Sustaining mobile learning: theory, research and practice* (pp. 43-56). Routledge.

Kusanagi, K., Abe, D., Fukuta, J., & Kawaguchi, Y. (2015). Developing multi-function software for recording, visualizing, and analyzing learners' writing process: WritingMaertiX. *LET Journal of Central Japan, 26*, 23-34.

Waragai, I., Kurabayashi, S., Ohta, T., Raindl, M. (2012). An experience-oriented language learning environment supporting. Japan Society for Educational Technology, 36, 91-101.

Waragai, I., Kurabayashi, S., Ohta, T., Raindl, M., Kiyoki, Y., & Tokuda, H. (2014). Context-aware writing support for SNS: connecting formal and informal learning. In S. Jager, L. Bradley, E. J. Meima & S. Thouësny (Eds), *CALL Design: principles and practice – proceedings of the 2014 EUROCALL Conference, Groningen, The Netherlands* (pp. 403-407). Research-publishing.net. https://doi.org/10.14705/rpnet.2014.000253

Waragai, I., Ohta, T., Raindl, M., & Kurabayashi, S. (2013). An experience-oriented language learning environment supporting informal learning abroad. *Educational technology research, 36*(1), 179-189.

Waragai, I., Raindl, M., Ohta, T., & Miyasaka, K. (2016). Mobile assisted language learning and mnemonic mapping – the loci method revisited. In S. Papadima-Sophocleous, L. Bradley & S. Thouësny (Eds), *CALL communities and culture – short papers from EUROCALL 2016* (pp. 462-467). Research-publishing.net. https://doi.org/10.14705/rpnet.2016.eurocall2016.607

ICALL's relevance to CALL

Monica Ward[1]

Abstract. The term Intelligent Computer Assisted Language Learning (ICALL) covers many different aspects of CALL that add something extra to a CALL resource. This could be with the use of computational linguistics or Artificial Intelligence (AI). ICALL tends to be not very well understood within the CALL community. There may also be the slight fear factor around ICALL, as it may seem very complicated and hard to understand. There is also the fact that ICALL resources tend to not be widely used in CALL as they may not be sufficiently robust enough for learners or they may not address a specific pedagogical need (Heift & Schulze, 2007). This paper looks at how some (basic) ICALL resources can be used in CALL. There is a need for ICALL and CALL researchers to work together to ensure that both benefit from each other's knowledge and expertise. ICALL has progressed in recent years and it is important for the ICALL community to raise awareness of what ICALL can bring to the CALL toolbox and to encourage CALL researchers to dip their toes in the ICALL waters.

Keywords: intelligent computer assisted language learning, ICALL, natural language processing NLP, computational linguistics, CL, artificial intelligence, AI.

1. Introduction

Intelligent CALL is a broad term that covers many different facets of extended or enhanced CALL, including Artificial Intelligence (AI), computational linguistics, Natural Language Processing (NLP) techniques, and speech processing techniques in CALL resources. ICALL materials can refer to resources that make extensive use of advanced techniques to support the language learning process or those that combine some extra elements to enhance a straightforward CALL resource. While in theory, the use of AI and NLP techniques in CALL should and can improve CALL resources, in practice, the development and successful

---

1. Dublin City University, Dublin, Ireland; monica.ward@dcu.ie

How to cite this article: Ward, M. (2017). ICALL's relevance to CALL. In K. Borthwick, L. Bradley & S. Thouësny (Eds), *CALL in a climate of change: adapting to turbulent global conditions – short papers from EUROCALL 2017* (pp. 328-332). Research-publishing.net. https://doi.org/10.14705/rpnet.2017.eurocall2017.735

deployment of ICALL resources is very challenging and few are sufficiently robust enough to 'escape' out of the world of academia and pilot studies to actual in-classroom and informal use by real-world learners. This is not due to lack of determination or willingness on the part of ICALL researchers, but rather due to the inherent difficulties in developing such resources (Heift & Schulze, 2003; Tschichold, 2014). Another challenge is that AI and NLP researchers are generally focussed on dealing with AI and NLP domain-specific issues and do not have an ICALL application in mind from the beginning of the research project, and often, the AI or NLP tools have to be adapted or retro-fitted to the CALL domain. This paper outlines some of the ways, despite the difficulties, in which ICALL can contribute to CALL.

2. ICALL Overview

ICALL resources range from simple grammar checkers and verb conjugation tools through to complex, rich language learning environments with automatic speech recognition and enhanced AI features. Many language learners may not think they use ICALL resources, but many do, e.g. word processors with spelling and grammar checking functions. Most ICALL resources tend to focus on one particular component of the language learning jigsaw, as resources are not available to develop comprehensive ICALL systems. For example, Volodina, Pilán, and Alfter (2016) focus on a system to automatically classify Swedish learning essays, while Digichaint (Ní Chiaráin & Ní Chasaide, 2016) is an AI system for learning Irish that focuses on simple sentences. Text input is easier for ICALL systems to deal with, but speech input systems are emerging in recent years. Voice recognition systems available with smartphones show that the technology is becoming more robust and better at dealing with a variety of different accents.

Many learners use online systems for vocabulary learning. For example, Duolingo is a vocabulary learning system which uses AI to incorporate a spaced repetition component for vocabulary acquisition. Duolingo is an example of a system that started with a different goal (language translation) and has morphed into an ICALL resource.

ICALL resources can be beneficial to learners. For example, ICALL systems can provide immediate and tailored feedback to learners. It is challenging to develop these types of resources and ICALL developers spend a considerable amount of time and effort on their design, development, and implementation. Speech processing is one area that has shown a lot of promise in the ICALL arena. Students can articulate words and the ICALL system can provide them with graphical feedback on their speech, perhaps with a comparison to that of a native speaker.

There are several basic ICALL tools and resources that can be used and developed by CALL researchers and practitioners without the need for extensive knowledge of advanced AI or NLP techniques. Many in the CALL field are unaware of what ICALL tools and resources are available to those outside the ICALL community. However, the ICALL curtain ranges from a complete blackout to a barely-there, almost transparent net curtain. While the blackout variety may be only penetrable by those with deep knowledge of advanced techniques, there are ICALL resources that could and can be used by CALL researchers and practitioners with basic linguistic knowledge of the target language. For example, there are some simple glossing tools available which CALL researchers can use to develop their own CALL resources, tailored to the needs of their learners. There are several features in learning management systems or online learning environments that can facilitate directed learning pathways through a language learning course, e.g. the conditional access feature in Moodle (Rice, 2015). While these features do not have the complexity of a customised AI system, they can approximate some of the decision tree features in AI systems. There are open source grammar checkers that CALL researchers can customise for their learners. For example, Gramadóir (Scannell, 2017) can be modified so that specific parts of the output are filtered so that the learner focus is directed to language learning goals.

3. Discussion

ICALL resource development is difficult (Heift & Schulze, 2007). It has to balance the technically challenging needs of NLP and AI, which tend to assume correct language input, with the reality that language learners will not provide correct language when interacting with an ICALL system. CALL researchers mainly have a language and pedagogy background, being less familiar with NLP and AI. They may be slightly apprehensive when interacting with ICALL researchers (and vice versa), as both communities speak a different language. ICALL researchers want to develop useful systems and input from CALL specialists can help them in this regard.

It is important to demystify ICALL and provide non-ICALLers with the confidence to try and experiment with ICALL tools. What is difficult for programmers can be easy for CALL specialists and vice-versa. This is not to say that it will be easy to develop ICALL resources or that they will be sufficiently robust for all language learners, but it is possible to develop ICALL resources that could be used by some language learners and be helpful for them on their language learning journey.

There is a need to manage expectations around ICALL resources. They are unlikely to be completely error-free and work exactly as the learner might expect them to. However, if learners and their teachers are aware of the limitations of a given ICALL resource, it is possible to develop and use reasonably useful ICALL materials. For beginner learners, limitations on the input language 'understood' by an ICALL system may not be too problematic, as beginners generally have a limited vocabulary. For more advanced learners, unexpected outputs or reactions by the ICALL system may foster discussion around why the error occurred and encourage them to understand the complexity of the language they are learning. Heift and Schulze (2007) provide a good overview of ICALL projects that have been successful with different learner groups.

4. Conclusions

When ICALL first emerged, along with Intelligent Computer Assisted Learning (ICAL) systems, there was great hope that it would revolutionise language learning. However, the reality is that ICALL development is much more complex and challenging than was first envisioned. Disappointment and the emergence of new avenues of research have meant that ICALL research has not been very prominent in recent years (Heift & Schulze, 2007). In order to address this, it is important for ICALL and CALL researchers to work together to develop practical resources that address real learner needs. ICALL researchers want to develop useful systems and they are torn between developing technically correct systems that do not match with the needs of learners in the real world. CALL researchers can help them in this regard by giving ICALL resources another chance. ICALL resources will not replace teachers, but they can augment the resources available to language learners.

References

Heift, T., & Schulze, M. (2003). Error diagnosis and error correction in CALL. *CALICO Journal*, 20(3), 433-436.
Heift, T., & Schulze, M. (2007). *Errors and intelligence in computer-assisted language learning: parsers and pedagogues.* Routledge.

Ní Chiaráin, N., & Ní Chasaide, A. (2016). The Digichaint interactive game as a virtual learning environment for Irish. In S. Papadima-Sophocleous, L. Bradley, & S. Thouësny (Eds), *CALL communities and culture – short papers from EUROCALL 2016* (pp. 330-336). Research-publishing.net. https://doi.org/10.14705/rpnet.2016.eurocall2016.584

Rice, W. (2015). *Moodle e-learning course development.* Packt Publishing Ltd.

Scannell, K. (2017). *An Gramadóir.* https://borel.slu.edu/gramadoir/

Tschichold, C. (2014). Challenges for ICALL. In *Keynote speech, 2nd workshop on NLP for computer-assisted language learning NoDaLiDa workshop, May* (Vol. 22, p. 2013).

Volodina, E., Pilán, I., & Alfter, D. (2016). Classification of Swedish learner essays by CEFR levels. In S. Papadima-Sophocleous, L. Bradley, & S. Thouësny (Eds), *CALL communities and culture – short papers from EUROCALL 2016* (pp. 456-461). Research-publishing.net. https://doi.org/10.14705/rpnet.2016.eurocall2016.606

Developing multimedia supplementary materials to support learning beginning level Chinese characters

Lisha Xu[1]

Abstract. Studies investigating beginner Chinese learners' character learning strategies found that learners considered orthographic knowledge the most useful factor (Ke, 1998; Shen, 2005). Orthographic recognition correlates with character identification and production and can be used by advanced learners to solve word identification problems (Everson, 2007). The central question, then, is how learners and educators can develop this ability. Component analysis and semantic radical instruction throughout the process of teaching beginner learners of non-character background can help learners create meaningful content out of seemingly disconnected information (Zahradníková, 2016). The multimedia material presented in this paper is specially designed with this in mind. A future research study will be conducted to understand the efficacy of modules and practices.

Keywords: Chinese character learning strategies, Chinese L2 beginners, multimedia material.

1. Introduction

Automatic identification of around 2,000 Chinese characters is required to understand the average written text, which makes developing "Chinese writing system competence" crucial before learners can proceed to "reading competence" or "writing competence" (Guder, 2007). Thus, the teaching of specific features of *hanzi* at the beginning level is often considered the most important step for reading or writing competence. Specifically, the typical curriculum includes the units of Chinese character formation, types of structure of compound characters,

---

1. Mount Holyoke College, South Hadley, United States of America; lxu@mtholyoke.edu

How to cite this article: Xu, L. (2017). Developing multimedia supplementary materials to support learning beginning level Chinese characters. In K. Borthwick, L. Bradley & S. Thouësny (Eds), *CALL in a climate of change: adapting to turbulent global conditions – short papers from EUROCALL 2017* (pp. 333-338). Research-publishing.net. https://doi.org/10.14705/rpnet.2017.eurocall2017.736

and stroke order. While moving on to the daily instruction of characters, however, the instructor usually faces the challenge of time constraints when attempting to fully elaborate upon character formation and learning strategies used for character retention, recognition, and production. Instead, mechanical copying and mindless memorization are often the main strategies adopted, which may lead to confusion in retrieval and production (Zahradníková, 2016).

Recently, some online materials and apps have been developed to support Chinese character learning, many focusing especially on conventional stroke sequence. The improvements help learners observe and recall characters better. However, there has been lack of digital material specifically designed to support the development of orthographic recognition for beginner learners.

The multimedia material presented in this paper was created to fill this gap. The overarching goal is to develop the integral knowledge and effective strategies for learning Chinese characters. This paper will introduce the design and the examples of multimedia materials created, and outline the methodology for a future research study.

2. Multimedia material

The learning material is novice level HSK (Chinese proficiency test) vocabulary which includes a total of 300 words with 450 characters. Using this as a starting point means that the materials developed are based on widely-accepted standards. The materials mainly focus on the details of each character, including its type (pictogram, ideogram, compound ideograph, phonogram), pronunciation, meaning, etymology, stroke order, components, and use of image-based annotations.

The theories and research findings for multimedia CALL design, cognitive theories and Chinese character learning, character learning strategies, and CALL-assisted vocabulary-learning techniques were all considered in the design.

2.1. Theoretical model

The principle for the design follows Chapelle's (1998) interactionist model. The model guides the CALL design and research on effectiveness based on the hypotheses about SLA. Table 1 demonstrates the components of the multimedia material applied to help learn Chinese characters.

Table 1. The structure and components of the multimedia material

Interactionist Model	Components	
Input	Present the learning materials in multimode content	• text • pronunciation in audio • image annotation • character handwriting sheet • character handwriting video demonstration
Apperception	Prompt learners to notice important aspects of the Chinese characters	• character's type • pronunciation • meaning • etymology • components
Comprehension	Decode the components of the characters	• semantics and cognitive analysis
Intake	Recognize the characters and their components	• formation and structure • stroke • stroke orders • meaning and pronunciation
Integration	Develop the learning strategies for Chinese characters	• analyze radical components and morphological structure of the characters • establish association among sounds, shapes and meanings • create images of the characters
Output	Get observable results about character retention and production	• flashcards • games • exercises

2.2. Multimodal content

Cognitive information processing theories are used to guide the design, since the character learning process necessarily involves the brain's ability to process information; the learner uses a variety of strategies to encode the characters' information for comprehension and memorization (Shen, 2011). This multimedia material has its roots in the framework of dual coding (Paivio, 1969), level-of-processing (Craik & Lockhart, 1972), and multi-modalities theories (Engelkamp, 2001). The content aims to create diverse effects with the multimodal input of text, etymology, image annotations, and audio and video to encode cues to aid information recall and deepen the information process. Table 2 presents the examples from the content created[2].

Table 2. Cognitive information process theories and pedagogical examples

Cognitive information process theories		Pedagogical examples
Dual coding theory	"Any information can be encoded as verbal or imagery presentation. If both methods are used, it will result in better learning and memorization than signal coding"	The top part likes character 日 sun 最 adv, most
Level-of-processing theory	"A deeper processing of the information is meaningful, with which the information will not be easily forgotten."	The top part means "hole" 穿 The bottom part means "tooth" Primary meaning: make a hole Extended meanings: to break through and to wear
Multi-modalities	"If we use multi-modalities instead of a single modality to encode information, when we recall the information, each model will contribute a unique cue to the recall of the information."	The bottom part 日 means "sun" 香 adj., sweet-smelling Story: In Spring, the grain is growing, exuding sweet-smelling. The top part 禾 means "grain"

---

2. Examples of multimedia material created can be found at https://research-publishing.box.com/s/i2gnd0ljb3gc7k8ntsw885lif9uenx57

2.3. Proposed study

The proposed study aims to investigate overall effectiveness of the digital components. The qualitative analysis will be conducted using a questionnaire and interviews. The experimental group consists of about 400 beginner learners. The statistical information will be summarized and student feedback will be analyzed by inductive procedure (Seliger & Shohamy, 1989). The study seeks to answer research questions including: to what extent do the modules help beginner-level learners develop the orthographic recognition and self-elaboration skills required to learn Chinese characters?; to what extent do the modules help beginner-level learners to recognize, retain, and produce the 450 most commonly used characters?; and how do learners reflect on their materials' use to support effective self-study of Chinese characters?

3. Discussion and conclusion

For novices, especially learners who use an alphabetic writing system, Chinese characters may appear to be a meaningless tangles of lines. It is crucial for the instructor to help illuminate the characters' shape, pronunciation, and meaning, as well as to help learners develop effective strategies to learn the characters. This can be a big challenge for both instructor and learners, due to a large amount of characters and limited short-term memory. In addition, if there is a lack of opportunity to practise and frequently review newly-learned characters, the characters may never enter the learner's long-term memory, nor will they be automatically recognized (Shen, 2011).

As a large variety of CALL materials become more accessible to learners, the demand for effective self-paced study in informal learning environments increases dramatically. To this end, to fill in the gap of pedagogically-sound multimedia material to help learners to learn beginning-level Chinese characters, the aforementioned learning materials were developed. Data collection and analysis will be conducted, from which the materials may be enhanced with better insight into learners' perceptions thereof.

4. Acknowledgements

This program is financially supported by the Five College Innovative Language Teaching Fellowship, 2015-2016.

References

Chapelle, C. (1998). Multimedia CALL: lessons to be learned from research on instructed SLA. *Language Learning & Technology, 2*(1), 22-34. http://llt.msu.edu/vol2num1/article1/

Craik, F. I. M., & Lockhart, R. S. (1972). Levels of processing: a framework for memory research. *Journal of Verbal Learning and Verbal Behavior, 11*, 671-684.

Engelkamp, J. (2001). Memory for action: a distinct form of episodic memory. In H. D. Zimmer et al. (Eds), *Action memory: a system-oriented approach,* (pp. 49-96). Oxford University Press.

Everson, M. E. (2007). Developing orthographic awareness among CFL Learners: what the research tells us. In A. Guder, X. Jiang, & Y. Wan (Eds), The cognition, learning and teaching of Chinese characters (pp. 33-50). Beijing Language and Culture University Press.

Guder, A. (2007). The Chinese writing system as third dimension of foreign language learning. In A. Guder, X. Jiang, & Y. Wan (Eds), The cognition, learning and teaching of Chinese characters (pp. 17-32). Beijing Language and Culture University Press.

Ke, C. (1998). Effects of strategies on the learning of Chinese characters among foreign language students. *Journal of the Chinese language Teachers Association, 33*(2), 93-112.

Paivio, A. (1969). Mental imagery in associative learning and memory. *Psychological Review, 76*, 241-263.

Seliger, H. W., & Shohamy, E. (1989). *Second language research methods.* Oxford University Press.

Shen, H. H. (2005). An investigation of Chinese character learning strategies among non-native speakers of Chinese. *System, 33*, 49-68.

Shen, H. H. (2011). Cognitive theories and vocabulary learning. In H. H. Shen, C. Tsai, L. Xu, & S. Zhu (Eds), *Teaching Chinese as a second language: vocabulary acquisition and instruction* (pp.67-92). Peking University Press.

Zahradníková, M. (2016). A qualitative inquiry of character learning strategies by Chinese L2 beginners. *Chinese as a Second Language, 51*(2), 117-137.

Roles of mobile devices supporting international students to overcome intercultural difficulties

Xiaoyin Yang[1] and Xiuyan Li[2]

Abstract. Sociocultural theory emphasises the mediational role of tools in learning. International students usually find themselves in a vicious cycle, experiencing difficulties when engaging with local people and culture which might provide the mediation necessary to develop their intercultural communicative competence. Yang (2016) further points out that "mobile technologies provide alternative mediational tools that might help students to break this cycle" (p. 2). This paper, developed from Yang's (2016) doctoral research, examines the roles of mobile devices in overcoming international students' intercultural difficulties during study abroad. Eight international students participated in the study and were asked to keep diaries and attend interviews for four weeks. A content analysis approach was applied to examine the students' use of mobile devices and situations. The findings revealed that for overcoming intercultural difficulties, the international students utilised mobile devices as search tools, social tools, service providers, presentation tools, and capture tools. Although the students showed some awareness of mobile devices as mediational tools, the problems that require the ability to analyse sociocultural contexts need further support from educators and technologies.

Keywords: intercultural difficulties, mobile devices, mediational tools, diary-and-interview methods.

1. Introduction

International students are usually neither native speakers of the target language nor members of the local culture. They need to develop their Intercultural Communicative Competence (ICC) to adapt to the study-abroad life. As discussed in Yang (2016, p. 37), ICC refers to the knowledge, skills and attitudes of another

---

1. Independent researcher, York, United Kingdom; xiaoyinyang@hotmail.com
2. Shenyang Normal University, Shenyang, China; lxyyyw@sina.com

How to cite this article: Yang, X., & Li, X. (2017). Roles of mobile devices supporting international students to overcome intercultural difficulties. In K. Borthwick, L. Bradley & S. Thouësny (Eds), *CALL in a climate of change: adapting to turbulent global conditions – short papers from EUROCALL 2017* (pp. 339-344). Research-publishing.net. https://doi.org/10.14705/rpnet.2017.eurocall2017.737

language and culture to communicate effectively and appropriately in intercultural situations (Byram, 1997; Deardorff, 2012). Sociocultural Theory (SCT) suggests that individual mental functioning is mediated by cultural artefacts, activities, and concepts in social interactions (Lantolf & Thorne, 2006). Mediation is the process through which mediational tools are employed to master the physical, psychological, and social world (Lantolf & Thorne, 2006). Therefore, international students are suggested to immerse into intercultural contexts for learning another language and culture and eventually develop ICC. Nevertheless, international students usually fall into a vicious cycle, experiencing difficulties in intercultural communication with people and surroundings (Lin & Scherz, 2014; Spencer-Oatey & Xiong, 2006) which might provide the mediation necessary to enhance their ICC. Mobile technologies provide alternative mediational tools that might facilitate students breaking this cycle. The devices could support ubiquitous learning with information from databases, more experienced people, and the surroundings to fulfil the user's specific needs.

This study, as Yang's (2016) doctoral research, aims to explore international students' use of mobile technology to mediate intercultural difficulties for ICC development during study abroad. This paper highlights one of the three research questions in the study, namely: what role do mobile devices play in dealing with intercultural difficulties?

2. Method

This research is a qualitative multiple case study focussing on the critical period of intercultural adjustment, namely the first few months after arrival into a new country. Diary-and-interview method was employed to collect descriptive data about the students' everyday life for four weeks, including their difficulties, situations, solutions, and use of tools. The students were interviewed every week to examine the diary-reported issues profoundly and check the researcher's interpretation of the data.

Eight Chinese international students participated in the study. They were doing one-year taught masters' courses in a UK university. It was their first time in the UK. Each student had at least one mobile device. All in all, the students contributed 192 records to the study, including 160 diary entries, and 32 interview transcripts.

The content analysis approach was adopted, which refers to data analysis via seeking items that fall into predetermined categories of a systematic framework or categories from the literature (Krippendorff, 2013). The schedule and coding manuals are the main tools for the approach. The coding schedule was structured according to elements in SCT and the research questions (see Table 1). As for coding manuals, for example, the manual for *role of the tool*, the focus of the present paper, included search tools, social tools, service providers, presentation tools, and capture tools based on previous studies on technologies as mediational and cognitive tools (e.g. Churchill & Churchill, 2008; Clough, Jones, McAndrew, & Scanlon, 2008) and the patterns of the data from the present study.

Table 1.   Coding schedule (Yang, 2016, p. 101)

Student	Issue No.	Nature of difficulty	Difficulty in ICC	Situation	Solution	Devices	Role of the tool	Note

3. Results

The present study identified 167 issues caused by difficulties in ICC. The students attempted to solve 134 (80%) of them. 71 (43%) of the solutions involved mobile devices for mediating the problem-solving. Mobile devices were used as search tools, social tools, service providers, presentation tools and capture tools (see Table 2).

Table 2.   The roles of the tools (Yang, 2016, p. 171)

Role of the tools	Frequency
Search tools	35
Social tools	20
Service providers	12
Presentation tools	4
Capture tools	4
Total	71

Search tools mainly consisted of search engines, dictionary apps and online databases. When the students encountered difficulties, their first intentions to use mobile devices were to find references, such as looking up words and searching for explanations online and in apps. The search function was applied in about half of the situations involving mobile technologies for solving problems (see Table 2). It revealed that the students were familiar with the role of mobile devices as search tools. Difficulties in linguistic and cultural knowledge associated with collective memory (i.e. big 'C' culture) were most likely solved with search tools. However, the difficulties involving small 'c' culture, namely the practices of a culture hidden behind thoughts and behaviours, were not solved thoroughly with mobile technologies. The students' reports indicated that the efficiency of search tools depended on the students' abilities to understand the sociocultural contexts and precision of keywords to describe the situations for searching.

Mobile devices as social tools were utilised to contact the more experienced individuals, so that the students could ask for help or advice. The students utilised emails, social networks, visual and audio calls, and text and voice messages through apps (e.g. iMessage, Facebook, and WeChat). The social tools enhanced the problem-solving by engaging the more capable people who were physically out of the contexts to help with the challenging situations. According to the students' reports, the success of solutions was usually decided by the student's unbiased interpretation of their situations and their selection of more experienced people who were able to reply in time.

Service providers sought by the students often referred to apps and websites that offered particular services such as navigations, online stores, and music players. The apps simplified intercultural communication as they avoided the face-to-face interaction with other people. The students could use the apps in L1, and had abundant time to figure out the meanings of L2 on the screen.

The students also reported that they used presentation tools, such as PowerPoint and photos, to present their ideas for explanation and knowledge exchange, while capture tools, such as the camera and the recording functions of mobile devices, to seize the instant containing crucial information concerning their difficulties. Presentation and capture tools were usually exploited to mediate issues in academic situations, such as reading papers, explaining ideas and recording academic activities.

4. Discussion and conclusions

The international students of this study already realised the mediational roles of mobile devices for overcoming their difficulties during study abroad, especially search tools and social tools. They usually exploited the devices ubiquitously when they encountered troubles without helpers or supports from the situations. The students observed and interpreted the surroundings to search online or consult more experienced people via mobile devices, and received some useful information for solving problems. Thus, mobile devices as the above five types of mediational tools could mediate the exchange of knowledge and some practical skills. However, the unsolved and partially solved difficulties demonstrated that the capacity of mobile devices to allocate ICC skills was limited. The skills contain the abilities to discover, interpret, and practise new cultural knowledge and practices from everyday interactions (Byram, 1997; Deardorff, 2012). Therefore, international students usually have to analyse and react to the situations with their ICC skills but no technical support. It implicates that educators could provide ICC training to international students with a focus on discovery, interpreting, and interaction skills, as well as let the students realise the roles of mobile devices for ICC development. Also, this study points out that educational technologies and app designers need to explore and apply the functions of mobile devices for mediating thinking and behaviours in sociocultural contexts that might mean applying artificial intelligence for ICC development.

5. Acknowledgements

We would like to thank Dr Zöe Handely for her feedback and the students for their participation.

References

Byram, M. (1997). *Teaching and assessing intercultural communicative competence*. Multilingual Matters.

Churchill, D., & Churchill, N. (2008). Educational affordances of PDAs: a study of a teacher's exploration of this technology. *Computers and Education, 50*(4), 1439-1450. https://doi.org/10.1016/j.compedu.2007.01.002

Clough, G., Jones, A. C., McAndrew, P., & Scanlon, E. (2008). Informal learning with PDAs and smartphones. *Journal of Computer Assisted Learning, 24*, 359-337. https://doi.org/10.1111/j.1365-2729.2007.00268.x

Deardorff, D. K. (2012). Framework: intercultural competence model. In K. Berardo & D. K. Deardorff (Eds), *Building cultural competence: innovative activities and models*. Stylus Publishing.

Krippendorff, K. (2013). *Content analysis: an introduction to its methodology (3rd ed.)*. SAGE.

Lantolf, J. P., & Thorne, S. L. (2006). *Sociocultural theory and the genesis of second language development*. Oxford University Press.

Lin, S.-Y., & Scherz, S. D. (2014). Challenges facing Asian international graduate students in the US: pedagogical considerations in higher education. *Journal of International Students, 4*(1), 16-33.

Spencer-Oatey, H., & Xiong, Z. (2006). Chinese students' psychological and sociocultural adjustments to Britain: an empirical study. *Language, Culture and Curriculum, 19*(1), 37-53. https://doi.org/10.1080/07908310608668753

Yang, X. (2016). *Mobile devices supporting international students to overcome language and cultural difficulties during study abroad*. Doctoral thesis. University of York.

Enhancing grammatical structures in web-based texts

Leonardo Zilio[1], Rodrigo Wilkens[2], and Cédrick Fairon[3]

Abstract. Presentation of raw text to language learners is not enough to ensure learning. Thus, we present the Smart and Immersive Language Learning Environment (SMILLE), a system that uses Natural Language Processing (NLP) for enhancing grammatical information in texts chosen by a given user. The enhancements, carried out by means of text highlighting, are designed to draw the users' attention to specific grammatical structures and thus help them to notice their occurrence in authentic contexts. To assess the quality of the enhancements, we carried out an evaluation of 48 structures in terms of precision in different text genres. This diversity approximates the contexts in which a language learner should immerge.

Keywords: NLP, SLA, input enhancements, syntactical highlighting, SMILLE.

1. Introduction

Computer-Assisted Language Learning (CALL) systems have recently started to use NLP applications for aiding in reading activities (Azab et al., 2013). Those systems base their approach to Second Language Acquisition (SLA) on the findings that the presentation of raw input to a language learner is not enough for ensuring that something will be learned (Meurers et al., 2010). So, the learner may not notice the grammatical content that is present in a text and, therefore, not convert the input into intake, as stated by Schmidt (1990, 2012). To address the lack of salience of information in input, the notion of input enhancements was created (Smith, 1993; Smith & Truscott, 2014).

Among the CALL systems that use NLP for identifying relevant SLA information in texts, the Smartreader (Azab et al., 2013), the FLAIR (Chinkina & Meurers, 2016), and the WERTi (Meurers et al., 2010) systems employ syntactic highlighting

---
1. Université Catholique de Louvain, Louvain-la-Neuve, Belgium; leonardo.zilio@uclouvain.be
2. Université Catholique de Louvain, Louvain-la-Neuve, Belgium; rodrigo.wilkens@uclouvain.be
3. Université Catholique de Louvain, Louvain-la-Neuve, Belgium; cedrick.fairon@uclouvain.be

How to cite this article: Zilio, L., Wilkens, R., & Fairon, C. (2017). Enhancing grammatical structures in web-based texts. In K. Borthwick, L. Bradley & S. Thouësny (Eds), *CALL in a climate of change: adapting to turbulent global conditions – short papers from EUROCALL 2017* (pp. 345-350). Research-publishing.net. https://doi.org/10.14705/rpnet.2017.eurocall2017.738

as a means of enhancing raw texts. All of them preprocess texts using the Stanford parser (Manning et al., 2014) and then apply rules with different granularities to get grammatical information and present them to the language learner[4].

This paper presents SMILLE, a system that automatically enhances grammatical structures in English texts chosen by the user. Since the detection of pedagogically relevant grammatical structures cannot be only based on parser information, we developed rules to cover them. In this study, our main focus was to evaluate the precision of these rules in different genres.

2. SMILLE

Using a similar approach to the systems already presented, SMILLE[5] uses input enhancements to draw the reader's attention to specific language structures. The user is free to choose any web-based text that will then be processed with Stanford parser and submitted to a rule-based processing that lists the existing grammatical structures for the language learner, who can choose on the fly which structures are to be enhanced. The enhancements are made by means of color-coding, highlighting, and boldface formatting (based on Simard, 2009), as illustrated in Figure 1. The system can enhance various types of grammatical structures that are based on Common European Framework of Reference for languages (CEFR) recommendations and are pedagogically organized according to Altissia's English curriculum (www.altissia.com). The system also provides access to grammar explanations, which are automatically linked to Altissia's course, and to word definitions from online dictionaries (e.g. Merriam-Webster's dictionary, at https://www.merriam-webster.com).

Figure 1. Example of highlighted quantifiers

---

4. A comparison between SMILLE and other systems is presented in Zilio, Wilkens, and Fairon (2017).
5. For a more complete description of the system, see Zilio and Fairon (2017) and Zilio et al. (2017).

3. Methodology

To assess the system's reliability in showing information to the user, a precision evaluation was conducted with 48 grammatical structures that do not rely solely on parser's information for being detected, requiring complex rules.

For that purpose, we selected four corpora of differing genres (Table 1): BBC: complete news articles from the BBC (2004-2005) corresponding to stories in five topics (entertainment, sports, business, politics, and technology) (Greene & Cunningham, 2005); GUT: selection of books from Project Gutenberg covering different literary genres (The Turn of the Screw, Wastralls, The Picture of Dorian Gray, The Phantom of the Opera, The Certain Hour, Greenmantle, Corpus, The Lair of the White Worm, Animal Ghosts, and The Shunned House); MOV: Cornell Movies, a collection of fictional conversations extracted from 617 raw movie scripts (Danescu-Niculescu-Mizil & Lee, 2011); and SCI: corpus of scientific papers (Jaidka, Chandrasekaran, Rustagi, & Kan, 2016).

Table 1. Description and average precision per corpus

Corpora	Tokens	Types	Sentences	Documents	Average Precision
BBC	978k	38k	41k	2,225	78%
GUT	826k	31k	41k	10	79%
MOV	4,246k	72k	481k	617	81%
SCI	660k	46k	29k	219	72%

All corpora were annotated with SMILLE and then we extracted samples of 25 random instances[6] for each corpus and for the 48 grammatical structures, and evaluated them in terms of precision. This evaluation was carried out by one language specialist[7].

4. System evaluation

The system achieved an overall average precision of 81%, but the median was 91%, indicating that most of the structures (67%) actually scored above the average. After removing outliers (beyond two standard deviations), the actual overall average is 85%. The similar average scores per corpus, as shown in Table 1, also hide the differences among the corpora and the distribution of the phenomena. For

---
6. If the corpus did not present 25 instances of a given structure, all of them were evaluated.
7. For reasons of space constraints, the complete table of results for all 48 grammatical structures is presented in https://goo.gl/CybVPE.

instance, BBC presented no occurrences for 1/3 of the structures and SCI had less than 10 occurrences for 1/4 of the structures, while GUT and MOV presented at least 25 instances for most of the structures.

Considering the individual structures, we saw that six structures scored below 50% precision, while 26 of them scored above 90%. Some of them had a very low precision score in all corpora, like the connectives of purpose (average 20%), and the connectives of reason and result (average 22%), while others had influence of the genre, like the ellipsed infinitive (0% in SCI, 17% in GUT, and 64% in MOV).

These differences between corpora arise from the preference of distinct forms related with the same grammar structure, as discussed by Roland, Dick, and Elman (2007). This means, for example, that the distribution of the ellipsed infinitive present in SCI are different to those used in MOV.

5. Conclusions

The evaluation of SMILLE showed us where we need to focus our attention for improving the system's performance. While a few of the grammatical structures present low precision scores that need to be addressed before presenting the system to a language learner, most of them had scores above 90%, which is comparable to systems of grammatical labeling (Cer, De Marneffe, Jurafsky, & Manning, 2010).

SMILLE is designed to be used along a regular language course, so, to approximate the variety of texts that a language learner can be in contact with, we used different genres, presenting a broader range of contexts for testing the developed rules, and we observed, for instance, that genre affects the detection of grammatical structures and should be considered for parsing purposes. This result can be used to optimize the system to consider text genres, so that rules could be specialized and applied to certain genres. In general, this allows us to improve SMILLE to better address the user needs.

6. Acknowledgements

We thank the Walloon Region (Projects BEWARE 1510637 and 1610378) for support, and Altissia International for collaboration.

References

Azab, M., Salama, A., Oflazer, K., Shima, H., Araki, J., & Mitamura, T. (2013). An NLP-based reading tool for aiding non-native English readers. *International Conference Recent Advances in Natural Language Processing, RANLP.*

Cer, D. M., De Marneffe, M. C., Jurafsky, D., & Manning, C. D. (2010). Parsing to Stanford dependencies: trade-offs between speed and accuracy. In N. Calzolari et al. (Eds), *Proceedings of the Seventh International Conference on Language Resources and Evaluation (LREC'10)*. European Language Resources Association (ELRA).

Chinkina, M., & Meurers, D. (2016). Linguistically aware information retrieval: providing input enrichment for second language learners. In *Proceedings of the 11th Workshop on Innovative Use of {NLP} for Building Educational Applications, BEA@NAACL-HLT 2016, June 16, 2016, San Diego, California* (pp. 188-198). https://doi.org/10.18653/v1/W16-0521

Danescu-Niculescu-Mizil, C., & Lee, L. (2011). Chameleons in imagined conversations: a new approach to understanding coordination of linguistic style in dialogs. In *Proceedings of the 2nd Workshop on Cognitive Modeling and Computational Linguistics* (pp. 76-87). ACL.

Greene D., Cunningham, P. (2005). Producing accurate interpretable clusters from high-dimensional data. In A.M. Jorge et al. (Eds), *Knowledge Discovery in Databases: PKDD 2005. Lecture Notes in Computer Science, vol 3721*. Springer. https://doi.org/10.1007/11564126_49

Jaidka, K., Chandrasekaran, M. K., Rustagi, S., & Kan, M. Y. (2016). Overview of the CL-SciSumm 2016 Shared Task. In *BIRNDL@JCDL* (pp. 93-102).

Manning, C. D., Surdeanu, M., Bauer, J., Finkel, J. R., Bethard, S., & McClosky, D. (2014). The stanford corenlp natural language processing toolkit. In *Proceedings of 52nd Annual Meeting of the Association for Computational Linguistics: System Demonstrations* (pp. 55-60). Association for Computational Linguistics.

Meurers, D., Ziai, R., Amaral, L., Boyd, A., Dimitrov, A., Metcalf, V., & Ott, N. (2010). Enhancing authentic web pages for language learners. In *Proceedings of the NAACL HLT 2010 Fifth Workshop on Innovative Use of NLP for Building Educational Applications* (pp. 10-18). ACL.

Roland, D., Dick, F., & Elman, J. L. (2007). Frequency of basic English grammatical structures: a corpus analysis. *Journal of memory and language, 57*(3), 348-379. https://doi.org/10.1016/j.jml.2007.03.002

Schmidt, R. W. (1990). The role of consciousness in second language learning. *Applied linguistics, 11*(2), 129-158. https://doi.org/10.1093/applin/11.2.129

Schmidt, R. W. (2012). Attention, awareness, and individual differences in language learning. In W. M. Chan, K. N. Chin, S. Bhatt & I. Walker (Eds), *Perspectives on individual characteristics and foreign language education* (pp. 27-50). De Gruyter Mouton. https://doi.org/10.1515/9781614510932.27

Simard, D. (2009). Differential effects of textual enhancement formats on intake. *System, 37*(1), 124-135. https://doi.org/10.1016/j.system.2008.06.005

Smith, M. S. (1993). Input enhancement in instructed SLA. *Studies in second language acquisition, 15*(2), 165-179.

Smith, M. S., & Truscott, J. (2014). Explaining input enhancement: a MOGUL perspective. *International Review of Applied Linguistics in Language Teaching, 52*(3), pp. 253-281. https://doi.org/10.1017/S0272263100011943

Zilio, L., & Fairon, C. (2017). Adaptive system for language learning. In *2017 IEEE 17th International Conference on Advanced Learning Technologies (ICALT)* (pp. 47-49). IEEE. https://doi.org/10.1109/ICALT.2017.46

Zilio, L., Wilkens, R., & Fairon, C. (2017). Using NLP for enhancing second language acquisition. In *Proceedings of Recent Advances in Natural Language Processing (RANLP 2017) in Varna, Bulgaria, 2-8 September 2017* (pp. 839-846).

Author index

A
Aizawa, Kazumi 1
Alizadeh, Mehrasa 7, 205
Allen, Christopher 46
Alzahrani, Sahar 13
Arnbjörnsdóttir, Birna 116

B
Baird, Robert 19
Bárkányi, Zsuzsanna 24
Bartram, Lorna 40
Baten, Kristof 86
Beirne, Elaine 30
Belletti Figueira Mulling, Alessandra 35
Berbyuk Lindström, Nataliya 40
Berggren, Jan 46
Bieri, Thomas E. 51
Bione, Tiago 56
Borthwick, Kate xii, 19
Bown, Andy 271
Bradley, Linda 40
Brückner, Stefan 277, 322

C
Canals, Laia 62
Cardoso, Walcir 56, 67, 135, 217
Chinkina, Maria 73
Choi, Sung-Kwon 79
Clark, Jill 242
Collins, Laura 135
Cornillie, Frederik 86

D
De Hertog, Dirk 86

Dey-Plissonneau, Aparajita 92

E
Elliott, Darren 51
Enokida, Kazumichi 99
Enticknap-Seppänen, Kaisa 105

F
Fairon, Cédrick 345
Fluck, Andrew 271
Forti, Luciana 110
Friðriksdóttir, Kolbrún 116

G
Gimaletdinova, Gulnara 184
Gimeno-Sanz, Ana 122
Godwin-Jones, Robert 128
Grimshaw, Jennica 56, 67, 135
Grounds, Patricia E. 140

H
Hendry, Clinton 146
Huang, Jin-Xia 151

I
Iso, Tatsuo 1

J
Jauregi, Kristi 157, 163

K
Kaplan-Rakowski, Regina 170
Kasami, Naoko 177
Kawahara, Tatsuya 211
Kayumova, Albina 184
Kebble, Paul 271
Khalitova, Liliia 184

Kida, Shusaku 99
Kim, Young-Kil 79, 151
Kiyoki, Yasushi 277, 322
Koby, Cory J. 189
Koguchi, Ichiro 7, 205
Kurabayashi, Shuichi 322
Kuure, Leena 312
Kwon, Oh-Woog 79, 151

L
Laurie, Anne 283
Lee, Kyung-Soon 151
Li, Chen 194
Li, Chenxi 194
Li, Xiuyan 339
Loranc-Paszylk, Barbara 170
Lyddon, Paul A. 200

M
Mehran, Parisa 7, 205
Melchor-Couto, Sabela 24, 157, 163
Meshgi, Kourosh 211
Meurers, Detmar 73
Mirzaei, Maryam Sadat 211
Misher-Tal, Hagit 222
Moore, Caroline 140
Morita, Mitsuhiro 99
Moussalli, Souheila 217
Mozgovoy, Maxim 254

N
Nadasdy, Paul 1
Namouz, Rana 222
Nic Giolla Mhichíl, Mairéad 30
Ní Chasaide, Ailbhe 229
Ní Chiaráin, Neasa 229

O
Ó Cleircín, Gearóid 30
Ó Doinn, Oisín 235

Ohnishi, Akio 99
Ohta, Tatsuya 322
Ostrowski, Boguslaw 242

P
Page, Mary 19
Papadima-Sophocleous, Salomi 248
Purgina, Marina 254

Q
Quere, Nolwenn 260

R
Robbins, Jackie 62
Rueb, Avery 67
Ruiz, Simón 73

S
Sadoux, Marion 265
Sadykova, Gulnara 184
Sain, Noridah 271
Sakaue, Tatsuya 99
Sato, Yukiko 277, 322
Sela, Orly 222
Selwood, Jaime 200
Sheepy, Emily 146, 283
Sikkema, Eline C. 289
Sofkova Hashemi, Sylvana 40
Strobl, Carola 294
Sundberg, Ross 283

T
Takemura, Haruo 7, 205
Tang, Jinlan 194
Tian, Yan 300
Titova, Svetlana 306
Tumelius, Riikka 312

U
Underwood, Joshua 317

W

Waragai, Ikumi 277, 322
Ward, Monica 254, 328
Wilkens, Rodrigo 345
Wina Rachmawan, Irene Erlyn 277
Windeatt, Scott 242
Wu, Ligao 194

X

Xu, Lisha 333

Y

Yang, Xiaoyin 339

Z

Zilio, Leonardo 345